D1576045

Colonial Habits

Colonial Habits

Convents and the Spiritual Economy of Cuzco, Peru

K A T H R Y N   B U R N S

D U K E   U N I V E R S I T Y   P R E S S

Durham and London, 1999

© 1999 Duke University Press
All rights reserved. Printed
in the United States of America on
acid-free paper ⊗   Typeset in Joanna by
Tseng Information Systems, Inc.
Frontispiece: The first cloister of Santa
Catalina de Sena in Cuzco. Photo by K. Burns.
Library of Congress Cataloging-in-
Publication Data appear on the last
printed page of this book.

To my family,
especially Roland

Contents

Acknowledgments

In the last several years Cuzco's colonial convents have been for me rather like Borges's Aleph: if I concentrated enough on this one, very particular spot, I could see that it held an entire world of vivid significance. Writing about what I saw involved crossing many boundaries, disciplinary and otherwise. I could not even have begun, much less completed, this book had it not been for the generous institutional support I received and for the warmth and help of my family, friends, and colleagues, whom I take great pleasure in thanking here.

For institutional support in Cuzco, I am grateful to the directors and archivists of the Archivo Departamental del Cusco, who helped me locate an abundance of relevant documents. I could not have read them all without Margareth Najarro Espinoza and Ingrid Patricia Vivanco Pérez; my warmest thanks to them for their excellent research assistance. The camaraderie that formed among the researchers ranged around the tables of the archives in Cuzco was very special, and I want to thank my friends John Rowe and Patricia Lyon, Charles Walker, Marisa Remy, Thomas Krüggeler, and Pedro Guibovich, who gave me invaluable help as I began, and David Garrett, Donato Amado and other members of the Taller de Historia Andina, Jean-Jacques Decoster, Carolyn Dean, Manuel Burga, Leo Garofalo, Neus Tur-Escandell, and Sabine MacCormack, who shared many ideas, archival leads, and coffee breaks with me. Madre Rosa Victoria Vega, prioress of Santa Catalina de Sena in Cuzco, gave me permission to consult colonial papers from her convent's archives, and her confidence and trust in me are deeply appreciated. I thank Madre Juana Marín Farfán, abbess of Santa Clara in Cuzco, for letting me consult her convent's early land titles, and I thank the directors and staff of the Archivo Arzobispal del Cuzco for facilitating my access to many pertinent records. I also relied on the fine library of the Centro de Estudios Regionales Andinos Bartolomé de Las Casas in Cuzco; my thanks to the directors and staff of the Centro for their support.

In Lima my oldest debts of gratitude are to the Pontificia Universidad Católica del Perú and the Comisión Fulbright. I especially want to thank Franklin and Mariana Pease and Marcia Koth de Paredes for their hospitality and for encouraging my earliest *investigaciones*. For helping me find useful sources in Lima, I am grateful to the directors and staff of the Archivo General de la Nación, the Sala de Investigaciones of the Biblioteca Nacional del Perú, the Archivo Arzobispal de Lima, the Archivo de San Francisco, and the Archivo de Límites del Ministerio de Relaciones Exteriores. I am also indebted to Félix Denegri Luna, who gave me access to his extraordinary library of rare books.

Much of the work on this project was done at Harvard University after my advisor, John Womack, Jr., encouraged me to develop a tangent-laden seminar paper on the *mestizas* of Santa Clara. I am very grateful to him for his wisdom and support in the years since then. I also thank Olwen Hufton, who was likewise generous with encouragement, and my fellow graduate students, especially Emilio Kourí, Elizabeth Fowler, Brodwyn Fischer, Aurora Gómez, and Renée Baernstein, who made doctoral studies much richer for me. During those years I became indebted to the work of Asunción Lavrin and Jodi Bilinkoff, who became enthusiastic supporters of my work, and I thank them warmly for their help. I received summer travel funding from Radcliffe College and Harvard University, a Fulbright-Hays fellowship from the U.S. Department of Education for dissertation research in 1990–91, a grant from the Real Colegio Complutense for travel to Spain in 1992, and a Charlotte W. Newcombe fellowship from the Woodrow Wilson National Fellowship Foundation to complete my dissertation in 1992–93.

Since joining the faculty of the University of Florida in Gainesville, I have also received generous assistance. Funding from the University of Florida allowed me to make two crucial research trips to Peru in the summers of 1994 and 1995 and to share portions of my work with scholars in Mexico City in the spring of 1995. Comments on my dissertation from John Rowe, Patricia Lyon, Arnold Bauer, and my Florida colleagues Murdo Macleod, Anna Peterson, and Carol Lansing greatly assisted my thinking about how to turn my dissertation into a book. A fellowship from the Shelby Cullom Davis Center for Historical Studies at Princeton University in 1995–96 enabled me to read more widely and rethink the implications of my work; I am very grateful to William Chester Jordan, Natalie Zemon Davis, Stanley Stein, Jeremy Cohen, Penny von Eschen, Kevin Gaines, Kari Hoover, and my fellow Davis Center fellows for making my Princeton stay so productive, and to my Florida colleague Louise Newman for her invaluable criticism and generous support during that year. As I have begun circulating my work more widely, many students and colleagues have given me constructive readings and ideas, and I want to express my sincere thanks to them for their help—particularly to Rebecca Karl and Mark Thurner for their stimulating intellectual company.

It has been a pleasure to bring out this book with Duke University Press. I am especially grateful to my editor, Valerie Millholland, for her patience, responsiveness, and good humor, and to my readers for the press, Brooke Larson and Charles Walker, whose insightful suggestions greatly improved the book's final version. I thank copyeditor Charles Purrenhage for his careful work, and managing editor Jean Brady and her staff for making the production process swift and smooth. I would also like to thank Duke University Press for permission to present here, as Chapter 1, a slightly revised version of my article "Gender and the Politics of Mestizaje: The Convent of Santa Clara of Cuzco," *Hispanic American Historical Review* 78:1 (February 1998).

It is hard to know where to begin to thank the many other friends who have helped me during the last ten years. The companionship of Gabriela Martínez, César Itier, Aurelia Fuertes, and those who came after them in the house on Saphy in Cuzco was vital to me during some trying times. For helping me to keep perspective on work and life, and to bridge the distances that separate Cuzco, Lima, and Gainesville, I am immensely grateful to Marisol de la Cadena, who has supported and inspired me since we roomed together on calle Suecia, and to María Emma Mannarelli, Kate Raisz, Stephanie Stewart, and Marianela Gibaja. I could not have completed this project without the intellectual companionship and love of Sheryl Kroen and Holly Hanson. Finally, I want to dedicate this book to my family. The patient, loving support of my parents, Ned and Martha Burns, my sister Stephanie, my brother Michael, and my dear friend Roland Greene has meant the world to me.

Introduction

Today anyone who wants to see Santa Clara has to get up early in the morning. Situated in the heart of Cuzco's market district, the oldest cloistered convent in South America is definitely not a tourist attraction. Thousands of tourists a year trundle by on their way to catch the predawn train to the Inca ruins of Machu Picchu without giving the convent's old stone walls so much as a sleepy glance. The church of Santa Clara opens for mass only briefly as day breaks and vendors begin stirring the market to life. After the small group of worshippers departs, the front gates are locked, leaving only an inconspicuous side door to admit the occasional visitor or deliveryman. Meanwhile the streets outside fill with lively exchanges: bargaining, buying, the comings and goings of maids and stoop-backed porters. By midmorning vendors have completely outfitted the perimeter of Santa Clara with the multicolored canvas of their market stalls, and from the vantage point of the street outside, the old convent practically disappears.

It is hard to imagine that the nuns were once at the center of city life. Now that the market and the convents turn their backs to each other, and commerce and spirituality seem to go separate ways, it is easy to think this was always the case and that cloistered nuns in general were always withdrawn, "in this world but not of it." The historiography of the colonial and postcolonial Andes does little to contradict these impressions. Convents are marginalized mostly by omission.[1] To the extent that nuns and convents have been written about, the point has often been more hagiographical than historiographical: to praise the monjitas for their edifying example.[2] The fascinating involvement of cloistered women in everything from conquest to the making of postcolonial nations has in the process been set aside, and the axis of

Fig. 1. Map of southern colonial Peru, formerly the heartland of the Inca state of Tahuantinsuyo

understanding stood on end, the grasping of a (seemingly timeless) spiritual essence privileged over the investigation of local histories.

Yet if we take some cues from the colonial nuns' contemporaries, it is readily possible to imagine things otherwise. Consider, for example, that Santa Clara was one of the first institutions the conquistadores of Cuzco decided they needed once their conquest of the Inca city was more or less secure—and that the six-year-old daughter of an Inca ruler was among the convent's first entrants. When Dominican nuns founded Santa Catalina in Cuzco half a century later, in 1605, they built atop the site of the *acllahuasi*, once home to virginal young women dedicated to serving the ruling Inca.[3] Thereafter both cloisters would receive numerous "Indian nobles," daughters of the indigenous elite whose collaboration made possible Spain's indirect rule over the Andes. A third convent, Santa Teresa, was approved by the Habsburg bureaucracy after it was determined that Cuzco's two existing convents were bursting with women: not only the nuns, but hundreds of servants, children of all ages, and slaves.

Clearly the colonial nuns' contemporaries knew what we have all but forgotten: that convents were vital to the securing of Spanish hegemony in Peru and to the erecting of a colonial regime on Inca foundations. The three colonial convents of Cuzco—Santa Clara (1558), Santa Catalina (1605), and Santa Teresa (1673)—have been in continuous existence ever since. Today their communities are much smaller than they once were (around twenty to thirty women each), but their central locations and imposing structures reflect the place they formerly occupied in the imaginative and practical geography of the city. Santa Clara and Santa Catalina were Cuzco's *conventos grandes* after the fashion of the largest, most aristocratic European convents of their day: virtual cities within the city, places where (to borrow a chronicler's description of one of Lima's convents) "the site is so large that if a servant flees from her mistress, it may be days before she is found, because there are streets, and neighborhoods, like a town."[4]

From the sixteenth century well into the nineteenth century, these imposing institutions were central to the way local people produced and reproduced themselves. *Cuzqueños* invested heavily in their convents. For centuries they sent their daughters (sometimes formally, sometimes furtively) to be raised and educated in the cloisters, paying dowry for their daughters, sisters, and cousins who professed. Nuns, in turn, invested heavily in local people, spending long hours praying for their souls and loaning them funds from convent coffers. The credit the nuns extended—mostly through contracts that have been out of use so long they have become notarial relics—enabled propertied cuzqueños to conduct thriving businesses and still avoid the moral traps of usury. The result of centuries of accretion of such practices was that cuzqueños—principally but not exclusively the region's elites—created for themselves a dense weave (as we will see) of historically specific kinds of exchanges that were indissociably economic and spiritual, distinctly colonial, and utterly habitual.

The making of this early modern tapestry, this dense network of interests and investments, is my subject, and I have chosen to call it Cuzco's spiritual economy. I do so to denote the inextricability of the material and the sacred, relying on a very old sense of "economy" as the managing of a house (Greek *oikos*) and pointing to the spiritual goals orienting such activity. In this kind of economy, spiritual "goods" circulated and might be bought for money with no perceived contamination or contradiction. In Cuzco, for example, prayers were once routinely bought and sold in very precise terms, and no one with enough income thought twice about endowing a clergyman with a certain amount of pesos per year to say a specific number of prayers. And nuns might seize the collateral property of a debtor and note simply that it "was spiritualized" (*quedó espiritualizada*).[5] I am asking after the history in which such things were simply common sense. In short,

I am investigating a colonial *habitus*: the "generative principle of regulated improvisions" that Pierre Bourdieu describes as the "immanent law" of a group or class, producing its common sense, the "conductorless orchestration" of its practices.[6] Nuns were of course not the only ones who recreated and moved authoritatively within this habitus. But their own accounts of their activities are few, fragmentary, and inaccessible—part of the reason historians have almost invariably depicted nuns, if at all, as decidedly off to one side of the main colonial action.

My telling gives Cuzco's nuns the leading parts. And in these introductory pages I will sketch the consequences of this move to make cloistered women the center of things. From the vantage point of the convent, each major period of Cuzco's storied past looks significantly different, its actors and aspects more connected. We can see the forging of a distinctly colonial elite—a hybrid provincial aristocracy whose members cultivated a profound attachment to the Inca past, even as they were riven by deep, increasingly "racialized" divisions. And as I hope will become clear, the legacies or habits of colonialism lingered long, shaping Peruvian postcoloniality—the "imagined community" of a new, secularizing Peruvian republic.[7] By considering nuns' agency we get to see this *longue durée* of the social reproduction of power and privilege. The insights gained here can be extended well beyond the bounds of the Andes, to the relationships articulated by convents across much of Europe, the colonial Americas, and beyond.[8]

* * *

First, some notes on the making of this version of the cloistered past. When I began research in 1988–90, fascinated with the seeming paradox of Santa Clara's founding, I planned to do a tightly focused case study of the Clares' earliest years. Why a convent, of all things, in the midst of Spanish wars of colonial expansion? How, in a century or less, had Santa Clara changed from an impoverished orphanage for *mestizas* into a wealthy, stratified haven for *criollas*? I expected to see pieces of the story narrated by the nuns themselves, for I knew from important work in recent years on convents from Mexico City to Avila that nuns did make narratives (often of their own lives, at the urging of their confessors: hence the hagiographical genre of the *vida*).[9] I hoped I might locate nuns' vidas, perhaps refracted in the prism of baroque compositions like those of the extraordinary Mexican nun Sor Juana Inés de la Cruz (1648?-95).

I eventually found answers to my questions, and along the way located fascinating traces of the lives of hundreds of nuns. Instead of meeting Sor Juana in the archives, however, I encountered (over and over again) the Spanish-Andean counterparts of Bartleby the Scrivener —the copyists and notaries whose elaborate procedural template shaped many if not most of the documents in Peru's rich colonial archives.[10] The hand of Cuzco's notaries seemed to be everywhere. When I eventually gained some access to the colonial papers of Santa Clara and Santa Catalina, these too turned out to be mostly Bartleby's work: they consisted overwhelmingly of notarial instruments of one kind or another, sales and wills and leases and rentals, most dating from the late seventeenth century or after.[11]

Thus I met the nuns of Cuzco mainly at the points of their intersection with the secular world they called *el siglo*. Put a different way, I met Sor Juana's lesser-known side, for she was often treasurer of her community, known for her agility at handling her convent's financial affairs.[12] And I could not help but notice that the nuns were actively undoing the categories and concepts many scholars have used to describe them: "repositories" of excess daughters; "islands of liberated women." The seeming dichotomy of conventual insiders and outsiders came further undone the more I read. Clearly these women were running their communities' affairs very much along the lines Asunción Lavrin disclosed in her pathbreaking studies of the financial activities of Mexico City convents.[13] So I changed the design of my project. My questions about the founding of Santa Clara remained, but my investigations expanded to include all three of Cuzco's convents and assumed a different temporal frame: a truly longue durée spanning several centuries. By keeping periodization simple here, framing things on the conventional arc of a rise and fall, I hope to provoke and focus reflection elsewhere—on the intensity of engagement between and among historical actors practicing their everyday rites and negotiations, and on the meanings of these practices.

My focus is thus on what Michel de Certeau has called "the practice of everyday life": everyday colonial life and its legacies.[14] By showing at this level how the "spiritual" pervades the "economic," and vice versa, I hope to expand our notions of both. Here "production" and "reproduction" become inseparable. They are not merely two sides of the same coin; they *are* the same coin, the very alloyed stuff of it. This insight enables us to recast even some of the most stock actors and activities of colonial history while adding new ones to the repertory. Conquistadores are featured here as anxious fathers, for example, painstakingly shaping their lineages along with their fortunes; chaste, cloistered women appear as purposeful dealmakers, creating fruitful, productive relationships with uncloistered men and women through the conduit of credit. We get to see, in and through the convents, the creation of both material and symbolic capital.

Gender becomes an indispensable tool at this everyday, practical level of historical analysis. For while men's and women's religious houses relied on many of the same customs and credit mechanisms, their practice of religious poverty was different, and distinctly gendered. Women, unlike men, formally entered the religious life through the trope of marriage. A nun was symbolically a bride who pledged fidelity to a divine spouse and brought a dowry to sustain her in spiritual matrimony. Understanding this trope reshapes our image of convent life as apart from, and opposed to, marriage and family life: we can reimagine the colonial nun's profession as a kind of marriage—a spiritual marriage to Jesus, involving a careful economic calculus and uniting the nun's family with the convent community in a richly significant bond. The study of convents thus contributes to our understanding of gender, family life, marriage, and motherhood.

Moreover, I hope to contribute here to resolving what has been identified as a weakness of "practice studies" (and of cultural history more generally): namely, such histories' ability to explain how, when, and why things change. Cuzco's convents, studied over several centuries, show remarkable practical and discursive continuities, but also disclose large, tectonic shifts. Gradually keywords emerged, and I began to see long-term patterns in their usage: *dominio*, an ancient term signifying "sovereignty" and linked to the strange, mutable history of property; *forastera*, "outsider" or "foreigner," an especially polyvalent term in the Andes for designating one's Others; and *libertad*, "liberty," a term people seemed to use more frequently by the turn of the nineteenth century to speak about something they felt they needed but did not have. And sites emerged: especially the convent *locutorio*, or visitor's parlor. In this book I work these practices, sites, and keywords together in an archivally informed—necessarily provisional—interpretation of Cuzco's spiritual economy. I suggest historical reasons why its workings, once entirely logical to cuzqueños and central to their well-being, came by the nineteenth century to represent an irrational burden and a fetter to their liberty, and how in that process nuns lost a great amount of cultural authority.

* * *

Some results of this study are unique to Cuzco, where for centuries convents were a crucial site of Spaniards' struggles to contain and control Incas, and of Incas' struggles for self-definition and authority. However, this study also offers important new insights into the workings of colonialism more generally—particularly the economic logic and the gender politics at work in the creation and reproduction of a colonial elite. Those engaged in theorizing the intersections of gender, race, and class will find much of interest here. So, too, will those interested in the major periods and themes of colonial Latin American and Andean history, from conquest and mestizaje to late colonial crises and the making of republican nations. In the pages that follow I signal the aims and contributions of each chapter and locate them in the context of relevant historiographies.

Chapter 1 unfolds the paradox of Santa Clara's founding in Cuzco during the 1550s. As we will see, the city was still caught up in intrigues and vicious fighting. What led Spaniards to create a convent in such an agitated time and place? Their recorded desire was to protect mestizas—daughters of Spanish men and Andean women—by separating the girls from their Andean mothers and raising them amidst Spanish religion and customs. Situating these founding acts in their charged political context, I argue that in these crucial years Cuzco's leading Spaniards saw in their daughters—and not, significantly, in their mestizo sons—a means of ensuring their own reproduction as well as that of the Spanish city they were trying to erect. In Chapter 1, then, we explore not only the founding of South America's first convent, but the complicated history of mestizaje. This chapter also contributes to the study of "spiritual conquest" by suggesting that cloistered women played a vital part in the Christianization of the Andes.

Chapter 2 also starts with a paradox, this time concerning property: Santa Clara by the 1560s had acquired local assets rivaling those of the region's encomenderos. How was this possible, if nuns were supposed to be poor? The Clares' rules did not prohibit the nuns from holding assets collectively, and I suggest we view their religious poverty as a gendered practice, predicated on strict enclosure, male proxies, and a measure of collective prosperity. Drawing on trial records—

particularly land disputes from the 1550s over "lands of the Inca and the Sun"—I examine the nuns' role in acquiring, and imposing, private property in the Andes. Local ethnic lords (kurakas) resisted their claims through the Spanish legal system. Underlying these conflicts were profoundly divergent cultural goals, and resolving them required the parties to engage in contentious rounds of thoroughly hybridized negotiations. Thus the nuns, in the process of staking their claims, helped not only to consolidate a new understanding of "property" in the Andes but to privilege a new set of local lords: culturally ambidextrous kurakas and criollos.

Chapter 3 uses the unusual case of Santa Catalina to explore the limits and contingencies of the spiritual economy, a distinctly local construct predicated on the relative stability of the assets it attached. In 1605, the Dominican nuns of Santa Catalina migrated across the Andes from Arequipa to Cuzco after natural disasters destroyed their property base. Cuzqueños greeted the nuns cordially at the end of their hard journey, but regarded them as outsiders, forasteras. Finding new supporters and resources took the Dominicans years of diligent effort. Eventually they succeeded in remaking themselves convincingly into cuzqueñas. They achieved this in part by taking in a female descendant of the Incas—thus symbolically, if belatedly, participating in the project undertaken by the Clares a half-century earlier, that of containing politically significant, thus potentially dangerous, Inca children. By the time a seismic disaster hit Cuzco in 1650, Santa Catalina had struck sufficiently deep roots in the city to remain where it was: atop the old Inca acllahuasi.

Chapters 4 and 5 treat the late-seventeenth-century zenith of the complex relationships that constituted Cuzco's spiritual economy. Daily life inside the cloisters is explored in Chapter 4; I show how, within Santa Clara and Santa Catalina, the nuns created and maintained their own thriving households (complete with children, servants, and slaves), redefining the institutions of marriage and family to meet their purposes. They also created a strongly hierarchical order that placed criollas and Spaniards at the top of the convents' affairs and relegated kurakas' daughters to a lower status. Andean elites thus could not aspire to see their daughters ascend to positions of control over important convent business. Instead, their daughters inhabited the middle ranks of the convent hierarchy; with the nuns' numerous servants and slaves, they made up the vast majority of the inhabitants of Cuzco's conventos grandes—houses grown so capacious and boisterous by the 1670s that cuzqueños moved to create a third, more austere Carmelite convent, Santa Teresa.

Chapter 5 details the cultural and economic circuitry that made it possible for all three convents to deploy their assets in the local economy in ways that facilitated the nuns' collective prosperity as well as the spiritual health of their benefactors. Debt created relationships: it made important, mutually sustaining bonds, not simply burdens. Together with the previous chapter, Chapter 5 advances my argument that Cuzco's convents played a vital role in the creation of a divided colonial elite: propertied criollos on the one hand; propertied Inca nobles and kurakas on the other. For the nuns forged relationships with both—accepting their daughters, extending them credit, and praying for the good of their souls. This important new perspective helps us to understand why, for centuries, kurakas consented to act as linchpins of Spanish colonial rule, even as it impoverished their communities and produced clearly discriminatory treatment of their daughters. Convents gave these indigenous members of Cuzco's elite access to credit, that all-important element of colonial enterprises of every sort. We thus gain new insight into the symbiotic arrangements that underwrote Spanish colonial rule—and the high cost at which they operated.

By the early eighteenth century, however, these relationships were showing clear signs of trouble. In Chapter 6, I consider several developments that gradually undermined the nuns' position over the course of the century, including mounting pressures for ecclesiastical and imperial reform, a surfeit of debt in the region, and the massive Túpac Amaru rebellion of 1780–81. Slowly, almost imperceptibly, the place of convents changed: their perceived wealth—long a sign to cuzqueños of their city's and their society's spiritual health—came into question, and the propertied classes that for centuries had supported the nuns were increasingly convinced that the "dead hand" of the church was responsible for agricultural stagnation. I explore the ironies and contradictions of the nuns' late colonial predicament and show how the perspective of convent finance enables us to trace out a new level of instability underlying Peru's late colonial crises.

Chapter 7 investigates the language and stakes of secularization in postcolonial Cuzco. In the wake of Simón Bolívar's 1825 progress through their city, cuzqueños were prepared to hurl sharp attacks at the convents' age-old practices, financial and otherwise. They began

The Plaza de Armas of Cuzco, hub of today's tourist traffic. Popular spots to visit include the cathedral (right foreground) and the Inca fortress of Sacsayhuaman on the hill overlooking the city. Photo by K. Burns.

aligning *Dios*, God, with the new republican state that Bolívar and others were working to erect, and placing nuns rhetorically on the other side of a great divide, as enemies of liberty. The nuns defended themselves vigorously in this vehement war of words, but their communities shrank and their structures began to crumble around them. All the while, cuzqueños came to see activities long controlled by the church — charity, the care of orphans, children's education — as responsibilities of the new Peruvian state. Thus there were few protests (except, of course, from the nuns) when Cuzco's convents were partially expropriated to endow new republican institutions like the Colegio de Educandas, one of Peru's first state-sponsored schools for girls.

Yet Cuzco's convents never closed, or were closed, down. Cuzqueñas continued to profess solemn vows and dedicate their lives to ancient rounds of prayer, even as their fellow citizens enacted land reforms, fought over the meaning of church and state, reinvented Inca traditions, and assisted ambivalently their city's transformation into an exoticized tourist destination, continually reconfiguring the terms of property, liberty, Indianness, and decency.[15] None of this kept women from devoting themselves to spiritual matrimony inside Santa Clara, Santa Catalina, and Santa Teresa. Nor does it keep the occasional visitor today from finding the convents' side doors after mass and entering, bearing small gifts for the nuns and perhaps a bit of news. These durable rounds disclose a spiritual economy that is still meaningful, if more inward in observance; they invite questions we have only begun to ask.

Part One

FOUNDING ACTS

No hay más claridad que si nunca viéramos . . .

—Juan Polo de Ondegardo, 1571

1 Gender and the Politics of Mestizaje

When the city council of Cuzco met on April 17, 1551, its members, all battle-hardened Spanish veterans, were enjoying a respite from seemingly endless rounds of war. Soon they would pick up their weapons and charge back into battle, for the fighting in the strategic center of the Inca heartland of Tahuantinsuyo was far from over. But on April 17, the Spanish city fathers of Cuzco had other business on their minds. That day they decided to buy a piece of city property and found a cloistered nunnery. Two weeks later, on April 30, the price of the property was donated by councilman Diego Maldonado "el Rico," a shrewd survivor of many battles and the wealthiest Spaniard in Cuzco.[1] Very few Spanish women were available to set the tone for the new foundation, yet rather than delay and send to Spain for nuns, the councilmen eventually found a local widow named Francisca Ortiz de Ayala to serve as abbess for life—which she did, as Abbess Francisca de Jesús.[2] So began one of the first religious houses for women in the Americas, Santa Clara, still operating today more than four centuries later.

Why a cloistered monastery, of all things, in such a turbulent time and place? The minutes of April 30, 1551, record that Diego Maldonado made his gesture to ensure the actual founding of a monastery to "remedy" mestizas—the children of conquest, daughters of Spaniards like himself and Andean women.[3] Writing to Francisca de Jesús in 1560, the *corregidor* of Cuzco, Juan Polo de Ondegardo, gives an expanded account of the motives behind these founding acts. He begins by linking the nunnery directly to the fighting: since so many Spaniards had died far from home, Christian charity obliged the survivors to care for the orphans of their fallen comrades.[4]

But why not care for the orphaned mestizo sons as well? Did mestizas hold—at least momentarily—greater promise or value in their fathers' eyes? Seeming to anticipate the question, Polo de Ondegardo

[handwritten marginalia: mestizaje faced a greater / girls must be / risk, protected / be more / for their / virginity]

writes that "although it appears the same should be done for the orphaned boys, *they run less risk than the girls*, and . . . it is fitting to provide for the greater need."[5] A masterpiece of patriarchal succinctness, Polo's statement expresses the gendered logic of his culture, according to which girls' virginity, a prized token of male honor and the means of shaping lineages, was constantly at risk and had to be protected at all costs.

Yet that was only part of the story. As he continues, Polo de Ondegardo conveys the special urgency that attended the founding of Santa Clara, only two decades after Spaniards first arrived in the central city of the Incas. In the cloisters of Santa Clara, Francisca de Jesús would win these young women from their Inca mothers and save them for their Christian fathers. The corregidor congratulates the abbess on the many (mestiza) souls he expects her to save:

> and I have no doubt they will be many, because the people born of this land, I have observed well, are all possessed of a very humble nature, which is excellently suited to receive the imprint of the truth, removing them from all communication with their mothers, as you do, which was an impediment to instilling anything good in them.[6]

Polo goes on to depict the abbess as engaged in a tug-of-war for the souls of mestizas with the devil himself, whose temptations "cannot fail to be great." He suggests Santa Clara help advance the cause of Christianity in the Andes, tearing girls away from their mothers in what he and his companions considered a necessary violence.

Not only do we glimpse the devil through Polo de Ondegardo's eyes, but he points us in the direction of a major revision of the story of conquest: toward seeing women as both subjects and objects of Spanish evangelizing drives. For evangelization this certainly was, of a gender-specific, strategic kind. Moreover, Santa Clara was designed to play an explicitly reproductive role, redirecting the energies of child-rearing to increase the numbers of female Christians in Cuzco. The point was not simply to populate the city with nuns. Abbess Francisca de Jesús was to take the place of the children's Andean mothers and keep the girls in the cloisters until they were old enough either to profess or to leave the monastery and assume a role (*estado*) in the Christian society their fathers planned to erect in the city.[8]

We are not used to thinking of cloistered convents as sites of reproduction. Thanks to an unusually detailed source, however, we can gain insight into the importance and outcomes of this seemingly incongruous project. In 1560, Polo de Ondegardo gave Francisca de Jesús a book for her to inscribe basic information about her young charges.[9] The records she kept are limited to the convent's first entrants, and many entries are incomplete. Nevertheless, this *libro de la fundación* indicates that Santa Clara in its earliest years succeeded in annexing to Spanish culture a number of mestiza girls, who grew up to become not only nuns but wives and servants in the Spanish households of Cuzco. In short, the project initially worked: it obeyed its founders' designs, at least for the space of a few critical years.

This information opens up new analytical angles on the Spanish conquest, enabling us to draw new connections: to see conquistadores and encomenderos as fathers; to take nuns into account as significant historical agents, involved in social reproduction; and (not least) to see a gendered dimension to the remote historical antecedents of what we now call race. I will argue that Santa Clara and its earliest entrants were vital to the production and reproduction of Spanish hegemony in Cuzco, helping remake the former capital of the Incas into a center of Spanish colonialism. For it was not enough for Spanish men to seize the Inca heartland. To gain firm control over the Andes, these would-be lords had to find the means to reproduce themselves—their lineages, authority, culture. Cloistering their mestiza daughters at a particularly sensitive moment in the consolidation of Spanish rule gave the leading Spaniards of Cuzco the means to do this, and thus stake a permanent claim to power in the Andes.[10] *The cloistered mestizas were raised to be Spanish.*

Appreciating fully the significance of these founding acts requires us to situate them in their notoriously turbulent historical context. Diego Maldonado and his companions were engaged in a ferocious struggle to control their *encomiendas*, those grants of Andean labor and tribute which they had won by acts of conquest and which had enriched them beyond their wildest imagination. Their best hope of establishing glorious legacies in the Andes lay in transmitting these prestigious and valuable grants to their heirs. Ironically, the very privileges afforded men by Iberian-style patriarchy made mestizos a threat to the consolidation of Spanish control at this volatile, politically charged moment in Andean history. By attending carefully to the gender politics of this critical juncture, we will see why the Spaniards increasingly came to see mestizos as "others," dangerous rivals to be feared, whereas their mestiza daughters might, if properly raised, help them to consolidate their power—why, in other words, Spaniards at this point developed a kind of gendered double vision of their own progeny.[11]

The Historical Context: A Protracted Conquest

To understand why the leading Spaniards of Cuzco were obsessed with inheritance and concerned about mestizos in mid-sixteenth-century Cuzco, we first have to examine who these men were and how they got there. Spaniards first saw Cuzco in 1533, the year Francisco Pizarro and a group of several dozen followers reached the city. At that point they had been inside the vast Inca state of Tahuantinsuyo for more than a year, and had long since realized they had had the good luck to intervene just as the Inca leadership was emerging from a bloody succession crisis. They had made the most of their fortuitous timing by seizing, ransoming, and then killing the Inca ruler Atahualpa at Cajamarca in a sequence of events that would be argued over for centuries.[12] Pizarro had rewarded his followers by distributing precious metals and Inca women: Diego Maldonado, one of the most abundantly rewarded, got thousands of pesos' worth of gold and silver and a woman later baptized as Lucía, a sister of Atahualpa.[13] Eager to see and acquire more, most of the "men of Cajamarca" then followed Pizarro as he made his way higher into the Andes toward the central city of the Incas.

Cuzco made an enormous impression on the first Spaniards who saw it. Pero Sancho, secretary to Pizarro when the Spaniards entered the city in 1533, observed that Cuzco was so large and beautiful a city that it would stand out in Spain. As for its principal fortress, Sacsayhuaman, he marveled that human beings could erect such impregnable walls.[14] Pedro de Cieza de León, who arrived in the 1540s, emphasized that nowhere else was such a noble city to be found; all other towns in South America looked insignificant to him by comparison.[15] The population of Cuzco at the time of the conquest can only be guessed at, but the city was probably the largest in South America at the time of the Europeans' arrival, with perhaps 150,000 to 200,000 residents.[16] An impressive network of roads led to it. The carefully preserved bodies of former Inca rulers exercised remarkable power from their central palaces, and stunningly majestic rituals filled the main plaza. To a people accustomed to finding power in cities, Cuzco was clearly the center of gravity of Tahuantinsuyo.

In this awesome place Pizarro staked his claim, formally refounding Cuzco as a Spanish city on March 23, 1534. Pizarro and his men enacted rituals of their own, performing a city into existence by transplanting to this terrain the fundamental institutions of a Spanish city: the *picota*, or pillory, symbol of Spanish justice; a church, for which a site was designated; and a *cabildo*, or city council. Eighty-eight *vecinos* were enrolled with the understanding that each would receive a portion of Cuzco's land and the labor power of its inhabitants.[17] Word of the riches of the conquered Inca empire reached an eager audience in Spain and elsewhere in the Americas with little delay, and a sixteenth-century gold rush was on.[18]

However, Pizarro decided to found his seat of government elsewhere, a decision that would have enormous historical ramifications. He settled ultimately on a coastal site and founded Lima, the "city of Kings," in January 1535. That left an open door to conflict in Cuzco. No sooner had Pizarro left than a vigorous Inca resistance took shape under the leadership of Atahualpa's brother Manco Inca, culminating in a massive attack on Cuzco in mid-1536 that nearly overwhelmed the Spaniards, followed by a devastating, year-long siege. When his efforts to retake Cuzco failed, Manco Inca retreated north in 1537, establishing himself in the *montaña* stronghold of Vilcabamba. From this "neo-Inca state," resistance to Spanish control of the region continued for decades under Manco and his sons Sayri Túpac (1557–60), Titu Cusi (1560–71), and Túpac Amaru (1571–72). The Inca elites who stayed in Cuzco after 1537 sought to accommodate the Spaniards, but the city remained a welter of bitter enemies.

For almost two decades, rival Spaniards raised forces against one another in a brutal series of civil wars in which Francisco Pizarro and countless other combatants died. Increasingly, these contests revolved around the fate of the encomienda as a means of organizing Spanish access to Andean wealth. An encomienda—often the grant of an Andean ethnic lord (kuraka) and those whose labor and tribute prestations he supervised—guaranteed its holder tremendous prestige and a lucrative material stake in settling the Andes for Spain.[19] But there were only a few hundred encomiendas, hardly enough to satisfy all Spanish comers. Men who had managed to obtain grants tried desperately to keep them, arguing that they should be awarded perpetual, heritable rights. However, the Spanish Crown, faced with numerous denunciations of arrogant, ruthless encomenderos who abused "their Indians," feared these men would create a seigniorial Spanish American aristocracy defiant of royal control. After a disastrous attempt in the 1540s to abolish encomiendas, the Crown fell back on a less drastic strategy: that of meting out encomiendas in men's lifespans, giving Spaniards rights for two *vidas* or more. Encomenderos were thus strung along over the issue of inheritance, kept in a state of perpetual uncertainty, with just enough at stake not to rebel (most of the time).[20]

Cuzco was central to the prolonged struggle over encomiendas. For although Lima was the capital, Cuzco at midcentury continued to be the heart of Peru, the prize over which successive waves of conflict broke. Cuzco was the richest region in terms of the Andean labor power and tribute goods that could be commanded there. European diseases caused great disruption and death in the region, but did less damage in the highlands than elsewhere.[21] Thus both the number of encomenderos and the tribute totals they received were higher in Cuzco than anywhere else in Peru.[22] And by the 1550s, Cuzco's encomenderos had hit upon new ways of using Andean labor to enrich themselves. Precious metal had been discovered in a great silver-veined mountain at Potosí in 1545, and the trade in coca leaf and other supplies from Cuzco to the mining city grew remarkably thereafter, as did Potosí itself. Despite all the warfare and uncertainty of the 1540s and 1550s, many encomenderos of Cuzco exploited their encomiendas to become rich.[23]

These years were marked by extreme violence, not least of it Spaniards' violent treatment of Andean women. The conquerors' imperious actions were only barely checked by the handful of Catholic clergy who had made it to Cuzco by midcentury. Vicente de Valverde, Cuzco's first bishop, was present in the city only sporadically, but made some effort to control individual Spaniards' excesses. In 1539 he punished two Spaniards with fines and brief jail sentences for holding Indian women against their will. Francisco González admitted to the bishop in January 1539 that he had kept a woman named Pospocolla in his house for a month and a half, and that "the other day he yanked her by the hair because the Indian said she wasn't his." Pospocolla testified that she had been beaten and taunted. The following month, Juan Begines appealed the bishop's sentence against him, even while admitting that he had kept a woman named Mencia, "an Indian who said she was a Christian," chained up inside his house and had whipped her many times—he couldn't recall how many—with a stick or whatever he found close at hand.[24]

Meanwhile, Spanish authorities (from the king down) were trying to settle Spaniards and convince them to stop their licentious ways and "bad example," preferably by marrying Spanish women. Earlier the monarchs had entertained the idea of intermarriage as a vehicle of conquest, suggesting that some Spanish women and men marry Americans "[so] that they may communicate with and teach one another . . . and the Indians become men and women of reason."[25] However, by the time Spaniards reached Peru, this notion had long since been dropped in favor of a new approach, one more in keeping with the monarchs' propensity to treat Spaniards and Americans as irreducibly different kinds of people who should be kept apart in separate "republics" (*repúblicas*). The new strategy relied on the trope of mirroring, the idea being that malleable Americans, like children, would imitate their conquerors. The Crown exhorted Spaniards to set "good examples": to stop keeping Andean women in their households, form legitimate Spanish households, and demonstrate to Andeans the benefits of Iberian-style civilization. And deadlines were set for encomenderos to marry or risk losing their encomiendas.[26]

But encomenderos did not want to marry just anyone; the decision was too important to the propagation of their lineages. It might take months to go over and find a wife in Spain or to arrange for a partner to bring over his marriageable kin. Instead, many encomenderos put off marriage and lived with elite Inca women. Diego Maldonado is one example. Another is Captain Sebastián Garcilaso de la Vega, who, while serving a term as corregidor in the 1550s, lived and had two children with an Inca noblewoman named Chimpu Ocllo; their eldest son was the eloquent mestizo author best known by his adopted name, the Inca Garcilaso de la Vega (1539–1616). Spaniards were quick to grasp the benefits of such arrangements. The Inca nobility regarded them as kin and assisted them accordingly.[27] But like Garcilaso's father, the encomenderos did not marry their Inca partners.[28] Almost to a man, they eventually wed Spanish women—often the daughter or sister of a fellow encomendero—and married off their Andean partners to less prominent Spaniards, as though tossing down scraps from a banquet table.[29]

Various Spanish accounts note one result of these turbulent years: the proliferation of mestizos. The etymology of the term "mestizo" is uncertain. The Inca Garcilaso asserts in his *Royal Commentaries of the Incas* that the term was initially used as an insult.[30] "Mestizo" soon became in Spaniards' mouths a synonym for "illegitimate," since almost all mestizos were natural children (*hijos naturales*), born to unmarried Andean women and Spanish men.[31] Some of the boys were taken into the religious orders to serve as *lenguas,* translators in the campaigns of evangelization that were launched across the countryside from cities like Cuzco. Others accompanied their Spanish fathers on expeditions to extend Spanish claims to new territory. But Garcilaso and his mestizo companions occupied an unsatisfying, in-between position. They were arguably twice noble, the children of both Spanish and Andean elites, yet the Peruvian viceroyalty had made no special place for them, no republic.

By midcentury, a first generation of mestizos was nearing adulthood and beginning to worry Spanish officials. As early as the 1540s, the occasional Spaniard had registered apprehension about the mestizo population. By the 1550s, the warnings in letters and reports to the Crown were becoming sterner and more paranoid. These boys and girls needed to be attached somehow: mestizo boys to learn *oficios* or trades, girls to be domesticated into Spanish homes (i.e., made auxiliaries, supportive players).[32] The boys in particular were starting to appear dangerous. Many had learned how to wield Spanish weapons, and some of the older ones, like Diego Maldonado's son Juan Arias Maldonado, had fought alongside their fathers in the midcentury wars.[33]

The encomenderos of Cuzco were also in a quandary at midcentury. While they had grown rich from their encomiendas, and had municipal offices firmly in their grasp, they were nevertheless increasingly insecure about the future. The Crown had left it far from clear whether their prized encomiendas could be inherited, even if they did manage to leave behind legitimate, Spanish heirs. And their eldest, mestizo children were growing up and beginning to realize, like Garcilaso, the vulnerability of their own position.

The position of the Mestizos was percarious, though of noble blood they were illegitimate & couldn't get inheritance. But they

Founding Acts *were a prevelant group.*

This was the charged context in which Cuzco's cabildo pursued its goal of establishing a cloistered monastery. On April 17, 1551, the assembled members bought a piece of property from the estate manager of Hernando Pizarro, stating that the cabildo would assume the role of patron of the new foundation. It is not clear whether the desire to protect mestizas was a part of the plan from the start. Probably so, since the Audiencia of Lima had ordered on October 8, 1550, that the corregidor of Cuzco report on the situation of mestizos living among the natives, and had stipulated that they be placed in the care of Spaniards until something more definite should be decided.[34] In any case, on April 30, 1551, Diego Maldonado galvanized his fellows into action by donating the 550 pesos the property had cost on the condition that the nuns pray for his soul and those of his successors.[35] The cabildo responded by naming him mayordomo of the new foundation for a year, setting down its intention to promulgate statutes to regulate the nuns' existence, and setting out to find additional property to donate to the new convent. With their notary public in tow, the cabildo members proceeded to the site bought by Maldonado and agreed on the spot to donate an adjoining tract.

Santa Clara was not the first monastic house to be established in Cuzco. The Dominicans, Mercedarians, and Franciscans had already established their institutional presence in the city, and the Augustinians and Jesuits would not be far behind.[36] But while the men's orders were founded by groups of friars sent over from Spain specifically for that purpose, Santa Clara was a homegrown institution, constructed by the city's founding fathers at the same time they were constructing themselves as such. The foundation has about it a distinct air of improvisation. During the 1550s Santa Clara appears to have functioned as a recogimiento under the leadership of Francisca Ortiz de Ayala, a pious widow who also attended to patients in the local hospital for Indians.[37] As the new foundation got under way, local Spaniards supported it with donations, and toward the end of the decade the cabildo sought royal permission to elevate Santa Clara formally to the rank of monastery.[38]

To found a monastery in sixteenth-century Spanish America was not unusual, nor was it unusual to shelter mestizas. Examples of these activities can be found throughout the region. In the viceregal center of Lima, for example, the Spanish widow of an encomendero and her widowed mother had by the late 1550s formed a monastic community under Augustinian auspices. This house, La Encarnación, was intended for widows like themselves, and mestizas were not allowed to profess in it.[39] About the same time, a separate institution was taking shape in Lima specifically to shelter orphaned mestizas: the recogimiento of San Juan de la Penitencia.[40] In Lima, as elsewhere in the region, professed nuns and their mestiza charges were clearly intended to be two quite separate categories.   *date 1550's*

To found a monastery in *order* to remedy mestizas, who might in time become nuns—this was distinctly out of the ordinary. The occasional mestiza might make her way into monastic life, but such cases were more the exception than the rule and might provoke heated debate. For example, when the corregidor of Cuzco, Alonso de Alvarado, offered La Encarnación the rich sum of 20,000 pesos to accept his mestiza daughters, the nuns defied their male superiors and accepted one of the young women, creating a major conflict between the convent and the Augustinian hierarchy in Lima.[41] Across Spanish America the preferred vehicle for the care of mestizas was the recogimiento, a flexibly defined institution readily adapted to welfare purposes. No royal approval was necessary for such a foundation, nor any monastic rule, and entrants were not required to bring a large dowry or profess solemn vows.[42]

Monasteries were a different matter. As in Spain, they were considered a reflection on the communities around them; Spanish ideals of honor and feminine purity were powerfully represented and reinforced by these bulwarks against evil, dishonor, stain.[43] If the nuns' honor was upheld, a city could hold itself in esteem, and vice versa. Thus founders consistently phrased their motives in terms of "giving greater authority" to their cities.[44] Following Spanish practice, criteria for entrance into Spanish American cloisters were more rigorous than for less formal enclosure: an initiation period was observed, and a substantial dowry required. By the sixteenth century, issues of legitimacy were already starting to make their appearance in Peru, as the scandal in La Encarnación over Alvarado's daughters shows. To admit mestizas was (almost by definition) to admit illegitimacy, people of mixed and still indeterminate status. The Augustinian overseers of La Encarnación were quite unexceptional in their objections to mestizas. The gesture of Cuzco's cabildo on behalf of mestizas was a noteworthy exception.

For a cabildo to sponsor a convent was also a striking departure from the norm. Most foundations in the Americas, as in Spain and throughout Catholic Europe, were initiated by individuals or families. Endowing a religious foundation was expensive, and thus typically the act of an aristocratic, wealthy lineage seeking to enhance its members' status while ensuring them spiritual benefits. For a cabildo to get involved suggests something vital was at stake in Cuzco, some collective interest of the encomenderos too important to be left up to individual piety and charity. If Santa Clara can be read as a sign of how greatly it mattered to these men that mestizas have a respectable place, be "remedied" and not lost, they must have had compelling reasons indeed.

We have seen the explanation of Juan Polo de Ondegardo for the new foundation: a combination of Christian charity exercised on behalf of fallen Spanish comrades, the protection of vulnerable girls, and the saving of souls. At this point, it is worth examining the historical context more closely. In 1551, the Crown was reiterating its insistence that encomenderos marry in order to retain their encomiendas, the implicit message being that they marry Spanish women.[45] Almost all the encomenderos of Cuzco, including all of the members of the cabildo, had by this point taken Spanish wives. To judge from the writings of the Inca Garcilaso, by the 1550s the remaining holdouts were noteworthy exceptions. However, many (if not all) of the encomenderos had fathered mestizo children before marrying, and were obliged to reconcile the needs of two distinct families—one Andean and informal, from the paternal point of view; the other recent, legitimate, and Spanish.

Some encomenderos, like Diego Maldonado "el Rico," had only mestizo children to whom they might leave their privileges and fortunes. Maldonado, who did the most to ensure the founding of Santa Clara, did take a Spanish wife around midcentury, Doña Francisca de Guzmán.[46] However, the couple never had children. Thus Maldonado's only potential heirs were his mestizo son and daughter, Juan Arias and Beatriz, born to the noble Inca he received at Cajamarca, Doña Lucía Clara Coya. And he was not the only founder of Santa Clara to father mestizo children: Alonso de Alvarado, who presided over Cuzco's cabildo in 1551, had at least two mestiza daughters. While there is no evidence that their own daughters entered Santa Clara, the cabildo members' connection to this project of "remedying" mestizas was clearly very close, at once political and personal.[47]

More insight can be gained from Santa Clara's "Libro original," a fairly detailed account of the convent's foundation and its earliest entrants and ground rules, kept from around 1560.[48] The picture of convent entrants that emerges is one of astonishing diversity. The circumstances of the girls' entry into Santa Clara vary widely, as do their backgrounds (see Appendix 1). In fact, it is quite possibly the most heterogeneous group ever to populate a colonial Spanish American monastery on terms of theoretical equality. Most prominent among them was Doña Beatriz Clara Coya, the only child of Cusi Huarcay and Sayri Túpac (d. 1560), one of the last Inca rulers of Vilcabamba. Only three of the sixty initial entrants are clearly identified as Spaniards. Two of these, apparently orphans, were allowed to become nuns in spite of the fact that they brought no dowry, "so that the convent might begin to be populated with Spanish nuns that there may be an abundance of them (*para que aya copia dellas*), and to give greater authority to the convent."[49] One girl by the name of Beatriz is listed as a *morena*, and thus may have been of African descent.

However, most of the sixty original entrants seem to have been mestizas, those Santa Clara was founded to favor.[50] Some had been plucked from Andean villages by passing Spaniards:

> JUANA. Poor, orphaned, father unknown, found in an Indian village, brought to this Monastery in early [fifteen] sixty-one, with no dowry or board; she is to be catechized and remedied for the love of God, and it shall be set down on this page what becomes of her.[51]

Like Juana, eighteen other young women were listed as "orphans," meaning that they were fatherless. Their Andean mothers are never mentioned. At least seven were daughters of Spaniards killed in the midcentury wars and their aftermath; these included the daughters of "Arias, who died at Villacurí" (in 1554) and those of "Medina, who died in the battle of Guarina" (in 1547). Many had been brought to Santa Clara by people who were not their parents, usually a priest or a merchant. One example is Francisca Arias, "brought by the priest Father Baltasar de Armenta, of the Order of Saint Augustine, who was among the Indians"; another is an orphan named simply Ana: "Juan Moreno, the merchant, brought her."

Twice as large, however, was the contingent of girls whose fathers were alive when their daughters entered the convent. Of the thirty-six who appear to fit this category, the most prominent was Doña María de Betanzos, the daughter of the chronicler Juan de Betanzos and his noble Inca wife Doña Angelina Añas Yupanqui (niece of the Inca Huayna Cápac and a former mistress of Francisco Pizarro). A few young women seem to have been abandoned, like Luisa Pizarro, whose father Mateo Pizarro left her destitute in Cuzco while going off to seek his fortune in Chile, and Ana Téllez, classified as "poor; she has a father; he has to be contacted, so that he may provide her board." But the majority were interned in Santa Clara by their fathers, many of whom gave their daughters a modest annual stipend. The phrase "her father brought her" (*metióla su padre; trájola su padre*) occurs frequently in connection with fathers who could afford a respectable amount for their daughters' maintenance. Some of these men were encomenderos of the region, like Diego de Uceda of La Paz. Some fathers were engaged in commerce—for example, Gerónimo García, "merchant," and Antonio Hernández, who "does business in Potosí" (*trata en Potosí*). Others were artisans—Hernán González, a smith, and "Góngora, tailor." One was a manservant of Captain Sebastián Garcilaso de la Vega. And at least one mestiza's father was a priest.

The majority of the first young women to enter Santa Clara were thus interned, either by a Spanish father or by an unrelated Spaniard. The "Libro original" notes that they were to be raised Christians and to receive *buenas costumbres* (literally, good customs or manners), shorthand for an education in Spanishness that probably included everything from prayers to stitchery, perhaps literacy. After receiving the imprint of Spanish culture—after being "remedied," to use Polo de Ondegardo's gloss—the young charges of Santa Clara might choose either to profess or to leave the convent. The point was not simply to create nuns, but to create culturally Spanish young women.

Thus in its earliest years, Santa Clara had as its principal mission an activity that was, for most other South American convents of roughly equal vintage as well as most Spanish convents, an adjunct: the Christian education of girls. Although the monastic rule stipulated that nuns should live apart from those not under formal vows, the young women of Santa Clara mixed indiscriminately in the early years. Papal exemption for this was sought, but not until the 1570s was a separate part of the convent set aside for the *doncellas*, or "maidens," who were being boarded and raised there. Given the midcentury context in which Santa Clara's educational activities were carried out, this "remedying" represented more than mere education. It was a program of acculturation, probably in many instances a painfully abrupt cultural reorientation.

This is particularly evident in the case of Doña Beatriz Clara Coya, the only fully Inca child among the convent's initial residents.[52] Beatriz was born around the time her father, Sayri Túpac, left the unconquered stronghold of Vilcabamba in 1558 and made peace with the Spanish authorities, receiving in return generous estates in the rich Yucay valley north of Cuzco. When her father died suddenly in 1561, Beatriz inherited the estate he had been granted, becoming one of the richest people in Peru. In 1563, when only five or six years old, she was taken from the care of her mother, Doña María Cusi Huarcay, to be raised inside Santa Clara. The "Libro original" notes that "she was brought to this house by friar Melchor de los Reyes of the Dominican Order, to be raised and to learn proper manners (*buenas costumbres*) in said house; the amount to be given towards her upkeep was not set."[53] Meanwhile, Beatriz was at the center of delicate peace negotiations be-

cristiana   Ias

Guaman Poma (1615) writes that Christian Indians "enter nuns' convents. They learn reading, writing, music, and sewing. They work, cook like Spaniards, sew and clean, bake," but are also sent into the streets late at night, where they "see all the bad" and end up "whores." This complex passage discloses his high anxiety about evangelization and acculturation inside Cuzco's cloisters.

tween the Spanish authorities and the new Inca ruler in Vilcabamba, her uncle Titu Cusi. The strategy hit upon to guarantee peace in Cuzco involved marrying Beatriz to Titu Cusi's six-year-old son, her cousin Quispe Titu.

Beatriz would eventually be married, but not to her young cousin. At the age of about eight or nine, she was taken out of Santa Clara to join her mother Doña María Cusi Huarcay in the household of one of Cuzco's wealthiest encomenderos, Arias Maldonado, who promptly tried to engage the girl to his brother Cristóbal.[54] Rumor soon spread that Cristóbal had raped Beatriz to enforce his claim on her. Alarmed by the implications of such a marriage alliance, Governor Lope García de Castro wrote to the Crown:

> I am afraid that he [Arias Maldonado] might marry her to his brother Cristóbal Maldonado, and I think that this has been done. . . . They tell me that he has been intimate with her, but I do not know whether this is true. This man must not be allowed to have the *repartimiento* [i.e., encomienda] that the girl possesses. For his brother has Hernando Pizarro's repartimiento, and they would become so powerful that no one could oppose them in Cuzco.[55]

The child was hastily returned to the convent. Still Philip II sought papal dispensation to marry Beatriz to Titu Cusi's son. By the time this was granted, it was too late: Titu Cusi was dead, and the Spaniards had again gone to war against the Inca, Túpac Amaru, who was captured and killed in 1572. Beatriz would eventually be given in marriage to Captain Martín García de Loyola, the man who captured her uncle Túpac Amaru, the last Inca ruler of Vilcabamba.

Santa Clara appears several times in the course of this violent and convoluted history. It served as the site of the hispanization of the young Beatriz in preparation for her projected marriage to Quispe Titu, a union the Spanish authorities wanted to domesticate as thoroughly as possible in order to make use of a pliant Inca to pacify the highlands. After an unsettling interlude with the Maldonados jeopardized the outcome of marriage negotiations, Beatriz was returned to cloistered life in Santa Clara. Her betrothal in 1572 to Loyola was contested by Cristóbal Maldonado, who had managed to return to Peru and who continued to insist he was her rightful husband. Not until the late 1580s would the legal dispute be resolved in favor of Loyola. Doña Beatriz Clara Coya was finally wed in her early thirties, decades after the bargaining over her marriage began, having spent most of her life in a convent.[56]

It is hard to determine much about the adult lives of the rest of Santa Clara's earliest residents. Eighteen young women—a third of those about whom the foundation records provide information—eventually professed as nuns. But almost twice as many, thirty-three, left Santa Clara after receiving a Christian upbringing. Ten of these young women were married to Spaniards. Of the other twenty-three, we know only that they were removed from the cloisters—most by their fathers, some by people seemingly unrelated to them. The daughters of the first abbess, for example, acquired three undowered orphans from Santa Clara; perhaps they became household servants, a fate not uncommon for mestizas in this period.

Santa Clara thus fitted numerous mestizas for a livelihood in the Spanish society that was just taking root in Cuzco, not only as cloistered nuns but as wives and auxiliaries in Spanish households—virtually the only honorable roles available to culturally Spanish women at a time when female honor was closely associated with domestic seclusion. Whatever course their lives took after their entry into the monastery, the girls to whom Santa Clara imparted Spanish religion, language, dress, manners, and mores became part of the reproduction of the Spanish culture in whose midst they had been raised. This was the point, as the corregidor Polo de Ondegardo observed in 1560 when he expressed to the new abbess his optimism that Santa Clara would save many souls by removing mestizas from their mothers, who represented "an impediment to instilling anything good in them." Obviously the successful consolidation of Spanish control in Cuzco depended on the Spaniards' ability to reproduce themselves and propagate Spanish ways in the heartland of a conquered empire. Polo de Ondegardo clearly appreciated the significance of the new convent in this long-term project. Although he would have put it differently—as a triumph of truth over falsehood—Polo grasped that the young women of Santa Clara represented a kind of cultural capital, the potential for reproducing Spanish dominance in the hybrid Spanish-Andean society that was taking shape in Cuzco.

A creative composite of monastery, orphanage, and school of Spanish culture, Santa Clara was a place where marriage-minded Spaniards could look for wives at a time that unmarried Spanish women had not yet arrived in large numbers.[57] The mestizas of Santa Clara were Christians—that is, culturally Spanish in the sense that mattered most—and of an age to reproduce: in terms of the demographics and cultural logic of conquest and settlement, they were in the right place at the right time. While it is hard to quantify Santa Clara's importance in the marriage market of early Spanish Cuzco, given the paucity of early parish and notarial records and the impossibility of accurately reconstructing the demographic flows into Cuzco at midcentury, the hispanized young women of Santa Clara may have played a major role. At least ten of the earliest entrants were married to Spaniards, and undoubtedly more of those who were removed by their fathers went on to marry and run Spanish households. By contrast, in Lima—a city with a relative abundance of Spanish women—the recogimiento of San Juan de la Penitencia did not prosper. Santa Clara's Lima counterpart declined rapidly in the decades after its 1553 foundation and was closed in 1576 for lack of mestiza applicants.[58]

Yet as the case of Doña Beatriz Clara Coya shows, the point was not simply to marry the hispanized young "doncellas" to Spaniards, but to marry them to the right Spaniards. While receiving a Christian upbringing in Santa Clara, Doña Beatriz was used first as a bargaining chip to secure the loyalty of the Inca to the Crown, then as a prize to repay the services of the man who had subdued the last Inca. Her abuse at the hands of the Maldonados dramatizes the dangers to which a valuable young woman was exposed, as well as the weight such things carried with the authorities. Not even Santa Clara could protect Doña María de Betanzos, the daughter of Juan de Betanzos and his wife Doña Angelina Añas Yupanqui: she was abducted from the convent by a Spaniard. Despite her father's move to disinherit her, she was ultimately married to her captor.[59]

Santa Clara was, then, more than a school for mestizas. It was a ward, holding its young charges off the marriage market while it was decided exactly what role they would play in the new society taking shape in Cuzco. By 1560 this was very much up in the air. Like Doña Beatriz Clara Coya and Doña María de Betanzos, others in Santa Clara had encomenderos for fathers and might be expected to receive a sizable dowry—perhaps even inherit their fathers' privileges. These young women also represented the possibility of connections for enterprising Spaniards into what remained of the Inca command system at its highest level.[60] But their value and status depended on the outcome of spirited debates, coming to a head in the 1560s, over the future of the encomienda and the place of mestizos in Peru. The consequences, both for the young women of Santa Clara and for Peruvian society in general, would be enormous.

Politics Within, Politics Without: Controversies of the Late 1560s

With the new monastery officially under way, Diego Maldonado and his fellow encomenderos no doubt rested easier about the future of their mestiza daughters, thinking their "mestizo problem" at least partly resolved. Francisca de Jesús would see to it that these young women received the Christian faith and seamlessly merged with those teaching them "buenas costumbres." But if the encomenderos believed Francisca de Jesús would cooperate fully in turning their daughters into Spaniards, they soon found out they were mistaken. Only a few years after the new foundation, the nuns were defying the encomenderos' powers of command and disrupting their designs. On the last day of December 1565, the cabildo met in the convent to convey the encomenderos' frustration over a criterion of difference that had appeared among the nuns:

> [W]e understand that among the nuns presently in the Convent, there is a division in that some of them wear a black veil and others a white veil, and as they are all nuns of the Order of Saint Clare . . . it is not good for such a division to exist, but all should wear a black habit, like nuns of Saint Clare . . . and all those who are now nuns and those who profess in the future, Spanish or native . . . should take the same habit and veil and profess the same enclosure and rule as nuns of Saint Clare.[61]

The cabildo did not seek testimony from the nuns themselves, but the meaning of this boundary can be read clearly enough. In Iberian cloisters the black veil distinguished professed nuns from novices and servants, who wore a white veil.[62] By appropriating this signifier, Abbess Francisca de Jesús and the small minority of Spanish nuns in Santa Clara were unmistakably asserting their superiority over mestiza nuns. The Spanish nuns seem to be saying that the mestizas are permanent novices, a novice people—if not natural slaves, then natural servants.[63]

This case of a sartorial color line points to the way stereotyping often works, through the deliberate fudging of certain boundaries (in this case, those separating mestizas/novices/servants) to reinforce and reify others (Spaniards/mestizas). Unfortunately, none of the nuns is on record regarding the veil controversy, so the cultural logic at work inside Santa Clara in the 1560s must be puzzled out of other traces. No doubt the stigma of illegitimacy weighed heavily against the mestizas in the eyes of Francisca de Jesús. Legitimacy was normally required for admission to Spanish cloisters. But were the Spanish entrants legitimate? The "Libro original" does not say:

> LEONOR DE LA TRINIDAD. Spanish, received without dowry to populate the Convent with Spanish nuns, so that it will have greater authority. . . .
>
> CLARA DE SAN FRANCISCO. Niece of Pedro Valdés, [received] without dowry because she is a Spaniard, and so that the convent will start to be populated with Spanish nuns that there may be an abundance of them, so the convent will have greater authority.[64]

The only clear difference between the mestizas and these young women is that the mestizas had Andean mothers, whereas these two were native Spaniards and presumed capable of providing an "authoritative" example to non-Spaniards.[65]

Diego Maldonado and his fellow councilmen vehemently protested the new veil usage, saying that "by no means would they place their daughters in the convent unless complete equality and conformity regarding the aforementioned [i.e., the same veil and habit for all nuns] were observed in it."[66] In Spain, they argued, there was no such division. Moreover, the cabildo members pointed to the irony of the Spanish women's pretensions in thus setting themselves above their mestiza counterparts: the few Spaniards had entered without dowry, whereas the mestizas for whose welfare the convent had been founded had brought the convent most of its assets. It was decided that no division of veils would be permitted among the nuns, and that in the assignment of tasks all should be admitted equally, "so that the most capable and religious shall be admitted . . . without regard to whether she is mestiza or Spanish." Francisca de Jesús was charged to obey.[67]

The cabildo may have won the skirmish, but it lost the war.[68] Francisca de Jesús and a handful of Spaniards inside the cloisters had commandeered the encomenderos' project and imposed a hierarchical division among the nuns that, despite the cabildo's protests, would later reemerge and remain in place for centuries. Even the cabildo did not champion the mestizas' equality on all points. At its 1565 meeting, the cabildo further determined that for the sake of decorum ("por la utilidad y decoro del conuento"), no illegitimate daughter of a Spanish man and an Indian or other nonwhite woman could be elected abbess for a twenty-five-year period—that is, until December 31, 1590. Perhaps the councilmen believed they were buying time for the mestizas to prove themselves. If so, they miscalculated badly; by 1590 the election of anyone but a Spaniard or criolla as abbess of Santa Clara would be out of the question.[69]

Meanwhile, Maldonado and his companions were busy outside the convent's walls fighting another losing battle—one of high-stakes politics—over the right to bequeath encomiendas to their children. In 1555 they had joined encomenderos around Peru in sending an emissary to the court of Philip II to offer an impossibly large sum, 7.6 million pesos, to buy permanent encomienda rights for themselves and their descendants.[70] Finally they had won the king's serious attention. Philip II, bankrupt and desperate for revenue, allowed a bidding war to begin. The kurakas of Peru responded with an equally impressive counteroffer to free themselves of the encomenderos' control, and sent their own emissaries to Spain: two renowned Dominican defenders of Indian rights, Bartolomé de Las Casas and Domingo de Santo Tomás. With the debate thus freighted with expectations on all sides, Philip II elected to send a new viceroy and three commissioners to Peru, instructing them to negotiate the sale of encomiendas in perpetuity. When these men arrived in 1561 the contest over Peru's future reached new heights of intensity.[71]

The momentous visit by the royal *comisarios* set the stage for some remarkable politics, including an unprecedented show of kuraka unanimity. Partisans on both sides of the great debate crisscrossed the Peruvian viceroyalty in 1561–62, organizing and polarizing the countryside for and against encomiendas.[72] Not surprisingly, the encomenderos of Cuzco found themselves seriously outnumbered. Alarmed by the scenes of violent opposition that formed in front of them, they fumed anxiously about restless and defiant "commoners" trying to become their equals.[73]

To make matters worse for men like Diego Maldonado, the viceroy and commissioners determined after months of inquiry that encomiendas must not fall into the hands of mestizos. In a letter of May 4, 1562, they proposed to the Crown that one-third of the encomiendas be granted in perpetuity to "deserving persons," that another third be granted for a limited period to other pretenders, and that the remaining third revert to the Crown. The authors recommended that to qualify for perpetuity, an encomendero should be married to a Spaniard, and that encomenderos who married Andeans, Africans, or foreigners (persons not subject to the Crown) should lose their grants. They indicated that unions of encomenderos with Andean women were commonplace, and lumped mestizos and mulattoes together in a general assessment that no good could be expected of such people, but rather disorderliness, as they were "badly inclined."[74] As for the process of consultation by which they had arrived at their recommendations, the viceroy and commisioners noted that the encomenderos had conceded ground only reluctantly and after strenuous argument.

This particular battle must have left the aging conquistador Diego Maldonado rather desperate. To try and turn things his way, he had made sizable gifts to those in Lima who were in a position to help him.[75] But in the wake of the commissioners' visit the Crown was still in no hurry to take a definitive stance on the future of encomiendas. Philip II could gain more by leaving matters vague and continuing to deal with encomenderos individually, extracting handsome amounts from them in exchange for prolonging their descendants' tenure in their grants. Such a piecemeal, divide-and-conquer strategy might be especially lucrative in the case of encomenderos with illegitimate heirs, and Philip II seized this opportunity, instructing the Peruvian viceroy to negotiate deals with encomenderos interested in leaving their grants to their illegitimate mestizo sons for the duration of the sons' lives. The viceroy responded that many encomenderos were willing to make such a bargain.[76] No doubt Diego Maldonado was in the forefront of those who were eager to cut a private deal. To him it was less important to preserve encomendero unity than to buy his mestizo son a chance to inherit his privileges and extend the family line.

Ironically, just as the encomenderos were yielding to the Crown's tactics and abandoning a united front, their mestizo sons were joining together to contest their predicament under Spanish rule. No longer willing to await the results of their fathers' schemes, a group of young men began plotting in Cuzco to overturn Spanish authority and seize control of the Peruvian viceroyalty. Early in 1567, just as their frustrated murmuring was about to give way to action, the corregidor of Cuzco, Gerónimo Costilla, got word of their plans. Little is known about the plot, which seems to have involved Spaniards and Incas as well as mestizos.[77] But the blame fell most heavily on a handful of mestizos, who were rounded up and punished. Among them was Diego Maldonado's son Juan Arias Maldonado, as well as Arias and Cristóbal Maldonado, who had just failed in their attempt to forge a marital alliance with Doña Beatriz Clara Coya. Diego Maldonado, the proud old encomendero, was forced to humble himself before the authorities in Lima to gain his wayward son's release.[78]

The "mutiny of the mestizos," as it was called, seemed to confirm the most dire prognostications of the Spanish authorities. Thus even though the failed conspiracy involved Spaniards and Incas as well, and was hardly the only plot of its kind uncovered during these years, it honed the authorities' hostility toward mestizos in particular. The shaken Spanish governor García de Castro, whose life the conspirators had been planning to take, penned many complaints about a mestizo population he characterized as restive, highly dangerous, and growing by the hour.[79] He urged royal action to prevent mestizos from bearing arms, arguing that "since they are sons of Indian women (*yndias*), as soon as they commit a crime they dress as Indians (*yndios*) and hide among their mothers' kin and cannot be found, and there are many among them who are better shots (*arcabuceros*) than the Spaniards."[80] Thereafter, legal provisions restricting mestizos' rights multiplied as a stereotype coalesced in the minds of men like García de Castro: that mestizos as a lot were grasping malcontents, restless and prone to violence.

Thus by the late 1560s, it was growing very difficult for the children of Spaniards and Andeans to find an honorable place in Spanish Cuzco. And the gendered distinctions Spaniards had been willing to make only a few years earlier, favoring mestizas and according them special protection, were starting to collapse. The veil controversy at Santa Clara in 1565 and the 1567 mestizo "mutiny" point in the same direction: toward growing discrimination against mestizos in general and the waning power of Cuzco's encomenderos. The first signs of discrimination against mestizas inside Santa Clara occurred just as the encomenderos were losing their bid for permanent encomienda rights. This crisis of encomendero power meant a significant decline in the mestizas' value on the marriage market; their chances of inheriting and becoming vessels for the transmission of their fathers' fortunes and privileges seemed suddenly remote.

The continuing turmoil in Peru led the Crown to dispatch a demanding lawgiver to impose a greater degree of Iberian-style order in the Andes. Viceroy Francisco de Toledo would be much more definite than his predecessors on the mestizo question, one of many difficult issues he confronted in his drive to "pacify" Peru. In late 1571,

Toledo undertook to visit his jurisdiction personally, and during 1572 he made Cuzco his headquarters. The encomenderos of Cuzco rejoiced: finally, a viceroy was coming to them. But almost as soon as he arrived Toledo found himself in a dramatic confrontation with the cabildo. The new viceroy was utterly determined to break the encomenderos' hold on municipal power, and insisted that the cabildo elect one non-encomendero to its ranks. The cabildo members were equally determined to defy him, but he faced them down and won: a non-encomendero was elected and installed for the first time.[81]

This was but the first of Toledo's disciplining moves. After prevailing over the encomenderos, Toledo went on to win a military victory over the Inca resistance at Vilcabamba. The last Inca leader, Túpac Amaru, was captured and executed in a gory public spectacle in the central plaza of Cuzco whereby Toledo meant to extinguish all further resistance to Spanish rule. And to remove any threat from the relatively cooperative Incas of Cuzco, the viceroy personally brokered the betrothal of Doña Beatriz Clara Coya to Captain Martín García de Loyola, the Spaniard who had captured her uncle Túpac Amaru. As royal authority was rigidly imposed in Cuzco by this ruthless representative of the Crown, the high hopes of the encomenderos were frustrated; those of the mestizos were crushed.[82]

Conclusions

By 1572, a distinct phase in Cuzco's development under Spanish rule was coming to a close, an extremely fluid time of great opportunities and violence. A seemingly paradoxical move on the part of Cuzco's encomenderos—the founding of a cloistered monastery in the midst of war—is in fact fully intelligible in terms of these men's chief concern: to secure Spanish hegemony. By focusing on reproduction, we can see why Spaniards' treatment of mestizas differed from that accorded mestizos. Mestizas (as Polo de Ondegardo reminds us) could be annexed relatively easily to a patriarchal Spanish culture that organized the asymmetries of gender by enclosing females. As nuns, mestizas would lead cloistered lives and teach other girls Christian cultural ways; as wives, they would be enclosed within domestic space and subordinated to their husbands, and could (if married to Spaniards) become part of the *república de españoles.*

Mestizos, by contrast, posed obvious dangers to the reproduction of Spanish patriarchy. While they too might be raised culturally Spanish, they stood to gain a potentially destabilizing role as male adults. As heads of households they might, if fully admitted into the república de españoles, have a wide range of (gendered) cultural tools and weapons at their disposal: arms, horses, powers of command. And to the extent that they had a "mestizo consciousness" at all, mestizos might use these weapons to threaten Spaniards, plucking their guilty consciences with altogether logical, hence threatening, arguments: as sons of conquistadores and high-ranking Incas, did they not have a right to something, perhaps twice as much as anyone else? The irony of Garcilaso's position is poignant. By choosing to value both his parents' cultures, and to claim the dignity of his hybrid condition, he consigned himself to a no-man's-land of Spanish colonialism, exposing the violence by which it was instated in the Andes.

By comparison, things turned out surprisingly well for Diego Maldonado's son Juan Arias Maldonado. Even though he was implicated in a conspiracy that the Spanish authorities took very seriously, sent to Lima for punishment, and banished from the viceroyalty, he ultimately managed to do what his father wanted: he produced heirs to perpetuate the Maldonado family name and fortune in his native Cuzco. This was not accomplished by means of encomienda, however, but through an entail (mayorazgo) that his father Diego set up near the end of his lengthy, eventful life.[83] The crafty persistence of "el Rico" and his well-timed payments to a bankrupt monarch allowed at least one mestizo to slip through the maze of thickening prohibitions, and enabled his descendants to prosper.

Nonetheless, this complicated story of violent striving and destruction left relatively few people satisfied. So thoroughly do Spaniards and their discontents dominate the written record of these decades that it is easiest to regard conflicts from their perspectives, and to see their hopes rise and fall. What of the Andean mothers of the mestizas of Santa Clara who had seen their daughters stripped away from them? We cannot tell what happened to these women, whether the mothers were noble, or even whether they were Incas. They may have been Cañaris or Chachapoyas once subjected to Inca control, or from another part of Tahuantinsuyo altogether. Not only did these mothers lose their daughters, they became textually invisible, brutally expunged by Spaniards who seized and claimed their daughters as Spanish property by branding them orphans.

The mestizas themselves are also silent in the records that speak to historians. However, in light of the pressing procreative and patrimonial designs of their fathers, it is noteworthy that many of the mesti-zas—including many not classed as orphans—professed, vowing to be chaste, poor, obedient, and enclosed. Can we read their professions as "resistance" to Spanish patriarchy? Not in any simple way. Interpret-ing these women's acts is difficult, given the scant archival traces and the tense circumstances in which they pledged to be virgin brides of Christ. Whatever the case, many of these women did remove them-selves from the reach of their fathers and Spanish pretenders by vow-ing to spend their lives in the midst of a community that for a time contained mostly mestizas.

Even so, Santa Clara made a vital contribution to the reproduction of Spanish hegemony in the old Inca city. Many of the hispanized young women raised within the convent were removed from it and as-sumed roles in Spanish households. Doubtless the social reproduction of Spanish Cuzco was also served by the example of the young mes-tiza virgins who devoted their lives and prayers to the worship of the Christian deity. Yet Santa Clara's patrons were not able to ensure that the project would obey their plans. Between 1551, when the cabildo decided to create a monastery for the proper upbringing of mestizas, and the planned uprising of 1567, room for mestizos and mestizas at the highest levels of Cuzco society was narrowing rapidly, and the nuns themselves reflected this fact in their habit. Mestizas could still become nuns, but Santa Clara would institute a new category for them: monjas de velo blanco, nuns of a lesser rank, wearers of the white veil.[84]

In 1576, after Francisca de Jesús had died, an election was held and the office of abbess went to Clara de San Francisco, one of the few Spaniards received without dowry at Santa Clara's foundation. All the abbesses for generations thereafter would be Spaniards or criollas, the American-born daughters of Spaniards. And a process of historical era-sure got under way, for it no longer made sense to cuzqueños to regard Santa Clara in its founders' terms, as a "monastery for mestizas." In-stead the convent gained a distinguished place in accounts of the city's past as a place where "noble" young women, "the daughters of the first conquistadores," had lived and professed. When the Franciscan chroni-clers Diego de Córdova y Salinas and Diego de Mendoza published the first hagiographical accounts of Santa Clara in the mid-seventeenth century, they would not so much as mention the word "mestiza."[85]

How could a foundation have changed so dramatically in just a few years? This transition—in effect, the creolization of Santa Clara—is now largely unavailable to us as detailed social history. (The creolization of Cuzco itself still remains to be explored: we can see that men like Diego Maldonado had their seigniorial dreams pricked by the work of the viceroy and quintessential *letrado* Toledo, but we know little about those who succeeded thereafter in building criollo dynasties in the region.) However, a sketchy roll of women professing in the late 1570s in the "Libro original" suggests that the cloistering of daughters in Santa Clara remained vital to the construction and reproduction of local power long after Toledo had completed his Cuzco sojourn. Doña Mencia de Zúñiga, the criolla daughter of councilman Rodrigo de Esquivel—progenitor of a long line of imperious local aristocrats, the Marqueses de Valleumbroso—took the veil in 1579. If her profession is any indication, criolla ascendancy within the convent may have occurred within just two or three decades of its foundation.[86]

The early history of Santa Clara (sketchy and provisional as it must remain) raises as many questions as it answers. In any case, the convent's foundation records oblige us to regard the category "mestizo" as unstable and provisional. They thus provide us with a powerful reminder about the unnaturalness of race and the limits of racial thinking.[87] Mestizos were not born but made—and the making of mestizos was a saliently gendered, *historical* process. We cannot assume Spaniards saw the same thing every time they looked at the child of a Spaniard and an Andean: circa 1560, "mestiza" signified one set of possibilities to Spaniards in Cuzco, "mestizo" another. Nor can we assume that after Toledo's time the fate of mestizos and mestizas was sealed into a single, unchanging category of difference. Such categories were clearly fluid and merit more comparative study than they have thus far received. In places such as Cuzco—and for that matter, Quito, Huamanga, or La Paz—why, how, and when did Spaniards and criollos begin to relegate mestizos to positions of inferiority? How did those who were labeled "mestizos"—or *chinos, cholos,* or *castas*—respond? Answering such questions will mean taking stock of the diversity contained within these categories, and undoing their masculinized plurals to allow for the singularity of gender.

2 The Dilemmas of Dominio:
Reconciling Poverty and Property

Whatever the color of her veil, the professed nun was obliged to live a life of poverty. On this fundamental point, the thirteenth-century rule given by Pope Urban IV to the followers of Clare of Assisi was clear: "All who wish to leave behind the vanity of the world and enter into and persevere in your Religion," it began, "must keep this rule and instruction, living obediently, without property (sin proprios), and chastely, and also perpetually enclosed."[1] To judge from the hagiographical portraits that the Franciscan chronicler Diego de Mendoza sketched of notable sixteenth-century clarisas (Clares) of Cuzco, the nuns observed their vows strictly, and made sure their companions did, too. Mendoza praises the founding nuns for their extreme personal asceticism and humility, set against a hopelessly Babylonian Cuzco of opulence, gold fever, and plenty. He begins with Francisca de Jesús, who "always wore a poor habit" with coarse cloth next to her skin, "never linen, even during her most dangerous and acute illnesses; her bed was an old animal skin, and a blanket." She found worldly goods and the means of acquiring them distasteful, and "was never richer or happier than when she was poorest, asking for alms to support herself and her nuns." The exemplary poverty of Santa Clara's first abbess inspires a lengthy rhetorical effusion from Mendoza, who urges his reader to ponder weighty truths:

> Who could doubt that the gifts, riches, pleasures, and goods of this life are a heavy weight on the human heart? Who does not know that God is not to be looked for in the depths of the earth, but in the heights of Heaven? How, then, will those who busy themselves in such depths mount up to such a sublime eminence?[2]

Poverty had to be enacted, and it was the responsibility of each nun to do so. The daily practice of poverty meant *desprendimiento*, a constant letting go, divesting oneself of material things beyond those strictly needed to sustain life, and using only the rudest life-sustaining materials. The Constitutions of the Order of Saint Clare provided detailed instructions on the observance of poverty, the better to ensure that each nun would experience it constantly and through as many of her senses as possible. Her habit was to be made of rough, base material. Her bed was to be simple; her daily meals likewise. By Mendoza's account, the founders and first abbesses took great care to live poorly and set an edifying example for the new community of Santa Clara. Abbess Clara de San Francisco is portrayed as having experienced even more rigorous austerity than her predecessor Francisca de Jesús. Not only did she wear a coarse habit, she wore nothing more than sandals on her feet in Cuzco's chilly climate—and her bed was not only rude and uncomfortable, but had an adobe brick for a pillow.[3]

How then was it possible for Santa Clara to amass rights to significant resources in and around the city of Cuzco? The fundamental structure of the monastic life—its basis in poverty and enclosure—would seem to disallow it. Yet the convent's foundation records make clear that from the moment it was established, Santa Clara was acquiring precisely what its individual nuns actively disavowed: property. Detailed inventories show that the monastery had gained title to a variety of valuable properties by December 1565, mainly through donations and purchases (see Table 1). And the list includes a startling incongruity. Santa Clara had managed to obtain not one, but two encomiendas, those hotly disputed grants of Andean labor power and tribute which had by that time become highly controversial. Thus at the very moment that Dominican friars were crisscrossing the Peruvian countryside, rallying support for the abolition of encomiendas, Francisca de Jesús and the nuns of Santa Clara in Cuzco were busy securing their own such privileges—specifically, to the labor power and tribute of the indigenous population of Corcora, Sutic, and Cucucheray.

In short, however austere its individual nuns might be, by 1565 the convent of Santa Clara was on its way to amassing a rich resource base in the Cuzco region which rivaled that of the wealthiest local encomenderos. Diego Maldonado himself could not have done better. Subsequent entries in the "Libro original" from the years 1582–86 give lengthening lists of assets in real property, both urban and rural, located in and near the city of Cuzco (see Appendix 2). The lists also re-

Table 1 Santa Clara's holdings in 1565

House in which the convent is located, bordering the house of the heirs of Alonso Díaz purchased by the nuns in 1558 for 2,600 pesos;

House bordering the above, purchased by the nuns in 1558 for 1,000 pesos ensayados;

Corc[or]a, a cattle ranch (*estancia*) and "certain Indians" granted in encomienda to the nuns by the viceroy;

Land in the valley of Ollantaytambo, acquired in 1560 as the result of a lawsuit against the Indians of Ollantaytambo;

Adjacent land in Ollantaytambo, purchased from the Mercedarian friars of Cuzco in 1561 for 260 pesos corrientes;

Land in Jaquijaguana, purchased in 1563 from a priest for 1,450 pesos ensayados;

Houses adjacent to the convent, in which servants (*yanaconas*) of the convent live;

A store on the central plaza of the city, left to the nuns by Alonso de Hinojosa, and which rents for 80 pesos;

A gristmill in Capi, purchased from Juan Moreno for 1,012 pesos ensayados;

A lien (*censo*) on the house of Francisco Mexía, for 90 pesos corrientes annually;

A lien payable by Gaspar de Sotelo, for 72 pesos, 6 tomines ensayados annually;

A lien payable by Juan de San Miguel, for 21 pesos, 3 tomines ensayados annually;

Livestock in Corc[or]a (320 sheep) and Jaquijaguana (200 cattle, 14 mules for plowing, and 27 pigs);

Ornaments for the convent church and the mass (including a chalice, missal, vestments, crucifixes, religious canvasses);

Tribute from the Indians that belonged in encomienda to the Mercedarian friars [Sutic and Cucucheray], granted to Santa Clara by the viceroy at the urging of Gerónimo Costilla (to take effect January 1, 1566).

Source: "Libro original," ed. Angulo, 75–80.

flect the growing involvement of the nuns in providing credit to local borrowers through the mortgage-like transactions known colloquially as *censos al quitar* which were becoming increasingly common in the region. From three liens (*escrituras de censo*) in 1565, the number of liens the nuns held against specific people's property climbs to eighteen by 1582–86. By the turn of the century, income from censos accounted for around 43 percent of the yearly income of Santa Clara, and the convent was well on its way to becoming one of the largest creditors, as well as one of the largest landowners, in the Cuzco region.

These assets hardly seem to fit with the austere portraits drawn by

Diego de Mendoza of women who shunned worldly goods and basic comforts. How could Francisca de Jesús, Clara de San Francisco, and their successors possibly justify this growing stake in the local economy? Were these holdings not "a heavy weight on the human heart," to use Mendoza's stern locution? The increasing importance of the convent in the regional economy of Cuzco would appear, at first glance, to be an outright contravention of the nuns' monastic rule and constitutions, seriously compromising their professions. How did the nuns of Santa Clara reconcile their vows of poverty with the fact that they were becoming collectively propertied, even prosperous?

The difference between sin and salvation hinged, in this case, on the quintessential sixteenth-century issue of dominio, or sovereignty. Provided the convent of Santa Clara held title to, and thus sovereignty over, the resources in question, no particular nun was guilty of the sin of ownership. The Franciscan Antonio Arbiol illustrates the crux of the matter in his manual for nuns, *La religiosa instruida*:

> The nun who has taken a solemn vow of poverty may not in good conscience possess anything, even a needle. . . .
>
> From this manifest principle it follows that whatever a professed nun has for her own use, she must have it in such a way that she understands clearly that she does not have sovereignty (dominio) over anything, and nothing belongs to her, but only to the Convent.[4]

Arbiol does not say a nun cannot *use* a needle—or benefit from the labor of an indigenous servant, or from the fruits of an encomienda. Rather, a nun's poverty depended on her clear understanding of "property" and its boundaries. Each nun had to take responsibility for keeping her vows, which meant recognizing that anything that came into her hands—even a slight sewing needle—was not truly hers. If her abbess required her to relinquish it, she was bound to do so with obedient alacrity. As long as all the nuns were clear on such matters, disclaiming individual ownership, there was nothing to prevent their convent from becoming as rich as Croesus (or Diego Maldonado "el Rico").

Thus Francisca de Jesús and her community did not sin against their vows of poverty when they acquired title to the property listed in the convent's foundation book, because they did so in the name of the convent, not on their own behalf. Nor were the nuns simply slipping through a loophole in their vows. Their acquisitive activity was in line with the contemporary practice of most European communities of Poor Clares, and fully consistent with Franciscan poverty as it was pursued by women. For unlike their male counterparts, Franciscan women following the rule of Saint Clare had to live perpetually enclosed and could not canvass the city for almsgivers, manage property directly, or otherwise tend to their livelihoods. The point of endowing their monasteries with productive assets was to oblige the nuns to concentrate fully on their daily quest for poverty. For cloistered women, desprendimiento typically required a resource base; their religious poverty was predicated on control over property.[5]

Each cloistered nun was expected to contribute to the resource base of her monastery on entering monastic life. Just as a married woman brought her husband a dowry (dote) to help sustain her in marriage, so a nun brought a dowry to her community when she professed. For a nun, too, was a bride. Her days were spent worshipping her celestial spouse, and prayer also interrupted her nights at regular intervals: the canonical hours reminded her constantly of Jesus, her holy bridegroom. The nun's symbolic marriage was one of reciprocal obligation between gendered, complementary partners, just as worldly marriage was. It enabled her to "take estate" (tomar estado), to assume an honorable position in a patriarchal society predicated on men's control over their female kin. And like worldly marriage, the commitment of a nun to her bridegroom was sealed by ritual acts and sustained by material gifts.

Poverty thus had its gendered limits, its historically defined parameters. At the time of Santa Clara's foundation, nuns might "live poorly" while collectively controlling dowry funds and local property, and were fully expected to do so. Still, the burdens of dominio were weighty, and even the most clear-minded abbess had to struggle with property. For the goal of a monastic community was not to maximize the resources in its grasp, but to have enough income to ensure the maintenance of its members in their daily routines. This meant that the proper balance between edifying poverty and collective comfort had to be constantly negotiated by the nuns themselves. How many worldly, material things were enough to guarantee the sustenance of the community as a whole? Which kinds of assets were preferable, and how were they to be administered? And where were the initial pieces of an endowment to come from in the first place?

Few sources are available for tracing the historical formation of Cuzco's monastic finances from their sixteenth-century beginnings. Neither Mendoza nor Santa Clara's foundation records dwell on the struggles Francisca de Jesús must have faced as she tried to make a material foundation for the community she led for more than two decades, until her death in 1576. But her contemporary Teresa de Jesús (1514–82), the celebrated mystic of Avila and founder of numerous reformed Carmelite convents, had a great deal to say about the difficult early stages of a community's foundation. She devoted a book to the subject which richly illustrates the tension in convent affairs between the ideal of poverty and the demands of property.

Her account of the many foundations she carried out across Spain between 1567 and 1582 leaves little doubt that Saint Teresa was an exceptionally capable administrator of property and income. Most of her convents were given substantial assets by wealthy local people, for whom Teresa expressed admiration and gratitude. Yet she never stopped advocating extreme poverty, strongly preferring that nuns live on charity rather than on the income accruing from investments and property management (rentas). Such income represented the potential for a perilous dependency, she suggests: "I am a great believer in convents being completely poor, or else they should have enough so that the nuns are never obliged to importune anyone for what they need." [6] Elsewhere she spells out her meaning even more precisely:

> I have always insisted that convents founded with an income have enough so that the nuns need nothing from their relatives nor from anyone else, but have all they need to eat and dress themselves in the convent, and to care well for the sick; for many difficulties arise from a dearth of basic things. And I never lack courage or confidence to found many poor convents without incomes, from the certainty that God will not fail to provide for them. I do lack all [courage and confidence] to found convents with little income; I consider it best not to found them at all. [7]

On the dilemmas of dominio, Saint Teresa was strikingly uncompromising: a convent should either be generously endowed at its foundation or receive nothing at all. Only in this way could the nuns concentrate on prayerful lives of poverty. Better to depend fully on God or a local aristocrat than to fall somewhere in between and face a distracting struggle for subsistence.

The writings of Saint Teresa suggest the bind in which Abbess Francisca de Jesús found herself in the Peruvian Andes, on a contested frontier of Spanish colonial expansion. Simply covering the basic living expenses of the community must have posed quite a challenge. Iberian foodstuffs were still scarce and extremely expensive in Cuzco. Dowry funds were not available for these purposes in any case. The cabildo, following the constitution of the Clares, had required that the dowries brought by the early mestiza entrants be invested rather than used for day-to-day operating expenses. This requirement, intended to secure the long-term financial well-being of the community, did nothing to alleviate the short-term situation.[8]

Moreover, Cuzco had no entrenched Spanish aristocrats to whom the nuns might turn for a secure, generous endowment. Men like Diego Maldonado might make gestures on behalf of Santa Clara, but no local Spaniard was yet in a position to deliver the kind of largesse that could be expected of an Iberian *grande*. It was equally unlikely the convent could operate on the basis of charitable gifts alone. The Spanish population of sixteenth-century Cuzco was small and highly transient, and Spanish clergy had as yet done little to propagate or require Christian charity; in addition, the economy was only recently becoming monetarized, and the circuitry and currency of productive activity was in the midst of dramatic transformations. As for the cabildo, which had asserted its patronage of the convent in the 1550s, Diego de Mendoza would write a century later that its members had ignominiously failed to deliver on their promise of support for the nuns.[9]

Compared to many Iberian monastic foundations, the beginnings of Santa Clara would seem to have been quite precarious.[10] Yet the inventories of 1565 and 1582–86 show that Francisca de Jesús and the nuns were somehow managing from an early date to build an endowment for their convent—a distinctly colonial endowment. Entries in the "Libro original" hint of their engagement in disputatious events that could not have occurred in Spain. Chalices and crucifixes are juxtaposed in the 1565 inventory with a lawsuit against the Indians of Ollantaytambo, and an encomienda made over to the nuns "on the condition that if the Inca Tito Aya Yupangue [Titu Cusi Yupanqui] submits to His Majesty, the grant will become void." The very incongruity of cloistered nuns collectively taking the place of a Peruvian encomendero suggests it was somehow *because* of the precariousness of this juncture, rather than in spite of it, that the nuns could profit, quickly assembling a valuable property base in the span of a few short years.[11]

How did they do it? The early records of Santa Clara's foundation give a clear hint. One man's name, Gerónimo Costilla, comes up over and over in connection with the management of convent property.

Named by the cabildo in 1558 as the mayordomo of Santa Clara, Costilla would play an extremely important role in the nuns' affairs for the duration of his long life, staking their claims, overseeing their finances, presenting their petitions, handling their lawsuits, and generally representing their causes to the relevant authorities. Francisca de Jesús and her community, like their cloistered European counterparts, were obliged to work through male intermediaries like Costilla to transact business outside their cloisters. By means of a carefully made chain of representations and male proxies, the nuns could take action far beyond the walls of their convent—collecting returns on their investments of dowry funds in the local economy, for example, and laying claim to property in places like Ollantaytambo.[12]

Retracing these connections enables us to see colonial relations taking shape. For unlike their European counterparts, the nuns of Cuzco were situated in a place where a colonial market economy—predicated on Spanish control over both private property and unfree labor—was only beginning to emerge in the ongoing violence of a protracted conquest. Using their proxy Gerónimo Costilla, the nuns of Santa Clara intervened in the historic economic and social transformations then taking place. Ironically, in order to pursue lives of religious poverty, the nuns became participants in the wholesale reworking of "property" in the Andes, a process that thoroughly hybridized land tenure and local authority in the late sixteenth century, while ensuring Spanish hegemony.

Gerónimo Costilla, in turn, used his position with the nuns to fashion his own fortune in the new economic geography of Cuzco. The resulting symbiosis between Santa Clara and the Costillas reproduced in Cuzco a local, colonial version of the aristocracy and wealth that Teresa de Jesús could take for granted in Spain. The names and faces might change over the years, but the symbiotic bond between nuns and elite families like the Costillas would last for generations. These were not merely relations of economic convenience, as we will see, but relations of spiritual sustenance. By examining in some detail the interwoven histories of Santa Clara and Costilla and his descendants, we may trace the formation and the workings of the spiritual economy of Cuzco.

Dominio by Proxy: General Costilla Performs the Rites of Property

The close association between Gerónimo Costilla and the women of Santa Clara was forged in the 1550s during something of a lull in the

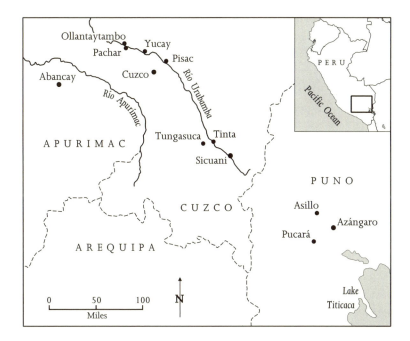

Fig. 2. Map of the region in which the nuns of Cuzco exercised dominio over resources. From the mid-1500s, the Clares held valuable properties from the hacienda of Pachar to the estancia of Caco, near Azángaro. All three convents extended credit to the sugar producers of Abancay, grain-growing hacendados along the Urubamba River, and other local entrepreneurs.

city's violent politics. The cabildo had lapsed in its attentions to Santa Clara in the mid-1550s when a serious rebellion against the Spanish Crown erupted, taking many months to contain. By the late 1550s, a precarious peace had been restored in the city and the cabildo had taken up the convent's cause again. The council members decided to buy Santa Clara a better site, in the house that had belonged to Alonso Díaz, an encomendero who had just been executed by the Spanish authorities for his role in the latest rebellion against the Crown. The cabildo also decided in 1557 to provide Santa Clara a food source, granting the convent a large rural tract of 200 fanegadas in the valley the Spaniards called "Tambo at a place called Pachar." [13]

The place the cabildo chose for Santa Clara had obvious attractions. It was close to the city, well watered, and suitable for growing the wheat that was increasingly in demand with the expansion of Spanish settlement in the region. Nor was this just any fertile valley. It lay near the center of the Inca empire, along the Urubamba (Vilcanota) River, and had long been the province of Inca panacas, the politically powerful kin groups of Inca rulers. Imposing terraces lining the sides of the valley yielded rich harvests of maize, making the region a granary for the Incas. Extensive Inca compounds secured the valley, at Ollantaytambo and Pisac, attesting to its strategic and symbolic importance.[14] So rich and attractive was the valley of the Urubamba River that several encomenderos had sought to have their base of operations moved there from Cuzco. The cabildo had seriously considered such a move, and might have followed through had it not been for Cuzco's venerable antiquity.[15]

Two hundred fanegadas was a very large amount of land to claim in a narrow Andean valley. Each fanegada was the amount of land a laborer could sew with a *fanega* of seed, about 2.9 hectares; so 200 fanegadas was roughly 580 hectares.[16] The cabildo deputized Gerónimo Costilla to carry out a careful inspection of the valley, along with additional Spanish witnesses and a notary, to determine which of its croplands might be given to Santa Clara "without harm to third parties." To this end, in October 1557 Costilla made the day's journey north of Cuzco to the valley to stake his first major claim on behalf of the new convent.

By this time Costilla, a native of Zamora in the old kingdom of Castile, was an authoritative man in his early forties, respectfully addressed as "General" by his companions. His advancing years could not have been comfortable, given the many rugged journeys and battles he had survived since his arrival in Peru in 1535. While accompanying Diego de Almagro south into Chile that year he had lost his toes to frostbite and nearly lost his life. After returning to Cuzco to help lift the siege of Manco Inca, Costilla had stayed and fought in several other battles, receiving as his reward for services to the Crown a share of the encomienda of Asillo, south of Cuzco in the province of Collao. During these years he became involved in the booming coca trade to the mining center of Potosí, like virtually everyone else of any means in Cuzco. By the time Santa Clara was founded, Costilla was among Spanish Cuzco's most honored vecinos. The cabildo entrusted him with the position of mayordomo out of respect for his status as the eldest council member.

Yet were it not for an accident of birth, Gerónimo Costilla would probably have spent his long life favoring the old Franciscan monastery in Zamora, where the bones of his ancestors were buried, rather than helping start a new one in far-off Peru. Costilla came from a noble family, and his parents had distinguished themselves as the benefactors of a chapel, known locally as "the chapel of the Costillas and Galli-natos," in the church of the Franciscan convent just outside the ancient city walls of Zamora.[17] But Gerónimo Costilla was a *segundón*, the second son of his parents Diego Costilla and Beatriz Gallinato. Ahead of him, and in line to inherit the bulk of the family estate and uphold its honor through various sorts of patronage and largesse, was his brother Antonio Costilla.[18] It was the firstborn son who would always take precedence over him, in life and in death, as long as Gerónimo Costilla remained in Zamora. He was ambitious enough not to. Although he would maintain financial and personal ties to his native province throughout his lifetime like many of his companions, Gerónimo Costilla would never go back to Zamora.

Instead, Costilla became deeply involved in promoting the pros-perity of the newly made monastery of Santa Clara, where he eventu-ally purchased a burial chapel in which he would be venerated as the honorable patriarch of a distinguished lineage, not a mere *segundón*.[19] Men, and some women as well, might remake themselves in this way in early Spanish Peru, and clearly Gerónimo Costilla took maximum advantage of the great distance that separated Cuzco from Zamora to jump off his family tree and strike a new root in fresh soil. He would accomplish quite a lot in his own lifetime, becoming a knight of the Order of Santiago in 1579 at a time when only a handful of men in Peru could boast of having attained knighthood in any order. And his six children by his Spanish wife, María Riveros, would accomplish more, combining canny marriage alliances, political officeholding, and noble titles to make Costilla one of the most solidly rooted and presti-gious family names in colonial Peru. Gerónimo Costilla's involvement with the new monastery would be continued by his descendants, sev-eral of whom would become distinguished benefactors and nuns of Santa Clara.

But in 1557 Costilla, like the monastery of Santa Clara, was just be-ginning to fix a firm material foundation on which to construct a prosperous future. Compared to his contemporary Diego Maldonado, he had made only modest moves toward becoming a wealthy *indiano*.[20] He and his wife had children to think about, four sons and two daugh-ters who would eventually expect an inheritance commensurate with the status of their father, a leader among the *primeros pobladores*, the origi-nal settlers. Not surprisingly, Costilla was among those applying pres-sure on the Crown in these years as the contest over permanent en-comienda rights gained intensity. Meanwhile, like many of his fellow encomenderos, he was hedging his bets by simultaneously entering into other productive activities, most notably the sale of coca leaf in Potosí. Among his ventures was the acquisition of attractive pieces of real estate. As he joined the veteran conquistadores Mancio Sierra de Leguizamo and Juan Julio de Ojeda on their October 1557 errand on behalf of Santa Clara, Costilla had his own interests in mind, and he began forming ideas about his own future stake in the valley that was Cuzco's granary.

So it was that on October 28, 1557, the kuraka of Ollantaytambo, Don Francisco Mayontopa, and his Inca kinsmen found themselves face to face with Gerónimo Costilla and his party. Whether a translator mediated their negotiations is unclear; none figures in the fragmentary record of these dealings. Only the Spanish side of the story survives. The account of the notary Luis de Quesada indicates that the first thing Mayontopa and his men did, on learning of the Spaniards' intentions, was denounce a previous usurpation of their land. Mayontopa declared that certain plots in the area already being tilled on behalf of Santa Clara, supposedly without harm to anyone, had been usurped from his people and should be returned to them. Ojeda and Sierra acceded on the spot, ordering that restitution of the land be made to the Indians of Ollantaytambo "as their own land and that of their ancestors." [21]

The encomenderos then proceeded to demarcate other lands in the vicinity which "by confession and declaration of the said *cacique* and Indians and *principales* were found and appeared to be lands formerly of the Inca and the Sun and not those of any third party." On that basis, Ojeda and Sierra claimed them for Santa Clara. They specified boundaries in the usual way, by detailed reference to local landforms and landmarks ("by a small door made of stone that is just beyond a wooden bridge"; "near the smooth boulders with white spots on them," and so forth), duly registered by the notary. According to Quesada's version, Mayontopa and his men assisted in the demarcation of the land "with their own hands" and pronounced it "well done." The land was then given over to Gerónimo Costilla in the accustomed Spanish ritual of possession. Ojeda and Sierra led Costilla by the hand onto the property, where he proceeded to tear up grass, break tree branches, and scatter stones, stating aloud "possession, possession, possession" to signify the right he claimed in the name of Santa Clara. According to Quesada, the kuraka and his men did not speak out against this ceremony ("contradecirlo"), so the Spaniards assumed the Incas' consent.

Costilla, Ojeda, and Sierra had performed into existence a valuable piece of property over which the monastery of Santa Clara could exercise dominio. In effect, the Spaniards had learned just enough about the Incas to use their terms of resource allocation against them. Land under the Incas had been distributed in accordance with a tripartite scheme: some had been used to support the Inca state ("the Inca"), some for maintaining Inca religion ("the Sun"); the rest had sustained local communities. By a kind of rough-and-ready Spanish logic, the first two types of claims had been rendered untenable by the Spanish conquest of Tahuantinsuyo, and the lands had become *tierras realengas*, royal lands. Thus, to show that a piece of arable land or pasture had been "land of the Inca and the Sun" was, from the Spaniards' point of view, the same as declaring the land uncultivated, vacant, and ownerless (*baldía, vaca, eriaza, sin dueño*), available for reassignment by Spanish authorities.[22] By getting the leading indigenous authorities to go on record to the effect that an area had been "land of the Inca and the Sun" prior to the conquest, the Spaniards were able to show to their entire satisfaction that local leaders had no valid claim to it.

However, in the wake of the events of October 28, 1557, Francisco Mayontopa took legal action to reverse Costilla's claim. At some point in the months following the rites enacted at Pachar, Mayontopa petitioned the corregidor of Cuzco, Polo de Ondegardo, for an order enforcing his and his people's right to possess the land that had been appropriated for Santa Clara. Although records of these actions seem not to have survived, other documents indicate that Mayontopa was simultaneously resisting the land hunger of another monastic order, the Mercedarian friars of Cuzco, who were likewise pursuing lands once dedicated to the Inca and the Sun. This was not simply Spanish land hunger, Mayontopa must have realized, but a growing ecclesiastical appetite for a particular kind of land.

Similar cases involving the Augustinians (1560) and Jesuits (1586) suggest a pattern to these claims.[23] The religious orders appear to have believed they deserved priority in the reassignment of *tierras del Inca y del Sol*, lands that once supported the very Andean "idolatries" they had been sent to eradicate. The monasteries needed resources to support the small but growing population of clergy that was spreading out across the countryside, waging a protracted campaign to convert native Andeans. What could be more appropriate in the friars' eyes than to reassign land from the false religion of the Incas to the evangelizing forces of the true faith? Charles V himself had raised this possibility in his 1543 instructions to the first Peruvian viceroy:

You will inform yourself as to which lands and *heredades* in that province were offered and applied by the natives to the houses of the sun, or to other rites and sacrifices of their gentility; and in what measure, and where located, and if it would be good to apply them toward the churches and monasteries that have been, or will be, erected in said province, and in what part and in what manner. And you will report to us the details and value of these, and the necessity that the churches and monasteries may have of them . . . so that we may weigh the matter and decide what is best.[24]

No decision on the matter is recorded. In any case, the idea of expropriating the conquered religion to benefit the conquering faith was clearly available by the 1540s, and the religious orders made use of it. By the time the Jesuits of Cuzco sought a grant of "land of the Inca and the Sun" in the 1580s, they would be told there was none left.[25] By then it was abundantly clear that the indigenous communities were not happy about such claims. In fact, a legalistic mess was the result: claims by Spaniards, counterclaims by kurakas, and seemingly endless lawsuits.[26]

Francisco Mayontopa was in the thick of the legal action. It was up to Mayontopa, as kuraka, to defend what the people of Ollantaytambo regarded as theirs.[27] He resisted the Mercedarians in the late 1550s and no doubt used the same arguments simultaneously against Santa Clara and Costilla. Through his legal representative, Gonzalo Rodríguez, the kuraka testified that he and the other leaders of Ollantaytambo had not spoken out against the initial claim of twenty-five fanegadas by the Mercedarians out of fear of the corregidor of Cuzco, Licentiate Bautista Muñoz, who had made the land grant. He and his men had not dared to dispute the ceremonies of possession, "even though they were very harmful." Mayontopa went on to state that his community needed the land to plant crops, that it was close to where the people lived, and that they had "held and possessed" it for several decades without interruption. Further testimony by Mayontopa and other witnesses is more specific on the harm done by the Mercedarians:

[A]bout four months ago, when [Mayontopa] and his community had sown about twelve fanegadas of the piece of land called Colcabamba with maize for the Collas *ayllu*, *mitimaes* of the said repartimiento, two [Mercedarian] friars . . . with no cause whatsoever let loose a herd of donkeys on the land to eat the maize that had grown there, then they plowed and sowed the land again, and sowed it with wheat.[28]

The scene the witnesses describe sums up much about the transition under way at Ollantaytambo and across the region, its complexity and indeterminacy, and its hybrid features. Even as the kuraka denounces the uprooting of Andean maize in favor of Iberian wheat, he is obliged to enter the terms of Spanish discourse (via his agent Rodríguez), and to fight for fanegadas and possession. His own definition of appropriate land tenure is neither solicited by the Spanish justice system nor offered by Mayontopa himself, and can only be imagined. Had Mayontopa been able to define the area in his terms, perhaps he would have spoken of the distribution of croplands among Ollantaytambo's ethnically diverse, hierarchically ranked ayllus (kinship groups), or noted where the people's huacas (sacred sites) were located. But this would have exposed the huacas to violent extirpation.[29] Mayontopa thus may have decided it was safer not to give away too much local knowledge to the Spaniards and to battle them instead on their own discursive terrain.

Yet Mayontopa may have performed an even more dramatic cultural crossover. The Mercedarians insisted he was lying when he said his people needed the land to grow crops. According to the Mercedarian representative, Alonso de Segura, the areas in question had been vacant and unpopulated "for many years" until the Mercedarians began working them, and had been "dedicated during the time of the Incas to the Sun and to the Inca, former lord of this realm, and never did Francisco Mayontopa or his Indians have or possess them as their own." The Mercedarian friar Miguel de Orenes testified a few days later that Mayontopa had entered into a commercial partnership with a man called "Xuarez,"

> who sows all the Indians' lands and harvests the wheat and brings it to Cuzco to sell, and what he gets for the wheat he divides with the aforesaid cacique [Mayontopa] without giving anything to the Indians . . . and it is Xuarez who has induced the cacique to demand and claim the aforesaid lands so that he, Xuarez, may take advantage of them and not because they are necessary to the cacique or his Indians.[30]

Orenes topped off his testimony by saying the friars had, "at great cost," laid an irrigation channel that benefited not only the land they claimed but lands of the "Indians" as well. In so many words, the Mercedarians argued that they were better to the people of Ollantaytambo than their own kuraka, who, manipulated by a mysterious Spaniard, had sold them out for his own private gain.

Did Mayontopa concoct his case to further a profitable deal he had made with a Spanish (or perhaps mestizo) business partner? Corregidor Juan Polo de Ondegardo apparently did not think so. Unimpressed by the Mercedarians' arguments, he ruled against them in 1559 and supported Mayontopa's claim to the land in question. The decision would be upheld the following year by a ruling of the highest viceregal court, the Real Audiencia in Lima. About the same time, Mayontopa also succeeded in getting Polo de Ondegardo to uphold his community's claim to the land at Pachar that the cabildo of Cuzco had assigned in 1557 to the nuns of Santa Clara.

Gerónimo Costilla then began launching furious allegations of his own to defend Santa Clara's right to Pachar. First came the familiar argument: the lands in question were not being worked because they belonged to the Inca and the Sun; Costilla was the first since the Spaniards' arrival to work the land, put in irrigation channels, and so forth. Next, Costilla asserted that it was entirely false that the members of Mayontopa's community were leaving for lack of land on which to plant their crops. He argued there was more than enough land, and that Mayontopa was being manipulated by Spaniards eager to take advantage of the community's land for their own profit.

What was really going on at Ollantaytambo? It is entirely likely that people were leaving the community, one way or another. Mayontopa must have seen a notable decrease in population, for reasons that are now well known if not yet adequately understood, including the impact of European diseases for which the Andean population had no resistance.[31] Mayontopa may have been defending land that his people once worked but that had fallen into disuse with a drop in the local population. He may also have engaged in commercial deals with entrepreneurial outsiders, as the region's maize and its wheat-growing potential had created a strong demand for both valley land and its grain.[32] Sometimes kurakas sold land to pay for legal proceedings, sacrificing some land in an attempt to safeguard the rest. Sometimes they made the kind of bargains of which Mayontopa was accused, making commercial deals (*compañías*) with mestizos and Spaniards and retaining part of the earnings, whether for their own profit or to meet the tribute obligations imposed on their communities.[33]

The particulars of Mayontopa v. Costilla are undecidable, but the case signals a historic transition under way in the Andes, a crisis of cultural categories and practices pertaining to property. Polo de Ondegardo denounced his fellow Spaniards' distorted understanding of the forms of tribute and resource use that had been customary under the Incas. True, under Inca rule land had been apportioned three ways: to produce maize and other produce for the Inca, the state religion, and the local population. But the "lands of the Inca and the Sun" had not been expropriated from the tributary communities; they went on "belonging" to the same indigenous groups as before.[34] If Spanish authorities, in their efforts to sort out the many judicial contests over land rights, would just take into account "that all those who worked the land in question reaped no personal gain from it, they would not try to decide who rightfully possessed it, but rather whose it was when the Inca dedicated it for a certain purpose."[35]

Polo de Ondegardo went to the heart of the conflicts over "land of the Inca and the Sun": namely, culturally different definitions and uses of vital resources. To men like Costilla, land was a thing (res) over which a single individual or institution might gain rights of sovereignty (dominio) by performing appropriately registered acts and receiving title, and might be obtained through purchase or by a grant from duly authorized authorities.[36] Improvements, such as building an irrigation channel, bolstered one's claim, as did permanence on the land. For the Incas, however, land was a token of very different kinds of relationships. Pasture and croplands were assigned and reassigned regularly within local-level arrangements of kinship and reciprocity, and were crosshatched by various—sometimes competing—claims.[37] Polo warned that when Spanish judges of land disputes ignored Inca usages, sticking instead to their own cultural definition of property, the Andeans ended up double losers: "[S]ince they used to pay tribute from the land, and it was theirs, if we now assess their obligation differently because it seems more convenient, clearly they face two tributes: first, the loss of their land, and second, the tribute amount we now demand of them."[38] Polo himself had seen his fellow Spaniards in action, imposing Spanish terms of land use and riding roughshod over those of the kurakas who attempted to stop them. He marveled at the resulting legal cacophony and lack of clarity.[39]

Polo de Ondegardo did what he could to support Don Francisco Mayontopa in his efforts to hold onto lands of the Inca and the Sun in Ollantaytambo. But Mayontopa decided to settle with his adversary

Gerónimo Costilla and the nuns rather than face an expensive legal battle. He agreed to cede some land to Santa Clara if Costilla would drop the case. The language of their agreement gives an ironic twist to the settlement: a "voluntary donation" of land to Santa Clara by the kuraka of Ollantaytambo hardly seems to accord with the spirit of what took place. The standard notarial protocols obliged Mayontopa to declare that his community did not need the land, and that losing it did not cause them harm.[40]

However, Mayontopa vastly reduced the amount of land he had to give the nuns by specifying an Andean unit of measurement for his grant to Santa Clara. The new terms called for him to give Santa Clara 150 *topos* rather than 200 fanegadas of land. The Andean topo varied from one place to another in the rugged highlands, and so Mayontopa was careful to insist in his bargain with Santa Clara that the topos at Pachar be measured in accordance with his people's customs.[41] This would have amounted to around 48 hectares, less than one-tenth the size of the initial grant of around 580 hectares. Thus the kuraka's astute interventions kept the nuns of Santa Clara and their mayordomo from getting the generous estates they desired at Pachar.

The people of Ollantaytambo had not seen the last of Costilla, though. As he grew more powerful in local politics, the mayordomo of Santa Clara could throw his weight behind even more ambitious efforts on behalf of the nuns. At some point in the mid-1560s, Costilla managed to persuade the viceroy to award Santa Clara an encomienda near Ollantaytambo, even though the Crown had decreed in no uncertain terms that monastic houses could not hold such privileges.[42] The people of Sutic and Cucucheray, who had previously been obliged to provide tribute to the Mercedarians, were required instead to give the nuns of Santa Clara an annual quota of pesos and a portion of the produce of their land and herds. Whether or not they were also required to perform agricultural labor for the nuns on their Ollantaytambo property is not clear. In any case, Santa Clara's possession of the encomienda of Sutic and Cucucheray was an obvious contravention of the rules, and it was not long before the next viceroy took it away from the nuns.

A few years later, Costilla was again making his presence felt in Ollantaytambo. He prevailed on the nuns of Santa Clara to sell him some of the same land he had wrested for the convent from Mayontopa in the late 1550s. In 1573, the land at Pachar was described in much the same terms as before—smooth boulders, white spots, and all— as part of the deed of sale transferring it from Santa Clara to Gerónimo Costilla.[43] The nuns' asking price was one thing, the purchase price another. It seems the nuns were convinced by their mayordomo to make him a special deal.

Costilla next managed to complement his new acquisition by obtaining another grant, this time in his own name. He petitioned the cabildo of Cuzco for land at Ollantaytambo in 1574, despite Viceroy Francisco Toledo's fresh prohibition of such grants. The place Costilla requested was the very one he had visited seventeen years earlier, alongside the Urubamba River at the point of its intersection with the same rushing stream: Pachar. A cabildo member, sent to conduct the usual survey, reported finding several corrals with broken-down structures inside them "from the time of the Inca." Walking about, he saw nothing that appeared to him to have been tilled or inhabited by Indians. His attention was drawn to "a large mound of earth above a boulder that appeared to have been a place of sacrifices (*sacrificadero*) and a sacred site of the natives." The Spaniard then called on the kuraka of Ollantaytambo, Don Gonzalo Cusirimache, and other local leaders to confirm his impressions. One man indicated that the large mound was "where the Inca had sat." Another said that the complex of broken buildings and corrals had belonged to Mama Ocllo, the mother of Huayna Cápac, and that his ancestors had told him *mamaconas* from the town of Maras on the plain above Pachar had once lived there. This detail must have suited Costilla, the mayordomo of the nuns of Santa Clara: the term "mamaconas" referred to women of Tahuantinsuyo chosen to serve the Inca, living virginal lives in enclosed communities (acllahuasis) which the Spaniards regarded as pagan "convents."[44]

The nuns of Santa Clara would later get back at least part of the highly symbolic land at Pachar. One of Costilla's sons, Don Gerónimo Costilla Gallinato, sold sixty-one topos at Pachar to the nuns in 1592, three years after purchasing the property from his brother Don Luis Costilla Gallinato, who had received it as part of his inheritance. By that time, the Costilla brothers had outfitted the property with a variety of Spanish-style means of production. The 1589 sale indiscriminately lumps together mules, plowing equipment, goats and kids, horses, "seventeen scythes, ninety-one fanegas of wheat, a black named Anton, and twenty grain sacks." Pachar figures as a combination of ranch (estancia) and cropland (*tierras de panllevar*). Apparently it was home to one African or African American slave named Anton. Pachar was also home to Andeans who provided labor, to judge from the 1589 sale, which excepts from the purchase "the services of the Indians."[45]

Thus the growth of Pachar did not proceed inexorably, or even steadily. Rather, the nuns of Santa Clara enlarged the property as opportunities presented themselves and in accordance with the wishes of their powerful patron Costilla and his relatives. The documents of the events at Pachar, while fragmentary, indicate a very close, symbiotic relationship between the nuns and Costilla—so close that it becomes difficult to disentangle the convent's property from that of its mayordomo. While Gerónimo Costilla actively consolidated a valuable property base for Santa Clara, the nuns helped him consolidate his successful departure from the ranks of the segundones of Zamora.

This pattern of mutual assistance and enrichment seems to have been repeated elsewhere. Costilla almost certainly brokered the acquisition by Santa Clara of another piece of property in 1559, just south of the city of Cuzco. Corcora appears in the 1565 inventory as "an estancia with certain Indians which belonged to Licentiate de la Gama and by his death became vacant," upon which "the Most Excellent Marqués de Cañete, Viceroy of these kingdoms, entrusted and granted it to the monastery." [46] The entry is puzzling: Was this a land grant (merced de tierras) or an encomienda? Santa Clara and Costilla seem to have assumed it was both, pressuring the local people to the point that they made a formal protest. In 1560 the viceroy revised the terms of the grant to Santa Clara, stating that

> certain Indians of the Pueblo of Colcora [sic] informed me that they have resided for a long time in the lands that were granted to the monastery and that they plant crops there for their sustenance, and that by the terms of the aforesaid grant they have been made to provide personal services, planting lands elsewhere and performing other tasks and services which occupy the majority of the few Indians who reside there, and that the services imposed on them are very harmful, as they should enjoy their liberty. [47]

The viceroy ordered the people of Corcora to provide only tribute instead, and he explicitly prevented Santa Clara from collecting it directly or claiming the land of Corcora as their own. [48] As in the case of Ollantaytambo, Costilla faced a defensive reaction from the Indians and did not obtain all he sought for the nuns, but he did not come away empty-handed. Santa Clara would be collecting pesos, maize, and chickens from the people of Corcora for decades.

It was probably around this time that Gerónimo Costilla managed to obtain possession of a small property just to the south of Cuzco for himself. Whether by grant or by purchase, Costilla ended up as the proprietor of an estancia called Suriguaylla just south of the city of Cuzco, and he eventually left that estancia to one of his sons in his will.⁴⁹ Costilla also obtained a small encomienda in the vicinity which figures in the archival record as "Culcora y Marasaca"—possibly an alternative rendering of "Corcora," which was located in the same place, in what is now San Gerónimo. Once more it proves difficult to separate the interests of the nuns from those of their mayordomo, so closely entwined were their business ventures.⁵⁰

Yet the close partnership between Santa Clara and its mayordomo was much more than a business association. It brought the self-styled general and his kin spiritual benefits as well, while enhancing the luster of the Costilla family name. In 1565, the cabildo had decided that Costilla should be given the opportunity to purchase a burial place in the church of Santa Clara for himself and his descendants. He did so in 1577, and the nuns pledged in exchange to pray fifty masses annually for the good of Costilla's soul. Now Costilla, segundón, had completed his own personal mission. He had created a pantheon for himself and his descendants like the one his ancestors had established in Zamora. Now he could go to his grave with the assurance that his deeds would be properly remembered.⁵¹

Business Without, Business Within: The Clares Manage Their Assets

While Gerónimo Costilla was busily helping Santa Clara acquire local land and labor, Abbess Francisca de Jesús and her successors were reaching complex decisions about how to deploy their assets in the rapidly changing economy of Cuzco. The Spanish population of the city was growing, and profiting from the even faster-growing city of Potosí to the south, where Indian miners were dragging an unprecedented bonanza out of a massive silver mountain. New commercial arrangements and labor demands were being made across the region to channel people and goods into the voracious economy of Potosí— for contemporaries, almost the platonic ideal of a post-Renaissance hell, as destructive of Andean laborers' lives as it was productive of silver riches. Cuzco's entrepreneurs sent regional products into this trade, particularly coca, the leaf chewed by Andean miners to ward off cold and fatigue. For those with access to the right resources and to the local levers of power, fortunes could be made in the boom times. Some entrepreneurs began venturing into more capital-intensive products, such as sugar.

Capital was in demand in late-sixteenth-century Cuzco, and the nuns of Santa Clara did not lack opportunities to invest the funds that came their way. These funds came from an increasing variety of people. One source was charitable donations, often made by local people in their wills. Another was inheritance: the monastery might receive legacies from the family members and benefactors of nuns. As the wrenching reorganization of Andean production enriched local entrepreneurs, the nuns gained many benefactors, including Spaniards, mestizos and mestizas, and Indians. Wills from the period range across a wide cultural and economic spectrum. Among the testators favoring Santa Clara with large amounts was Catalina Díaz, who stated in her 1584 will that she was the daughter of the encomendero Alonso Díaz and an Indian woman "whose name I cannot recall." Díaz left the Clares (one of whom was her sister Isabel) the unusually large sum of 42,000 pesos for the founding of a *capellanía*, or chantry.[52]

Dowry, too, was becoming a major source of investment funds for Santa Clara by the late sixteenth century. The amount and terms of payment of a nun's dowry had initially been left quite flexible by Santa Clara's founders; it might be paid in local produce, such as livestock or sacks of flour. After 1565, however, the cabildo—incensed at Francisca de Jesús for favoring Spaniards over the mestizas who had brought all of the dowry received to that point—ordered that all nuns professing in Santa Clara bring at least 1,000 pesos ensayados in dowry. By the early seventeenth century the dowry had been raised once more, to 3,312 pesos, 6 reales corrientes (the equivalent of 2,085 pesos ensayados), a level at which it was to remain fixed in Cuzco for centuries.[53]

A nun's dowry might be paid in a variety of ways, usually by her parents or a close relative. The dowry might be paid in cash, by imposing a lien on one's property in the amount of the dowry, or by donating a piece of property to the monastery of sufficient value to cover the dowry amount. Given the available opportunities for productive use of scarce capital, it is not surprising that many families met the dowry requirement for their daughters through liens, or by ceding property to Santa Clara, rather than part with their pesos.[54] However, cash did figure in some dowry transactions as well as in the payments on liens. And in Cuzco, as in Europe, the nuns had ready their strongbox (*caja de depósitos*) with the prescribed three keys—one for the abbess, one for the nun acting as treasurer, and one for the vicar or mayordomo—to receive the cash paid to them.

The challenge, for Francisca de Jesús and her successors, was how to place the monastery's money and property in an unstable, quicksilver economy so as to ensure a stable annual return. Managing property was relatively straightforward. Once the nuns found reliable individuals with whom to do business (no doubt with assistance from Gerónimo Costilla), they borrowed the time-tested strategies of European monastic orders, whose finances had long been based on deriving rents from property. One option was essentially a form of long-term lease, described in the *Siete Partidas* as the alienation of real property in return for a fixed annuity.[55] Through such dealings, often styled *ventas a censo* or *ventas enfitéuticas* in the notarial records of Cuzco, the nuns might divide their dominio over the property into two imaginary parts— literally, "use dominion" (*dominio útil*) and "direct dominion" (*dominio directo*)—and alienate the former to a buyer in exchange for an annual income. The nuns of Santa Clara appear to have used this type of censo to manage at least one of the rural properties listed in their sixteenth-century inventories, a small wheat farm in Jaquijaguana that by 1602 had been sold to two different people without ceasing to belong to the monastery. What was sold was the use value, while Santa Clara retained title to the property.

Such long-term leasing was well suited to the management of properties the nuns did not consider essential to their sustenance. With other properties, however, the nuns desired tighter supervisory controls, and might opt instead for short-term rentals (*arrendamientos*) or hire a specific person to run an estate for a specific length of time. Two of Santa Clara's earliest productive assets illustrate well the nuns' use of the latter management strategy: the grain-producing hacienda of Pachar and a livestock ranch called Caco, located south of Cuzco near the town of Pucará. Both were acquired in the late sixteenth century. For more than two centuries thereafter, Santa Clara either rented these properties or hired specific individuals to act as resident mayordomos, overseeing the work of indigenous shepherds and other laborers, seeing to general maintenance, and remitting specific amounts of goods to Cuzco. Clearly these two properties were too basic to the nuns' sustenance for their productive activities to be conducted carelessly.[56]

Disposing properly of cash was a more complicated affair. The Dominican friar Tomás de Mercado, in the 1571 edition of his popular manual *Summa de tratos y contratos de mercaderes*, warned those with money of the dreadful danger they might confront: the temptation to take interest on a loan. "No vice bears a greater likeness to the devil than this one," he wrote. "What is there more detestable and frightening for men to look upon than the devil? Yet there are few of us who do not usher him into our hearts a hundred times."[57] The insidious evil he denounces is usury (usura), defined in Mercado's time as lending at interest—any interest whatsoever. Earning interest on money was damnably immoral, almost as bad in Mercado's eyes as homosexuality: "No sin is more vile (besides the abominable sin) than that of usury."[58] The Catholic church considered homosexual acts barren and "against nature," a sinful contravention of the reproductive purpose of sex. Something similar was at the root of the usury prohibition: money, in the scholastics' conception, was also barren. Therefore, for money to reproduce itself through lending at interest was, in the eyes of Thomas Aquinas and others, contra natura, against nature.[59]

Lending at interest, like homosexuality, was condemned and prohibited in an Iberian-derived moral economy marked by abhorrence of usury. To be sure, people in sixteenth-century Peru did perform these "unnatural" acts. They lent one another money at interest, despite dire sermons and the risk of denunciation.[60] But this could hardly be the basis of a monastic order's finances. How then was it possible for the nuns of Cuzco to become major lenders, investing their accumulating dowry funds and earning a steady stream of income?

To gain a licit income, the nuns relied on a relatively new and controversial investment strategy that was becoming popular in Spain, the censo al quitar.[61] This form of censo, technically a censo consignativo, was a contractual arrangement resembling a modern mortgage. Typically, a prospective borrower offered to place a censo "in favor" of the monastery on a piece of real property that he or she possessed, receiving in exchange a certain sum of money from the nuns (the principal) and promising to pay a fixed percentage of the principal annually until such time as he or she might choose to repay the principal and cancel the obligation. These censos might appear to modern eyes to be loans at interest, yet they were carefully constructed to avoid the moral traps of usury. The monastery did not enter into loans, but rather contracts of purchase and sale in which the nuns purchased the right to collect an annuity.

For example, Bartolomé de Celada turned to the nuns of Santa Clara when he needed credit to purchase a house in Cuzco from Román de Baños. In 1581 Celada received 1,400 pesos ensayados from the nuns

censo al quitar—Instead of loans, the nuns 'bought' the right to collect annual payments from the purchaser

in a censo al quitar, agreeing to pay them 100 pesos annually (7.14%) until such time as he or his heirs chose to repay the principal.[62] By the terms of the contract, Celada was not taking out a loan but *selling* Santa Clara the right to collect an annual payment of 100 pesos from him and his descendants. The nuns, for their part, were not loaning him money at interest but *buying* the right to receive this annual income for the price of 1,400 pesos. The principal of a censo was thus also its price—the "just price" of the annual income being bought and sold. Celada was required to put up collateral for this deal, so he "imposed" the censo on two properties: the house he was purchasing from Román de Baños and a sugar-producing estate (*ingenio*) called Miraflores and its capital equipment, located in the valley of Marcahuasi. A marginal notation indicates that Celada canceled his censo contract two years later by delivering six silver ingots worth 1,400 pesos to the mayordomo of Santa Clara.

The annual rate of return on a censo—to modern eyes, the interest rate—was determined not by the nuns but by the Spanish Crown, which had considerable authority over the Catholic church in its domains. During the late sixteenth century the rate set by Philip II was 7.14 percent (expressed as *catorce mil el millar*). It was readjusted in Cuzco in the 1620s, and throughout most of the colonial period remained at 5 percent (*veinte mil el millar*).[63] These were probably very attractive rates, to judge from the sparse evidence concerning prosecutions for usury. Individual lenders might charge upward of twice as much for lending money.[64]

The nuns did not extend credit to anyone who needed it, however. Collateral had to be offered for a censo bargain to take place, and the acceptable collateral for such transactions was overwhelmingly of one kind: *bienes raíces*, real estate. The nuns of Cuzco made plain their preference for proprietors whose holdings were free of other obligations. Occasionally they would make an exception—as in 1588, when the nuns of Santa Clara lent Bernardo de la Torre four silver ingots valued at 1,500 pesos ensayados in a censo secured only by de la Torre's stake in unspecified mines. (The deal turned out to be a mistake: the nuns would fail to get their due from the miner's heirs, who argued that the censo had been improperly secured in the first place.)[65] Generally speaking, however, anyone without title to some piece of real property in this economy—a house, ranch, or farm—could not expect to avail himself or herself of the censo as a means to credit.

Controversy over the terms of the censo al quitar raged throughout the sixteenth century.[66] Objections centered on the rate of return, which was not brought under royal control until the 1560s, and on the dangers posed by the censo al quitar for those who fell behind in making payments to their creditors.[67] Anyone who failed to pay an ecclesiastical creditor for two consecutive years (three years in the case of lay creditors) was liable to seizure of the property he or she had put up as collateral. This meant that even if a censo al quitar had been paid up punctually for generations, and the original amount repaid several times over, an ecclesiastical creditor could still take legal action to seize collateral after two years of nonpayment of annuities. By contrast, older forms of censo had not posed the risk of property seizure (comiso) for nonpayment.[68] After the censo al quitar became widespread, as disgruntled commentator Bartolomé de Albornoz noted, people began losing their property to their creditors.[69]

Yet the advantages of the censo al quitar were also significant for a region's economy. Previous kinds of censo had included no provision for repayment of the principal and cancellation of the contract. They might be shifted to another property through traspasos, ventas, and reconocimientos de censo, but technically they were "perpetual" and could not be redeemed.[70] The censo al quitar gave a debtor the option of repaying and canceling the obligation at his or her convenience. Moreover, the new type of censo could set up a chain of loan-like transactions: when one person repaid and canceled a censo al quitar (like Bartolomé de Celada), the creditor could loan the money out again, and so forth. In other words, the censo al quitar could serve as the basis for a credit system.[71]

Through this triumph of casuistry and practical reason, Catholic institutions—including Santa Clara—would become heavily involved in providing credit in sixteenth-century Peru, and would remain major lenders well into the nineteenth century, independence and republicanism notwithstanding. Credit and morality were tightly bound together, albeit with some changes in interpretation over the years. Not everyone was happy about such changes. In Spain, the recalcitrant Albornoz was never convinced of the rectitude of the censo al quitar: he challenged his readers to tell him how it was any different from usury and protested that anyone could see censos were the ruin of the realm.[72] As early as 1548, the prior of the monastery of Santa María de Guadalupe in Spain had issued similarly dire warnings, encouraging people to avoid censos al quitar altogether.[73] But it was too late; the practice had already become a mainstay of the Iberian economy, just in time to be transported to the New World. It would become even more of a mainstay in local economies across Spanish America, including that of Cuzco.

Cuzco's nuns were certainly not the only investors to rely on the censo al quitar as a financial strategy. Other local institutions—including the men's monastic orders (the Mercedarians and Augustinians in particular)—extended credit through the same mechanism of the censo al quitar.[74] However, because of their steadily increasing dowry funds, cloistered nuns would gradually come to exercise a leading role in the heavily censo-based economy of colonial Cuzco. The rules of the orders required that they invest their pooled dowry funds, and the censo al quitar offered a ready means for earning a relatively steady income.[75] By 1602, enough women had professed to give the monastery of Santa Clara substantial amounts of dowry, the income from which seems to have accounted for around 43 percent of the convent's total annual income of 5,191 pesos in that year.[76] The censo-based economy of Cuzco was off to a solid start. In subsequent decades it would continue to expand, accompanying (and fueling) a period of relative prosperity that has been seen by historians as Cuzco's "golden age."

Conclusions

In this chapter I have argued that religious poverty was a gendered activity—a specific kind of performance that men and women were expected to enact differently, in accordance with a hegemonic Spanish gender system that aligned masculinity with mobility and femininity with chaste enclosure. Yet this by no means meant that cloistered nuns could not operate outside their convent walls. To the contrary: their entire way of life was predicated on securing a substantial endowment, a stable set of properties and investments that necessarily involved them quite deeply in the business of the people and communities around them.

In the process of gaining such an endowment, Santa Clara and its proxies participated in a profound redefinition of "property" in the Andes. As we have seen in detail in the case of Ollantaytambo, by the 1550s Inca ways of determining access to land were being rudely displaced under the onslaught of a very different, Spanish system of tenure, one based on reckoning land's value and making it possible for parcels to be bought and sold, held in private possession, and so forth. Cuzco's Spaniards were particularly intent on competing for choice pieces of the fertile, warm Urubamba river valley just outside the city, terrain that had long been choice in the eyes of the Incas as well: here lay many rich "lands of the Inca and the Sun," once dedicated to produce for the support of the spiritual and political leaders of Tahuantinsuyo. For many years, Polo de Ondegardo learned, the Indians had not dared to stop cultivating them as lands of the Inca and the Sun, in case the Inca should be fully restored to his powers of command.[77] But death, destruction, and migration had taken their toll and the land had begun to fall into disuse—and thus, by the 1550s and 1560s, to look more available to Spaniards' eyes.

Several things seem to have sharpened the Spaniards' land hunger: for one, the drive to secure arable land near the city, suitable for growing the crops Europeans prized; for another, the impetus to superimpose the conquering Christian faith on the symbolic heartland of the Inca religion. We should recall a third. Not until 1572 was Túpac Amaru captured by the Spanish captain Martín García de Loyola and the stronghold of Vilcabamba defeated. Thus the securing of the strategic valley of the Urubamba and the capture of its rich—and richly symbolic—lands during the 1550s and 1560s was not gratuitous. The Inca was still alive.

So, too, were his former servants, kurakas such as Don Francisco Mayontopa, whose very name in the documents reflects his hybrid condition, his Spanish-Andeanness, and the mestizaje of power structures under way in the Andes. We still know little about this process for several critical sixteenth-century decades, save what can be reconstructed from the fragments in conventual and public archives: namely, Mayontopa's legal actions to forestall the land claims of Santa Clara and other religious orders. Long after the last resisting Inca was dead, Mayontopa and his fellow kurakas would be dealing with the Spanish colonial administration. Mayontopa's actions and the words of Polo de Ondegardo, who once backed him in the court of Spanish law, serve as reminders that the endowment of Santa Clara did not proceed untrammeled.

Gerónimo Costilla was the man most responsible for Santa Clara's acquisition of a patrimony during the 1560s and 1570s. His own advancement was very much part of the process. As a noble segundón, who left his native Zamora at about age seventeen, he had much to gain by participating in the conquest of Cuzco, and his story gradually becomes inextricably bound up with that of Santa Clara. The convent, like convents in Spain and elsewhere, reflected powerfully on its patrons, and the good standing and general authoritativeness of one was mirrored in the other. For Costilla's stance as patron to be plausible, he had to both endow and be endowed. Santa Clara enabled him to do both. In fact, it is difficult to discern what was Costilla's and what was Santa Clara's: in the information gathered by Vásquez de Espinosa from *visitas* and *revisitas* of the late sixteenth and early seventeenth centuries, "Culcora" appears as the encomienda of Gerónimo Costilla.[78]

By the close of the sixteenth century, then, the Poor Clares of Cuzco had assembled a considerable endowment for their convent. Santa Clara was maintained not only by its crops, livestock, and tribute goods, but also—and increasingly, as women continued to profess in the convent and add their dowries to the general fund—by funds invested in the local economy. From its earliest years, and even into the twentieth century, Santa Clara was sustained by censos consignativos and in turn sustained others, providing them with generous infusions of credit.

However, the very structure of the censo consignativo, imported directly from Europe, meant that those with access to credit in the local economy of Cuzco would be the region's *nuevos ricos*, its new landholders—people like Gerónimo Costilla who were pushing their way into Iberian-style property rights, despite the best efforts of those who, like Francisco Mayontopa and Polo de Ondegardo, tried to stop them. The landowning individuals and families of Cuzco held precisely the kinds of assets that the nuns were seeking as collateral for the investment of their censo funds, and they struck the nuns as precisely the kind of people who could be counted upon to provide the convent with a safe, steady income. And the nuns could offer the credit terms that the landowners needed to maintain and expand their operations— obrajes, sugar ingenios, and so forth.

Thus Cuzco's nuns actively and deliberately reinforced the colonial ruling class of their region, the propertied elite with collateral to secure good credit terms. In return for their credit and prayers, the Clares were able to deploy their resources with people in Cuzco in the ways their order required. So it was that in the colonial society which cuzqueños built on these relationships, the availability of both credit and salvation became intimately related to women's decisions to profess. The colonial agrarian economy of Cuzco, in other words, became contingent on Santa Clara's successful "harvest of souls," *agricultura espiritual*.

3 Forasteras Become Cuzqueñas

Early in the seventeenth century, the city of Cuzco gained a second community of cloistered nuns. Like those of Santa Clara fifty years before, the founders of the monastery of Santa Catalina were responding to extraordinary circumstances, trying to maintain their balance in the midst of dramatic upheavals. But this time the upheavals were seismic. The first struck the highlands on February 18, 1600. By the account of Cuzco chronicler Diego de Esquivel y Navia, the volcano of Huayna Putina, near Arequipa, erupted "with such force that it threw down great burning boulders nearby and rocks and ash at a distance, which killed many men and animals in their path. The shaking of the earth nearby was horrible." Cuzco was spared the full force of the earth's tumultuous explosion in 1600, but "the noise could be heard at more than sixty leagues' distance. . . . [The effects] reached as far as Panama and Nicaragua by sea, and by land as far as the Yungas." [1]

The volcanic eruption of 1600 was a disaster for the southern Peruvian city of Arequipa, the first in a devastating series. Floods carried away carefully tended vineyards on which the local economy depended. Crops would not grow in the ash-covered fields for the next several years. And just as Arequipan property owners were beginning to recover from the damage, their region was tossed up in a fresh seismic surge. This time serious earthquakes struck in a series that lasted from early November through late December 1604, leveling much of the city of Arequipa. [2]

Among the many things shaken by the earthquakes of 1604 was the resolve of a Spanish widow named Doña Lucía de Padilla. She had invested years as well as several thousand pesos in establishing a convent in Arequipa, and the volcanic eruption of 1600 had severely damaged the properties with which she and her deceased husband had endowed the new foundation. But it took a second major upheaval of the earth's crust to convince Padilla to abandon the city of Arequipa altogether. Late in December 1604, without waiting for more apocalyptic events, she moved swiftly to arrange for herself and the nuns to migrate across the Andes to Cuzco.

The people of Cuzco turned out to greet this unusual company of migrating nuns as they made their way into the old Inca city in early 1605. Doña Lucía de Padilla was accompanied by her daughter the prioress, Doña Isabel de Padilla, and twenty-five other women, one of whom later wrote an account of the momentous day of their arrival. The welcome culminated in a tumultuous public embrace of the community as the women processed through the old stone streets, no doubt wide-eyed in amazement at the sturdy Inca masonry as well as all the "music and dancing and fireworks" whirling about them. Their route was thronged with "all of the important people of the city, both gentlemen and ladies, as well as a great many others—many from out of town, and a multitude of Indians—so that we could barely walk."[3]

As soon as the joyous welcome was over, however, the nuns found themselves in a difficult position. Doña Lucía de Padilla and her companions had to come to terms with the fact that even though they had traveled only a few days' journey from their home, they had moved beyond the effective range of the ties they had created to sustain them in Arequipa. The rules had not changed, nor had the contractual obligations made in support of the community ceased to exist; but they began to lose their meaning, the power to bind up people's words, intentions, and actions. Without intending to, the Padillas and their Dominican community had crossed over a subtle boundary not on any map: the imperceptible border separating the spiritual economy of Arequipa from that of Cuzco.

To cuzqueños, the new arrivals were not kin but forasteras, "outsiders" or "foreigners."[4] Greeting these women warmly was one thing; supporting them with donations and daughters was quite another. As the anonymous nun's account put it, the local people already had "their monastery," Santa Clara. By 1605 propertied families (like the Costillas) had woven a dense network of connections between and among themselves and the Clares, relations in which kinship, spiritual obligation, credit and debt were all inextricably bound up together. Their sense of themselves, and of what it meant to live in an authoritative city, was intimately wrapped around this institution which had made the transition from struggling shelter for mestizas to thriving school for aristocratic criollas. Getting into this increasingly elaborate spiritual economy would prove neither simple nor straightforward for the newcomers.

Nevertheless, the women from Arequipa did manage to make a place for themselves in Cuzco. In 1649 Vasco de Contreras y Valverde included them in his official survey of the ecclesiastical institutions of Cuzco—albeit in last place, outside the chronological order of his roll call of the convents, schools, and hospitals of the region.[5] His placement hints that the Arequipans had not yet entirely overcome their status as forasteras. Yet his description of their convent in 1649 tells a different story, one of Andean self-fashioning and rags-to-riches success. He begins by recounting the terrible impact of the turn-of-the-century eruptions, earthquakes, and floods. Then, counting on his readers to share his assumptions about the relationship between dominio and religious women's quest for perfection, Contreras y Valverde writes approvingly of the Dominican nuns: "[T]hey have been remaking and reforming themselves, so that in this year of 1649 there are more than one hundred professed nuns, and counting the lay sisters (*donadas*) and servants, the monastery has two hundred fifty people who support themselves comfortably with the real estate and haciendas they have acquired."[6]

Clearly the nuns had managed by midcentury to assemble a new endowment, in Contreras y Valverde's eyes the sine qua non for their dedication to prayer and the cultivation of stainless, exemplary lives. The logic of the spiritual economy described in the previous chapter would suggest they had also forged a new set of relationships with local backers, making mutually beneficial deals built to last for generations. How did the nuns do this despite their "foreignness"? Using the nuns' own records, we will now explore the diverse, inventive strategies—indissociably material and symbolic—by which the women performed this Andean act of self-fashioning, "remaking and reforming themselves" into cuzqueñas, merging their prayers and property into the spiritual economy of their new home. As we will see, they belatedly joined the ranks of the "conquerors" of the Incas, superimposing their convent on a still-resonant Inca site and containing Christian descendants of the Incas within their walls.

The Power of Wealthy Widows: The Padillas Found, and Move, a Convent

Thanks to the anonymous nun's account, it becomes possible to imagine, four hundred years later, how the nuns viewed the turbulent events that engulfed and transformed them (Appendix 3). Now stitched into the nuns' carefully preserved volume of papers relating to the Cuzco foundation, the draft—a kind of tug-of-war between hagiography and diary, revealing in its roughness—draws full-length word portraits of its protagonists, the founders. They not only bracket the narrative but carry it forward; their intentions are the dominant ones throughout. Even God is mentioned only in connection with them: they are the "zealous guardians of God's honor." At the story's beginning, larger than life, is Doña Lucía de Padilla, for whom the anonymous author expresses affection and fealty with a telling possessive:

> My lady Doña Lucía de Padilla, the founder of this monastery of Our Lady of the Remedies, advocation of our mother Saint Catherine of Siena, was from Antequera and of the Padillas. . . . She came to the city of Arequipa with her father or brother and a sister named Doña Beatriz de Casillas y Padilla along with the conquistador Juan de la Torre, *vecino de indios*. My lady Doña Lucía married Don Fernando de Ribera de los Perafanes, a conquistador and encomendero. In this marriage she had two children, Friar Antonio de Ribera of the Dominican Order and my lady the prioress, Doña Isabel de Padilla, our patron and founder.[7]

Clearly Doña Lucía de Padilla was among those early Spanish residents of Peru who, like Gerónimo Costilla, were not content merely to have been born noble, and who dreamed of enhancing their reputations by making a fortune in the Americas. Like Costilla, she would spend decades exploiting the labor power of Andeans held in encomienda, becoming in the process "highly esteemed in the city of Arequipa, a lady of great pomp, jewels, and riches." Because she was a woman, however, she could gain access to the chief means of extracting Andean wealth only by marrying an encomendero. This she would do more than once in the course of her long, eventful life.

Marriage proved the key to Padilla's success at fulfilling the Spanish emigrant's dream. Her first marriage, to Ribera de los Perafanes, probably took place around the time of her sister's marriage in 1551 to Juan de la Torre. Ribera was then in possession of two valuable encomiendas—the Arones and Ocoña—and no doubt seemed a good match for the young Spanish woman from Antequera. Yet he soon lost his encomiendas in legal wrangles, and on his death left Padilla with two children but no encomienda. Padilla did not remain unmarried for long. Her second marriage, to the Basque encomendero Juan de San

Juan, produced no children but made her enduringly wealthy. After his death she retained the right to collect tribute from his encomiendas (neighboring those of her previous husband), the Arones Yanaquihua, Ocoña de Pacheco, and Colani. Padilla then went on to marry and outlive a third husband, Pedro de Ahedo, by whom she had a son of the same name whom, the anonymous nun tells us, "she loved and adored in the extreme."[8]

Like most encomenderos, Padilla and her husbands were not content only to hold Andean labor and tribute. Gradually they began buying up land in the vicinity of their labor grants and applying the labor of "their Indians" to bring forth the fruits of their new investments. That Padilla and her husbands and kin had committed themselves to re-creating the imagined flavor of their homelands on new soil is clear from the names they gave the places where the Arones and Ocoña peoples were obliged to settle: pueblos called Granada, Antequera, and Porto.[9] When in 1575 Padilla married for the fourth and final time—to Gerónimo Pacheco, a Spaniard who had come to Peru in the retinue of Viceroy Toledo—she brought her husband, in addition to encomienda rights, several properties in dowry: houses in the city, two pieces of cropland nearby (chacras), and a vineyard in the Ocoña Valley.[10]

By this time Arequipa had become an important Spanish settlement, the center of a thriving wine business that had grown up not long after the city's foundation in 1540.[11] Unlike Cuzco, Arequipa was a new city; the Spanish founders had picked a site that suited them, along the banks of a river where good land for grain crops and fruit orchards was close by. Vineyards did well throughout this region, which was a great deal more like Doña Lucía's native Málaga than Cuzco could ever be. There was no Inca center with which to seek accommodation, although a wide variety of ethnic groups lived in the area and, through their kurakas, could be made to work the land. The attractions of receiving an encomienda in Arequipa were thus not negligible. According to the rates established in 1573 the Arones Yanaquihua, Ocoña, and Colani tributary populations were expected to provide their encomendero 710 pesos in gold and 850 pesos in silver annually, in addition to tribute goods.[12]

Arequipa was the center of business for Padilla and her husbands, but their sphere of action extended well beyond it. In 1567, Doña Lucía de Padilla arranged for her daughter Isabel—then only ten years of age —to wed an elderly Basque encomendero of La Paz named Pedro Basáez, who had been granted the encomienda of Tiaguanaco. The couple eventually had a daughter, who died very young. When Basáez himself died, there was suspicion that Doña Isabel de Padilla had been the agent of his death, sufficient that she was barred from inheriting any rights to the encomienda of her deceased husband.[13] Thus deprived, the young widow rejoined her mother and stepfather in Arequipa, perhaps in disgrace. The family then moved to the city of Cuzco, where from 1578 to 1581 Pacheco served as corregidor. There Isabel decided to enter religious orders.[14] Almost as soon as the family returned to Arequipa, she entered the city's newly established Dominican monastery of Santa Catalina, where she took the habit on July 15, 1582, at age twenty-five.[15]

While Isabel de Padilla spent the next several years working to establish the first cloistered convent in Arequipa, her mother struggled with the burden of a tragic loss. Her third child, the son on whom she had planned to settle a rich inheritance, died suddenly. The bereaved Doña Lucía decided to memorialize Pedro de Ahedo, the son she had "loved and adored in the extreme," by turning her house into a cloister. Gerónimo Pacheco supported his wife's initiative fully. In 1595, he drew up a will leaving 42,000 pesos for the construction of a new convent and giving ample latitude to Padilla in the execution of his provisions. He even made his own project, the founding of a Jesuit school for the Arones, secondary to the fulfillment of his wife's wishes. Pacheco would live just long enough to see her project realized.[16]

So it was that on August 1, 1599, Arequipa's second monastery began to function in Doña Lucía's house, with herself and her daughter in charge. Doña Lucía had wanted the nuns to be Conceptionists or Franciscans, but Doña Isabel had insisted that her mother found a Dominican community, else she would stay where she was. "Given the resistance of her daughter," the anonymous nun wrote, Doña Lucía "conceded that it should be as she wished, and so there were two monasteries in Arequipa of the same habit."[17] The new foundation was called Nuestra Señora de los Remedios—Our Lady of the Remedies—after the virgin whose name Doña Lucía's dead son had called out in his death throes, the patron of his mother's Iberian homeland, Antequera. When Doña Isabel de Padilla left Santa Catalina in 1599 to found the new monastery, disputes broke out between the two Dominican communities over her dowry and other property.[18] Nevertheless, she was allowed to leave and join her mother.

However, Doña Lucía herself never professed. Had she become a nun, she would have had to renounce her worldly belongings and would have lost the encomienda that provided a substantial part of the income on which the new monastery depended. Instead, following Pacheco's death late in 1599, she lived a strenous, in-between existence. "Living very austerely and dressing simply," according to the anonymous nun, Padilla only took part in the nuns' ritual observance of the canonical hours at night, attending matins, "because by day she attended to her business affairs." A combination of de facto prioress, encomendera, and administrator, Doña Lucía seems to have been an energetic woman and to have taken matters very much into her own hands.[19]

Early in 1600, matters escaped Doña Lucía's control. Unusually heavy rains fell; then, on February 18, two strong tremors shook Arequipa. Next, the nearby volcano of Huayna Putina erupted, spewing a thick layer of volcanic ash over the surrounding countryside and turning the following days into night. These natural disasters seriously disrupted the region's economy, since many vineyards and fields were rendered unproductive. As a result, when vineyard owners and other local producers failed to keep up payments on censos owed to Arequipa's two convents, much of the income on which the nuns depended dried up. Just as productive activities were starting to revive in the region, another serious earthquake hit. On November 4, 1604, much of the city of Arequipa collapsed. Both Santa Catalina and Nuestra Señora de los Remedios were seriously affected. The quakes continued, lasting late into the month of December. So it was that the Padillas wrote to the bishop of Cuzco, Don Antonio de la Raya, seeking his help to relocate the convent in Cuzco, given the ruin of its productive base in Arequipa. Convent records reflect an unusual turn of events: the nuns migrated across the rugged Andean mountains. After Bishop de la Raya gave his permission for Nuestra Señora de los Remedios to come to Cuzco, he dispatched trusted ecclesiastics to serve as an escort, along with mules, equipment, tents, and other provisions for the women's journey. Some twenty-five professed nuns and two niñas seglares (girls who boarded in the convent) made the difficult trip. The family names of most are not recorded, but at least four were Padillas: in addition to Doña Lucía and her daughter, Doña Andrea and Doña Lorenza de Padilla were part of the group. The women's leave-taking from Arequipa was, according to the anonymous nun's telling, deeply felt throughout the city, "with such clamor, tears, and sobs that it seemed like Judgment Day." On the bishop's instructions, priests and kurakas along the way made the women's progress as comfortable as possible. Their visitors did what they could to preserve monastic modesty in the most incongruous of circumstances:

> We walked in such religiosity, composure, and silence that whenever a reception party approached us we covered our faces with our veils, not allowing anyone to see us. The priests put on great festivities, the caciques gave us many gifts, and the rest of the people went out to receive us on their knees, with dancing and much music, and they kissed our habits and scapulars. . . . Once when it was necessary to camp outdoors, the priest was so attentive that he ordered a place to be dug out so that we might fit snugly inside; today travelers lodge there and it is called the Cave of the Nuns.[20]

When the nuns finally reached Cuzco, they received still more lavish greetings, no doubt carefully prepared by their new ecclesiastical superior, Bishop Antonio de la Raya. The day that would culminate in a dazzling parade through the city's streets began with a much quieter reception: a brief visit to the cloistered monastery of Santa Clara. According to the anonymous Arequipan nun, the Clares "had begged [the bishop] to allow them to receive us that day and welcome us." He had acceded, apparently hoping the gesture would extend beyond a simple courtesy call in the visitor's parlor. It did not. The nun recounts merely that "they welcomed us, but did not take us into their cloisters, which His Excellency much regretted." The newcomers ate a meal with the Clares, then went back into the thronged streets where more public celebrations awaited them.[21]

The Dominican nuns may not have considered this brief reception at Santa Clara an affront, but clearly Bishop de la Raya was disappointed on their behalf. As the aging bishop escorted them to their makeshift cloister adjacent to the Jesuit church, then waited patiently until workers finished sealing the entrance, he may have fretted over the incident and seen in it a worrisome sign of things to come. If local people would extend to the newcomers nothing more than courtesy, he would have a heavy load to bear in seeing to the comfort and security of the nuns. Somehow, new backers would have to be won for the arequipeñas in Cuzco.

Bishop Antonio de la Raya de Cuzco — Wanted the Dominicans of Santa Clara to be welcoming + accepting of the ? of Nuestra Señora de los Remedios to gain legitimacy ? financial backers.

The Cuzco the Padillas joined in 1605 was a city whose leaders were busily fashioning themselves a splendid provincial capital. Foundations of all kinds were multiplying: churches, hospitals, confraternities, seminaries, and schools, as well as monasteries and convents. Massive stone edifices were raised up, and when tremors split and shook them down, they were made to soar even higher.[22] Most of these events are known today much as they were when Diego de Esquivel y Navia completed his *Noticias cronológicas*: as chronologically ordered bits of news, items of worthwhile information in the rough, unassayed. Clearly, however, they suggest a convergence of powerful forces.[23]

The subsequent century has been called the "golden age" of Cuzco, its *edad de oro*. But perhaps this could more appropriately be called its silver period.[24] For behind the imposing seventeenth-century edifices that are still the city's landmarks—its enormous cathedral, churches, and monastic houses, with their baroque canvasses and splendid altars —was the silver of Potosí and the vast amounts of Andean labor necessary to extract it. The mines were producing millions of pesos in silver annually. By law one-fifth of the minted silver was destined for the treasury of the Spanish monarchy; much of the rest remained in regional circulation.[25] Potosí's silver yield declined steadily throughout the century, but the mining city continued to support a far-flung set of regional enterprises like those of Cuzco and Arequipa with its demand for goods and inputs of all kinds.[26]

Andean labor power, as well as profit gained from the flow of trade toward Potosí, was responsible for the quickening pace of institution-building in Cuzco. The notoriously burdensome labor draft (*mita*), reorganized by Viceroy Toledo in the 1570s to direct a steady supply of indigenous labor toward the silver mines, also helped quite literally to lay the foundations of Cuzco's ecclesiastical and charitable institutions, which received allotments of Indian construction workers. Capital for new initiatives came from the enterprises that began to thrive with the mines from the mid-sixteenth century, becoming mainstays of Cuzco's distinctive local economy. Three stand out: coca, the leaf chewed by Andean workers, particularly miners, to ward off cold and fatigue; sugar, shipped in "loaves" to Potosí and elsewhere, made into molasses, and otherwise used to sweeten the Spanish-Andean diet; and cloth, the kind produced in the obrajes that were becoming a major Cuzco industry by the seventeenth century.[27] These were coarse products, raw ingredients for insertion into other processes; they were to Potosí mining what reagents are to a chemical reaction. Coca, sugar, and textiles were not the only products brought to market by cuzqueños, but they were especially important in the transregional circuitry of trade and supply that kept the mines in business, and thus were especially profitable.

Who profited by these colonial arrangements? Not the tributaries of the Spanish colonial state who constituted the vast majority of the region's population; for Peru's so-called Indians, the seventeenth century would be anything but a "golden age." Around the turn of the seventeenth century, as the burden of labor drafts and disease sapped their strength and resources, communities also had to negotiate the disruptions of forced resettlement (reducciones) and fend off massive Spanish efforts to "regularize" land titles (composiciones de tierras).[28] Many thousands uprooted themselves and migrated in an effort to escape colonial exactions. Half a century after Viceroy Toledo's visit to the southern highlands, the Indian tributary population had fallen sharply, from an estimated 600,000 to around 350,000 by 1620, and the decline would continue throughout the century.[29] Not until the eighteenth century would the region's Indian population show sustained growth.[30]

The leaders of the Andean population of Cuzco fared better, including those of distinguished Inca descent and those whom the Spaniards recognized as ethnic lords, whether of Inca or non-Inca communities, and called "caciques." To Spaniards this was the Indian nobility, indios nobles—those who controlled the flows of Andean labor and who thus held the key to indirect rule over the Andes. Accordingly, Spaniards worked through them, cultivated relatively good relations with them, and taught them Christian customs. Sons of the region's kurakas were educated in special Jesuit schools, founded in Cuzco and Lima in the early 1600s specifically for that purpose. Indigenous elites used Christian names along with the honorific of "Don" or "Doña," maintained houses in the city of Cuzco, and wore a mix of Andean garments and the finest Spanish clothing they were able to obtain. Unlike commoners, members of this elite could ride on horseback, bear arms, and generally live much as Spaniards did—provided they could afford it.

Spaniards monitored and circumscribed the roles and range of this indigenous elite. Even the Incas who had assimilated themselves most assiduously to Spanish customs were not permitted to hold high office or otherwise exercise authority over Spaniards. Instead, the high-ranking Incas of Cuzco created their own ways of wielding authority, forming and leading their own honorary council, commissioning canvasses to exalt themselves and their communities, attaining a hybrid heraldry, and displaying the symbols of their power on public occasions. Christianity gave them a new, powerful medium for expressing their prestigious status. They used such important Christian pageants as the feast day of Corpus Christi to send messages to their fellow cuzqueños, parading the finery of their Inca forebears.[31] Their re-creation of Inca authority in Cuzco was successful enough to revive viceregal anxieties around the turn of the century: Viceroy Luis de Velasco, concerned that the highest-ranking Inca in Cuzco, Don Melchor Carlos Inca, would become a rallying point for conspiracies against the Crown, arranged in 1601 to send Don Melchor Carlos to Spain and made sure he would never return.[32]

Little is known about how the kurakas of Cuzco fared in these crucial turn-of-the-century decades under Spanish rule. If their experience resembled that of kurakas elsewhere in the Andes, however, they faced growing contradictions between their official role in enforcing Spanish rule and their traditional role of protecting their communities' integrity. Spaniards expected the declining Andean population to labor for them and meet tribute quotas, and they were not greatly inclined to sympathy when kurakas complained of their communities' decimation by labor drafts, migration, and disease. Andean communities, on the other hand, were not inclined to respect and obey kurakas who forced them to work beyond what they could bear, and were suspicious of kurakas who exploited their leadership position for personal gain. The lot of the kurakas of Cuzco was thus not easy. Materially their lives might be less difficult than those of Andean tributaries; politically and culturally, however, they occupied a very difficult, interstitial position, as numerous scholars of the Andes have pointed out.[33]

Arguably those who benefited the most from the colonial relations of production in Cuzco were the members of a small, tight-knit group of elite criollos, the Peruvian-born heirs of Spaniards. A new criollo aristocracy was emerging in the former capital of Tahuantinsuyo, dominated by men claiming legitimate descent from Spanish conquerors and primeros pobladores.[34] The encomiendas some of them had managed to inherit from their fathers and grandfathers were no longer as valuable as before. Their ranks were small. But this elite segment of the population exercised hegemonic power in Cuzco. They had inherited the wealth and privileges of their parents and grandpar-

Kurakas were in a percarious situation to (impress) their Spn. nobles? ... earn the respect of their Inca subjects

ents, and they had cornered most of the benefits and circumvented many of the exactions of the Spanish colonial regime.

Gerónimo Costilla's eldest son is a good example. Unlike his father, Don Pedro Costilla de Nocedo did not fight Incas. Other means to power and renown were available to him. Like his father, he was a member of Cuzco's cabildo. He also inherited his father's rights to the encomienda of Asillo, which gave him relatively little tribute income but valuable access to credit and labor (as well as prestige). Costilla's family had long since cultivated the relevant kurakas, no doubt plying them with gifts and favors in the kind of unequal exchange that had gradually created tightly bonded power groups in rural places across the region—the kind Felipe Guaman Poma de Ayala graphically denounced, in his caustic drawings, as ruinous to the well-being of ordinary Indians. Costilla used his connections with kurakas to bargain successfully for indigenous laborers to tend the herds of his nearby ranch.[35] Costilla probably also drew on his good relations with kurakas to tap into indigenous community funds (*cajas de comunidad*) for loans. Such loans were so seldom serviced, much less repaid, that aggrieved kurakas eventually began to register abundant complaints about the depredation of their communities' coffers. Whether or not Costilla violated his payment terms is unclear, but he did receive loans from Indian communities' cajas.[36]

Predictably, Costilla also married well, wedding Doña Inés de Vargas, the daughter of one of Cuzco's conquistadores and encomenderos, Tomás Vásquez. Costilla's sister, Doña Francisca, helped to seal the families' union by marrying the brother of Doña Inés, Pedro Vásquez de Vargas. By such extensive intermarriage the most privileged families of Cuzco criollos soon created their own charmed circle, a set of tightly interlocking dynasties that included the Costillas, Esquiveles, Maldonados, Valverdes, and a small handful of other extended kin groups. By the end of Don Pedro Costilla de Nocedo's life, many people of local power and prominence in his native city were either Costillas or the cousins or spouses of Costillas. Don Pedro's descendants would often require papal dispensations to marry each other, so close was their degree of kinship.[37] Thus men like Don Pedro and their families created the matrix from which Cuzco's elite would reproduce and renew itself throughout the colonial period, selectively admitting and absorbing well-positioned Iberians.

Cuzco's criollo aristocrats, following long Iberian precedent, gave lavishly in support of the Catholic church. We have seen that the spiritual investments of the Costillas began early; by 1577 they had a burial chapel in the church of Santa Clara. Thereafter, several wellborn Costillas would enter religious orders: the first, Doña Lucía Costilla de Umarán (a granddaughter of Gerónimo Costilla), rose to the rank of abbess in Santa Clara by the early 1630s (see Appendix 4). The Costillas continued to support the Clares with their donations as well as their daughters, as did Cuzco's other "first families," and by the turn of the seventeenth century patronage was no longer exclusively a male prerogative. Women like Doña Leonor Costilla Gallinato (another of Gerónimo Costilla's granddaughters) had begun to wield the power of religious patronage to make their mark on the city of Cuzco. Like the Padillas, Costilla was a wealthy widow without heirs to whom she might leave her fortune. Although her desire to found a new convent in Cuzco was not realized (she died before the license she sought was granted), Costilla made several gifts to the nuns of Santa Clara and received loans from the nuns' coffers to run the businesses she and her husband had built.[38]

Other families did much the same as the Costillas: they sent daughters to the Clares, prayed for the nuns' health, cultivated their friendship, received loans from the convent's coffers, attended mass in the convent church, sent the nuns donations of food, and left them sums in their wills. No doubt they cultivated the men's religious orders as well. In any case, by the early 1600s, Cuzco's emerging aristocracy was very thoroughly involved in supporting Santa Clara and, in turn, was supported by the nuns. Their constant engagement defined a spiritual economy of mutual assistance in which cuzqueños might, without any contradiction, seek and obtain property, profit, good credit, and salvation. The Dominican newcomers who stepped into this scenario in 1605 had left behind a similar set of close ties in Arequipa. As they were soon to find out, these economies, as they produced insiders like the Costillas, simultaneously demarcated a much larger circle of relative outsiders. In 1605 the Dominican nuns were among the outsiders.

The new elite of Cuzco was so entrenched by 1605 that even a new group of Dominican Nuns were not accepted.

"To Make and Unmake Many Things": Forasteras Become Cuzqueñas

Unfortunately for the nuns of Cuzco's second monastery, their most important patron died only a year after their arrival. The death of Bishop Antonio de la Raya in 1606 dealt the nuns from Arequipa a major setback. They had counted on this aristocratic Spanish prelate to help them as they uprooted themselves and moved from the periphery of his diocese to its center.[39] And Bishop de la Raya had given every indication that he would do for the Dominican nuns what the cabildo and Gerónimo Costilla had done for the Clares a half-century earlier: broker their first acquisitions of local resources. He may well have been the moving force behind the earliest large donations to the new community, many of which came from priests in his diocese. In 1606, for example, the parish priest of nearby Capi, Francisco de Aguilar Villacastín, donated 11,000 pesos to establish an endowment in support of the nuns' chaplains.[40] And the bishop himself gave generously. The anonymous nun writes wistfully that

> as long as our sainted father lived, he sent money for our monthly expenses along with some of the gifts he received, and did this with such love and charity that had he lived longer he would have left us very well cared-for indeed. He used to say that as soon as he paid what he owed for the foundation of the school in Huamanga, all the rest would go to this monastery. God soon took him from us.[41]

On the face of it, this might seem a wistful exaggeration, reflecting bereavement more than (actual or feared) material deprivation. Cuzco's hybrid economy was expanding, thriving; the political arrangements that guaranteed criollo and Spanish prosperity were much more firmly in place than before. But the problem was how to make an entrance into the local circuitry of power, credit, and prosperity. Bishop de la Raya, though a newcomer himself in a sense, had enjoyed a highly visible set of powerful connections in the Cuzco region. At his death the nuns lost their mediator, their go-between. His successor would not arrive in the diocese of Cuzco for several years.[42]

Doña Lucía de Padilla did her best to make up for the loss and to remedy the monastery she had founded. Taking advantage of the fact that she had never made vows of enclosure, she began waging a door-to-door campaign for donations. By the anonymous nun's account, however, the yield was slight: "People promised much but gave almost nothing, which was a great pity."[43] Matters reached an even more difficult pass when in 1608 Doña Lucía died. The nuns suddenly found themselves without a large chunk of their income: namely, the encomienda receipts of more than 2,000 pesos a year that had belonged to

Padilla. Almost to the end she had remained an encomendera rather than take the habit, precisely so that the monastery might benefit from the tribute of the Arones Yanaquihua and Ocoña peoples of Arequipa. The anonymous nun saw Padilla's strategic decision not as a grasping, selfish act but as part of her saintliness, and her founder as an inspired and holy businesswoman, adept in the ways and means of the spiritual economy. She composed Padilla's literary death mask accordingly:

> She did not take the habit until she was near death so that the King would not take her Indians, and thus she died a novice. Trusting God would give her life and so as not to lose the Indians, she died a novice like a saint, with great acts of contrition. She was very zealous of God's honor and was always an extremely Christian lady even while living in the world in the midst of such pomp and splendor. She did everything she could for the nuns. . . . Her death was deeply felt and mourned.[44]

Now Doña Isabel de Padilla had to manage the burdens of prioress without her mother's assistance. Income was urgently needed, not only to supply basic needs but to cover the cost of constructing new cloisters for the nuns. One of the difficulties Padilla faced was collecting the convent's remaining Arequipan income to finance construction in Cuzco. Several properties near Arequipa owed the nuns income, including the vineyard of Tintin, which had belonged to Lucía de Padilla and carried 9,000 pesos' worth of censos in the monastery's favor.[45] Here family ties helped. The nuns relied on the Padillas' kinship connections in Arequipa, authorizing Don Fabián Gómez de Tapia, the husband of Doña Juana de Padilla, to collect censo payments and remit them to Cuzco, which he seems to have done with some regularity.[46]

But Arequipa was too far away to provide the nuns a reliable sustenance. They soon began selling off Arequipa property to raise cash for the construction projects at hand in Cuzco.[47] The nuns kept some of their original assets for several more decades, doing what they could to collect income on them. Squeezing annuity payments out of these holdings often proved impossible, however. Mayordomos were driven to distraction trying to get Arequipans to honor the censos their properties still carried in favor of the nuns of Nuestra Señora de los Remedios — including the desperate, hungry Francisco López de Morla, who in 1668 wrote the monastery from Arequipa regarding his lawsuits to collect payments on the nuns' behalf. After six fruitless months away from home he was sick of wasting his time:

[T]here is no justice for the monastery in this city and though I have justice and Reason on my side it is of no use because they find laws where they want to find laws and although I have done everything in my power and spent many pesos pursuing these cases no one wants to move unless he is very well paid for it. I face twenty thousand vexations and disappointments daily with these gentlemen in this city . . . and the expense of daily meals cannot be avoided, yet I have not collected so much as one *real* in this city and every day I beg the *censuatarios* [debtors] at least to give me enough to eat but they pay no attention. . . . God give me strength to put up with the annoyance of these gentlemen.[48]

López de Morla's letter is quite explicit about the sources of his frustration. The city's lawyers had recused themselves from helping him with the suits; the judge, he wrote, was on the side of the contrary parties; everyone was attempting to dissuade him from going further, and all were against him because he was "a foreigner" (forastero). His claims were legally valid, yet nobody would pay any attention to, much less enforce, them. Not even the viceroy's order supporting the monastery in its efforts to recover arrears in Arequipa did any good. By relocating to Cuzco, the nuns—many of them natives of Arequipa—had definitively crossed a line and become foreigners, their claims unwelcome.

The Dominican nuns couldn't get $ b/c they were foreigners

Clearly the nuns required a new resource base in Cuzco over which to exercise dominio. But one could not easily secure land as Santa Clara and other religious houses had done a half-century earlier; grants of "tierras del Inca y del Sol" were no longer being handed out by the cabildo. Even if such grants had still been available, no Gerónimo Costilla or Diego Maldonado stood ready to help the Dominican newcomers negotiate local politics successfully. Instead, the nuns had to rely on other means of getting real property, and on Padilla relatives to administer their business as best they could.[49] The monastery picked up some important donations: the successor to Bishop de la Raya, Bishop Fernando de Mendoza, gave the nuns 7,000 ducados to buy a local wheat field, and in 1617 a local priest, Juan de Cabrera, gave the nuns the cattle ranches of Pallata and Chunoguana in Chumbivilcas.[50] To judge by a 1623 list of their property, however, the nuns had to rely heavily on purchases to assemble a range of resources in the Cuzco area to meet their basic needs.[51] Livestock was pastured on a ranch the convent had purchased, Churucalla, as well as on the properties in Chumbivilcas that had been donated. Grain crops were grown on the convent's properties of Sondor and Palpacalla near San Salvador; one had been purchased, the other given to the convent to settle a debt. The grain-producing hacienda of Capra, near Pisac, had been brought to Santa Catalina in dowry. A gristmill had been purchased in 1620.[52] Potatoes were provided by a small estancia above the parish of San Blas, Patallacta, also purchased by the convent. The pattern is a familiar one. Unlike the Clares, however, the Dominican nuns got their resource base through the local land market without benefit of land grants.

The Dominican nuns did seek favors in these years, asking the viceroy and the Spanish Crown not for land but mainly for Andean labor power to work their estates. The Crown responded by authorizing a grant of 1,500 pesos in 1608, but its terms were not carried out and the nuns were obliged to continue their petitions.[53] However, they did succeed in obtaining grants of Indians to tend the convent's cattle. Eight mita laborers were assigned to the estancias of Pallata and Chunoguana by order of the viceroy in 1617.[54] An additional grant in 1639 provided the convent with Indian labor for "domestic services." Further rights to Andean labor would be acquired by the monastery in subsequent years, as certain haciendas came into the nuns' hands along with mita allotments.

Getting local authorities to enforce the convent's right to mita labor proved difficult for the nuns, however. Competition for Andean labor was often stiff. In 1668, for example, Santa Catalina came into possession of haciendas that had belonged to a man named Pedro de Onor, carrying a mita allotment of twenty people from the pueblos of Catca and Oropesa. Local authorities consistently failed to provide the laborers assigned to the hacienda, leading the prioress of Santa Catalina to obtain a viceregal order compelling the kurakas in question to supply the allotted laborers.[56] Doña Lucía de Padilla might no longer be around to teach her successors about wielding the powers of an encomendera, but they clearly learned to do these things themselves, as part of their exercise of dominio. Like Santa Clara, and the other monasteries and convents that arose across the colonial Andean landscape, the Dominican cloisters depended on that dwindling, much-exploited resource, the labor power of Andeans.

The monastery of Nuestra Señora de los Remedios—which cuzqueños soon began to call familiarly by the name of Santa Catalina—could prosper in Cuzco only by putting down local roots and becoming a recognizably cuzqueñan community. This process involved much more than the acquisition of local property and labor power.

The nuns of Santa Catalina are particularly devoted to the Dominican saint by whose name their convent is known, Saint Catherine of Siena (1347–80), represented in this painting bearing a lily/crucifix and the stigmata (Peru? 16th–17th century). Courtesy of the Brooklyn Museum.

Local families had to be persuaded to entrust their daughters to the new convent. Only then would the Dominicans become fully integrated into the spiritual economy of Cuzco—and the Padillas seem to have understood this, as from the start they accorded high priority to the recruitment of local nuns. Dowry was reduced, both to raise cash and to attract local professions so that the community might overcome its "foreignness." [57] The strategy seems to have worked. Nothing so detailed as Santa Clara's foundation book survives, but the nuns have preserved a simple list that was made soon after the Arequipans arrived in Cuzco. It shows that, before long, several women from Cuzco had taken the habit. Among them was the daughter of the nobleman Don Diego Pérez Martel, one Doña Mencía, who, despite her illegitimacy, enjoyed the status and prerogatives of high birth.[58]

By the time a list of the nuns' properties was drawn up in 1623, dowry payments had already done much to alleviate Santa Catalina's financial difficulties. At least two of the professed nuns had brought property to satisfy the dowry, and the receipt of sufficient cash had made it possible for Santa Catalina to become involved in local lending. By the mid-1620s the nuns had extended credit to some of the most important encomenderos of Cuzco, including Don Juan Sierra de Leguizamo, General Damián de la Bandera, and Don Miguel Gerónimo de Cabrera—all of whom had female relatives in the convent. By 1684, when Prioress María de los Remedios drew up a list of the convent's censos for her successor, Santa Catalina was entitled to collect on a total of 166 separate obligations.[59]

It is tempting to see in the new location of Santa Catalina another powerful reason for the nuns' success at remaking themselves into cuzqueñas and securing a place in the local spiritual economy. The nuns were lodged alongside the church of the Jesuits, in a site of great symbolic resonance: the old acllahuasi, or house of the chosen virgins of the Sun. A more cuzqueñan site could hardly have been selected for cloistered virgins of the new religion. Endlessly fascinating to European chroniclers from Cieza de León on, this institution of Inca culture appears to have been both a linchpin of Inca domination of various ethnic groups within the empire and a symbolically central feature of Inca religious life. Cuzco's acllahuasi had been at the center of a far-flung network of smaller acllahuasis throughout the Inca's domain, all of which had served to collect, house, and train selected young women for a life dedicated to serving the Inca ruler. The preparation of fine cloth and maize beer was the main activity of Cuzco's acllas, who lived (according to various Spaniards' reports) under the strict supervision of a headwoman known as a mamacona—inevitably, to Spanish eyes, the functional equivalent of an abbess. Indeed, these institutions were almost invariably described by Spanish chroniclers as convents. That Inca virgins lived a closely supervised, cloistered existence in what appeared to be convents must have struck early Spanish observers forcefully: the demonic parody of the Catholic forms of observance must have seemed at its most wickedly ingenious in these temples of pagan purity and feminine virtue. To accord Santa Catalina this place was to

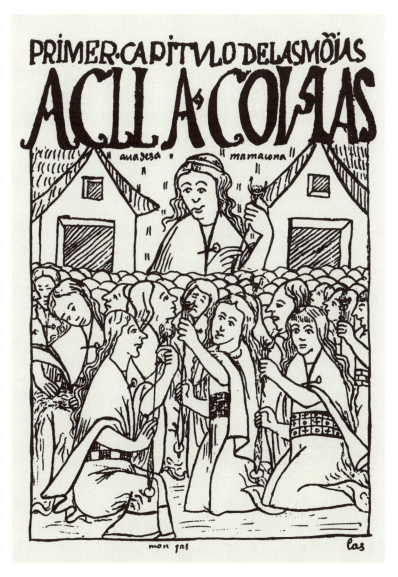

The acllahuasi, as imagined by Guaman Poma (1615), who identifies the acllas as nuns (*monjas*) living under an Inca abbess (*abadesa/mamacona*).

charge the new religious foundation with safeguarding an especially sensitive site. The Arequipans had been handed an Inca treasure.[60]

And just as Santa Clara could claim an Inca "princess" among its initial entrants, Doña Beatriz Clara Coya, Santa Catalina could boast of containing a different *coya*: Doña Melchora Clara Coya. She was the daughter of Cuzco's most noble assimilated Inca, Don Melchor Carlos Inca, great-grandson of Huayna Capac, and an Inca noblewoman named Doña Catalina Quispe Sisa. Doña Melchora seems to have gone by the name of Doña Leonor de Esquivel after her one Spanish grandparent, her paternal grandmother Doña María de Esquivel.[61] From the time she was young her father lived in Spain, owing to the anxiety of Peru's Spanish authorities about his potential involvement in plots with Cuzco "vagabonds." In a petition for royal support made soon after the nuns arrived in Cuzco, Santa Catalina's representative made sure to adduce the fact that the convent sheltered a descendant of the Incas: clearly this was considered an especially valid service rendered to the Crown, deserving of reward.[62]

Thus Doña Melchora (Leonor), like Doña Beatriz Clara Coya before her, became a bargaining chip, a trophy in the continuing cultural wars over the meaning and the political valence of Cuzco's Inca legacy. By the early seventeenth century, the threat of a major Inca revolt no longer hung heavily over the heads of elite cuzqueños as it once had. This position of relative security allowed them increased leeway to manipulate the Inca legacy, and cuzqueños began fashioning a variety of ways to honor and lay claim to the potent symbolism of the Inca past. To shelter an Inca "princess" inside the cloisters, atop the old acllahuasi—simultaneously containing and preserving the Inca past— was to tap the enormous symbolic resonance that was in the process of accruing to this glorious, "classical" past. How could a community carrying out such an exalted mission be considered foreign?

More Upheavals: Santa Clara Moves

Meanwhile, what of the original "insiders," the Clares, and the closely knit webs of kinship, belief, and credit that sustained them at the time the Dominicans arrived? How did they fare during the years in which the spiritual economy of Cuzco was expanding to accommodate a new monastery? The available record offers no more than hints, but it seems Santa Clara itself was undergoing rather dramatic change at this time, including the construction of new cloisters and a move. The Clares did not move across the Andes; they only moved across town, once the new site was completed in 1622. Yet the archival traces of this transition suggest that it precipitated an upheaval of a magnitude to rival that of the region's lively seismic events, because it shook up one of the most solidly reputable criollo families in all of Peru: the emerging Costilla dynasty.

All began innocuously enough, with a widow's pious bequest. In 1594 Doña Beatriz de Villegas—apparently a childless widow, like her Arequipan contemporary Doña Lucía de Padilla—formally donated all her possessions to Santa Clara.[63] Stating that she had already spent more than 34,000 pesos by that time to construct a new convent for the nuns, Villegas took the liberty of ordering in the terms of her donation "that the main chapel of the Church of said convent . . . be given to the Person who gives the largest donation for it," stipulating further that the winning donor as well as her brother Juan Zapata receive burial there.[64] Six years later Zapata appeared before the authorities to inform them of the death of his sister. The notary Juan de Olave was sent in April 1600 to certify that Villegas was indeed dead, and that inside her residence—then in the process of being converted into cloisters for the Clares—he had seen her body "laid on the floor on a black cloth, dressed in the habit of Saint Francis."[65]

Villegas had come as close as possible to the monastic life without actually professing solemn vows: like Padilla, she had turned her home into a monastery. She too had become an illustrious founder. But there was a problem: Santa Clara already had a *capilla mayor* in the church of the old convent, and the bones of the previous founders were buried inside it. Villegas and the nuns were conveniently ignoring the fact that this choice spot had already been claimed by the powerful Costilla clan. In June 1577, General Gerónimo Costilla had taken possession of the right to be buried inside the capilla mayor of the first church of Santa Clara, for which he had paid thousands of pesos.[66] His wife María Riveros had been buried there, and his remains had been placed alongside hers when he died a few years later. Had nobody thought of them? What would become of the burial place Costilla had bought to re-create the glorious tomb of his ancestors in Zamora?

Years passed before a crisis erupted over the conflicting claims of the heirs of Costilla and Villegas. If the Costillas learned the details of Villegas's donation, which threatened to undo the burial arrangement their progenitor had established, they must have assumed the threat could be countered effectively by their kinswoman Doña Lucía Costilla de Umarán, a granddaughter of Costilla and Riveros who ranked among the most powerful nuns in Santa Clara. Meanwhile, the construction project was running into difficulties. The site Villegas had donated turned out to be unsatisfactory. The cabildo approved a swap in 1603 for a different site, and construction was resumed.[67] The massive project dragged on for years and absorbed the energies of countless Andean workers. Building new cloisters also undoubtedly consumed many charitable donations, and the Clares may well have viewed the nuns from Arequipa as unwelcome rivals for the alms of the local populace—which would explain the less than effusive reception the Clares accorded the newcomers in 1605.

Finally, in 1622, the new cloisters stood ready to receive the nuns. Like the Dominicans before them, the Clares received a lavish public display of affection as they left the confines of their old convent and processed solemnly to the new convent. Wealthy cuzqueños hung rich tapestries from their balconies and looked on from above, while a popular crowd thronged the streets to celebrate the occasion. The Clares were accompanied on their brief journey by "all the nobility, important residents, and merchants" of the city, who formed "a lucid military squadron" in defense of the nuns' honor. The following day, the new convent church of Santa Clara was inaugurated with a mass and a eulogy.[68]

The Clares did not see fit to take the bones of Costilla and Riveros along, however. They left behind the chapel in which Gerónimo Costilla had arranged to be buried alongside his descendants, and began dividing up and selling off the premises that had once housed the community.[69] Not surprisingly, these moves provoked the Costillas to erupt in a burst of outrage. When Don Pedro Costilla learned his family would not retain its right to burial in the new church of Santa Clara, he flew into action, starting a furious and protracted campaign to compel the nuns to honor the terms of his parents' patronage. Powerful cuzqueños began choosing sides. The provincial leader of the Franciscan Order issued an order to stop Costilla from taking rash action. Heedless, and assisted by a prominent local clergyman, Costilla went so far as to disinter his parents' bones from the old chapel and move them into the new one himself.[70]

The ensuing legal battle would drag on for years. Costilla vigorously sustained that the privileged place the Costilla family had occupied in the old convent chapel should be theirs in the new one as well. The brother of Villegas, Juan Zapata, was somehow persuaded to enter into an agreement with Santa Clara by which he gave up his right to burial in the new chapel in exchange for a specific piece of real estate.[71] Yet the lawsuit was still unresolved when Don Pedro Costilla de Nocedo died in 1641, and what finally became of the Costillas' remains is not clear.

This obscure case is very revealing all the same. It provides a window through which we can glimpse the anxieties of aristocratic identity among local criollos—the heirs of men like Gerónimo Costilla—a century after their forefathers' arrival in the Andes. The stable, distinguished place Gerónimo Costilla thought he had ensured himself and his family was undone only a few years after his death. Surely, his son Don Pedro probably muttered to himself, this rude displacement would have been unthinkable back in Zamora, where the sediment of ancient tradition had settled its weight over such arrangements, preventing them, for better or worse, from being so brazenly disturbed.

Maybe so; but then Gerónimo Costilla had left Zamora precisely to escape the confines of such arrangements, and he himself had bought his way into the re-created perquisites of Spanish nobility in the Andes. He had managed to beat Villegas to it by a matter of decades. The need for a new convent had then provided her the opportunity to step in and rewrite Santa Clara's foundation story, displacing the Costillas and the cabildo and inserting herself in their place as "founder." In Cuzco, circa 1620, no Spanish benefactor's nobility was so deeply rooted as to deter the nuns from replacing him or her if a wealthier benefactor came along with a better offer.

Thus the social terrain for aspiring aristocrats might prove as unsteady as the geological landscape. Even the powerful Costillas could not simply take for granted their status as "insiders" in the spiritual economy of Cuzco; they had to maintain this position by investing in it constantly, else the privileges they regarded as the hallmark of their nobility might be bought out from under them. The Clares' move showed that important privileges could be had for the right price, as the widowed Villegas found out. Like many other things about this emerging colonial society, the role of noble benefactor was for sale.

Conclusions

The (re)founding of Santa Catalina in Cuzco reveals the limits and vicissitudes of what I am calling a spiritual economy. Instability could be a major problem for those attempting to operate within such a network (or, to borrow Pierre Bourdieu's lexicon, system of dispositions). A certain amount of instability could be accommodated, and was expected. Nuns and other investors did not put all their investments in one place, because crops might fail, a family's finances might give way, and so forth; instead, investors spread their investments around, building some flexibility into local finance. In general, however, the formal protocols of the spiritual economy were predicated on the long-term stability of the assets they attached; thus, natural disasters—such as the earthquakes that periodically hit the Andes—were a major problem. The available means of distributing the risks were overwhelmed by large-scale upheavals like those striking Arequipa around 1600.

It is by looking at times of such major disturbances that we can grasp the importance of a sturdy resource base (something the nuns of Nuestra Señora de los Remedios were not likely to attain easily in Arequipa's years of rebuilding). More than that: we grasp the vital enabling role of the informal protocols of the spiritual economy—those never committed to print, yet just as vital to transactions as the words on the notary's page (if not more so). In particular, we can deduce the crucial place of face-to-face, familiar connections between nuns and local families, fortified by lifetimes of sympathetic inquiries, prayerful concern, spiritual investment, and personal devotion. I am not suggesting that people were motivated to commend one another's souls in prayer, to ask after one another's health, to clothe altars, and so forth in order to lay away goodwill for the eventuality of an earthquake or some other disaster. They did these things because they seemed simply and utterly "natural." But such sustained bonds of ready familiarity came in handy in the event of an emergency. It helped for a family to have invested heavily over time in a sustained relationship with a monastery: the nuns might grant a grace period in time of need to those whom they considered close friends and supporters.

The story of volcanoes, earthquakes, and migrating nuns at the turn of the seventeenth century also raises to view more figurative varieties of instability, exposing the anxieties of identity in an emerging colonial aristocracy. The people of Arequipa who in 1605 wept so clamorously for the departing nuns that "it seemed like Judgment Day" would later treat the Dominicans' proxy López de Morla as a pariah, rendering his claims untenable. For the nuns, daughters of local Spanish property holders, had broken the unspoken contract that bound them to their locale, the invisible relationship that rendered the city more "authoritative," sheltering the virginal young women who would grow up to reproduce it. Quite possibly this was a gendered response: daughters were supposed to remain close to home, under the tutelage and control of their kinfolk.[72] In any case, the trajectory of the Padillas shows that for a monastic institution to uproot and transplant itself from one regional economy to another, given the spiritual obligations that its various contractual commitments entailed, was a risky move, as the play in the application of the term "foreigner" to the nuns of Santa Catalina demonstrates. By leaving behind their original site, the nuns voluntarily (albeit perhaps unwittingly) surrendered their passport to move familiarly within the spiritual economy of Arequipa.

In this case, the move paid off. Outsiders could "remake" themselves and become insiders in the space of a few decades. The nuns quickly acquired symbolic capital, as well as the more conventional kind. And they succeeded, by means of these strategies, in accomplishing their chief goal: winning the daughters of cuzqueños to the religious life. At the risk of some redundancy, we could consider this "reproductive capital" in a dual sense—for as we have seen, convents played a vital role in the reproduction of the cities around them; additionally, convent communities could reproduce only by attracting daughters from outside their walls and recruiting them to the religious life.

In 1649, when Contreras y Valverde wrote his account of the ecclesiastical glories of Cuzco, both Santa Clara and Santa Catalina were able to support well over a hundred inhabitants each. The Cuzco clergyman estimated that Santa Catalina held more than a hundred nuns, a figure the convent's records confirm. Santa Clara, by his estimate, held more than three hundred women, of which half were professed nuns. The two monasteries had become conventos grandes, like those in Lima and elsewhere: well-endowed, populous cities within cities.

Ironically, no sooner had the Dominican nuns succeeded in overcoming their status as "foreigners" and rooting themselves firmly in their adopted region than seismic disaster struck again. This time the epicenter was Cuzco. On the afternoon of March 31, 1650, wrote the chronicler Esquivel y Navia, the city suffered "an earthquake, the most formidable of all that had been felt in this region." The effects were devastating: "Almost all the buildings in the city were demolished, and most were left with little more than their foundations; those that did not collapse were so badly damaged that none could be inhabited safely." Cuzco's population began living in the streets and plazas as weeks of aftershocks further damaged their homes. Santa Clara "had better luck than the other convents," and the nuns could simply move to the patios of their cloisters while repairs began on their living quarters. Other churches and orders had to cope with varying degrees of damage. The women of Santa Catalina were the least fortunate of all:

Inca wall with geranium pots, a portion of the old acllahuasi inside Santa Catalina. Photo by K. Burns.

"their entire convent collapsed in ruins, and a sick nun was crushed by a wall."[73]

This time the Dominicans stayed where they were. The aftermath of the 1650 earthquake clearly illustrates how well they had succeeded at making themselves cuzqueñas, integral to the local landscape of spiritual and economic distinction: the nuns were led from their ruined cloisters in a solemn procession to the house of one of Cuzco's most powerful criollos, Don Pablo Costilla, great-grandson of the benefactor and former mayordomo of Santa Clara. Thereafter they moved, for lack of space, to the houses that had once belonged to a prominent conquistador. Despite the hard-hit economy of the following years, they were able to rebuild almost immediately. In December 1651 the first stone was laid in a ceremony marking the beginning of construction of the new convent church. The nuns would eventually return to their original site atop the old acllahuasi.

There the community remains to this day, and the nuns are proud of the fact that their community inhabits some of the most beautiful Inca stone walls in the city. Presiding over their modest garden, beyond the second cloister, is a row of astonishingly beautiful trapezoidal niches, the interior ornaments of an Inca wall, each now adorned with a flowerpot of pink geraniums. The stones of the old laundry look surprisingly like the face of an *intihuatana* (what guidebooks call an "Inca sundial"). Jumbled, this is the old acllahuasi, where virginal young women have lived and reproduced their respective cultures for centuries.

Part Two

ZENITH

En Madrid el Rey, en Lima el Virrey,
y en Cuzco el Marqués de Esquivel . . .
—pasquinade, ca. 1690

4 Reproducing Colonial Cuzco

To enter into contact with the nuns of Santa Catalina or Santa Clara—whether in the seventeenth century when their convents were new, or now, more than three centuries later—one must step inside the locutorio, or visitors' parlor. These rooms bear the name of their function, *locutio*, talk: they are the convent's listening posts on the world. But to enter a locutorio is to be impressed by its sights rather than its sounds. The visitor's eye is immediately drawn to the thick iron bars of a large grille, the *reja* (also *red* or *grada*), positioned so as to permit no physical contact between persons on either side. Even the gaze is impeded by the gridwork of the grille, which is the dominant feature of every locutorio.[1] Then, as now, only talk could pass freely between those seated on either side. Discipline is strikingly visible here, the separateness and discipline of the cloistered, contemplative life cast in strong bars.

The nuns referred to the world beyond the boundary of their grille simply as "el siglo," the secular world. The implication is clear: mundane projects had their ups and downs, beginnings and ends, while inside the cloisters time was different, advancing only to return to the point from which it started, through matins, prime, terce, lauds, and so forth. By entering the cloisters, the nuns had turned their backs on the world and tethered time to the wheel of ritual. But of course the exigencies of property and possession required of the nuns some engagement with secular people (*seglares*), those who lived in accordance with worldly hierarchies and by worldly time. The locutorio is thus a curious in-between place: it simultaneously acknowledges and denies the passing of the centuries. It is the in-between space of a necessarily delicate mission, the point at which the nuns interrupted their rounds of prayer to meet those living in el siglo.

The nuns heard constant warnings about the the dangers of such encounters. Their male superiors made sure of this, using such tools as

Nuns and their visitors before the grille of a locutorio, Santa Catalina. Photo by K. Burns.

Antonio Arbiol's manual on the proper observance of the religious life to convey stern lessons on the perils of the locutorio. "Our Seraphic Doctor Saint Bonaventure," Arbiol cautioned, "gives a horrifying description of conversation between Religious and Secular persons as contagious, and pestilential: because like the plague, it spreads from the sick to the healthy," never the other way around. Thus the nun in conversation ran a "great risk of catching something" worldly. Arbiol considered the use of the locutorio a necessary evil, "highly sensitive and difficult by its very nature for the true Brides of Christ. If it could be arranged for Nuns never to deal in temporal affairs with Seculars, this would be a great comfort to the happy souls who are consecrated to God, and very edifying for the World; but in accordance with the evil centuries in which we live, this is very unlikely."[2]

To make sure that as little as possible was left to chance, the orders carefully restricted the kinds of interactions that could take place inside the locutorios. Nuns might speak with visitors only during certain hours of the day and in the presence of an *escucha*, a listener delegated to monitor every conversation at the grille and to report any improprieties to her superior for disciplinary action. The bars of the grille were to be studded with sharp nails, in accordance with the rule of the Clares, and covered with a black curtain "in such fashion that the Nuns may not see those on the outside, nor be seen by them."[3] In short, everything possible was done to avert the dangers of outside penetration within the locutorios and to make them quiet, strictly decorous backwaters.

The locutorios of Cuzco were anything but backwaters, however. The notaries of Cuzco leave us a very different story. The archival record suggests that as Santa Clara and Santa Catalina grew into conventos grandes, their entryways and locutorios became alive, even boisterous, with activity. Through them flowed fathers and mothers, sisters, brothers, businessmen and businesswomen, bachelors, widows, and babies. Nuns were continually engaging with their visitors in "temporal affairs" of many kinds, sometimes using an interpreter for Quechua speakers whose business needed to be registered in the hegemonic Spanish language. And the grille might turn out to be a very useful asset. It could be employed to great effect when things were not going well: a nun might simply retreat into the cloisters when an affair was not working out to her liking. Or she might take advantage of the cloisters by refusing to appear at all and thus keep a would-be interlocutor waiting for days at the grille.[4]

Nor were locutorios always quiet. Those of Santa Clara and Santa Catalina might ring with the choral and instrumental music of an evening's entertainment.[5] Or with shouts and violence, as in 1682 when Francisco de Tapia sought ecclesiastical immunity inside Santa Clara and was dragged from the locutorio by local authorities in a raucous struggle.[6] Occasionally someone might go even further, as in the case of Don Antonio de Losada y Novoa, who rushed into the cloisters of Santa Catalina one morning in 1678 with his sword and dagger drawn, assaulting the nuns in order to attack one of his daughters in the cloisters for insulting his honor and turning her back on him. He had gone so far and raised such a scandal that his only hope of escaping severe punishment was to plead temporary insanity.[7]

Over the years many men have written about the world of the locutorio. For by the midcolonial period almost every important city in Peru had at least one monastery of cloistered women, and the viceregal capital of Lima had several, many of which seem to have maintained lively interactions with visitors at the grille. What these commentators have shared is a penchant for using the locutorio to gauge the nuns' supposed failure to live up to their vows of poverty, chastity, and

Guaman Poma (1615) depicts a nun receiving a donation (*limosna*) from a bilingual visitor. He praises nuns for the love and charity they show Indians, and contrasts their generosity with the vanity and selfishness of "worldly ladies" (*señoras del mundo*).

obedience. Male ecclesiastics scolded the nuns for "excessive" contact with secular people and periodically tried to impose stricter discipline. Others saw in the locutorios sites of sublimated desire, where men might make fools of themselves by engaging in platonic courtships with particular nuns.[8] And historians, to the extent that they have noticed convents at all, have likewise tended to fault the nuns for unruliness.[9] Such portrayals have served to relegate locutorios, nuns, and convents to the margins of colonial Peruvian historiography, where they appear, if at all, as mere sideshows to the central drama of colonial Peru.

Yet to see locutorios merely in anecdotal terms is to ignore a crucial arena in which colonial relations were forged. The nuns used these spaces to create richly textured alliances with cuzqueños of all kinds, extensively reworking the worldly protocols of marriage, family, and inheritance to suit their own purposes. And as Cuzco turned into a thriving colonial emporium with its own distinctive aristocracy, the monasteries reached a zenith of their own. Their locutorios became some of the most heavily trafficked sites in the city's center, vital to the making of aristocrats and commoners alike. To grasp fully the logic at work in these spaces, and their importance, we first have to go past them—to the structures and spaces of interaction within the cloisters. There, by the mid-seventeenth century, the nuns of Cuzco had made for themselves an elaborate reproductive role, at once reflecting and sustaining the baroque splendor of the criollo-dominated city flourishing around them.

The Order of Things

Beyond the locutorios of Santa Clara and Santa Catalina, inside the stone edifices that indigenous cuzqueños built for the nuns early in the seventeenth century, lay an ample world carefully shaped for ritual. Each monastery still occupies a great deal of space in the center of Cuzco, on the interior of large city blocks ringed by storefront properties. They used to occupy much more space. Apart from its church, where mass was celebrated for the public, each convent once contained not only extensive living and working quarters, but spacious patios, gardens, fountains and, in the case of Santa Clara, a large orchard. They were veritable cities within the city, enclosed behind high stone walls and massive wooden portals.

Most visible to the outside world are the splendid churches of Santa

Clara and Santa Catalina. These were among the most brilliant theaters in the region for the staging of one of the most lavish, spectacular cultural events of the day, the Roman Catholic mass. The nuns spared no expense to adorn their churches, commissioning huge, magnificent canvasses for their walls and baroque woodcarving and sculpture for their altars. To contribute to the enhancement of the convent church was a mother superior's fondest dream. In 1660 Prioress Isabel de la Purificación even refused to leave office on time so that the glory of completing a particularly splendid *retablo* for the church of Santa Catalina would redound to her benefit. (Her community lamented that the devil had tempted their prioress, whose term in office had otherwise been exemplary.)[10] The visual effect of such lavish expense of artistic energy is still dazzling. The nuns made sure that the music of the mass was equally sumptuous and moving: from their choir at the back of the nave, concealed by a curtain from the public's gaze, they provided elaborate choral and instrumental accompaniment to the priests' administering of the sacraments. So important was the quality of the music that the nuns went to great lengths to nurture exceptional singers and musicians, hiring music teachers to give daily lessons in the locutorio in harp and organ.[11]

Apart from their churches, the apex of convent architecture, the interiors of Santa Clara and Santa Catalina are seldom described in the archival record. However, it is clear that both convents were expanding during the seventeenth century. In 1655, only five years after the devastating midcentury earthquake had destroyed a substantial portion of the nuns' living quarters, Santa Clara was constructing an expensive new cloister. The nuns defrayed some of the cost by bartering: one artisan, Diego de la Cuba, contracted to install the floor in a portion of the new cloister in exchange for the Clares' commitment to furnish him Indian laborers and to accept two of his daughters as nuns.[12] Meanwhile the Dominicans of Santa Catalina, whose cloisters had been much more severely damaged by the 1650 earthquake, were not only rebuilding but enlarging their convent, purchasing and then enclosing several adjacent streets and houses.[13]

Inside these spaces were common rooms for cooking, eating, and sleeping: the convent kitchen, refectory, and dormitory.[14] There was also a special *sala de labores* where the nuns and novices kept busy practicing such skills of domesticity as embroidery, knitting, and flower arranging, producing *labores de manos* of various kinds for local consumption. Some women became expert cooks, enriching the cuisine of the city with their recipes. The monastic life permitted such labors on a small scale because they were, as Arbiol expressed it, "appropriate for delicate women . . . and the good Nun remains quiet, and alone, elevating her heart to the heights while her hands work and are not idle." [15]

Yet by far the most notable feature of the convents' interiors in an otherwise silent documentary record is the nuns' division of their living quarters into separate, private cells (celdas). By mid-seventeenth century this form of organization had become widespread as an alternative to the common dormitory, both in Cuzco and elsewhere in the viceroyalty.[16] Santa Clara and Santa Catalina clearly had many such cells, which might be quite large, including as many as eight rooms. Many cells contained their own kitchens, patios, even chicken coops. Some had altars for private devotions.[17] Large portions of the monastic compounds of Cuzco may have come to resemble neighborhoods of independent living quarters of this kind, which the documents often describe as "casas," houses.

A nun's comportment inside these spaces was extensively regulated by the rules and constitutions of her order, themselves a massive edifice of intricate prescription. To read these is to gain a sense of the cumulative weight of centuries of monastic practice, as every conceivable aspect of a nun's life seems to be covered, down to the details of how she must wear her habit. The particulars varied in accordance with the determinations made within each order over time. In 1639, for example, the Franciscan authorities who had convened to revise the constitutions of the Clares exhorted the nuns to sleep in a common dormitory and to "avoid the profane cells that have been introduced, on the pretext of having a place to meditate quietly (recogerse)." (This particular battle the Franciscans seem to have sensed they would lose, as a few passages later they instruct nuns with private cells "to try sincerely to make them reflect saintly poverty . . . contenting themselves with a Cross, and an Image," and avoiding decorative "curiosities and adornments.") [18] They sought also to impose stricter regulations in the locutorio, ordering the nuns "not to play harps, guitars, or other instruments, sing profane songs, or dance, even in their habits," as such activities went against "religious modesty." [19] Such prohibitions and prescriptions abound in the constitutions to which Clares and Dominicans were expected to adhere; no detail was too small to be beneath regulation.

Entering this carefully structured world meant a woman had to learn its rules in an extended apprenticeship known as the novitiate.

This period began with a ritual of separation from the world and submission to a new authority, the mother superior. The rules and constitutions of the Dominicans outline its steps carefully. The novice was to "prostrate herself in the middle of the assembled nuns, and when asked by the Prioress, 'What do you want?' she must respond, 'The mercy of God, and yours,' and then be ordered to rise, and the Prioress, after explaining to her the rigors of the Order and receiving her response that she wants to bear them, must say: 'The Lord who began doing good in you, let him finish,' and dress her in the Habit, assigning her a year of probation, and no less." [20] Each novice then took an additional step away from her worldly identity: she took a religious name, often that of a saint to whom she was especially devoted. Thus transformed, she might install herself in the novices' quarters, where she would live for a year with the other novices under the close supervision of a teacher, a nun known as the *maestra de novicias*, whose duty it was to instruct and discipline her.

During their year of probation novices were thoroughly versed in the rules and practices of their order. Their teacher might assign them spiritual readings, such as the lives of the saints, and examine them to be sure they had absorbed the right lessons. The novices of Santa Clara must have pored over the chronicle of Diego de Mendoza, obviously written for just such a didactic purpose. Mendoza upheld an ideal of extreme distance between the outside world and the cloistered, contemplative life: model nuns never went to the locutorio; they humbled themselves by performing manual labor, even though they might be daughters of important, wealthy people. And they always obeyed the orders of their superiors promptly and without question, no matter the cost to themselves. Mendoza praised the nun Bernardina de Jesús in particular for her exemplary obedience. One day, he recounted,

> a barber was brought to the cell of this servant of God [Bernardina], who was far from needing any molar or tooth of hers removed. When the barber said he had come on orders of the abbess to pull her molar, Bernardina replied that she did not need any molar removed. The nun acting as nurse thought Bernardina was excusing herself out of fear, however, and convinced that the abbess's orders superseded any fear of pain, reminded Bernardina that even though she did not have a toothache, her vow of obedience [to her abbess] obliged her to offer not one but all of her teeth to be removed. The barber then

asked Bernardina which molar he should pull, and she said he might pull any one he liked, since none of them hurt.[21]

So the man chose a healthy tooth in Bernardina's mouth and pulled it. The convent marveled when word of the incident spread: the barber had been conducted to the wrong nun's cell! But Bernardina, according to Mendoza, "was very happy at having obeyed her Superior, happier than she would have been with the tooth in her mouth."

Once a novice had learned such lessons to her teacher's satisfaction, she might be admitted formally to the community as a nun, a process that involved several steps. First for the Clares came a comprehensive examination: the abbess was to select "two Nuns to examine [the novice], to see that she knows her prayers, and how well she understands the Rule she is to profess; and if the said Nuns testify before the full community that she is well versed in everything, she may profess."[22] In both orders the assembled nuns voted on whether or not to admit the novice; a majority of the votes would enable her to proceed. The novice was further examined by a male ecclesiastical authority to determine whether she was old enough to profess and whether her decision expressed her "free will." (She had to be at least sixteen years of age for her profession to be valid, in accordance with the Council of Trent, and professing under no duress.) Along the way, payment of her dowry had to be guaranteed, as well as certain other customary expenses. If all these things proceeded smoothly, the novice would be allowed to profess in the prescribed ritual. On the appointed day, she knelt before her mother superior, placed her hand in her superior's, and took the solemn vows of poverty, chastity, and obedience, upon which the nuns gave her the black veil and she was received with songs and celebration as a symbolic bride of Christ.[23]

Thereafter, a nun's life revolved around an ancient central purpose: that of offering prayers on behalf of sinful humanity. The prayers of the spiritual bride of Christ were considered to have special efficacy; like those of the hermitic, desert-dwelling fathers of the church, a nun's prayers gained by her purity and dedication, her freedom from other, competing objectives. Her days thus consisted of constant movement back and forth between her cell and the church, guided by the ringing of bells. The canonical hours provided the basic structure of each day's activities. Nuns rose during the night and early in the morning to begin the day in prayer, and they went to bed after completing evening prayers; in all, each day included matins, lauds, prime, terce,

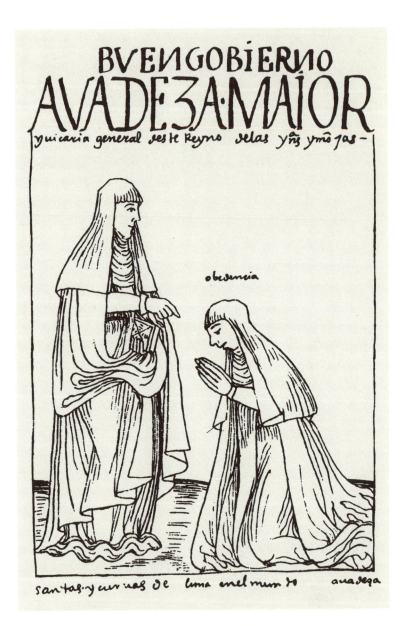

One of the images used by Guaman Poma (1615) to depict order and good governance (*buen gobierno*) is that of a nun kneeling before her abbess; she is literally under obedience (*obediencia*).

sext, none, vespers, and compline. Not all days were exactly alike, however. The monastic communities observed an extensive calendar of saint's days and other special occasions, including Christmas, the Lenten season of penitence and fasting, and Easter, or *semana santa*. On such occasions special sermons might be given by visiting priests, and fasts broken with festive meals. Each community also marked the day of its patron saint with celebrations in her honor.

Atop this busy world was the abbess or prioress, elected by majority vote of the nuns to serve a three-year term. The rules and constitutions accorded her enormous power. It was her responsibility to oversee convent finances and provide for the needs of all the members of her community "with discretion and charity, like a prudent and wise Mother of a Family."[24] She held the keys to the locutorio, and one of the three keys needed to open the convent safe, the *caja de tres llaves*. She received and disbursed payments, working closely with the convent's various male proxies, its mayordomos and *administradores*, as well as with its ecclesiastical supervisor (always a Franciscan friar in the case of the Clares, a high-ranking diocesan authority for the Dominican nuns). And responsibility for discipline in the cloisters ultimately rested with her. She assembled the nuns on a regular basis so that they might declare their faults publicly and be corrected and given penance by her. In cases of severe infractions, she might sentence nuns to a variety of punishments, ranging from a diet of bread and water to lashings and incarceration in the convent jail.[25] So powerful was the mother superior that the rules charged the nuns to choose a leader "of spotless virtue, who will lead more by her saintly example than by [authority of] her position. And let her care for her community honestly, so that the Nuns may be moved to obey her by love rather than fear."[26]

Responsibility for keeping order was also apportioned among a variety of other officers of the convent. Each triennium, the nuns elected a *supriora* or *vicaria* to serve as second in command to the mother superior. The mother superior relied heavily on her, and on the *madres de consejo*, a select group of nuns chosen for their experience and ability to act as her closest advisors. No important business decision was to be taken by the mother superior without first consulting the madres de consejo, most of whom had served a term as mother superior themselves.[27] The rest of the convent's officers were charged with supervising particular places or conducting specific tasks. Among the most strategic were those of the guardians of the convents' main points of contact with the public: the doorkeeper, or *portera*, responsible for opening and closing the convent's portals; the *torno* attendant, or *tornera*, who handled the cylindrical, revolving compartment, set into the wall by the convent entrance, by means of which small items could be passed into or out of the convent; and the grille-minders (*rederas*) and the listeners (*escuchas*), whose duty it was to watch and listen to all conversations in the locutorio. The *depositaria* was responsible for keeping track of money. Other officers were charged with ensuring proper ritual observance: the *sacristana* made sure all was in order for the mass; the *vicaria de coro* led the nuns' prayers; the maestra de novicias, as noted above, handled all aspects of the training and discipline of novices. Others saw to maintenance and provisioning: the supervision of the kitchen and refectory, the larder, the infirmary, and so forth.

To permit the nuns to concentrate on their prayers, the heaviest labor in the cloisters might be performed by lay sisters (*freylas donadas* or *hermanas legas*). These women, who wore the white veil permanently, were charged with performing "all the humble tasks" in the cloisters, "such as cooking, nursing, and laundry . . . without being excused from the most humble . . . since they entered the Convent to serve the Nuns, and not to be served."[28] Like the nuns, lay sisters were expected to complete a novitiate, profess vows, bring dowry to the community (albeit less than that of the nuns), and take part in daily prayers. However, their prayers were restricted so that they might devote more time to chores, and they were not permitted to vote in convent elections or hold high office. The constitutions of the Clares stipulated that there be no more than one such lay sister for every ten nuns.[29] The Dominicans' constitutions likewise instructed the nuns to have no more than a "moderate number" of lay sisters at their service.[30] Best of all, the rules indicated, was for nuns to do without such auxiliaries as much as possible.

Practices

Little wonder that Arbiol and others considered the locutorio a necessary evil and a place of danger: in dealings at the grille, the distance the nuns were encouraged to maintain from the practices of the secular world might collapse. Hence the strong bars and pointed iron nails, the curtains, the vigilant eavesdroppers. Novices might see family members only three or four times in the course of their year-long novitiate, as they were considered particularly vulnerable to mundane influences and attachments. Yet the rules and constitutions themselves provided for a partial undoing of the strict division (literally ironclad) between cloistered women and the outside world. Secular servants might assist the nuns with their chores, and secular boarders might be received "for urgent and serious reasons, or due to a person's high rank."[31] The nuns of Cuzco forged generous interpretations of these provisions over the years. They not only made extensive use of their portals and locutorios, but brought secular women into the cloisters for periods of residency which might last anywhere from a few days to several years. By the mid-seventeenth century, in fact, Santa Clara and Santa Catalina had taken in such large numbers of secular women and girls that professed nuns constituted a minority of the residents inside their own convents. According to the clergyman Vasco de Contreras, Santa Clara held more than 300 women by 1649, of whom 150 were nuns; Santa Catalina held 250 women, of whom about 100 were nuns.[32]

Who were these seglares? Most visible by far are the girls, the niñas seglares who abound in convent records. Some were deposited with the nuns for temporary safekeeping, like Francisca, daughter of a traveling merchant named Pedro Francisco de Abreu, who in 1655 agreed to pay board to the nuns of Santa Catalina until he returned for her.[33] Many young women took up residence with a cloistered sister, cousin, or aunt—as did Doña Ana de Losada, who in 1678 lived in Santa Catalina with her professed sister Doña Josefa.[34] Most were sent by their families for a period of schooling. A lengthy list from Santa Catalina shows nearly a hundred girls entered the convent between the years 1651 and 1658, including not only elite young criollas like Doña Catalina de Valdes y Zárate, the daughter of a wealthy local hacendado, but at least two "Indians" as well: Micaela B., daughter of the kuraka of Quiquijana, and Tomasa Sisa, a nine-year-old interned by her father at a rate of 30 pesos a year for "ratione educationis."[35]

Other girls arrived in more precarious circumstances: the baby girls who came into the nuns' care when a parent furtively placed them inside the torno. Still in use today in many convents, the torno was intended for the passage of letters, small gifts, and such. Because its rotating compartments were large enough to hold a baby, occasionally infants were passed through it, into the hands of the surprised nun on the other side.[36] These infants might still be known years later as expuestas, girls who had been abandoned and literally "exposed."[37]

Nuns thus became (adoptive) mothers, nurturing foundlings and orphans along with their female kin. They turned their cells into nurseries: "I raised and educated her from the time she wore diapers," claimed a nun of Santa Clara about a particular girl, and many others could say the same.[38] Seglares were supposed to be housed separately from professed nuns, but where children were concerned this separation was not strictly enforced—if it was observed at all.[39] A nun might tutor her young charges to read and write, and to sing and play musical instruments.[40] The strong attachment nuns developed to the children they raised is evident in myriad documents, such as the gifts many nuns gave their young charges. They referred to their girls as "mis muchachas" and "mi niñas."[41]

In short, the nuns of Cuzco redefined for themselves the social institutions of marriage and family. For them, mothering did not require conjugal sex or secular marriage, and family did not require a patriarchal head of household. Their experience of motherhood took place instead within a spiritual form of marriage, and their recasting of family relations placed them at the head of their own households (albeit under the authority of their monastic superiors). They broke neither their vow of chastity nor that of obedience. By mothering many girls of Cuzco to adulthood, the nuns also reproduced themselves. Many niñas seglares grew up to become novices and nuns, an outcome that in many cases was their families' stated intention. Others did not "find themselves," as one woman put it, and left the cloisters.[42]

Not all children raised by the nuns were free to leave upon reaching adulthood, however. This is particularly obvious in the case of children who entered the cloisters as slaves. In 1646, for example, a family quarrel broke out when Feliciana de San Nicolás, a nun of Santa Catalina, refused to give up an eight-year-old slave girl named Gerónima whom she had been raising in the cloisters. The nun insisted that Gerónima had been left to her in the terms of her brother's will, and that she would not have received the girl otherwise because Gerónima was only a year and two months old at the time.[43] Young boys as well as girls might be involved in such "gifts," as a different donation makes strikingly clear. In 1642 an Indian woman named María Panti made a gift to her cloistered granddaughter María Jesús of two children, both born slaves.[44] One was a two-and-a-half-year-old girl named Isabel; the other, her adolescent brother—Gaspar. María Panti specified that the girl was to serve her granddaughter inside the convent, while the boy was to work outside as a tailor and remit his wages to his mistress. The nun María Jesús may well have apprenticed him eventually—as did another nun, Inés de Terrazas, who in 1661 arranged through a Franciscan proxy to apprentice her slave Leonardo Terrazas to a master tailor.[45]

The nuns were thus actively reproducing the relations of servitude upon which the colonial society around them depended. They stretched the bounds of dominio to allow slavery inside the cloisters, making it possible by the mid-seventeenth century for Santa Clara and Santa Catalina to hold a panoply of servants, retainers, and slaves. That future nuns and their slaves might grow up together inside the same cell suggests the nuns saw no contradiction between their quest for spiritual purity and their control of other people as property — so long as such control was exercised in accordance with their monastic vows. If her superiors gave permission, a nun might have lifelong personal servants at her command. These things were entirely naturalized under colonial monasticism in Cuzco.

And what of the large population of servants and donadas so proudly pointed out by Vasco de Contreras? The ranks of the nuns' servants seem to have been far more numerous than those of their cloistered slaves or, for that matter, those of the niñas seglares. The servants no doubt had to bear the greatest responsibility for washing, sweeping, tending gardens and orchards, and cooking for the monastic community. Unfortunately, they are all but invisible in the archival record. Very little note was ever taken of them — how they came into the cloisters, and their motives for doing so; where they lived; how long they stayed; how they identified themselves. Occasionally a servant sealed her commitment to the cloistered religious life by professing simple vows as a donada. In 1652, Santa Catalina had eighteen such lay sisters, and probably dozens more unprofessed servant women and girls.[46]

Many of these dozens, even hundreds, of servants were probably orphans and foundlings brought up inside the cloisters. That nuns raised some orphans to become maids is clear from their petitions to reward their best servants. Gregoria de Santiago y Valenzuela, for example, sought in 1743 to bequeath her cell in Santa Catalina after her death to "two orphans I am raising," stating that "I owe them [for] their personal service." Her contemporary Josefa del Carmen made a similar request, specifying a detailed order of succession in which she extended control over the lives of "her girls" past not only her death but theirs. In her 1742 petition she seeks to grant "a little chicken coop and its cell" to Josefa Labaxonera, her favorite, "whom I have raised from infancy to sing in the choir, as she has been doing, so that she may have a place to live the rest of her days, and after her Tomasa

Meseta, together with all the girls I am raising, to whom I owe their personal services, and when all my girls have died, my Monastery shall receive the right to it."[47]

So the nuns of Santa Clara and Santa Catalina constructed their own complex, colonial households, with infants and toddlers, adolescents, maids, and slaves—perhaps all at once—inside their capacious cells. Nuns became the matriarchs of their own alternative families, which often included their nieces, sisters, and other female kin. They nurtured, schooled, and supervised; they spoke of "their girls" in affectionately patronizing diminutives: "una cholita ahijadita mía"; "una donadita"; "una indiecita que estoy criando." The abbesses and prioresses of Cuzco sanctioned these all-female families, even allowing nuns to leave behind the use of their cells and chicken coops to girls and women of their choosing—in short, refashioning inheritance within the protocols of the cloistered religious life.[48] Widows in particular seem to have benefited from this generous interpretation of the monastic vow of poverty. Many widows took the habit and brought their worldly possessions with them, reserving usufruct rights for themselves as long as they lived: for example, Doña Mariana de Rojas, a widow who became a novice and who in 1631 donated her properties to Santa Clara, "reserving to herself the usufruct of them during the days of her life."[49] Years later a widow and her daughter both professed in the same convent, then empowered a proxy to handle their business affairs: these two were in effect moving their household into the cloisters.[50]

How did these cloistered households and alternative families relate to the patriarchal households of Cuzco? By training generations of young women, did the nuns in effect serve as extensions of secular households, merely obeying the will of Cuzco's patriarchs? The language of the notarial records seems to suggest as much. "I interned them to be Nuns" ("las entré Monjas"), reads a passage in the 1633 will of Juan de Vargas, who had placed three of his nieces in Santa Catalina.[51] Diego de la Cuba in 1655 placed his daughters in the Dominican cloisters "with the intention and desire that they become professed nuns, God willing."[52] But the unusual case of Don Antonio de Losada y Novoa shows how the cloisters might also be used to frustrate and subvert patriarchal authority.

On the morning of April 30, 1678, Don Antonio had by all accounts violated the cloisters of Santa Catalina in dramatic fashion. Witnesses testified that he had rushed in brandishing his sword and dagger, in furious pursuit of his daughter the professed nun Doña Josefa de Losada, and had chased her into a cell where Feliciana de San Nicolás was lying sick in bed. Before the mayordomo could subdue him, Don Antonio had pinned his daughter beneath the bed and wounded the sick nun in the process. He himself admitted only to advancing "a few steps" inside the cloisters, "for an extremely urgent reason and in defense of my honor because I was told that they wanted to remove from said Monastery my daughter Doña Ana de Losada [a secular boarder] in order to marry her unequally to José de Quintana, a metalworker, and precipitated by my ire at such a grave insult, and without thinking, I went a few steps inside the door to prevent such great damage to my honor." The frustrated patriarch accused Doña Josefa of being the matchmaker. When asked how she could have arranged such a dishonorable match, he said, she had responded "brazenly and impudently, that her sister could do whatever she wanted, and not what [I] wanted"—and then turned her back on him. Don Antonio's representative argued mitigating circumstances: to defy one's father "in such a grave matter as the election of a spouse, on which the family honor depends . . . is the most outrageous provocation of the most severe punishment, and the most Just excuse of the worst crime." [53] Unfortunately the documents are truncated and the outcome in this case is unclear. Nevertheless, it is quite clear that at least one nun actively defied patriarchal authority from the relative safety of her cloisters.

Yet even as they used the power of motherhood to shape and control their own households, the nuns also acted in various ways to bolster the institutions of marriage and family in the society around them. For one thing, they accepted the occasional *depositada* or *penitenciada*, women sentenced by ecclesiastical authorities to the cloisters as punishment for allegedly violating or defying the bounds of propriety. Adultery, licentiousness, thievery—these infractions of Cuzco's officially sanctioned moral order, or the suspicion of having committed them, might land a woman in a convent against her will. For these seglares the convent was intended to be a bleak prison. And by all indications the nuns consented to their role as jailers, humbling and isolating the depositadas, who complained of being mistreated and poorly nourished. In 1704, for example, Petronila Serrano appealed her case to Lima, complaining that she had been kept prisoner ("reclusa y presa") in Santa Catalina for more than five months without being told the charges on which she was deposited there; her legal representative noted that she was several months pregnant, and at risk of aborting her child.[54]

The nuns of Cuzco also took in women who sought shelter from violent marriages. Women whose husbands beat them might take refuge in the cloisters, as did Cipriana Villalba, who complained of her husband's drunkenness and adultery as well as his violence: in the midst of the Corpus Christi procession, she testified, he had given her such a blow to the stomach that he had nearly killed her. She asked the ecclesiastical authorities of Cuzco to grant her permission to live in one of the city's convents with her three young children.[55] Cecilia Aymulo's case began very differently: she was deposited in Santa Catalina as punishment for having tried to kill her husband by throwing him into a raging river. When after three years her husband (who had somehow managed to extricate himself) tried to obtain her release, Aymulo resisted, saying she had never wanted to marry in the first place and had done so only because her parents had forced her. Aymulo had by that point become one of the convent's servants. She had changed from prisoner to refugee, gaining considerable range of movement in the process, and her "comings and goings" clearly displeased and aroused the suspicions of her husband, who succeeded in convincing diocesan authorities to give him back his wife against her will.[56]

These scant traces make all the more clear the cloisters' relationship to the social order of Cuzco. By accepting, containing, and disciplining women for whom marriage had somehow reached a breaking point—women whose lives were no longer governed by a husband, or who refused to be governed by one—convents made the conventions of worldly marriage easier to uphold. From time to time, convents may have served to thwart the desires of a patriarchal head of household, as in the case of Don Antonio de Lozada y Novoa and his daughters. In general, however, convents facilitated the workings of patriarchy at the level of Cuzco's households: they produced marriageable young women as well as nuns, provided an escape hatch for marriage's battered refugees, and punished female infractors when ordered to do so, reinforcing the authority of their male ecclesiastical superiors. Redefining marriage for themselves as a form of spiritual commitment did not, in other words, keep nuns from upholding the institution of worldly marriage. To the contrary: their convents were a bulwark sustaining it.[57]

Distinction: Making "Nuns" of More than One Category

By mid-seventeenth century, as the two conventos grandes of Cuzco grew and prospered, each became highly stratified. While the nuns made their rounds of prayer, called by the convent bells back and forth between their cells and the church, an equally large population moved at its own uncelebrated pace, describing with its movements the rounds of servitude. Servants and slaves hurried between the kitchen and the refectory, the laundry and the infirmary and the dispensary; Indian yanaconas who lived in the patios adjacent to the cloisters came and went with cargoes of food and supplies. Parents periodically called at the grille and brought news, gossip, and gifts to their cloistered children. And through these variegated dealings, the monastic order of things not only mirrored the increasingly baroque complexity of colonial Spanish-Andean society but produced it.

The nuns constituted the privileged elite of their enclosed worlds, yet they too were hierarchically divided. By midcentury one did not simply become a professed nun, but a nun of the black veil (velo negro) or the white veil (velo blanco). This criterion of difference was the very one that had deeply incensed the founders of Santa Clara in 1565; they had objected to its being used to organize unequal relationships between mestizas and Spaniards inside the cloisters. The cabildo of Cuzco had insisted the nuns all wear the same habit and veil, because "to do otherwise would foment division, discord, schism and perpetual enmity among the nuns." [58] The nuns had nevertheless revived the once controversial distinction between wearers of the black and white veils. Despite the fact that their constitutions prescribed only two categories of professed women, nuns and lay sisters, the women of Santa Clara and Santa Catalina had created a third, intermediate category—a permanent class of nuns of lesser rank. A list of women professing in Santa Catalina from 1654 to 1679 shows that while nuns of the black veil were the most numerous group, the category of white veil was also quite large: the ratio between the two groups was about 5:2 (see Appendix 5).

What did it mean to belong to the intermediate category of the white veil? In terms of dowry, it meant paying exactly half the dowry required of the nuns of the black veil. The full dowry had by the mid-seventeenth century been fixed at 3,312 pesos, 4 reales; thus, a nun of the white veil was expected to bring 1,656 pesos, 2 reales. [59] (Donadas

brought significantly less, typically 500 pesos.) Nuns of the white veil
received less than nuns of the black veil when the community distributed Christmas gifts and got smaller food rations as well. They were
not allowed to vote in convent elections, nor could they hold high
offices.[60] Among the clearest archival indications of the status of nuns
of the white veil comes from Santa Clara in 1683. The nuns, having purchased and enclosed some houses to enlarge their cloisters, decided
to convert part of the additional space into a new infirmary for nuns
of the black veil and to use the old infirmary for treating nuns of the
white veil and donadas.[61]

Nuns of the white veil thus appear to have filled the role of lay sister
spelled out in the constitutions of their orders. They were part of the
substantial corps of housekeepers in their cloisters, presumably supervising the numerous ranks of donadas, servants, and slaves ranged
beneath them in the conventual hierarchy.[62] Their decisionmaking was
restricted to this quotidian level of convent affairs; like those placed
beneath them, they had no voice in the governance or business matters of their communities. However, they might control property if
given the proper permission. Many nuns of the white veil had private
cells, in which they might form their own households with children
and servants. In 1735, for example, Ignacia de San Martin, "monja de
velo blanco," donated her cell inside Santa Catalina to her niece Doña
Francisca Sampac, "whom I have raised since childhood and to whom
I owe her personal service and the many favors of her father Don
Matías Sampac, my brother, and Doña Martina Guariloclla, his legitimate wife." Ignacia went on to state that the donation left her sufficient
resources to provide for herself and her servants.[63]

Why organize such unequal relationships within the convent elite?
Certainly the nuns of Cuzco were not alone in doing so: Luis Martín,
whose work concentrates on Lima, shows that during the course of
the seventeenth century the conventos grandes of the viceregal capital
became similarly stratified. Martín sees the difference between nuns of
the black and white veils as more social than economic. The black veil
he characterizes as a "closed aristocracy" of women who "belonged,
if not always to the economic elite of the viceroyalty, certainly to the
upper social strata of colonial Peru."[64] Simply being able to pay the
full dowry did not guarantee acceptance at this level. Belonging to a
distinguished family, on the other hand, might be enough to attain the
black veil even for a woman with no dowry.

In Cuzco, too, the distinctions reinforced by the black and white veils tended to be more social than economic. The case of Doña Martina de Ugarte helps clarify the boundary between the two categories. After she was received in Santa Catalina as a novice to become a nun of the white veil, a local clergyman came forward with 3,312 pesos, 4 reales for her dowry so that she might take the black veil instead, "in recognition of her noble blood."[65] Similar cases confirm that in Cuzco, as in Lima, poverty was not necessarily an impediment for women seeking to become nuns of the highest rank, so long as lineage compensated.[66]

Nor was illegitimacy an insuperable obstacle for those considered noble. The contested election of Doña Mencía de San Bernardo as prioress of Santa Catalina led to a landmark decision on this issue in 1644. The losing candidate (by only one vote), Doña Juana de los Remedios, charged that Doña Mencía should not have been admitted as a nun of the black veil in the first place, much less allowed to run for prioress, as she was a natural daughter (hija natural), born to parents who could have been legally married but were not at the time of her birth.[67] The irate Doña Juana went on to charge that Doña Mencía had wielded family connections to get around the fact that she was an "unqualified and incapable person on account of not being legitimate, born of a legitimate marriage." Those who joined her suit accused Doña Mencía of using bribes, promises, and other pressure tactics to court the vote, including musical entertainments ("músicas y saraos") in her cell. They went so far as to allege a conspiracy among the illegitimate nuns to seize power, asserting that "the majority of the votes Doña Mencía received were likewise those of illegitimate persons who manifested their support with a view to [the time] when their turn might come, which is sufficient cause to annul said votes as a form of simony." When the case reached Lima on appeal, Doña Mencía's representative argued that her alleged impediment was "easily overcome" by her lineage: she was noble, the natural daughter of Don Diego Pérez Martel. Under Castilian legislation, he argued, the natural children of hidalgos enjoyed all the privileges due their parents. The ecclesiastical authorities apparently agreed with him: Doña Mencía's election was upheld.[68]

Thereafter, illegitimacy of this variety seems not to have troubled the nuns of Santa Clara and Santa Catalina, so long as candidates for the black veil were the daughters of high-ranking parents. While most nuns of the black veil were legitimate, the archives also contain many examples of nuns who were hijas naturales, including a descendant of the conquistador Gerónimo Costilla, Doña María Costilla Gallinato, who became a nun of the black veil in Santa Catalina.[69] Perhaps her illegitimacy influenced her family's choice of convent, however: most (if not all) of her cloistered kin had taken the black veil inside Santa Clara.

Thus in Cuzco as in Lima, nuns of the black veil included many women of the "upper social strata," in the words of Martín. Certainly there were also nuns of the black veil whose families were not wealthy or prominent; in the 1680s, for example, Doña María Tristán de Najera painstakingly pieced together her own dowry by making and selling peach preserves inside Santa Clara.[70] However, those most visible in the archival record are the legitimate criolla daughters of the region's most aristocratic and powerful families: women like Doña Lucía Costilla de Umarán and Doña Constanza Viviana Costilla, descendants of the conquistador Costilla; like Doña Ana María Arias Maldonado, a descendant of the wily conquistador Diego Maldonado "el Rico"; and like Doña Catalina de San Alejo and Doña Juana de Salas y Valdes, descendants of Juan de Salas, one of Cuzco's earliest Spanish settlers. Many of these women held high office in the convent. Both Costillas, for example, became abbesses of Santa Clara in the course of the seventeenth century.

Meanwhile, outside convent walls, the families of these women were busily monopolizing Cuzco's choicest resources and colonial posts: estates, slaves, and managers, benefices, *corregimientos*, and positions on the city council. By the 1670s, a new claim to status was making its appearance among the most wealthy criollo lineages: titled nobility. The first cuzqueño to gain a title for himself and his family was yet another descendant of the conquistador Costilla, Don Antonio de Mendoza y Costilla, who in 1671 was made the first Marqués de San Juan de Buenavista. He was joined in 1687 by Don Pedro de Peralta y de los Ríos, a native Arequipan who had lived most of his life in Cuzco and who in 1687 was made the first Conde de la Laguna de Chanchacalle, and his brother-in-law Don Diego de Esquivel y Jaraba, the first Marqués de San Lorenzo de Valleumbroso. The amount these men spent for their privileges is not known, but they must have paid the Crown handsomely, for such exalted titles did not come cheap.[71] All the while they were wielding their various resources and connections to consolidate extensive business interests in the region—large enterprises like the maize- and textile-producing estate that the Esquiveles had constructed just south of the city of Cuzco. The elite women of Santa Clara and Santa Catalina and this worldly elite were clearly (and quite literally) related, and mutually reinforcing, reproducing a social order which they dominated.

Yet in Cuzco "nobility" was defined differently than it was elsewhere in the viceroyalty, and had been since the conquest of the Incas. Noble Indians were a numerous and highly status-conscious component of the elite of midcolonial Cuzco, as attested by their dress, their titles and property, and their prominent role in the city's public ceremonies.[72] At the Jesuit school that had been founded in 1622 specifically to train them, sons of the region's kurakas learned how to comport themselves as Christian gentlemen while reading the memorable words of their predecessor Garcilaso about the glories of the Incas. Each parish of the city had its own Andean *alcaldes ordinarios*, and each year the parishes chose an *alférez inca*, or official Inca standard-bearer, to represent the Inca nobility in the annual Corpus Christi procession and on other important occasions. The weightiness these institutions and actors had assumed by the late seventeenth century may be glimpsed in the fact that in 1696 the bishop of Cuzco complained about them to the Crown: "The Indian Alférezes that are elected each year by the Parishes of this City . . . are accustomed to offer very expensive banquets, thereby indebting themselves to the point of ruin . . . [and] they invite all of their companions, Spaniards as well as Indians."[73]

As the bishop's concern suggests, "noble Indians" and local "Spaniards" were not isolated groups. They literally spoke the same languages, since children of the criollo elite learned Quechua from their Andean wet nurses and children of the indigenous elite learned Spanish from their religious teachers (whether Jesuits or nuns).[74] And, of course, interlocking interests as well as a kind of firmly and genealogically rooted "imagined community" set this native elite against those born elsewhere. They were the inheritors of the Inca legacy. They even had a name for the native Spaniards sent to exercise colonial power in their region: these distasteful people were *guambos*. Although criollos might marry their daughters to such men to gain a competitive advantage, peninsular Spaniards remained outsiders and might easily arouse the hostility of their in-laws.[75] In one of his better-known (though perhaps apocryphal) moments of high-handedness, the Marqués de Valleumbroso claimed publicly that he was an *apu*—implying that he properly ruled Cuzco—and that Spanish officials were sent to the region only to rule over its guambos.[76]

Given their noble heritage and their parents' vital role in sustaining colonial rule over the region, we might expect to find "indias nobles" among the elite of Cuzco's convents. After all, both Santa Clara and Santa Catalina had in their earliest years assertively claimed Incas as members of their monastic communities, and by 1619 a daughter of the assimilated Inca Don Melchor Carlos had been accepted as a nun in Santa Catalina.[77] Some years thereafter the Dominican nuns received a second descendant of the Incas, Doña Feliciana Pinelo, the natural daughter of Doña María Manaria and granddaughter of Doña Magdalena Mamaguaco.[78] And in at least one subsequent case the Dominicans accepted a member of the indigenous elite into the category of velo negro: in December 1660, they extended credit to Don Diego Quispe Guaman, the kuraka of the pueblo of Pausa in Parinacochas, so that his legitimate daughter Doña Antonia Salinas might take the black veil.[79]

By the turn of the century, however, the veil was again becoming a salient boundary separating Andeans from Spaniards and criollas in the practical life of the cloisters. Of the women who professed in Santa Clara and Santa Catalina around that time and who were clearly identified as relatives of kurakas and other indigenous leaders, almost all took the white veil. This was the case, for example, with Doña Antonia Viacha, described as an "Indian novice" and as a niece of the kuraka of Colquepata in Paucartambo, Don Gaspar Viacha. In 1708 she professed as a nun of the white veil in Santa Clara, although she was able to bring only 1,000 pesos in dowry. The nuns decided that discounting the remainder was "very just [in order] to remunerate her in some fashion" for her many years of service to the convent as a music instructor.[80]

Other women came from more distinguished and prosperous families of caciques than Doña Antonia, yet their legitimacy and their parents' wealth did not ensure them a place in the ranks of the convent's decisionmaking elite. Doña Ursula Atau Yupanqui, who took the white veil in Santa Catalina in 1713, was the legitimate daughter of Doña Petrona Cusi and Don Francisco Atau Yupanqui, the latter a principal of the parish of San Sebastián who belonged to the Sucsso ayllu and described himself as "one of the twenty-four electors from the eight parishes [of the city] of noble Incas and the Royal Alférez." Don Francisco was able to set aside for his daughter's dowry 2,500 pesos in cash, significantly more than she needed for the white veil.[81] The profession of Doña Josefa de San Cristóbal in Santa Catalina in 1717 is similar: although she was legitimate and had inherited the entire estate of her parents Doña Juana Tomasa Cusimantur and Don Cristóbal José Sinchi Roca, "cacique y gobernador" of the parish of Belén, she too was received into the category of velo blanco.[82]

Such cases show that by the turn of the eighteenth century, legitimacy and prosperity were not enough to guarantee the black veil even to the highest-ranking daughters of the Andean elite of Cuzco. As nuns of the white veil they might control property, and regularly did so. The notarial archive contains numerous examples of such women at the grille, making deals in Quechua through the services of an interpreter —Doña Josefa de San Cristóbal, for example, who went to the locutorio of Santa Catalina more than once to conclude the sale of properties that her father had left her.[83] But their status excluded them from high office and from the important business decisions of their communities. Thus while their families invested in Santa Clara and Santa Catalina, increasing the dowry resources on which the convents depended, indigenous nuns had no role in electing convent leaders or in making their communities' investment decisions. Their purview was limited— increasingly, it seems—to the "humble offices" of the convent.[84]

Why did these women's families not send their daughters to a local recogimiento, or *beaterio*, instead? By the late seventeenth century Cuzco held several, ranging from small, precariously endowed communities to the more stable and populous beaterio of Las Nazarenas. The *beatas* of Las Nazarenas required a dowry of 500 pesos of their professed entrants to be invested in the local economy, and they seem to have specialized in educating girls; thus, in many respects, their institution closely resembled Santa Clara and Santa Catalina.[85] Typically beaterios were smaller, more dependent on alms and the earnings of the beatas, and comparatively poor. Some operated literally at the margins of the formal religious life, to judge by a 1689 survey of the diocese, which turned up a total of nine beaterios in the parishes of San Blas and the Hospital de Naturales alone—all poor, and many attached to the churches of mens' orders. Yet in such institutions, an Indian woman might occupy a position of importance, and might even become abbess.[86]

Kurakas and other indigenous leaders did in fact avail themselves of this alternative, as did Don Manuel García Cotacallapa, the kuraka of two pueblos in the province of Carabaya who resided in Cuzco with his wife Doña Marta Puraca. By 1761 the couple had sent four daughters to Las Nazarenas. One had professed as a beata; another was on the point of doing so, and two more were being raised inside the beaterio.[87] Had their daughters brought these dowries to one of the city's convents instead, they would have been received as donadas, far below the professed nuns of the black and white veils in the conventual order of things. At Nazarenas they did not face this kind of structural subordination.

However, the beatas of Cuzco might be treated with extreme disrespect by cuzqueños who would not think of spewing insults inside the locutorios of Santa Clara or Santa Catalina. A suit brought in 1689 by the "Indian abbess" of the beaterio of Nuestra Señora del Carmen suggests why placing one's daughter in a convent might appeal to indios nobles more than the alternative of the beaterio. Abbess Magdalena de San Juan Bautista charged Don Pedro de Balbín with having inflicted verbal wounds of a most injurious kind. On the evening of October 30, 1689, she recounted, Balbín had sent "some mestizas" who had pounded on the doors of the beaterio but were not admitted. Balbín himself then came demanding entrance, but as it was a "suspicious and indecent hour for a recogimiento of so many maidens to open," the doors remained locked. He then began shouting in indignation, "publicly calling us all whores and saying that at night we let men climb over the roof and that we bore their babies inside [the beaterio], all for the purpose of dishonoring the beaterio and stripping away the honor and prestige of us all."[88] Witnesses confirmed and added to the record of Balbín's vituperations: "that if they did not open the door he would throw them out, whipping them first"; that the beatas were drunks, that he would kill them, beat them, and so forth. Ironically, Balbín was at the time the city's official Protector of Natives!

Perhaps the beatas of Las Nazarenas were spared such offenses. Yet they were clearly marginal to the conventos grandes in another sense: to a greater extent than Santa Clara or Santa Catalina, Las Nazarenas disciplined the marginal women of the society around it. When in 1704 the pregnant Petronila Serrano appealed for release from her confinement in Santa Catalina, for example, the ecclesiastical authorities had her transferred to Las Nazarenas instead.[89] Over time, Las Nazarenas became the favored repository for local authorities sending female infractors into confinement, although the authorities still called on Santa Clara and Santa Catalina to accept some depositadas well into the nineteenth century. Gradually, it seems, Las Nazarenas (and perhaps other, less visible beaterios as well) took over the roles of prison and asylum for women fleeing abusive relationships of various kinds.[90]

In sum, beaterios were significantly closer to the secular world than were the convents, at least in certain respects, and this contributed to making convents the more attractive option for kurakas seeking to place their daughters in positions commensurate with their rank.[91] The beaterios represented the somewhat frayed margins of the religious life. For cuzqueños concerned about their own reputation and that of their daughters, the cloisters of Santa Clara and Santa Catalina were the most honorable alternative. The vecinos of Cuzco, after all, did not measure themselves by the status and authority of their city's beaterios, but by that of its convents.

So it was that the nuns of Cuzco became actively, thoroughly involved in reproducing a distinctly colonial elite in Cuzco. Esquiveles and Costillas, Quispe Guamans, and Atau Yupanquis all sent their daughters into the cloisters, and all proudly traced their genealogical roots back to the sixteenth century and beyond: to the Incas, to Spanish conquistadores and, in some cases, to both. Perhaps some of these elite criollos and indios nobles considered themselves blood relatives; they may have imbibed the mother's milk of the same Andean wet nurses. Of course, under Spanish colonial rule they shared local power very unequally. Criollo families such as the Esquiveles were expanding their claims rapidly by the late seventeenth century, taking advantage of a favorable conjuncture to buy their way across new thresholds of power and prominence.[92] By contrast, kurakas, who had long consented to their contradictory role in the local structures of power, were seeing their privileges slip from their grasp in significant ways, even as Spanish colonialism continued to reduce and impoverish their communities. And convents helped secure these increasingly lopsided bargains. They reflected the distance between Cuzco's unequal lords in the distinct veils with which the nuns dressed the city's aristocratic daughters.

Colonial Chiaroscuro: Baroque Excess and the Desire for Austerity

By the late seventeenth century the cloisters of Santa Clara and Santa Catalina were brimming, and the convents' size and opulence were giving rise to a certain amount of anxiety. The quintessentially baroque appeal of the intricate, richly adorned interiors of the convent churches, with their gold-encrusted altars set with mirrors that played with the light and the images of worshippers, and that seemed to be deliberately picked up by the nuns in the eye-catching adornments they wore stitched to their habits—all this was experienced, at least by some cuzqueños, with an attendant unease.[93] When was richness carried to dangerous excess, and the nuns' vows of monastic poverty stretched beyond recognition?

As early as 1656 the Franciscan Diego de Mendoza had implied that the nuns of Santa Clara were moving beyond the range of permissible interpretation and into sinful reaches of sensual excess. His descriptions of the austerity of the convent's founders speak to his seventeenth-century readers in pointed, cautionary detail. By his telling, the founders busied themselves with the humblest tasks, not allowing servants to perform them. They abjured rich food, disapproving of "treats from the kitchen" and of nuns who spent too much time cooking ("hechas perpetuas cozineras, y ministras de la gula"). Indeed, the noblest among them were the humblest and most self-abasing of all. When changes were introduced which threatened to soften the nuns, they protested. Catalina de los Angeles, for example, "wept (burning with zeal for her holy rule) when she saw [nuns] introduce fine and costly habits . . . and [she] exclaimed, 'What does luxury have to do with penitence? What does profane glamor seek in mortification? Poor us, the world has entered our Religion!' "[94]

Diego de Mendoza was not alone in his fear that the nuns of his day had abandoned the path of austerity.[95] Concern about the nuns' lax observance of their rules and constitutions was registering indirectly in cuzqueños' increasing devotion to Nuestra Señora del Carmen and to the austere reformer of the Carmelite order, Teresa of Avila.[96] The influential Spanish nun (cited frequently by Mendoza) had just been canonized, in 1622, and her widely read works resonated with spiritual authority. Teresa condemned worldliness in the cloisters with particular vehemence. In many convents, she warned, "the path to salvation is more dangerous than in the world." Therefore parents "should prefer a marriage of much lower status for their daughters to placing them in monasteries like these." Her denunciations built to a ringing crescendo: "Oh, tremendous evil! Tremendous evil of religious—I am not speaking now more of women than of men—where religious life is not observed. . . . True religious life is practiced so little that friars, or nuns, who are indeed about to follow wholeheartedly their call must fear those of their own house more than all the devils."[97]

The first cuzqueña moved to action by Teresa's admonitions was Doña Leonor Costilla (1592–1662?), a granddaughter of the conquistador Gerónimo Costilla. Like the founders Francisca de Jesús, Doña Lucía de Padilla, and Doña Beatriz Villegas before her, Costilla was a wealthy widow. After her husband's death in 1641, she had made a fortune administering the thriving sugar plantation of Pachachaca and supplying sugar loaves to Cuzco and Potosí. By the late 1640s her properties were worth 200,000 pesos. And although her family had long supported Santa Clara, where her younger sister was a madre de consejo, Costilla decided instead to devote half of the value of her assets to founding a new convent of reformed Carmelite nuns. The first step was to seek formal approval from the Crown. Unfortunately for Costilla, the royal decree of 1651 authorizing her foundation was lost somewhere on its way to Cuzco, and by the time a duplicate arrived in 1664 Costilla had been dead for two years.

By this time the project had gained local momentum. The bishop, stressing that a Carmelite convent would be of "great importance for serving God and reforming local practice," recruited another founder to make the necessary investment: a wealthy Spaniard, Don Antonio de Zea (1612?–1699). Zea, a native of the villa of Salteras near Seville, had spent most of his life in Peru since arriving as a boy around 1625. Zea had made his fortune by obtaining lucrative corregimientos: when only twenty he became corregidor in Abancay (1632–36), then held the same post in Yucay (1642–46) and Andahuaylas (1653–56). He settled in Cuzco, serving several times as an alcalde ordinario and petitioning successfully for knighthood in the prestigious military order of Santiago. Late in life Zea married a local criolla named Doña Ana María de Urrutia Matajudios (1624–1702). Like Doña Leonor Costilla and her husband, the couple had no children. They too would make a monastic foundation their heir.

Founding ceremonies began on March 9, 1673, with the laying of the first stone of the convent church in the presence of Cuzco's assembled dignitaries. Carmelites had been sent from Charcas in Upper Peru to establish the new convent, and six had arrived in Cuzco by mid-October, three professed nuns and three novices. During the afternoon of October 22, 1673, a solemn procession accompanied them from the cathedral to their new quarters. Local notables escorted the nuns, two señoras principales and two city councilmen to each nun, as they made their way around the central plaza to take up residence in a building still under construction.[98]

Thus in a fitting counterpoint to Cuzco's increasingly baroque opulence, the most austere of its convents, the reformed Carmelite monastery best known simply as Santa Teresa, was founded as the city was reaching the zenith of its "golden age." The third and last of Cuzco's convents would long be its smallest and most unassuming.[99] In accordance with the terms of Teresa's strict rule, there could be no more than twenty-one nuns in the community at any given time. The nuns did not accept and educate secular girls as their Franciscan and Dominican counterparts did. The convent church of Santa Teresa was (and is) the simplest, the least ornate of the three convent churches. And the nuns may well have been strict about observance of their rules, since local archives contain few cases of conflict inside their cloisters.

Yet in many fundamental ways, the Carmelites' practice of the monastic life resembled that of the other two orders. If austerity defined a distinctive, Carmelite style of desprendimiento and set the nuns apart from those of other orders, that did not prevent the Carmelites from being served or from prospering collectively.[100] Their observance of religious poverty also relied upon the accumulation of substantial assets and claims to indigenous labor. The nuns of Santa Teresa expected the same amount of dowry from new entrants, and invested their dowries in censos to generate a steady income. They acquired a variety of urban and rural properties through donations and purchases, managing these through mayordomos in the usual ways, renting and leasing to local people. And the Carmelites also drew distinctions within their community between nuns of the white veil and nuns of the black veil. Even the strictest, most austere monastic rule might be shaped by its practitioners in Cuzco to the colonial order of things.[101]

Conclusions: Matters of Interpretation

Did the nuns of Cuzco break their rules and go against their vows as they turned their cells into elaborately stratified households and their locutorios into lively visiting parlors? It might seem obvious that they did. For example, the constitutions of the Clares explicitly limited them to one lay sister for every ten nuns and instructed them to use servants only in the absence of lay sisters. Yet the nuns of Santa Clara clearly regarded servants as complements to lay sisters rather than alternatives to them, admitting dozens of women into both categories by the middle of the seventeenth century. They even multiplied the ranks of these women, creating a complex hierarchy of service within their cloisters: nuns of the white veil, donadas, servants, and slaves. Is this not clear evidence that the nuns broke their own rules? Perhaps so, from the late-twentieth-century vantage point of certain legal cultures—but not if we attend to the historically specific relationship of seventeenth-century cuzqueños to law, including the rules and vows of the religious life.

The nuns of midcolonial Cuzco clearly understood their rules not simply as interdicts to be obeyed or violated, but as occasions for acts of interpretation, for the case-by-case application of theory to practice.[102] In short, they understood the thoroughly casuistic *medio* in which they lived, and took full advantage of it. Their rules and constitutions empowered them to act as competent interpreters and make countless daily decisions about how best to perform their vows of poverty, chastity, and obedience. As they did so, the nuns used each vow to recast a fundamental social institution to serve their purposes. Practicing poverty thus meant not rejecting property, but taking a collective approach to it in order to further the monastic community's mission. Practicing chastity likewise meant redefining marriage as a spiritual commitment, one that by no means excluded motherhood. And obedience, as practiced by the nuns of Cuzco, meant redefining family, relocating the source of authoritative command from patriarchal father to mother superior.

All of these moves could be performed without breaking or necessarily straining kinship ties. While the patriarchal fathers of Cuzco might not always get the results they expected from their ties to the convents (as Don Antonio de Losada learned the hard way), the nuns in fact depended upon close ties to their kin in order to rework their relationships to the institutions of property, marriage, and family. Through these mutually sustaining relationships, they reproduced both themselves and their families. This much we can see especially well in the business transacted in the convents' locutorios, which were constantly busy with visits between the nuns and novices and their various guests. The grille was very permeable, regulating rather than inhibiting the flow of words, daughters, dowries, and credit, and the intensity of their circulation is apparent in the archival record.

Over time these practices created much more than strong, reciprocal bonds between convents and local families. They also inscribed profoundly hierarchical relationships among the native elite of colonial Cuzco: the city's criollo aristocrats and the "Indian nobles" on whom their fortunes depended. The nuns and convents thus played a vital part in producing an off-center Spanish hegemony in the provincial Andes, anchoring colonial rule at a highly strategic point in Spain's American empire. As we shall see in the following chapter, very substantial material interests were at stake in this long-running imperial production.

5 Producing Colonial Cuzco

If a visit to the locutorio was not a trivial affair for the nuns of Cuzco, neither was it trivial for their visitors. People approached the grille to create sustained bonds with the nuns, often investing their daughters and dowries in the process. The anxiety that might attend these encounters can be seen in the influential 1611 dictionary *Tesoro de la lengua castellana*: Sebastián de Covarrubias defines "locutorio" with deft synecdoche as "the grille through which the nuns do business (*libran*)." *Librar* still resonates with the first sense Covarrubias gives—"to liberate"— but he gives two more that pertain not to liberation but to specific confines, those of the cloisters and the business deal. The verb turns out to have been a semantic crossroads for liberators, merchants, and nuns: "To *librar* and give a *libranza* is to respond to a written order. . . . *Librar* [also] signifies a nun going out to the grille to speak, which at times could more properly be called *enredar* than *librar*." So begins a Cervantine romp through the definitions for Covarrubias's takers. *Enredar* could mean many things, including "to catch with a net," but its common figurative sense was (and is) "to mix things up": to tell a story backward or mix up the parts of a proverb, like the addled Sancho Panza of *Don Quijote*. It could also mean getting entangled with someone so thoroughly that one could not easily get loose. The wordplay of Covarrubias thus conveys, with a touch of misogynistic humor, a sly hint that confusion and entanglement might await the visitor seeking to deal with nuns.[1]

At least one cuzqueño might have penned Covarrubias's definitions himself. On December 23, 1678, the Marqués de Buenavista Don Pablo Costilla, great-grandson of Gerónimo Costilla, lent several valuable pieces of jewelry to his sister Doña Constanza Viviana Costilla, the abbess of Santa Clara, "for a fiesta that she gave."[2] Among them was an extraordinary ring set with thirty-one diamonds which never came back to him. Instead he received a much less valuable ring, whereupon he started making "various contacts (*diligencias*)" to get back the diamond-encrusted original. None of his informal contacts worked. Then suddenly the ring reappeared before his wife's eyes almost five years later, when in 1683 she asked a local man to arrange for her to borrow "some finery to adorn the [altar of the] Holy Trinity for the fiesta that was given in the Church of the convent of San Agustín." To her surprise, among the pieces her broker borrowed from local people at her request was her husband's lost ring. She promptly notified her husband, and this time Costilla brought suit to recover his valuable property.

The case of Don Pablo Costilla's purloined ring created a veritable knot of *enredos*, with conflicting testimony and a truncated ending. On one thing the witnesses could agree: Costilla had lent the ring to his sister the abbess in December 1678 so that she might dress his daughter, the nun Doña Juana Rosa Costilla, for a fiesta. The whole affair thus arose because of the Costillas' desire that Doña Juana Rosa attend Christmas festivities in the locutorio of Santa Clara resplendently attired. This particular investment made sense for several reasons. Lavish display on solemn occasions was crucial to a noble family's defense of its honorable reputation (and dress was an especially critical kind of display, to judge by the level of sumptuary anxiety in colonial Cuzco). The Costillas were also upholding family tradition: they had been distinguished benefactors of the nuns since the time of Gerónimo Costilla. But why then was it so difficult for Don Pablo Costilla to recover his property from Santa Clara? After all, his sister was abbess. Still he spent five years of fruitless contacts before initiating a lawsuit, and when he did so he did not move against the convent. Why did this powerful patriarch avoid conflict with the nuns?

The Clares were family, for one thing. But Costilla's moves also make perfect business sense. He was willing to go to great lengths to avoid risking his family's good credit with Santa Clara. His ancestors had grown wealthy by creating a close association with the convent, and the Costillas had continued to invest in Santa Clara over generations, sending their daughters to live there and burying their dead in a place of honor inside the convent church. The nuns had amply reciprocated, investing in the Costillas by extending them credit in the form of censos secured by the hacienda Suriguaylla. Late payments on the Costillas' censos were not a problem for the nuns as long as the overall balance of favors and goodwill kept the family in good standing. (Having Costillas at the highest level of convent affairs helped: between them,

Doña Lucía Costilla and Doña Constanza Costilla served many terms in the course of the seventeenth century as abbess and madre de consejo.) By the late seventeenth century, however, the relationship was clearly strained. Costilla's son was falling behind in making censo payments to the nuns on the hacienda Suriguaylla, which had been in the family for generations. Don Pablo Costilla's efforts to cultivate good relations with the nuns ultimately failed to keep Santa Clara from filing suit to collect back payments.[3]

As this particular set of entanglements suggests, being on good terms with the nuns of Cuzco was worth a great deal to families like the Costillas. The Costillas, Valverdes, and others needed credit to keep their families and businesses afloat. By means of the censos they negotiated in the locutorios of Santa Clara, Santa Catalina, and Santa Teresa, they financed the funerals of their relatives, the purchase of municipal offices, and the expansion and improvement of their obrajes, ingenios, and haciendas. The nuns, for their part, needed trustworthy borrowers. Their rules sternly forbade them to spend their dowries and required them to invest dowry receipts instead. All three cloistered convents thus constantly sought opportunities to invest with cuzqueños who could meet their terms. Structurally, nuns and credit-hungry cuzqueños were a perfect match. Yet within these large structures of engagement there was always sufficient maneuvering room to keep participants from taking one another for granted. The nuns might do so by offering an extra measure of financial flexibility to their important clients: grace periods for censo payments, for example. The Costillas did their part, too, performing services and favors for the nuns, such as lending jewels to increase the luster of an especially important fiesta.[4]

Once we see the logic of these flows—this circulation of daughters, dowry, and credit—it becomes possible to see how production became vitally linked to reproduction through the locutorios of Cuzco, and spirituality to the nuns' economy. Through their daughters and their dealings in the locutorios, kurakas and criollos produced and reproduced themselves, sought good credit and obtained grace. The result of these myriad contacts was an economy saturated in debt that sealed and sustained spiritual bonds. In a way, this saturation may have been as much a sign to elite cuzqueños of their spiritual health as the baroque splendor of their churches.

The convents was almost religous to maintaining favorable relations w/ those who gained status from them

It has long been a truism that colonial Spanish American economies were cash-poor, exporting their silver to Spain. Yet the implications of this (macro) situation for the regional economies of the Americas have not been fully explored, especially the extent to which the dearth of "good money" led people and institutions to form credit relationships with one another.[5] The scholastic complexity of the contracts that mediated these relationships may account for this, as well as the fact that these instruments changed over time, and across regions, as they were modified strategically by their users. Contracts also took place orally, so the written record does not reflect all the give-and-take among colonial creditors and borrowers, especially loans linking individuals.[6] The archives nevertheless give rich insight into the making of colonial relationships through credit. By peering into the microeconomic intricacies of relationships expressed through censos and other kinds of obligations, we can draw important connections between forms of economic agency and colonial exploitation.

The enormous importance of credit in the colonial Spanish American economy is now becoming increasingly apparent.[8] Over time each city and region forged its own set of practices and institutional alternatives. Where mercantile activity was at its most dense, as in Lima or Mexico City, the institutional apparatus of credit became especially complex. The merchants of Lima were active lenders individually as well as collectively. Men like Juan de la Cueva might work their way up from relatively small-scale commercial activity to engaging in large-scale lending and in the creation of "banks." In addition, ecclesiastical institutions in Lima were expanding and prospering by the turn of the seventeenth century. As professions, donations, legacies, and (in the case of the Holy Office of the Inquisition) expropriations channeled large amounts of resources into their coffers, the regular orders became active lenders.[9]

In Cuzco, the first major institutional source of credit was the region's indigenous communities. A portion of their tribute went into community coffers (cajas de comunidad) each year, theoretically to help meet the needs of the community itself; soon, however, such funds were being tapped for loans by outsiders.[10] By the late sixteenth century, local-level cajas in the region had been integrated into a larger entity known as the *caja de censos de indios*, based in Cuzco and administered by Spanish and criollo officials, who did no better at ensuring

Españoles borrowed on Credit from Indian community but didn't repay or were late etc.

Thus indians couldn't pay their tribute

indigenous communities' economic security (although a centralized location no doubt made it easier for Cuzco's criollos to obtain credit).[11] Credit operations transferred large amounts of resources from the caja de censos de indios to families like the Costillas and Esquiveles, who borrowed heavily from Andean community resources without bothering to keep up their annual payments. The resulting depletion of the caja created serious problems for the Indians of Cuzco. By 1599, according to the official Protector of Natives Luis de Montemayor, the indigenous communities were owed more than 50,000 pesos, and had spent large sums in fruitless legal efforts to collect on unpaid censos. To make matters worse, the amounts that had been collected on these communities' behalf were never turned over to them, making it impossible for them to meet their tribute quotas.[12] The recklessness of the borrowers in this case is profoundly expressive: certainly they did not cultivate the Indians as they did the nuns. (Ironically, these fundamentally hostile relations seem to have done no harm to the borrowers' credit for future loans!) Men like Don Diego de Esquivel y Jaraba groused as Spanish officials reacted to the scandal in the 1650s by tightening up collection practices and squeezing delinquent debtors. It would be decades, however, before this particular source of credit rebounded.[13]

As indigenous communities' funds were being exhausted, the city's ecclesiastical institutions were taking in large amounts of resources and becoming important sources of credit in their own right.[14] The nuns would continue to extend credit just as they had since the founding of Santa Clara. First, they permitted cuzqueños to fulfill their daughters' dowries by placing liens on specific pieces of property. This enabled men like Rodrigo de Esquivel to use their resources for other purposes. Placing a censo al quitar on his property in 1582 so that his daughter Doña Mencía might take the black veil in Santa Clara meant Esquivel did not have to pay the nuns 3,312 pesos, 4 reales in dowry (and if he held that amount he could invest it in his obraje of Quispicanche instead); he had only to pay them 5 percent of this amount annually (165 pesos, 2 reales). Second, the nuns used the mechanism of the censo al quitar to make loans from their coffers, investing significant amounts of the monies they received from dowries and censo payments. "Loan" and "lien" censos, all of which were contracted as censos consignativos, are notoriously hard to tell apart in the written record.[15] Both can be seen, in any case, as credit operations. Liens and loans gave cuzqueños much-needed flexibility in a cash-poor economy, enabling them to get something they desired—a daughter's profession or a loan—without having to lay out large sums.

Nuns were hardly the only important creditors in Cuzco. There were many institutional alternatives, including men's monastic orders, which like those of the nuns were expanding in the seventeenth century, both numerically and in terms of the resources they controlled. The Costillas, for example, clearly cultivated not only the Clares but the Augustinians of Cuzco, who were developing extensive financial ties to the region's propertied elite much as the nuns were.[16] These bonds were strengthened by the professions of male Costillas: the marqués Don Pablo Costilla had a brother in the monastery of San Agustín in Cuzco, Fray Lorenzo, as well as a sister inside Santa Clara, and he eventually named one of his own children Agustín.[17] The Mercedarians, Dominicans, Jesuits, and Bethlemites also maintained large houses in Cuzco and availed themselves of the contractual mechanism of the censo to extend credit to local people.[18] Cuzco's secular clergy made credit available too, through diocesan institutions like the *fábrica de la catedral* and the *juzgado eclesiástico*. And a variety of *cofradías* and capellanías (many of which were administered by nuns and friars) took in and loaned out resources.[19] All of these ecclesiastical institutions employed the censo al quitar as a crucial part of their long-term investment strategy. Through censos they deployed their funds in support of a variety of regional economic activities. This can be seen clearly in the credit history of countless properties in the region—haciendas, obrajes, ingenios.[20]

By the second half of the century, however, Santa Clara and Santa Catalina appear to have been the largest institutional creditors in Cuzco.[21] Decades of dowry receipts, donations, legacies and other income had gradually built them an impressive assemblage of resources to invest. The annual income of Santa Clara, for example, increased nearly fivefold in the course of the century as successive generations of nuns professed (see Table 2). In the wake of the severe 1650 earthquake Santa Clara's income had fallen sharply—to only 10,000 pesos a year by one account—and had not yet recovered by 1690, when it stood at around 24,000 pesos. Still the nuns were taking in 17,900 pesos' worth of censo payments in that year. As for Santa Catalina, a 1684 list of contracts payable to the convent (mostly censos al quitar) contains 166 separate entries, totaling more than 297,433 pesos in principal. If the nuns managed to collect on these at the standard 5 percent rate, then they took in more than 14,870 pesos that year.[22] By comparison, the

Table 2 Annual income of Santa Clara, selected years

Year	Income	Censo Income (as % of total)
1602	5,191 pesos	2,230 pesos (43%)
1650 (ca.)	31,000 (est.)	—
1690	24,000	17,900 (75%)

Sources: For 1602, "Libro original," ed. Angulo, 170–76; for 1650 and 1690, Archivo de Santa Clara, Cuzco, "Volúmen de varias escrituras que pueden servir de títulos," fols. 466–67, July 19, 1690, report of the abbess Gerónima de Villena y Madueño to the king.

monastery of San Agustín, perhaps the richest of the men's monastic houses, was collecting 11,116 pesos' worth of censo payments on 78 separate obligations in the year 1676.[23]

Individual nuns were a source of credit as well. With their superior's permission they might lend sums from their *peculio* or *violario*, personal funds given them by relatives or benefactors. Such dealings appear frequently in the notarial records. In 1668, for example, Doña Feliciana de San Nicolás y Pinelo, a descendant of the Incas and a nun of the black veil in Santa Catalina, arranged (with the bishop's approval) to lend 1,000 pesos to a local clergyman.[24] The Dominican nun Juana del Carmen had extensive business interests by the time she died in 1688: an inventory itemized five separate loans she had made to local borrowers, ranging from 500 pesos to 1,500 pesos, amounting to a total of 4,600 pesos.[25] These nuns' dealings were transacted through censos, giving them (at least in theory) a steady annual income with which to support themselves and those who lived in their cells. Occasionally nuns might use their personal funds to extend short-term credit, through contractual *obligaciones*.

Credit-hungry cuzqueños moved quickly when credit became available. No sooner did a woman profess and bring dowry to the convents' coffers than a local borrower came forward to take the money out again. On Sunday, December 19, 1700, for example, Manuela de San Bernardo took her vows to become a donada in Santa Catalina, bringing a dowry of 500 pesos. The next day, December 20, Doña Gerónima de Carranza y Urrutia arranged through a censo to receive the 500 pesos, offering her house and land as collateral.[26] Many censos likewise feature the exact amount of a nun's or a donada's dowry: 3,312 pesos,

4 reales (the dowry of a nun of the black veil); 1,656 pesos, 2 reales (that of a nun of the white veil); and 500 pesos (donada). The nuns kept track of how each woman's dowry was invested. A nun's dowry, in other words, did not simply disappear into a common fund (at least, not at first); years after it had been paid and invested, it might still be known as a particular woman's dowry. Sometimes a nun's dowry was split and loaned to more than one local borrower; this was noted in the convent's books so that the mayordomos might collect the right amount of annual payment from the right people.[27]

Having relatives inside the cloisters could help secure a family's credit terms, particularly if a daughter was elected the head of her community. Thereafter she would remain powerful for years as part of the advisory council that handled the community's business affairs. Her family might gain many things by this association: for one, inside information about credit. To get a loan ahead of one's competitors meant knowing who was about to make payments into the convents' coffers. The nuns themselves probably facilitated the flow of information by notifying those with whom they had close working relationships. Notaries were in an excellent position to do this, too: since they were called upon to formalize the making and unmaking of censos, they knew who was in the process of repaying loans, and they could spread the word to interested parties.[28] The administrators and mayordomos of Santa Catalina or Santa Clara would also have been a very valuable business contact to know—or, better still, to have in one's family circle. Not surprisingly, abbesses and prioresses often put close male relatives in these critical positions, thereby keeping vital financial information in the family. Nuns also sealed close relationships with their notaries by extending them credit and accepting their daughters as nuns of the highest rank.[29]

It was not necessary, however, to have a highly placed relative inside the convent to receive credit. Nor did a close relationship with one convent preclude close relationships with others. The six Dueñas Castillejo brothers are a good example. In 1644, they began contracting for loans from the nuns of Santa Clara, securing the loans with their haciendas in the rich croplands to the south of the city. Twenty-six years later, when they sold "hatun Lucre," the property carried censo obligations amounting to 32,000 pesos—almost two-thirds of its value of 50,000 pesos.[30] These censos had been arranged in eight separate transactions with the nuns (see Table 3). All but one of the contracts of these censos al quitar are now missing from the notarial

Table 3 Dueñas Castillejos' censos from Santa Clara, 1644–70

November 19, 1644	9,000 pesos
February 6, 1645	7,000
December 19, 1646	4,000
January 9, 1647	5,000
April 30, 1647	1,000
February 11, 1648	3,000
September 22, 1660	1,000
January 16, 1669	2,000
Total	32,000 pesos

Source: Archivo Departamental del Cusco, Protocolos Notariales, Lorenzo de Messa Andueza, 1670, fols. 805–9v.

records. The one that remains, from December 1646, indicates that the Dueñas Castillejo brothers were in the process of expanding Lucre by purchasing more than 200 fanegadas of land from the Crown. When the Crown's representative came through on his tour of duty to regularize titles and garner income for the royal treasury, the brothers took the opportunity to buy titles to attractive neighboring land, more than doubling the size of their holdings (formerly only 120 fanegadas).[31] Quite possibly, then, Santa Clara's loans gave them the resources they needed to buy more land. The brothers sold some of their property in August 1670, perhaps unable to afford the high payments they had incurred (1,600 pesos annually). But only three months later, Gerónimo Dueñas Castillejo was back in the locutorio taking out yet another loan from Santa Clara, and loans from Santa Catalina as well, this time securing his deals with a property called Chinicara. These loans also proved unsustainable in the long run, and by 1675 Dueñas Castillejo had to agree to split his harvest with the nuns of Santa Catalina, since he was otherwise unable to cover his debt to them. Eventually the brothers' properties ended up among the estates of the Costillas and the Esquiveles, who assumed payment on the censos that had fueled both the rise and fall of the Dueñas Castillejos.[32]

What else did cuzqueños do with the loans they obtained in the locutorios of Cuzco? Unfortunately, contracts rarely specify the purposes for which people sought loans from the convents. But some do disclose their purposes. Doña Antonia Siclla, for example, borrowed 1,500 pesos from the nuns of Santa Catalina in 1673 to pay for the funeral of her deceased husband Don Gerónimo Uscaquiguartopa, cacique of the pueblo of Pumaquiguar.[33] The would-be regidor Don Manuel Soriano de Lezama approached the nuns of Santa Catalina in 1679 for money to buy his municipal office. His deceased father had left him the title of regidor, but Lezama lacked funds to pay the royal treasury the requisite third of the office's value, and so he hastened to borrow 1,500 pesos from Santa Catalina before the title could be put up for auction.[34] Sometimes monastic orders turned to one another for credit to finance major endeavors. In 1747, for example, the Franciscan provincial explained to the Clares his "urgent need" to borrow 10,000 pesos to underwrite the transatlantic travel of "missionaries and Spanish subjects for the alternative (*alternativa*)"—the practice within his order of alternating Spaniards and criollos in high offices. The nuns agreed to loan him the entire amount.[35]

Many of the loans that disclose an intention show the borrower planned to make capital improvements on an hacienda, ingenio, obraje, or homestead. The borrower (*censuatario*) might simply indicate that the credit was destined to "equip" or "renovate" a property (e.g., "aviar mi hacienda," "refaccionar estas fincas"). The nuns of Santa Clara remained on this level of contractual generality when in 1676 they borrowed 13,500 pesos from the Colegio de San Buenaventura, in part to "equip" (*aviar*) Pachar.[36] Don Felipe Sicos, a principal of San Sebastián, borrowed 1,000 pesos in 1718 to "renovate" (*refaccionar*) his 48-topo farm in San Sebastián.[37] In other instances, however, the borrowers were more specific. The Jesuits turned to the Dominican nuns of Santa Catalina in 1647 for 1,000 pesos they needed "for the purpose of conducting water to the Colegio de San Bernardo."[38] Captain Dionisio de Osorio and his brother Juan de Osorio, hacendados in Limatambo, borrowed 1,000 pesos in 1709 from a nun of Santa Clara to purchase mules, plowshares, and other equipment for an hacienda they had just inherited.[39]

An especially illustrative run of transactions comes from the registers of the notary Pedro de Cáceres, who handled the bulk of Santa Clara's business in the waning years of the seventeenth century. In 1696 and 1697, he was near the end of his career and more than a little careless about the documents to which he affixed his rubric. These included a set of censos entered into by the abbess and nuns of Santa Clara with various Cuzco landowners, all of whose signatures the notary got but whose business he neglected to write down. Their signatures in Cáceres's records grace the bottom margin of several empty pages. Years later, abbesses of Santa Clara discovered to their chagrin that they

Table 4 Santa Clara's censos, December 1696–July 1697

December 14, 1696	Don Andrés Arias Sotelo and Doña Agustina de la Borda	8,000 pesos
January 26, 1697	Don Lucas de Navia and Doña Antonia de Aller	5,312
January 29, 1697	Don Diego de Almonasi and Doña Catalina Alvares	2,000
March 5, 1697	Don Andrés Tecse and Doña María Suta Asa	1,656
March 13, 1697	Blas Montalvo de Herrera	3,000
July 7, 1697	Don Pedro Mijancas Medrano and Doña Bernarda de Ibarra	1,500
Total		21,468 pesos

Source: Archivo Departamental del Cusco, Protocolos Notariales, Pedro de Cáceres, 1696, fols. 403–4v; 1697, fols. 441–57v.

Note: These lists, compiled in 1712 and 1728, contain other activity as well. The six censos appear in both, and all but the fifth are clearly loans.

were unable to adduce details of these censos, thanks to the negligence of Pedro de Cáceres. They set about putting the record right. Lists were made of all the transactions Cáceres had failed to execute properly, and these were then completed and retroactively authorized. Many of the contracts are now missing from the notary's registers, but those which remain indicate that the people in question received loans from the nuns. This sequence of censos also suggests the volume of convent lending. In just over seven months, it appears that at least 21,468 pesos entered and then left the convent's coffer, loaned to a variety of local people (see Table 4).

Links between the nuns and specific sectors of the region's economy are unusually clear in these transactions. Don Andrés Arias Sotelo and his widowed mother Doña Agustina de la Borda sought 8,000 pesos from Santa Clara to improve their sugar-producing estates along the Apurimac River, declaring that they would use the money to install cane-crushing equipment and fix irrigation channels. (They declared the value of their properties to be 90,000 pesos, with 13,000 pesos' worth of outstanding debts, mainly to other ecclesiastical creditors.) Blas Montalvo de Herrera, of Abancay, may well have been making capital improvements on a sugar estate himself, as he too was an hacendado in the region. For their part, Don Diego de Almonasi and Doña Catalina Alvares arranged to borrow 2,000 pesos to expand their *chorrillo*, or urban textile-manufacturing workshop.[40] By making their funds available as credit, the nuns were assisting the growth of some of the region's leading productive activities: during the seventeenth century both sugar and textiles were major regional exports to the market of Potosí.[41]

Loans and liens were not the only contracts the nuns made in their locutorios. They also handled large amounts of real estate, most of which by the seventeenth century served the same purpose as the nuns' dowry funds: that of generating a steady flow of income. The nuns contracted their urban property to cuzqueños through short-term rentals (arrendamientos) and long-term leases (commonly styled ventas a censo or *ventas por tres vidas*).[42] Rentals often proved disadvantageous. The streams that ran through the city made many properties vulnerable to flooding, and high turnover from one tenant to the next might also lead to serious deterioration. Such was the case, for example, with a residence on the main plaza that Santa Clara sold in 1697 after having rented it for many years. The house is described as "old and mistreated," and the contract notes that many renters had simply left without paying the convent.[43] The nuns understandably developed a preference for the long-term lease, usually styled venta a censo. Should the lessee wish to be released from the contract, he or she could, with the nuns' approval, make the lease over to someone else. Or the lessee could formally renounce the contract and allow the convent to start over, as did Pedro Rodríguez, who in 1631 left Cuzco for the mining camp of Cailloma, renouncing his lease on a house he had occupied since 1627 and enabling the nuns to lease it instead to Marcos Falcón, a master sculptor and gilder, and his wife.[44]

Rural estates required the nuns to use some of the same managerial strategies. Some were not valuable enough to merit the hiring of an overseer, and these the nuns and their proxies preferred to lease rather than rent. Such was the case with the hacienda Yanaguara, for example, which the Dominican nuns leased in 1648. (The nuns' administrator noted in an attached petition that leasing was distinctly preferable to renting because renters mismanaged properties and stripped the fields and houses bare, stealing farm equipment and "taking locks, keys, and even the doors when they leave, and making it necessary to spend more than the amount of the rent to fix them up again.")[45] Other properties were worth the trouble and expense of closer management, as

some holdings of a convent provided the nuns w/
everyday living necessities

they supplied the nuns directly with beef, milk, cheese, grain, sugar, and other products. The nuns hired mayordomos to run these "mainstay" properties and remit supplies to the city on a regular basis. Such was the case with a ranch called Caco. Located south of Cuzco in the province of Azángaro, this ranch belonged to the nuns of Santa Clara from the sixteenth century until the late nineteenth century.[46] For three centuries the Clares depended on Caco, its mayordomos, and its indigenous shepherds and livestock handlers to send the convent cheese, dried beef (charqui), lambs, calves, and tallow.[47] Santa Catalina and Santa Teresa had similar "mainstay" ranches and haciendas that produced and remitted such supplies to their communities. Those of Santa Catalina included the grain-producing hacienda of Guambutio and the sugar- and molasses-producing ingenio of Yllanya, the latter valued at 100,000 pesos by the late seventeenth century.[48]

The nuns and their proxies managed their most valued estates closely, even quite aggressively. Long after Gerónimo Costilla had assertively staked the Clares' first claim to Pachar, for example, the nuns were still vigorously expanding the hacienda. In 1621 they sold excellent farmland in the Urubamba Valley in order to purchase land adjacent to Pachar that was "more useful and beneficial."[49] Pachar also grew by means of less savory practices. During the 1650s two Indians of Huarocondo, Juan Quicho and his son Pedro Quicho, fought hard against the encroachments of two haciendas on their land: Pachar and Silque (the latter belonging to an hacendado named Alonso de Soria). According to charges filed by the Quichos, the mayordomos of both haciendas harassed them, even sending henchmen to drag them off to work during the planting season in Silque, despite the fact that the Quichos could produce valid title to their land, which Juan Quicho's father Sebastián said had been granted him by Pachacuti Inca Yupanqui. The remarkably resilient Quichos pressed their case all the way to Lima, and in 1654 the viceroy granted them formal protection from harassment. Still they were not left alone. Finally the elderly Juan Quicho, in poor health and having spent most of his assets, made a deal with his adversaries. He agreed in 1658 to donate six topos of land adjoining Pachar to Santa Clara in exchange for a comparable plot of land elsewhere, where he and his grandchildren might live undisturbed. The Clares agreed to receive two of his granddaughters in the convent as part of the deal.[50] (We can only wonder if the impoverished Quicho ever approached the locutorio to visit them.)

Occasionally the nuns arranged to sell the surplus produced on their

nuns as marchants

estates.[51] Did they have a hand in other local enterprises? The nuns of Santa Clara in Huamanga did: by the late seventeenth century, they were operating their own obraje. According to a petition by their administrator in 1666, the nuns asked "that in a site belonging to them named Pomacocha they be allowed to mount two or three looms and with these produce coarse woolens for tunics and white baize for sheets, so that they do not waste linen on bedclothes or petticoats, and blankets for their beds and some coarse cloth (*jergas*) for bedding and for sacks to haul flour and vegetables."[52] The request was apparently granted, for a later account shows Santa Clara of Huamanga earning up to 15,000 pesos a year from the sale of coarse woolens.[53] In Cuzco, where obrajes were a mainstay of the colonial economy, it is entirely possible that this kind of arrangement existed, although no evidence of it has yet turned up.[54] The Huamanga case serves as a reminder of the wide range of roles that nuns came to play in the economic activities of their regions. They themselves engaged in production, while also enabling others to produce by extending credit.[55]

Once bonds like these were established, they were not ties the participants were eager to break. Quite the contrary. Cuzqueños like Don Pablo Costilla and Don Diego de Esquivel considered their interests well served by long association with the nuns, even when the original amount of their censos had been paid back several times over. The nuns, as we have seen, did much more than lend them money, and maintaining good relations was thus a long-term goal. In addition, 5 percent was not only the standard rate for ecclesiastical lending, but a good rate, to judge from the sparse evidence concerning prosecutions for usury. Individual lenders might charge twice as much for lending money.[56] For their part, the nuns certainly did not want frequent redemption of censos. Nor did they want to engage in lengthy, expensive legal procedures to recover back payments from their censuatarios if these could be avoided.

They didn't want complication?

Thus the nuns were willing to show considerable flexibility when times were hard and people fell behind on payments. The nuns could resort to legal action against anyone who failed to make two consecutive years' worth of payments on a censo; the Castilian Leyes de Toro had made this clear. When such suits were carried out successfully, the property the debtor had offered as collateral for the censo was auctioned off in a *concurso de acreedores* to satisfy his or her creditors. Sometimes the nuns initiated such proceedings with relative alacrity. However, in many cases they were willing to wait several years—even decades—before resorting to legal proceedings.[57] They were especially forgiving if the tardy censuatario was a powerful, supportive kinsman like Don Pablo Costilla or Don Diego de Esquivel.

The Marquéses de Valleumbroso are a good case in point. By the close of the seventeenth century, the Esquivel properties had accumulated some 25,000 pesos' worth of debt to Santa Clara and more than 28,500 pesos' worth to Santa Catalina through various censos, and the Marqués de Valleumbroso was not punctual with his payments: in January 1707 he gave the abbess of Santa Clara more than 8,300 pesos to cover more than six years' worth of arrears. Such irregularity must have made it difficult for the nuns to manage their finances, since a year in which the marqués failed to pay his debts meant a year in which Santa Clara either had to do without 1,255 pesos of income or find them elsewhere. Yet hardly more than a year later, in March 1708, the marqués was back in the same locutorio taking out an additional 8,500 pesos.[58] The tightly knit web of kinship, local power, and influence kept the convents and the Esquiveles intimately connected. The Esquiveles' daughters and kin were, after all, among the women overseeing the convents' decisions. And the very closely related criollo aristocrats of Cuzco were the biggest landowners around—those whose assets could secure one censo after another.

Family Strategies: Why Families "Married" Convents

By frequenting the locutorios of Santa Clara, Santa Catalina, and Santa Teresa, propertied cuzqueños could satisfy several needs at once, pursuing profit and salvation without any contradiction. They were supporting not only themselves but the nuns who raised their daughters and prayed for the good of their souls. To see these connections enables us to revise several common assumptions about nunneries: for one, that nuns' dowries were not economically productive and that convents generally "froze" assets and took them out of economic circulation.[59] (A close look at seventeenth-century Cuzco shows precisely the opposite.) It is also assumed that convents constituted a kind of fallback option for elites, an honorable way out for families with too many daughters or too few resources to arrange advantageous marriages.[60] This certainly may have been the case for many families. Yet the actions of cuzqueños also suggest a different logic.

Given the benefits they might receive by placing their daughters in the cloisters, elite families might seek, through their daughters, to *marry convents.* The spiritual benefits were obvious. A daughter or kinswoman in the cloisters would constantly offer prayers for the salvation of her extended family. The material benefits might be substantial, too. As we have seen, the convents were in the business of providing credit from their coffers, and having kin inside the convent may well have increased one's chance of competing successfully for a portion of the available loans. Should one's daughter gain position among the convent's leaders, as abbess or prioress or as a member of the advisory council, she might control the distribution of tens or hundreds of thousands of pesos among Cuzco's prospective borrowers. And for those unable to meet censo payments she might, in several senses, intercede and obtain grace.

The decision to place children in the cloisters might also benefit a family well into the future. Since novices of both sexes typically renounced their inheritance rights, placing sons and daughters in religious orders was one strategy a family might use to consolidate a patrimony. Under Castilian family law, practiced in the Spanish American colonies, every legitimate child received part of his or her parents' property, a portion of which had to be reserved for this purpose.[61] Within the legal framework of partible inheritance, however, there were ways to pass along most of the family's wealth to a particular child. One way was for the parents to designate an heir to receive the bulk of the inheritance through a practice known as the *mejora* (which might proceed by thirds, by fifths, or both in the case of the *mejora del tercio y del quinto*). Another was for children to join religious orders and renounce their right to an inheritance.[62] *then all the $ went to the others*

Both strategies were employed by the Peraltas, who had purchased the title of Condes de la Laguna de Chanchacalle in 1687, thereby joining the recently established ranks of Cuzco's titled aristocrats. In her will the first countess had chosen her daughter Doña Petronila de Peralta to inherit the bulk of her property by means of a mejora del tercio y del quinto, specifying that the property be managed by specific Dominican nuns so as to generate an income to cover Doña Petronila's living expenses. A later modification settled the entirety of the family's property on Doña Petronila's brother instead. The new terms obliged Don Diego de Peralta to honor a 20,000-peso lien on his estate, paying his sister 1,000 pesos annually, and also to send her specific food supplies: "thirty loaves of bread and two *borregos* a week, and each year twelve *cargas* of maize, including *paracay*, black *culli*, *la sacsa*, *la chochoca*; twelve cargas of potatoes, and twelve more of *chuño*, and it is understood that this bread and produce [shall be provided] as long as Doña Petronila shall live." Doña Petronila seems clearly enough to have supported not only herself but an entire household within her cell.[63]

Even in the best of times, a well-to-do family might send daughters to the convent—perhaps even an only daughter. Doña Petronila de Peralta, the only sibling of the second Conde de la Laguna de Chanchacalle, is one example. Doña Mencía de Esquivel, sole sibling of Don Rodrigo de Esquivel y Cáceres, is another. And the Costilla family tree shows that in almost every generation, men and women entered the regular orders of Cuzco. By the late seventeenth century, the wealthiest, most powerful criollo clans of Cuzco had frequently employed the time-tested strategy of allying themselves with monastic communities by sending their children into the cloisters. To them, these alliances represented much more than the absence of better alternatives. They were actually a form of advantageous marriage.

Did a daughter's will affect these decisions? Church decrees insisted that women's "free will" be respected in matters of spiritual as well as temporal marriage. According to the Council of Trent, no one could oblige a woman to enter a convent against her will.[65] No doubt many women entered the cloisters with a strong religious vocation that coincided with their parents' desire that they profess. Yet some women were clearly pressed by their families to act against their desires. Don Pedro de Guemes's daughter, the nun Doña María Juana de Guemes, protested in 1677 that her father, a wealthy regidor, had obliged her to renounce her property in terms that conformed to his will rather than her own.[66] And in 1720, Rafaela Centeno recounted that her father had coerced her into becoming a nun. After the death of her mother Tomasa Martínez de la Paz, Centeno's father had taken her and three sisters to reside in the obraje of Taray. He married her older sister, Luciana, to a local man. Then, she recalled, he "began to beg her with tears and endearments to become a nun . . . promising her a large income in the division of his assets and those left by said Tomasa Martínez de la Paz, and she obeyed her father with due submissiveness out of love and respect for him and entered this convent, where she professed, and the promised division of assets was never made . . . and Doña Luciana kept everything." [67] While Centeno's case certainly cannot be taken as representative, it shows the forceful role parents might play in their daughters' decisions to profess. With temporal marriages it was often no different: the paramount object was preserving the family's best interests.

European patriarchs had, of course, long acted in similar fashion. Patriarchal heads of elite households put the family's interests first, and arranged their children's marriages accordingly—whether the marriage was a temporal or a spiritual one. By moving to reinforce women's right to decide whether or not to profess, the sixteenth-century Council of Trent was responding to deeply entrenched European practices of social reproduction (including child oblates and the betrothal of prepubescent children). The family strategies cuzqueños enacted through their children and their city's convents inscribed these old European practices in new, Andean terrain.

In Cuzco, however, these strategies would reproduce a divided elite and produce contradictory, intensely colonial results. We can appreciate this best by returning to the convents' visiting parlors. On the way to and from the locutorio, an Esquivel or a Costilla might have met with Don Andrés Tecse Amau Inca, a master silversmith and principal of San Sebastián. In early 1697 Don Andrés and his wife, Doña María Suta Asa, learned that someone had just canceled a censo by paying the nuns of Santa Clara the principal of 1,656 pesos, 2 reales, and they moved quickly to take the money out themselves. As collateral they offered the house they possessed in the city's center as well as the house, cornfields, and orchards they owned in San Sebastián, one of Cuzco's eight "Indian" parishes. The contract (one of those authorized years later, owing to the negligence of the notary Pedro de Cáceres) reflects that this was not the couple's first trip to a locutorio. Their properties already bore a previous censo in the amount of 2,000 pesos in favor of the nuns of Santa Catalina.[68]

What kinds of relationships did Andean nobility like Don Andrés Tecse Amau Inca and Doña María Suta Asa cultivate with the nuns? Did these relationships differ from those created by criollos like Don Pablo Costilla? The archival evidence, most of it from the eighteenth century, indicates that kurakas, principales, and their spouses often approached the nuns for many of the same reasons that Cuzco's criollos did. Doña Antonia Siclla needed a censo to pay for her husband's funeral and settle his debts. Doña Petrona Cusi, the wife of Don Francisco Atau Yupanqui, principal of San Sebastián, purchased a cell ("una celda y su solarsito") inside Santa Catalina for her daughter Doña Ursula Atau Yupanqui, a nun of the white veil.[69] Don Cristóbal Mancoturpo, the kuraka of Azángaro, arranged with two Dominican nuns to purchase the haciendas Llaullicancha and Llaullipata in the parish of San Cristóbal. When he died without paying the price of 6,000 pesos, the nuns made preliminary moves to sue but then reached a settlement with his son Don Alejandro Mancoturpo. These and other cases show that indios nobles who were prepared to offer acceptable real estate as collateral might receive credit from the nuns, and regularly did. They might also rent property from the nuns. For example, in 1741 the cacique principal of the parish of Belén, Don Antonio Díaz Uscamaita, acted through an interpreter to rent a house in Cuzco from Nicolasa de los Remedios, a nun of Santa Catalina who served as mayordoma of the cofradía of Nuestra Señora de la Encarnación.[71]

In addition, many kurakas and principales arranged before the grille to place liens on their property to enable their daughters to enter the religious life: women with such family names as Atau Yupanqui, Guaman Cusitopa, Quispe Guaman, Sinchi Roca, Guampu Tupa, Tecse, Tamboguaso. Their daughters made deals in the locutorio, too, often transacted in Quechua and duly registered in Spanish by means of an interpreter. They sold land, sold houses, and lent money, frequently to people who appear to have been criollos.[72] And like many of the elite criollas inside the convents, the Andean nuns lived in their own cells and formed their own households. They might even be supported and attended by slaves. This much is indicated by the widow María Panti's 1642 donation to her granddaughter, cloistered in Santa Clara: namely, the services of two Afro-Peruvian slaves, the adolescent tailor Gaspar and his two-and-a-half-year-old sister Isabel.[73]

But the relationships established with the nuns by the families of Andean elites were also different in crucial ways from those established by the region's criollos. The daughters of kurakas and principales were not in charge of convent business. Only rarely did they become nuns of the black veil, and none became abbess or prioress. As we have seen, the criolla nuns by the turn of the eighteenth century increasingly kept these women locked out of the highest level of convent affairs. Women of the Andean elite were permitted to profess mainly as nuns of the white veil, even when their families were relatively prosperous and could have afforded the full dowry of the black veil. While their families contributed substantial resources to the convents of Cuzco, then, (Indian) their daughters could play no direct part in deciding how credit and other convent resources were apportioned among local people. They could manage only their personal funds, provided they obtained their superior's permission.

By the early eighteenth century, Andean elites may well have been putting more resources into convents than they were getting out.

Moreover, the nuns may have been less flexible and forgiving with them than with other borrowers. There is a hint of this in the case Santa Teresa brought against Don Melchor Queso Yupanqui, principal of Belén, and his wife Doña Josefa Pilco Sisa. The couple had received credit from the nuns in two separate censos of 200 pesos each, one recent and the other more than twenty years old. The Carmelite nuns sought to place an embargo on the couple's residence after just three years of nonpayment, citing their failure to pay 60 pesos (20 pesos annually on the principal of 400 pesos). For Cuzco's convents this was very small change indeed.[74]

Why did kurakas consent to what appear to be increasingly unfavorable terms in their relationships with the nuns of Cuzco? More than an honorable reputation might be at stake, as a fascinating contract of 1746 shows. In that year Don Tomás Thopa Orcoguaranca, the kuraka of Guayllabamba in nearby Yucay, sought and obtained 500 pesos in a censo from the nuns of Santa Teresa to pay back tribute owed to his corregidor, who had threatened to embargo his and his wife's assets and imprison him if he did not deliver.[75] No further details are provided, but Don Tomás's predicament can be imagined: he might defy the corregidor (and land in jail), force his community to come up with the unpaid sum (and risk straining his ties with his kinsmen), or go into debt himself. When pressed too hard, a community might resist its kuraka. Under pressure from the colonial authorities, and perhaps afraid of this kind of outcome, Don Tomás approached the locutorio instead, and the nuns came through.

At a certain abstract level, this deal of 1746 was just business as usual. The flexible symbiosis of convents and local elites was proved and renewed once again, keeping an elite family afloat and colonial relations working. Just as a Costilla might get out of trouble by special pleading in the locutorios of Cuzco, a Thopa Orcoguaranca might, too. Both families had carefully cultivated good relations with the nuns of Cuzco, sealed by the professions of young women. In 1743, three years prior to the run-in of Don Tomás Thopa Orcoguaranca and the corregidor, a daughter of Don Alejo Thopa Orcoguaranca Lan de Bisnay (a principal of Guayllabamba, no doubt related to Don Tomás) had been received as a nun in Santa Clara.[76] In all likelihood the nuns of Cuzco's convents had seen Thopa Orcoguarancas in their locutorios before and felt comfortable helping them out of a difficult situation.

Yet no criollo noble was ever in Don Tomás's position (although

Indians were still liable for tribute

criollos might face their own debt crises). The 1746 incident could only have befallen an indio noble, structurally vulnerable to a corregidor's demand for tribute. Seen in this way, in terms of the structural, colonial *differences* among Cuzco's elites, the case points to the embattled, contradictory situation of many kurakas by the 1740s. Tensions in Cuzco and across the Andes were rising sharply by this time, and as Scarlett O'Phelan has shown, rebellions were breaking out constantly; Steve Stern has proposed calling the mid-eighteenth-century decades after 1740 an "Age of Andean Insurrection." Obtaining loans from the nuns of Cuzco may have assuaged the profound contradictions of colonial rule for Don Tomás Thopa Orcoguaranca, but for many kurakas the situation had become untenable. The price of consent to Spain's indirect rule of the Andes was one that many indios nobles were no longer willing to pay.[77]

Conclusion: Long-Term Economic Consequences

In this chapter we have seen Cuzco's convents and nuns flexibly perpetuating the colonial order of things, kurakas borrowing from the nuns to pay tribute, criollos borrowing for capital improvements to expand some of the region's largest and most valuable properties, and both elite groups placing their daughters in the city's convents, albeit on unequal terms. By the late seventeenth century, this flexible symbiosis had been nurtured by hundreds of deals struck in the locutorios of Cuzco. Several generations of women had professed, increasing the convents' investment funds with their dowries. No sooner did a woman profess and bring a dowry to the convent coffers than a local borrower stepped up to take the money out again. Through hundreds of such dealings, at this microeconomic, microdevotional level, the "golden age" of Cuzco was laboriously constructed.

money creation

From this vantage point, moreover, we can gain insight into a little-noted paradox: how, in a matter of just a few years, Cuzco plummeted from the zenith of its supposedly golden age into the turbulence of Stern's "Age of Andean Insurrection." The border of one period almost touches that of the other, even overlaps it.[78] How is this possible? How did a prosperous period in Cuzco's past suddenly give way to startling upheaval and sharp decline? This seemingly precipitous fall makes better sense if we take care to specify *whose* rise and fall we actually mean—that of the region's propertied elites—and if we think closely about the long-term consequences of the bonds they created by means of a slow accretion of obligations, many of them carefully tended over generations in the locutorios of Cuzco (at what Michel Foucault would have called the capillary level of power). Underneath the prosperity of many families lay increasingly debt-saturated, unstable foundations. To a dangerous extent they had come to rely on the kinds of obligations we have examined here.

We have seen that among propertied, elite cuzqueños, *debt created relationships*—important, productive ones. Censos represented a bond, not simply a burden. The closeness of elite cuzqueños and convents was expressed in gestures that were performed over and over again in the locutorios: the pledging of daughters, the getting and giving of various kinds of resources. If each generation wanted to reaffirm the connections through a new performance, while maintaining and even expanding the family estate, one logical strategy was to place layer upon layer of censos on the family's houses, farms, and ranches (a strategy practiced to an extreme by the Dueñas Castillejo brothers).

The cumulative results could eventually prove devastating to a family's finances, however. The more obligations family members placed on their principal productive properties, the higher the annual payments they had to make, whether to nuns, friars, secular clergymen, or others, and the greater the risk of falling dramatically behind when a run of bad years hit—when droughts dried out the land and killed the crops, for example, or when hail thundered down, or when earthquakes broke up the irrigation channels in the fields. By occasionally canceling a censo, a debtor might relieve his or her situation, but coming up with large sums of cash was not easy. Even kinship with one's creditors did not guarantee indefinite grace on tardy payments. Under pressure, cuzqueños might shift their censos around: through transfers (traspasos), censos could be lifted from one especially burdened property and placed on another instead. Some people consolidated their debts, incurring one large obligation to cover and cancel a variety of smaller ones; cultivating one creditor made energy-saving sense, concentrating one's risk in one place. But these were tactics of expedience, not viable long-term strategies.

Heavy reliance on censos could (and did) prove ruinous for particular families, and it posed an even more serious threat to the extent that it became regionwide. By the early eighteenth century, Cuzco's abbesses and prioresses could see this danger, and they registered deep concern about the increasing saturation of the region's properties in dense layers of debt. Charitable donations and dowries might sit for months in the convent coffers, they complained, for there was no secure place to invest them: the region's haciendas and houses were already covered in censos, *acensuadas*. Soon their complaints would swell into a chorus.

Part Three

CRISIS AND DECLINE

No ay con que costear aun el papel sellado . . .

— Ignacio Mariano Maldonado,

administrator of Santa Catalina (1790)

. . . habiendo arrasado la epidemia general de la pobreza . . .

— Madre Paula de los Remedios, prioress

of Santa Catalina (1835)

6 Breaking Faith

Had it been up to Don Francisco de Goizueta Maldonado, there would have been a fourth nunnery in Cuzco. The dean of Cuzco's cathedral chapter was a wealthy man, an Arequipa-born criollo who had come to possess extensive holdings in livestock on various ranches in the Cuzco region.[1] On his death in 1700, he left a sum considerably larger than that given by Don Antonio de Zea in 1673 for the founding of Santa Teresa, specifying that his bequest be used to found a Conceptionist convent. Almost immediately, claims and litigation began to diminish the legacy, however, and nothing was done to effect Goizueta's design.[2]

In 1718, another would-be founder began proceedings to obtain license for a new foundation. Again the initiative came from a member of the cathedral chapter of Cuzco, this time from Don Agustín de Larrazabal, who wanted to found a convent of Discalced Trinitarians.[3] The Crown first sought the opinion of the bishop of Cuzco. What was his assessment of the current state of Cuzco's convents? Santa Teresa was well provided for, responded Bishop Gabriel de Arregui, because of the small number of nuns and because its foundation was "opulent." Santa Catalina was able to celebrate the mass and the sacraments decently, but otherwise appeared to him to be suffering: the wardrobe (vestuario) was not adequately looked to, and little was provided for the nuns' sustenance. Too many servants came and went. Hacendados failed to pay the nuns what they owed, and when they did, it was neither on time nor in cash. With Santa Clara, he wrote, it was the same. Even Santa Teresa was affected by the general hardship, but there "it is felt less than in the others." Under the circumstances, Bishop Arregui could not begin to understand the pretensions of Larrazabal. "I have advised Your Majesty of the situation," he concluded, "because there are some optimists who with great facility recommend new foundations, without the kind of firm basis in rents for lack of which many irregularities occur, and they evince certainty of imaginary assets, as I see in the case of the Maestre Escuela Don Agustín de Larrazabal, whose ingenuous reports and zeal I entirely fail to understand."[4] Larrazabal, too, failed in his efforts.

In 1730, Bishop Arregui's successor Bernardo Serrada decided to distribute what was left of Goizueta's donation among various other charitable projects in Cuzco.[5] The 100,474 pesos that remained after three decades of lawsuits were far from enough to purchase a site and construct a convent, even if one were necessary—which, according to Bishop Serrada, was not the case. He wrote the Crown that it would be impossible to found a convent in Cuzco in 1730, owing to the insufficiency of Goizueta's bequest and "on account of the decadence and poverty to which this City is reduced in its funds, along with all of its Provinces, so that it is unable to sustain itself; nor is a new Convent of Nuns necessary, in view of the fact that the three existing nunneries, all founded with very substantial rents, at present manage only to obtain what they need for their sustenance with great difficulty."[6]

These failed attempts at foundations point to a problem that would plague Cuzco's convents throughout the eighteenth century: getting sufficient income. While it is still hard to gauge the accuracy of Bishop Serrada's 1730 assessment of Cuzco's "decadence and poverty," the nuns were clearly struggling by then to maintain themselves in their accustomed fashion. The symbiotic arrangements on which they had relied for centuries had saturated much of the region's property in debt, leaving many cuzqueños little or no margin of error for making their censo payments with reasonable regularity. By midcentury the complaints of Cuzco's mother superiors had an edge of desperation. No amount of gentle persuasion could get debtors to pay what they owed.

Under such pressure, the old, reliable arrangements of the spiritual economy began to break down. The distressing state of their business affairs drew more and more of the nuns' attention toward "el siglo," as their business spilled over from their locutorios into the courtrooms of Cuzco (and as far away as the Audiencia de Lima) and from their hands into those of lawyers. Meanwhile, relations inside the cloisters grew tense as accustomed ways of doing things became too expensive to maintain. Common spaces like the refectory and the novices' quarters became too costly to operate and fell into disuse. Incoming and outgoing mother superiors quarreled over convent accounts. Their communities reproached them for distributing too little food, clothing, and money. And nuns blamed and baited one another in frustration. After the dowry of the Dominican nun Doña Gabriela de Meneses was lost in a bad real estate investment, for example, she became known inside Santa Catalina as Wasted Bread ("Pan de balde"). Some even claimed she had died of shame.[7]

Ironically, as the nuns of Cuzco were spending increasing amounts of their time trying to coax an income out of their failing investments, "enlightened" Spaniards were developing a forceful critique of the church as excessively worldly and unduly rich. Influential royal advisors like Pedro Rodríguez de Campomanes and Gaspar Melchor de Jovellanos were convinced that the church held far too much property and should be stopped from amassing any more. For them, the church represented an obsolete obstacle to what truly mattered: the advancement of agriculture and industry. This goal, they believed, could best be attained by the efforts of individual farmers and artisans with their own, relatively small holdings—certainly not by priests, monks, or nuns. "It is a timeless maxim," Campomanes argued, "that population is greater and more permanent where real property circulates with more ease among the secular subjects, without being withdrawn from them, because it is the indispensable basis for their general prosperity." His disciple Jovellanos warned ominously that failure to limit the concentration of land in entail and in the hands of the church would "open up a terrifying abyss" that could eventually "swallow up the entire landed wealth of the state."[8]

This new, secularizing economía civil preached in the salons of Madrid threatened monastic livelihoods as far away as Cuzco. For (simply put) it made convents' exercise of dominio look like a threat to the prosperity of the realm. Almost anything the nuns did to try and collect something on their investments—foreclosing on debtors' property, for example—could be seen to illustrate the dire predictions of Jovellanos. Thus, even though it was articulated in response to Iberian circumstances, the enlightened critique of church wealth appeared to increasing numbers of cuzqueños to fit the scenario they saw around them: one of worldly priests and nuns with a seemingly voracious appetite for an income.

Moved at least as much by financial expediency as by the power of enlightened thinking, the Bourbon monarchs of Spain began to curtail the power of the clergy on both sides of the Atlantic, particularly after Charles III came to power in 1759. Reform of the church was but one area of the so-called Bourbon reforms, measures that by the 1770s had seriously exacerbated the strains of colonial rule in the southern Andes. Andean communities across the region were notoriously burdened by the escalating demands of their corregidores, kurakas, and priests, and such demands, combined with demographic and other pressures, created a tense, combustible situation in the countryside. Cuzco's established elites were also under strain—the elite criollo and "Indian" families on which the nuns of Cuzco depended for their livelihood (and who, in turn, depended on them).

Thus the convents of Cuzco were already in an embattled position, structurally speaking, when in 1780 the kuraka of Tinta killed his corregidor and set off a massive explosion of popular discontent. The movement led by Don José Gabriel Túpac Amaru (Thupa Amaro) began with appeals to the criollos of Cuzco to join a common Andean cause and free the highlands from Spanish corruption. Instead, the city's leading criollos scrambled to put themselves on the side of the Crown, where they were joined by many loyalist indios nobles. The loyalists won: the rebellion failed to undo colonial rule. Yet the bloody "Great Rebellion" made nearly all elite cuzqueños appear seditious and suspicious in the eyes of Spanish authorities. Even the city's cloistered nuns were suspected of vague, scandalous conspiracies that involved illicit affairs and strange, amorous whisperings in Quechua.

Well after 1780 much about Cuzco still seemed upside down. For the nuns the situation was increasingly desperate. The censo-driven symbiosis of the spiritual and the economic had been slowly coming apart for decades, and the elite families that had been around for generations had in many cases gone bankrupt or otherwise been displaced. (The decline of the Costillas had been the most spectacular of all: by 1765 the Marqués de Buenavista had become a drunken highwayman.) In the aftermath of the rebellion of 1780, even more aristocratic criollos fell from their high positions, and Cuzco's indios nobles were abruptly stripped of their privileges. Kurakazgos were abolished altogether. Whose authority were the convents to reflect and reproduce, and on whose graces and annual payments were they to rely? By the end of a turbulent century of decline the answer was far from clear.

Censo Saturation, Bad Faith, and Bourbon Reforms

There is reason to believe that Bishop Serrada was not exaggerating for effect—that in 1730 the convents of Cuzco were, in fact, experiencing serious economic difficulties. A massive, deadly epidemic had swept across the Andean region in 1720, killing tens of thousands—at least 20,000 in Cuzco alone, according to Diego de Esquivel y Navia, who survived to give a graphic account of "the fever." The countryside was hit especially hard. A survivor's account of the ravaged town of Quiquijana, for example, reported that all but two of its caciques, principales, and other indigenous leaders had succumbed, along with 7,000 "common people of the town and its district." Maize and wheat crops had spoiled "because there was no one to harvest them."[9] Across the Cuzco region the epidemic created such serious labor problems that the labor draft for the mines (the infamous mita) was temporarily suspended.[10] Meanwhile, production in Potosí was reaching its nadir in the mid-1720s. The ability of Potosí and the other mining centers of Alto Perú to absorb the sugar, maize, and textiles of the Cuzco region may well have diminished during these years.[11]

Convents could absorb some of the economic impact of times such as these by temporarily reducing the obligations of those who owed them. Even though debtors were liable for the full amount of their censo obligations unless their property had been almost completely destroyed, the nuns often reduced payments or suspended them altogether after a catastrophe struck; they had done so following the earthquake of 1650. Thus the nuns moved to do so in the 1720s, assisting Cuzco's hacendados as they struggled to rebound after the disastrous epidemic. Concessions were granted to enable some of the censuatarios to revive production and meet censo payments. The nuns also made terms more flexible by agreeing to receive payments in kind rather than in cash.[12]

Yet such measures worked only if enough debtors rebounded quickly, particularly those who owed substantial amounts. Unfortunately for the nuns, by 1720 some of their most powerful allies were facing severe difficulties of their own. Don Diego de Esquivel had become entangled in a ruinous lawsuit with a Spanish merchant that began in 1716 over a perceived insult.[13] Esquivel was dead by the time he was finally acquitted in 1732, and his only daughter, Doña Petronila, was left to settle her father's debts as best she could. This was not an easy task, since Don Diego, in addition to being Cuzco's leading criollo aristocrat, had been one of the city's heaviest borrowers. By the early 1700s he had accumulated more than 53,700 pesos' worth of censo obligations to Santa Clara and Santa Catalina.[14] The convents struggled to collect on these, and the Dominicans even wrote off 8,000 pesos of unmet payments in 1733 in view of the "general calamity of the times."[15] Yet in 1784 the nuns would calculate that the heirs of the marqués still owed nearly 83,000 pesos in back payments.[16] His kinsman the Conde de la Laguna de Chanchacalle became similarly overwhelmed by debt. When Don Diego de Peralta died around 1727 without leaving an heir, dozens of creditors fought to recover what they had invested in his estate, including all three of Cuzco's convents.[17]

The burden of accumulated debts and a lack of male heirs was gradually eclipsing the Costilla family as well.[18] Don Pablo Costilla's granddaughter Doña Josefa Martina Costilla and her husband Don Fernando Venero had payment problems of their own by the early 1740s.[19] By the 1750s their son Don Fernando Venero y Costilla, heir to the title of Marqués de Buenavista, had become the terror of nearby Pisac, indulging in drunken rampages and mounting assaults on those who happened to take the road by his estate. Several witnesses testified to having been robbed and severely beaten at his orders. In 1765 his exasperated mother asked the authorities to arrest him for becoming a drunken highwayman.[20]

The nuns of Cuzco thus saw some of their oldest and strongest allies severely weakened in the early eighteenth century. After the Marqués de Valleumbroso succumbed to lawsuits, his descendants managed to revive the family's fortunes, shifting their alliances—and eventually their residence—to Lima. The Esquivel surname was subsumed into an elite family network of limeños, and by the late eighteenth century the Marqueses de Valleumbroso were no longer administering their affairs from Cuzco, but from Lima.[21] Obviously it became harder for the nuns to exercise their "urbanas reconvenciones" at such a distance, or with the family's proxies. The nuns of Santa Catalina seem to have had great difficulty extracting payments from the Esquiveles. The family remained rather more responsible in its obligations to the Clares, however, probably because two Esquivel women were in command of the convent's affairs for decades. The seemingly indefatigable Magdalena and Bernarda de Esquivel served a total of eight terms as abbesses of Santa Clara between 1740 and 1776, and when they were not abbesses they were madres de consejo.[22]

As the old criollo dynasties of Cuzco declined, other families took their place, perhaps most notably the Ugartes. They too claimed roots stretching back to Cuzco's mythical sixteenth century, and they took pride in their connection to the Inca past, earning a reputation among local Spaniards for insolence.[23] (Doña Juana Josefa de Ugarte was called "la coya" in reference to the family's distant kinship to Inca nobles.)[24]

The family intermarried with other prominent local families.[25] Like the Esquiveles and Peraltas before them, the Ugartes also formed alliances with Cuzco's convents, borrowing heavily from the nuns to finance their haciendas and obrajes in the Cuzco region.[26] Their access to credit was facilitated by the high places occupied by Ugartes inside the cloisters. At least three Ugarte women were elected leaders of their communities in the course of the century, and at least one member of the clan, Don Antonio de Ugarte, served as administrator of Santa Catalina.[27]

Not surprisingly, it was the Ugartes to whom the nuns of Santa Clara turned for help when their problems with censuatarios did not improve. The Clares sought a special judge empowered to compel payments, and in 1724 the viceroy deputized Don Gabriel Urtarán Pérez de Ugarte to visit the convent's debtors throughout the region and oblige them to pay the nuns the amounts they owed.[28] Even such exceptional measures did not resolve the difficulties. The convents continued to suffer shortfalls and were obliged to borrow money to meet their expenses. In 1744 the prioress of Santa Catalina went so far as to seek permission from diocesan authorities for an act she knew was strictly prohibited by the rule of her order: namely, borrowing from the convent's investment fund to meet operating expenses. Prioress Catalina de San Estanislao stated that income was stagnant ("en decadencia"); the convent's debtors, engaged in harvesting their crops, had resisted all her entreaties and she had "no money with which to maintain the Community." Her urgent request to withdraw 1,000 pesos from the convent's coffers was approved.[29]

Inflation and soaring legal expenses exacerbated the nuns' cash flow crisis. In 1743 Melchora Luisa de San José, having just completed a term as prioress of Santa Teresa, listed the "unavoidable expenses" that had left her no choice but to borrow thousands of pesos from local people. Maintaining the splendor of the mass had been most costly: she had borrowed 5,000 pesos for "a monument," possibly an altar for the convent church. A variety of urgent repairs to the cloisters had absorbed some 2,000 pesos more in borrowed funds. Then there had been the cost of food and clothing, the provisioning of the sacristy, and the upkeep of the church, "all of which cost much more than it used to, because of the scarcity of things and because of the high price of food during my term." Finally, to complete her litany of unusually large expenditures, Sor Melchora included legal fees, starting with the lawsuit to recover from the estate of the deceased Conde de la Laguna. "I have sent 1,700 pesos thus far to the city of Lima to resolve it," she wrote, "in addition to spending more than 500 pesos a year on lawsuits over censos in this city, because everything ends up in embargoes and lawsuits, so poorly do they pay my monastery."[30] If debtors would only pay what they owed!

But as Sor Melchora and her counterparts were in the process of discovering, the censo economy itself was in crisis. The profound underlying cause might best be called "censo saturation." Years of symbiotic relations between the nuns and local borrowers had left the Cuzco region layered in debt, and by the early eighteenth century the burden was becoming untenable for many families. Many obrajes and ingenios of the region still produced enough income for proprietors to cover their operating expenses and meet all their taxes, tithes, and censo payments.[31] Haciendas, on the other hand, did not generate a high rate of return, so as censos mounted, receipts on crops covered annual payments less and less successfully.[32] Some families simply gave up their properties to the nuns to avoid expensive lawsuits; the archives contain numerous examples of such *dejaciones*.[33] Others allowed year after to year to pass without paying what they owed, probably frequenting the locutorios all the while to forestall legal action by the nuns. This route courted danger: the family's property might be seized, embargoed, and auctioned off for failure to make censo payments.

Gradually the problem that had preoccupied sixteenth-century Castilians was manifesting itself in Cuzco: considerable property was accumulating in "dead hands" owing to local borrowers' failure to meet the terms of their censos. Such seizures were not a new development in Cuzco.[34] However, the abundance in the eighteenth-century notarial record of legal actions by creditors (concursos de acreedores) suggests they were indeed becoming a more common occurrence, as indicated by the ex-prioress of Santa Teresa.[35] Eager to shed their debts and their creditors' demands, some cuzqueños resorted to strategies as ingenious as they were full of bad faith. In one case, Don Pedro de Hermosa y Mendoza arranged for a friend of his to buy his hacienda Sondor after it was seized and auctioned to pay debts to Santa Catalina. The friend then turned Sondor back over to Don Pedro, who seems to have neatly sidestepped his onerous arrears![36]

When convents did manage to collect significant amounts from those who owed them, they had trouble finding sound opportunities to invest their pesos. Many large, valuable properties were already heavily encumbered with censos and could bear no more.[37] For this reason, in 1754 the nuns of Santa Clara actually refused to allow the

Mercedarian friars to pay off a 10,000-peso censo on the hacienda Callapuquio. The Clares insisted a pact had been made that the censo would "always" remain in place: they wanted to continue receiving the yearly payment of 500 pesos on the censo and did not relish the idea of having to invest the 10,000 pesos of principal somewhere else. "At present," they noted, "all the estates (fincas) in this Bishopric are burdened with Censos and there is no place left to invest [the money] without the risk of losing it."[38]

The nuns knew that the logic of the concurso de acreedores worked against those who had made the most recent investments. When a debtor's estate was sold to satisfy the claims of his or her creditors, the first debts to be paid were not the largest but the oldest ones.[39] By midcentury the danger of losing a large sum (like the Mercedarians' proffered 10,000 pesos) was very real. The money might evaporate in a concurso if invested in a troubled property that went into foreclosure. Concerned hacendados, for their part, fretted about the danger of missing too many payments and losing valuable estates to their creditors. By the early 1760s, the deeply worried sugar producers of the Cuzco region joined together and dispatched a representative to the capital "to ask that the Sugar Producers of the City of Lima and its Jurisdiction not be allowed to sell [sugar] to be transported to the Provinces of the highlands," else the cuzqueños would not be able to sell their own, with "the unfortunate result that we will not be able to pay the Censos Imposed on our property, in favor of the Religious Orders, and the Chaplaincies and pious works and pensions, which we pay by selling said Sugar."[40]

The nuns adjusted as best they could. By midcentury Cuzco's abbesses and prioresses, faced with the enormous difficulty of guaranteeing a steady income flow by the usual means, were resorting more often to short-term lending (obligaciones). In 1751, for example, Don Ignacio de Arriola borrowed 9,000 pesos from the Clares in a one-year loan at 5 percent, offering as collateral the sugar estate he had just bought at auction. (Worth more than 53,000 pesos, the estate already carried 34,000 pesos' worth of debt to ecclesiastical creditors.)[41] Soon thereafter, Don Gabriel de Ugarte y Celiorigo took out the impressive sum of 12,799 pesos, 7 reales for a year and a half from the Clares, whose abbess Doña Rosalia de Ugarte was no doubt a kinswoman.[42] Although such arrangements meant the nuns had to seek new investment opportunities for their money every year or so, this was distinctly preferable to letting the money sit in the convent safe. To counteract this destabilizing shift and preserve relatively stable, long-term relationships, the nuns relied heavily on the long-term lease or "emphyteusis" (venta por tres vidas; venta enfiteutica).[43] And they joined the vehement protest by the city's ecclesiastical institutions when in 1776 the cabildo of Cuzco asked the viceroy to make censos and capellanías payable at 3 (rather than 5) percent.[44]

Meanwhile, in order to compensate for their communities' precarious finances, individual nuns resorted to private, relatively small-scale business dealings, carried out with the assistance of their servants and slaves. Many nuns made loans, and some rented or leased real estate with the assistance of the convent's administrator. Others relied on whatever they and their servants could produce inside convent walls and sell in the city: fine stitchery, sweets, and so forth. This was what caught Bishop Gabriel de Arregui's attention in 1718: the incessant coming and going of servants, disturbing the peace of the cloisters and making it hard for the nuns to keep their minds off worldly affairs. The bishop's complaint would be heard again and again in subsequent years, as those with an eye to reform of the church seized on the nuns' lively involvement in worldly "traffic" as evidence that their spiritual vocation had been seriously compromised.

Ironically, the very things that enabled the nuns to get by as their income contracted also made them targets of criticism. In 1768, the cabildo of Cuzco protested to the Crown about the misconduct of the region's clergy, closing with a few choice words on the state of Cuzco's convents as full of "secular persons and a multitude of servants, who . . . turn what should be houses of edification into houses of commerce."[45] Such complaints were heard around the Peruvian viceroyalty. When a council of bishops met in Lima in 1772 (the first in several generations), one of its aims was to strengthen the monastic discipline of the regular clergy by obliging them to obey their rules more closely, in keeping with the direction of Bourbon reforms in Spain. The bishops sought to reinforce discipline in Peruvian convents in various ways: by limiting the number of nuns allowed in each convent in proportion to its income, restricting the number of secular inhabitants, and reinforcing the control of male ecclesiastical authorities over the nuns' spiritual and financial affairs.[46]

By the 1770s, then, Peruvians were feeling the effects of "enlightened despotism" in church affairs. Reactions around the viceroyalty varied. The expulsion of the Jesuits by Charles III in 1767 no doubt caused alarm among the superiors of the other orders at the tactics of their increasingly heavy-handed monarch. The Jesuits' expulsion struck at some of the region's oldest and most solid institutions of learning, including three in Cuzco: the Universidad de San Ignacio de Loyola, the Colegio de San Bernardo, and the Colegio de San Francisco de Borja, the latter dedicated to the education of the sons of Andean kurakas. Some of the largest haciendas in the region—including the sugar ingenio of Pachachaca, which had been left to the Jesuits after the death of Doña Leonor Costilla—passed into secular hands. The Ugartes must have been pleased, however: they picked up not only Pachachaca but the neighboring ingenio of Ninamarca as well.[47]

Ecclesiastical property was not yet an issue in Peru in the sense that Spanish reformers had proposed. Nor would educated Peruvians argue, when they did begin to advocate measures against the "dead hand," on behalf of the progress of an abstract common man or agriculturalist. In their view, the majority of those who lived on the land in Peru were little better than beasts, lazy and wholly undeserving of education or reform. But they would eventually adapt the enlightened reformers' goals to a colonial American setting, arguing against church wealth on behalf of the progress of agriculture in the abstract. When this late-blooming physiocracy took root in the Andes, it was less a tribute to the power of Enlightenment ideas about liberty and the rights of man than it was a pragmatic response to the destruction caused when war broke out in 1780.

The Great Rebellion and Its Aftermath

Convents were but one of the many institutions that Bourbon monarchs sought to reform during the eighteenth century. In fact, the scope of the reform effort under Charles III was so wide-ranging—encompassing corregidores, priests, fiscal agents of the Crown, and almost everyone else in any position of authority over revenue-producing colonial subjects—that its effect on the American viceroyalties has been characterized as a "second conquest."[48] As compared with Habsburg rule, which could often be circumvented or safely ignored in the Americas, Bourbon rule proved very demanding. In particular, more revenue was demanded for the support of Spain's extensive military involvements. The end was not new to the Crown's American subjects, but some of the means to it were; there were new taxes, and the old ones were extended and more exactingly enforced.[49]

The effects of the Bourbon fiscal and administrative reforms across the urban and rural landscape of Cuzco were various and marked. Ironically, their success in obtaining the Crown's goal of increasing the flow of revenue from the colonies hastened the end of Spain's control over the Indies. By stretching and cracking old structures of collusion, held in place for generations by densely interwoven local interests, they destabilized and irritated almost everyone who was not a native-born Spaniard, from the local criollo elites on down. The travelers Jorge Juan and Antonio de Ulloa had noticed in the 1730s the virulence with which Peruvian criollos attacked the peninsular Spaniards among them, many of whom had arrived with little and managed to put together considerable wealth by starting in commerce at a lowly level, working their way up to positions of greater solvency and prestige, and marrying opportunely into the local power structure. The "general sickness" of criollo resentment was, according to Juan and Ulloa, "noted particularly in the cities of the mountains" because of their provincial isolation.[50] This aspect of their account was paid little heed, however, in the Bourbon drive to reduce corruption and diversion of resources by cutting viceregal authorities' ties to local criollo interests. Peninsulares were systematically favored and the presence of criollos in high places was reduced, aggravating local sensitivities.

At the same time, the role of kurakas and other indios nobles as guarantors of Spanish rule was increasingly undermined. These elite Andeans were deeply offended by the viceregal authorities' refusal to recognize and honor many of the privileges they claimed, and they sought (but did not necessarily receive) legal redress of their grievances.[51] Meanwhile, the forced sale of merchandise to their communities by corregidores, a practice known as reparto, grew especially abusive and burdensome after the Crown decided to legalize it in 1751.[52] This attempt to control corregidores did not achieve the desired result. Corruption continued, as did complaints. By the 1770s, matters were reaching a breaking point in rural Cuzco.[53] The reparto was well in excess of stipulated limits. Priests also made abusive exactions of their indigenous parishioners.[54] Making an aggravated situation more volatile, maize prices fell markedly in Cuzco in the 1770s, a factor that may well have intensified the pressure on kurakas and their communities.[55]

Outbreaks of rebellion were already occurring around the Peruvian viceroyalty when new Bourbon measures aggravated the already strained situation in Cuzco.[56] In 1776, the Crown created the new viceroyalty of La Plata out of what had long been Peruvian territory, giving it the rich silver mining jurisdiction of Upper Peru. Thus Potosí, the market toward which Cuzco's economy had been oriented for more than two hundred years, came more firmly into the orbit of Buenos Aires, its port, and its merchants. Cuzco's products were by no means shut out: an estimated 10 percent of the total value of Potosí's imports still came from Cuzco in 1794.[57] But the effect of the administrative reordering of the colonial territories was not neutral.[58] Moreover, the sales tax was raised and customs houses were established in the late 1770s for direct tax collection at strategic points along the main transportation routes. These measures affected not only producers but arrieros, those in charge of running the mule trains between Cuzco and Potosí, who found it harder to make a profit from carrying local merchandise to Potosí.[59]

On November 4, 1780, Don José Gabriel Túpac Amaru, the kuraka of three small towns in the province of Tinta and a moderately prosperous owner of mule trains (piaras), ignited the most momentous and far-reaching rebellion in the history of Spanish colonialism in the Americas.[60] He imprisoned the local corregidor, Don Antonio Juan de Arriaga, and on November 10, 1780, presided over Arriaga's execution, after which he announced his grievances and goals: an end to the hated repartos and alcabalas and to the corregidores who enforced them. Thousands of rural people rallied to support Túpac Amaru, and together they launched what came to be known as the Great Rebellion.[61] The rebellion spread rapidly from its beginnings in Tinta, located to the south of Cuzco along the royal road connecting the city to Potosí. When the rebels won their first major victory on November 18 at the battle of Sangarara, several thousand rebels took part in the defeat of a much smaller Spanish militia.

The defeat at Sangarara left the elites of Cuzco terror-stricken. Suddenly the tense rivalry of criollos and peninsular Spaniards was dwarfed by the threat of imminent Indian invasion and an end to a world in which whites, whatever their rivalries and secret fears, assumed they were on top and acted accordingly. Rumors flooded the provincial city with the most horrendous scenarios of butchery and cannibalism.[62] People hurried to hide their valuables from the hordes that might descend upon them. The bishop of Cuzco hastily called on Santa Clara, Santa Catalina, Santa Teresa, and the ecclesiastical court to move the contents of their coffers to the monastery of San Francisco for safekeeping. When the nuns objected, the bishop relented, instructing them to hide their money and valuables in the safest possible place they could find; Santa Teresa, which turned out to have by far the largest sum of cash on hand, made a special cache in the cellar into which nearly 38,000 pesos were sealed.[63]

Túpac Amaru had hoped he could count on the criollos of Cuzco, knowing that the provincial capital was a key to his success. One of his earliest moves in search of support was to write to the Ugartes asking for their adhesion. Specifically, he addressed Don Gabriel and Don Antonio de Ugarte as his "cousins" and as "the principal leaders of the City," and he asked them to place the corregidor of Cuzco under arrest and confiscate the funds in the royal treasury.[64] Instead, the Ugartes chose to participate actively in the movement against Túpac Amaru. Although they had previously encouraged their fellow cuzqueños to defy peninsular Spaniards, the dramatic events of 1780 caused the Ugartes to perform a sudden about-face.[65]

The general reaction of Cuzco's criollo families followed the same lines as that of the Ugartes. They found themselves in the position of joining the Spaniards they scorned and resented in order to avert a prospect even more hateful: that of a Túpac Amaru monarchy. As they rushed to demonstrate their loyalty to the Crown and to protect and distance themselves from the dreaded "rebel hordes," Cuzco's criollo aristocrats seem to have undergone a striking reorientation of allegiance. Those who, like the Ugartes, had considered themselves the proud inheritors and continuers of the Inca past scrambled to prove themselves staunch defenders of the king. The reactions of the kuraka leadership in the Cuzco region were more diverse. Some joined the kuraka who had proclaimed himself Inca, but many others decided to join the Spanish forces in putting down the Great Rebellion.[66] Particularly effective was the kuraka of Chinchero, Don Mateo García Pumacahua, who rose to the rank of colonel through his activities on behalf of the loyalist cause.

While Cuzco was reinforced and defended in late 1780 and early 1781, the countryside was being torn up by the conflicts that raged and ranged from one part of the southern highlands to another. Haciendas and obrajes that lay in the path of the combatants were stripped of their resources, both by the rebels and by the troops attempting to subdue them. On January 4, 1781, for example, the bishop of Cuzco reported to the viceroy concerning the rebels' uncontested entry into the major towns of the vicinity of Lampa, followed by Túpac Amaru's return to his base in Tungasuca: "In the course of their journey they took with them all of the livestock from the surrounding area . . . the greatest harm being done to the estancia Quehue belonging to the Carmelite convent of this City, which contained more than fifteen thousand sheep." [67] The rebel leader paid many of his debts in kind, using the stock he seized from the region's productive properties to compensate his troops. [68] Royalist forces likewise took what they needed when they swept through the region in pursuit.

Both sides built toward a major confrontation in Cuzco, but it never came. When the rebels laid siege to the city in early January 1781, they were unable to carry off their prize. Thereafter the rebellion under José Gabriel Túpac Amaru lost momentum, pursued by Spanish troops and unable to replicate the triumph of Sangarara. In early April, Túpac Amaru and his wife and close collaborator Doña Micaela Bastidas fell captive, along with many members of their family, and were brought to prison in Cuzco. There they were tried and executed in a gory public spectacle on May 18, 1781. The Túpac Amaru family was extinguished in the bloodiest possible fashion, and the severed parts of their bodies were distributed to various towns so the highland population would learn a gruesome lesson.

Still the rebellion continued, moving south under the leadership of Don Diego Cristóbal Túpac Amaru and a handful of survivors of the defeated kuraka's family, including his adolescent son Mariano. In the subsequent phase of the rebellion, the largely Quechua forces from the Cuzco region joined with Aymaras of Upper Peru, who had risen in revolt under the leadership of Túpac Catari. The continuation of the Great Rebellion was, according to some observers, more ferocious, bloody and destructive than ever; it included a devastating siege of the city of La Paz. Hostilities would not cease until a royal pardon was offered to Don Diego Cristóbal and his nephews, who in 1782 cautiously agreed to give up the fight in exchange for guarantees of their security.

By 1782 Cuzco was considered more or less pacified. Túpac Amaru, Bastidas, and many of their relatives were dead. The remaining rebel leaders had accepted a royal pardon, and as a result Don Diego Cristóbal Túpac Amaru and his young kinsmen Andrés Mendigure and Mariano Túpac Amaru had laid down their weapons in January 1782, promising to live peacefully in the small town of Tungasuca and to remain faithful to the king and his representatives. [69] The city of Cuzco had undergone significant changes in the shocking turn of events of 1780–81. It had become an armed camp, full of regular troops, militiamen, weapons, and ammunition. These were expensive to deploy and maintain, and the royal treasury had run dry. Forced loans were thus assessed of the local institutions assumed to have funds to spare—including, of course, the cloistered nunneries. The nuns were obliged to pay, despite their protests that they could ill afford to do so. Santa Catalina was so short of cash that the nuns had to borrow from the diocese to meet their assessed contribution of 2,000 pesos toward the war effort.[70] Painful as these exactions may have been, the nuns would find the long-term impact of the rebellion even more painful and profound.

Spanish authorities obliged the nuns to play a role in securing the Spanish victory over the rebellious Túpac Amarus. On August 8, 1782, the corregidor of Tinta ordered Santa Catalina to receive a prisoner: María Mejía, a woman from the town of Sicuani. She arrived escorted by a sergeant, four soldiers, and a notary, and was entrusted to the prioress Rivadeneyra.[71] The young woman was under arrest because she had been pursued by Don Mariano Túpac Amaru and, by her testimony as reported secondhand to ecclesiastical authorities in Cuzco, forced to agree to an elopement:

> [S]he exclaimed . . . loudly, and repeatedly, that it was not her desire to enter into that state [i.e., matrimony] by any means, even though Don Mariano had pressured her in all possible ways, both in the town of Sicuani and later in this City, going to the Convent, attempting first to seduce her with tender words, then threatening to kill her if she did not go along with his intent, as when she went on one occasion to Tungasuca to pick some potatoes and he made her go into the church, and obliged her to swear [her troth] before the image of the crucified Christ of that Town, and she was compelled and forced to do so, as she feared for her life.[72]

Whether or not she had once desired marriage to the nineteen-year-old son of the great rebel leader, the nuns' prisoner appears to have been a humble woman. She might be found picking potatoes in a field; witnesses described her as "half *zamba*" and a "prostitute."[73] Yet despite the best efforts of everyone from the bishop of Cuzco to his uncle Don Diego Cristóbal Túpac Amaru, Mariano persisted in his intent. On the night of September 9, 1782, taking advantage of the fact that the nuns had left the main entrance open later than usual, Mariano descended on Santa Catalina with "eight or nine men who accompanied him, all of them armed with swords," and stole María Mejía from the cloisters. She was promptly recaptured and committed to another convent in Cuzco, this time to Santa Clara, and found to be pregnant. Thereafter

Mejía seems to have become increasingly ill, and the outcome of her pregnancy and her confinement is not known.

The scandal in which the convents were caught up was a very public one, and a source of consternation to the local authorities. It contributed to the Spanish authorities' sense that the pardoned survivors of the Túpac Amaru family represented a live danger to the peace of the viceroyalty, and it heightened their desire to destroy what was left of them. Not long after the scandal involving María Mejía, a pretext was found for arresting Don Diego Cristóbal and the surviving members of the Túpac Amaru family network. Those who were not tortured and killed were sent into exile. Mariano would die in 1784 aboard a ship while on his way to exile in Spain.[74]

That year Cuzco received a severe and easily excitable Spanish governor, the intendant Don Benito de la Mata Linares, to whom the city seemed only barely under control.[75] The incidents involving Mejía and Túpac Amaru only confirmed his suspicions of the local elite, Incas and criollos alike—especially criollos who appeared connected to Túpac Amaru or the Inca past. Mata Linares suspected the criollo bishop of Cuzco, arequipeño Juan Manuel de Moscoso y Peralta, of having secretly aided and encouraged the rebel leader, even though Moscoso had excommunicated Túpac Amaru and even ordered priests into battle against him. Despite Moscoso's protestations of loyalty, Mata Linares succeeded in having him sent to Spain pending the outcome of a thorough investigation. The criollo bishop defended himself vigorously, and was ultimately given the bishopric of Granada, but was not allowed to return to Peru.

The Ugartes were likewise unable to free themselves from suspicion, as Mata Linares was convinced their house was "a seminary of murmurings and doctrines against the Spanish Nation."[76] The brothers Gaspar, Gabriel, and Antonio de Ugarte had served in the Cuzco militia against Túpac Amaru, but accusations of their collaboration with the rebel leader were raised against them nonetheless. One of the charges made against the Ugartes was that their haciendas had been left untouched as the rebels moved through the countryside. Also adduced against them were their reputation for insolence and disrespect for the king; the respect they commanded from the Indian population and the nickname "la coya" by which Doña Juana was known; that Don Gabriel and Don Gaspar had hidden behind a boulder in the height of battle. And other charges were leveled, reflecting the Spanish authorities' heightened state of fear and paranoia more than anything else.[77]

Although no charges could be proved against them, the Ugartes were sent into exile in Spain and were not permitted to return.

The persecution of the Ugartes resulted in years of upheaval inside Santa Catalina. Tensions centered on Doña María de la Concepción Rivadeneyra, a sister-in-law of Don Antonio de Ugarte who had been prioress of the Dominican nuns at the time of the Túpac Amaru rebellion. Mata Linares regarded Rivadeneyra with intense suspicion. He had heard she had attempted to flee her convent with her brother-in-law Don Antonio de Ugarte after the rebellion failed, and that her scandalous conduct had created a state of agitation inside the convent. Rivadeneyra was also accused of having maintained a scandalously intimate friendship with Bishop Moscoso, and thereafter with the prior of Santo Domingo, Friar Juan de Medina. Moscoso had joined in the allegations against her. Perhaps in an effort to defend his own difficult position, he had come forward in 1783 with juicy bits of hearsay: "Once the Prioress [Rivadeneyra] used in one of her notes some sort of amatory phrase in the general language of the Indians which is so common in this city, and unable to understand it Father Medina had to ask the monk Sequeyros what it meant."[78]

Inside the cloisters, Rivadeneyra had gained some virulent detractors as well. Tensions over the conduct of convent business had been building for years, and by 1783 a bitter conflict was raging between two factions of nuns, the supporters of Rivadeneyra and those of her most powerful rival, the ex-prioress Francisca del Tránsito y Valdes. The conflict shows, in fascinating detail, that the nuns were acutely aware of precisely how much their standard of living had deteriorated. In a long, aggrieved letter, Rivadeneyra's rivals accused her of having deprived them of food—luxuries as well as the basics—in order to marginalize them:

> The Cell of Mother María de la Concepción [Rivadeneyra], which in accordance with the common life should be a Pantry of Provisions for all the Nuns, is only for those who belong to her party. At six in the morning, they all gather there to drink Punch, Chocolate, and mate. At nine they gather again to lunch, at eleven they have mistelas, and then at noon they reconvene to eat splendidly; at five in the afternoon there is a sumptuous snack provided for them, and at nine at night, an abundant supper. Such is the zeal with which she keeps them

prisoners. . . . [Our] food is reduced on Fridays to a portion of poorly cooked Greens, the kind that is used here only to feed beasts, and [a dish] called *Locro*, with three or four potatoes swimming in Water, and on a meat day our only meal is a dish of ground corn commonly known as *Lagua*. It was always the custom to give us a Borrego each week . . . [but now] we receive one peso, and the rest of the Nuns [of the white veil] six reales, and the Legas and Donadas three reales, even though the price of a *Carnero* is twelve reales.[79]

The detailed denunciations went on at length, focusing on Rivadeneyra's alleged substitution of paltry amounts of money for the nuns' accustomed supplies of food. Each nun of the black veil used to receive twelve large loaves of bread a week, they explained, which the poorer nuns would sell outside the convent for a real and a half per loaf. Rivadeneyra instead gave each nun of the black veil only four reales every two months or so. So it went with sugar, sweets, and so forth. Rivadeneyra excused her sleight of hand, they charged, "with the specious pretext that the Rebellion has ruined the income of the Monastery." Instead, they claimed, the prioress and her brother-in-law had sold off convent properties clandestinely and looted Santa Catalina's coffers.[80]

In 1786 Mata Linares finally found the pretext he needed to attack Rivadeneyra's authority. That year a majority of the Dominican nuns reelected Rivadeneyra as their prioress, sending Mata Linares into a predictable frenzy: here was a powerful criolla who, because she was a cloistered nun, could not be summarily exiled to Spain. After a series of clumsy manipulations, Mata Linares arranged for a *presidenta* to be installed in Rivadeneyra's place. Yet that, too, failed to contain her influence within Santa Catalina. Finally Mata Linares resorted to the only available form of exile, ordering that Rivadeneyra be forcibly removed to the cloisters of Santa Teresa. He conferred at length with the convent's diocesan overseer José Pérez about how best to "avoid a noisy scene of tears and screaming and other irregularities from the Nuns, as well as from the large number of Servants of all Castes." Pérez recommended intervening "shortly after the Avemarias, and before they shut the Doors, because those Women would rather let them be broken down than open them willingly." So it was that Mata Linares sent soldiers into the convent to remove Rivadeneyra by force—a task he supervised personally, and that did in fact require the men to break down the convent doors. The violence would not be played out until years later, after many conflicts over jurisdiction, and must have kept the convent in an uproar.[81]

As the documentation on the case and the high level at which it was handled make clear, the troubled state of Santa Catalina was taken quite seriously, as it was seen to reflect the troubles of Cuzco as a whole. The most apt commentary on the situation seems to be that included in the gloss of the case when it reached the Crown for final review in 1794. The anonymous author singled out for censure the incompetence of Intendant Mata Linares, who saw "in every rumor, however ridiculous, the threat of a new rebellion" and who fretted that Cuzco would succumb to a dangerous "illness . . . born of nothing more than foreboding."[82] While Charcas and Peru in general were tranquil, he wrote, "Cuzco alone with its intrigues recalls the tragedy of the recent revolutions, the memory of which has to be extinguished as quickly as possible"—a task for which Mata Linares and the military commandant Gabriel de Avilés appeared unsuited ("they should have inspired in that citizenry complete confidence, rather than resentment"). By allowing incidents such as that at Santa Catalina to flare up, they kept the overall situation from settling down, "because it is useless to multiply troops if at the same time the reasons for having them present also multiply."

But such censure came years too late to stop the energetic Mata Linares. He bent with particular eagerness to the task of crushing what John Rowe has called "Inca nationalism": the careful cultivation by men like Túpac Amaru of their noble Inca heritage, through such means as legitimating their noble genealogies and sending their sons to be schooled in the stirring words of the Inca Garcilaso de la Vega. Mata Linares zealously monitored and reported in minute detail on the practices of the indios nobles. He was alarmed to find them still using the *mascapaycha*, the red "imperial fringe" that was among the most potent visual signifiers of Inca authority.[83] Nor had they stopped electing their own Inca alférez. "They used to vote by Houses in accordance with an insidious system of their own devising," wrote Mata Linares to his superior José Gálvez in 1786. Each voting group "supposed itself to be descended from a Royal House, some distinguishing themselves as the house of Manco Cápac, others as that of Sinchi Roca," and so forth, "believing there to be twelve Royal Houses; and what will most surprise Your Excellency is that they continued to do this even after the rebellion."[84]

As the Spanish authorities learned the practices by which Andean elites reproduced themselves, they moved to contain all appeals to the glory and authority of the Inca past. Reading the Inca Garcilaso's *Royal Commentaries* was prohibited, as was the use of the mascapaycha. Many kurakazgos were abolished altogether. The indios nobles tried to limit the damage. In 1791 they empowered Don Diego Cusiguaman to go before the judges of the audiencia and other viceregal authorities in Lima and defend "the privileges that belong to them by virtue of their nobility." [85]

Meanwhile, a new audiencia was created in Cuzco to oversee the administration of Spanish justice in the southern highland region. The judges were native Spaniards.[86] The ceremonious welcome and installation of the new audiencia took place in early November 1788 in the accustomed fashion: an elaborate procession of local notables in hierarchical order moved through the streets of the city; then came days and nights of feasting, bullfighting, fireworks, and other forms of public spectacle. Ignacio de Castro, the official chronicler of the occasion, described the scene and its participants at length. Noble Indians led the formal procession, taking their accustomed place—but no longer dressed as Incas. Castro carefully records that they wore "the Spanish uniform." When it came time to dance, nothing Incaic was allowed, only the most fashionable dances of the day: English, French, and German.[87]

But no amount of bureaucratic reform could treat a deeper malaise that afflicted Cuzco in the aftermath of the Great Rebellion. Ignacio de Castro seems to be hinting at it when, around his florid descriptions of the elaborate festivities of 1788, he remarks on the decline of the city's "distinguished families." [88] The installation of a new audiencia was clearly part of an overall plan to gain a firm imperial grip on the city of Cuzco, but the local aristocracy was suffering problems much more profound than the loss of precedence. The bases of their power and prestige, the operations of their haciendas and obrajes, had been hit hard by the months of fighting and the aftermath of rebellion.

Bending and Breaking Faith

The convents' affairs reflected the deeply distressed state of late-eighteenth-century Cuzco. The prolonged crisis had affected not only the livelihood of cuzqueños, but their most engrained habits, allegiances, and beliefs. Old ways of constructing an elite identity could certainly not be counted upon any longer. To boast of a noble Inca heritage, for example, might imperil one's household and lead to exile. Traditions and connections that families had long cultivated thus became a terrible burden for them. Increasingly, the same was true of the old ways of constructing an elite family fortune.

Propertied cuzqueños began to wonder about the heavy burden of their debts. Some had been incurred more than a century earlier by their grandparents and great-grandparents. Hadn't they already paid the creditors enough? At 5 percent, people reasoned, it took twenty years to pay the original amount, so why continue to pay for decades? People began to imagine ways to gain more than temporary relief from their censos. The spreading doctrine of the day was not exactly the one Mata Linares had feared (the "doctrines" against "the Spanish Nation"). It was French, after a fashion. The nuns started to hear pieces of it in their locutorios as their debtors began to frame their excuses in terms of Reason and the privileged place due the Farmer.

Their debtors had, of course, become even more unreliable in the wake of Túpac Amaru's rebellion. Many came to the grille seeking grace periods from their censo payments to enable their properties to recover. Among those who approached the nuns of Santa Catalina was Don Francisco Bernales, a sergeant in the infantry and an hacendado of Quispicanchis, who in 1785 asked to be excused for the payments he owed on his hacienda La Hermita for the years 1780, 1781, and 1783. Bernales told a sad story. He had been taken prisoner at the battle of Sangarara, and his foreman had been killed in a separate conflict. In the course of the rebellion, rebels and loyalists alike had damaged La Hermita, carrying off maize and livestock. Then a freeze had hit the region in 1783, and he had been able to salvage only about a quarter of the usual harvest. The nuns were unmoved. Citing the *Siete Partidas*, Prioress Cecilia de San Sebastián responded that Bernales must "pay what he owes . . . [and] if he does not he will face legal proceedings and embargo." Arguments then flew back and forth, based mainly on the medieval Castilian code of Alfonso X. But Bernales's lawyer invoked a more recent authority on his client's behalf: Louis XIV of France and his defense of "the privileged place of the *agricultor.*" Proclaiming that "Reason is the soul of the Law," the lawyer insisted once more on his interpretation of Alfonso's wise measures, then jumped forward several centuries to extol the art of Agriculture: "This art, fomented and protected by all Nations, has been the concern of Sovereigns. Louis XIV succored with his Treasury the needs of the Farmers of France, and our August Monarch, has supported [farmers] with numerous decrees, making their protection one of his first concerns on issuing his Instructions to Intendants." The fiscal authority who ultimately settled the matter was more flexible than the nuns, recommending that Bernales should pay Santa Catalina for only one of the three lean years.[89] As the result of such cases, the convents learned to add specific clauses to their censo contracts stipulating that no reductions in the annual payments would be granted under any circumstances, even in the event of earthquake, floods, fires, or other disasters.[90]

Bernales was but one of many willing to be aggressive with the nuns to get relief. In many cases the nuns turned out to be the heaviest losers. For example, Santa Teresa was owed annual payments on 11,000 pesos' worth of censos on an hacienda called Guaylla, just south of Cuzco in Andahuaylillas, which was "entirely ruined by the Indian Rebels who rose and in one night destroyed all of its buildings without leaving a serviceable threshold or roof tile," and which in 1786 was "still without any equipment or livestock." When the nuns managed to lease Guaylla in 1786 in a venta a censo, its value stood at only 6,000 pesos. Still the censuatario failed to pay, claiming that he had not received the entire property because parts of Guaylla had been invaded by "common Indians." While the hacienda stood empty, the Carmelites and their lessee fell to arguing over who was legally responsible for evicting the land invaders.[91]

The destruction caused by the rebellion of 1780–81 was most evident in the estates and obrajes of the provinces most heavily traversed by the rebels, militia, and troops—provinces such as Tinta and Quispicanchis, particularly the areas bordering the royal road linking Cuzco to Upper Peru. In the wake of the destruction, hacendados would be trying to make arrangements with the convents through the 1780s and into the 1790s; in some cases they ended up ceding their property to the convents, unable to continue meeting payments. The heirs of Don Ramón Vicente Tronconis and Doña Rafaela Mioño Pardo de Figueroa are one such case: even after receiving a reduction in the burden of censos weighing on their haciendas, they could not pay; they elected instead to give their extensive properties up to Santa Clara in 1789.[92]

The crisis also extended to areas that were not the scene of looting or fighting. According to the report of a provincial bureaucrat posted to the sugar-producing region of Abancay, that province had not yet recovered in 1794 from the loss during the rebellion of some 1,200 to 1,500 mules, which had been used for the transportation of troops and baggage.[93] The haciendas of Abancay, he wrote, were heavily burdened by indebtedness, there being "few or no Haciendas without Censos, and . . . most [are] unable to bear any more charges of this type, or any other."[94] Moreover, competition from sugar produced elsewhere had succeeded in crowding Cuzco's sugar out of its former markets. The overall effect was conveyed ironically by Concolorcorvo in 1793: *cañaverales* had turned into *engañaverales* and *trapiches* into *trampiches*.[95]

The convents were obliged to adapt as best they could, and the kinds of contracts they entered into in the years after the rebellion reflect the changes in their circumstances. The notarial archives show a rise in the convents' rentals of small stores (*tiendas*) and market stalls (*cajones*, *cajoncitos*) by the month, often for negligible amounts—as little as 2 or 3 pesos monthly.[96] In general, rentals multiplied during these years, both for urban and rural convent properties. The notable proliferation of such arrangements appears to be a symptom of the overall instability of the times: the convents complained that rentals exposed their properties to greater risk of deterioration, since tenants were notoriously less attentive than lessees, but the nuns were unable to strike better deals for the administration of their resources. As a result, they often had to borrow, both from local people and from their own permanent investment funds.

In sum, convents were getting more property, by means of various forms of legal action (dejaciones and concursos), but were able to do less with it. The nuns were caught like almost everyone else in the general hard times. When cash came their way, it was more difficult than ever to "situate" it on a piece of property: the nuns' complaints multiplied to the effect that every valuable property in the area was burdened with debt. All the ecclesiastical lenders of Cuzco were suffering the same problem.

It is worth considering the situation from another angle, however: that of the outsider looking to make a start. Structurally, the debt burden on the region's estates made it relatively easy for newcomers to move in and take a chance on a property.[97] With sizable debt piled on many haciendas, the cash amount needed to buy them was often quite low. For example, an estate worth 50,000 pesos and carrying censos in the amount of 45,000 pesos might be had for only 5,000 pesos in cash, so long as the purchaser agreed to assume payment of the annual 5 percent (in this case, 2,250 pesos) on the property's outstanding obligations. The annual payments might prove in a year or two to be too heavy a load to bear, but if the investment did not work out, relatively little was risked and lost. Moreover, so long as the property still had some portion of its value free of censos (in this case, 5,000 pesos), the purchaser could still seek another loan, up to the full amount of the property's value.

This logic seems to be borne out by the available documentation. Tenancy of many properties in the Cuzco region became a revolving door. A good example is that of the hacienda Guallgua, located near Pisac in the province of Calca.[98] In 1755, Santa Catalina purchased the property from Felipe Pardo for 22,000 pesos and began leasing it.[99] After the Túpac Amaru rebellion, the lessee Don Andrés Gras gave the property back to the nuns, saying he had lost more than 800 fanegas of wheat and maize in the rebellion. All the sheep, oxen, mules, and equipment had been taken from Guallgua by the rebels, and the property had been unsupervised ("acephalous" [acéfala] was the word Gras used) for many months owing to the threat of rebel incursions. The hacienda was then made over by the nuns to Lorenzo Carmona, who promised to pay (in sacks of wheat flour) 5 percent annually on 10,000 pesos' worth of censos.[100] A year later, Carmona declared he had bought the property for someone else, the priest of Pomacanchi, Don Gregorio Yepes y Valdeiglesias. The priest kept up his payments for a time, but by 1789 he was three years behind and Santa Catalina was initiating a concurso to recover the property.[101] No wonder both Santa Catalina and Guallgua were in bad shape: in thirty years, the hacienda had lost half its value, changed hands three times, and produced more headaches than anything else.

Many other estates in the Cuzco region seem to have had a similar history of unstable tenancy during the difficult final decades of the eighteenth century. As a result, the nuns' clientele became less stable as well as less reliable. Some of the old criollo aristocrats were still around—the remaining Ugartes, and assorted Jaras, Valdeses, Centenos—but others had migrated to Lima or had been exiled. New surnames appeared in Cuzco in these years—Garmendia, Astete, Letona, Ocampo—as newcomers arrived and struck root, taking on some of the region's largest productive properties. In a sense, this was nothing terribly new. Cuzco's wealthiest and best-connected families had always attracted and accepted outsiders by offering their daughters in marriage, particularly to peninsular corregidores and ministers of the Audiencias of Lima and Charcas. But these outsiders—who probably also married into the local families—seem to represent a new breed, less connected to the old viceregal structures of governance (and misgovernance), more exclusively commercial in derivation and orientation.[102] Probably the increased militarization of the Cuzco region brought new propertyowners to the region as well. In any event, the abbesses and prioresses of Cuzco must have seen many new faces in the locutorio, and more than usual, as the unstable economic situation obliged them to deal with a rapidly changing clientele of borrowers, renters, and tenants.

Conclusions

The bishops who in the early 1700s had decried the decline of Cuzco's convents would have been far more distressed by the state the nuns were in a century later. To a prelate's eye the situation was alarming. The common life had completely disappeared inside Santa Clara and Santa Catalina; because convent assets fell far short of generating enough income to run the kitchen, the refectory, and the novices' quarters, these spaces gradually fell into disuse.[103] Each nun had to fend for herself and for whatever household she maintained inside her cell as best she could. One strategy was to dodge expensive convent offices like that of sacristan, which involved considerable personal outlays.[104] Another was petty commerce. Not only did the locutorios hum with small-scale deals transacted in Quechua and Spanish, but the entryways were busy as well: servants and slaves were constantly being dispatched into the streets of the city to find small jobs or sell things their mistresses had made or could spare. This was worse than simply indecorous, and the nuns were well aware of it. Their rules and conduct manuals warned sternly against making and selling large quantities of anything. Production within the cloisters should be limited, wrote Antonio Arbiol, to a few sweets or biscuits to give to the sick, nothing more. "To produce such things in large quantities, deliberately in order to sell them, and make a profit on them (*hacer notables grangerías de ellos*), is a very serious matter." [105] Yet the nuns had little choice but to look beyond their locutorios in search of a living.

So it was that the convents of Cuzco—for centuries a mirror to the region's elites of their own prosperity—began to resemble the city's beaterios. Cuzqueños were accustomed to seeing beatas and their attendants moving about the city in search of humble tasks to perform. Everyone knew that beatas lived off the income from sewing, embroidery, and other labores de manos. Nuns were expected to spend their time and energy in prayer, however, not scrambling for an income. And they were certainly not expected to give rise to scandal. By the turn of the nineteenth century, word of conflicts among the nuns seemed to spread around the city quite frequently, as it did in 1805 when the determined ex-prioress of Santa Catalina, Francisca del Tránsito, brought furious suit against two of her sisters on charges they had defamed her. She testified that Martina de San Miguel and Alberta de la Trinidad, "on one of the days of Carnaval . . . fixed to the door of my cell libels full of the most grotesque and audacious injuries and affronts," and she brought forward a local artisan who testified how the two nuns had secretly commissioned an offending likeness of her. The result was a portrait of "an old nun, seated, with her head wrapped in a cloth, a basin in one hand, and in the other a bag of coins, and the Devil posed at her side as though speaking to her, and on the right a Franciscan beata handing her a bag of coins, and on the left a secular woman with a bottle of strong drink in one hand and a glass in the other"—not an especially legible image, but hardly a flattering one.[106]

The convents were in the process of losing much of their cultural authority, their power to reflect to cuzqueños a portrait of their spiritual and economic health. But whose authority were the convents to reflect? Long before 1780 this was becoming unclear; after the Great Rebellion, it became even more so. The nuns must have been dismayed to watch old, mutually sustaining relationships with long-standing allies and supporters—families like the Costillas—gradually come undone under the strain of the times. Those who, like the Esquiveles, could move away to more prosperous (or at least more diversified) economies might establish new relationships and regain their balance. The nuns could not move.

The old forms and the old families did not simply collapse.[107] But the marks of decline were everywhere in late-eighteenth-century Cuzco. The convents continued to make loans through the censo mechanism, but the pace slowed and the amounts diminished. Redemptions and cancellations became relatively few and far between; only once in a great while did someone step forward to pay the nuns a large sum of cash and thus free himself or herself from a censo obligation on real property.[108] In 1793, José Hipólito Unanue's *Guia política, eclesiástica y militar del virreynato del Perú* gave the annual income of Cuzco's convents as follows:

Santa Clara	24,994 pesos, 3 reales
Santa Catalina	12,844 pesos, 1 real
Santa Teresa	6,509 pesos, 5 reales [109]

Santa Clara, the wealthiest convent by this account, was taking in 20 percent less than it had a century earlier, when its annual income had reached some 31,000 pesos.

One root of the nuns' difficulties was censo saturation. The region's economy had reached an impasse: its properties lay saturated in debts that left local people unable to borrow further and local institutions unable to lend further. The linchpin of the spiritual economy, the censo mechanism, was failing the nuns—not because of its inherent nature or logic, but because of the workings-out of that logic in the specific context of late-eighteenth-century Cuzco. One way out was an influx of new people with enough money, initiative, and inclination to assume local properties, restore them, and pay off some of their debt. To some extent this appears to have happened. However, the same conditions might (and did) attract buyers with less to give, leading to frequent turnover and rapid deterioration of assets, as in the case of Guallgua. In such cases, the convents had to spend considerable amounts of time and money in legal proceedings while their estates languished.

Another way out of the impasse was to undo the burden of debt itself—the terms of which seemed completely unreasonable to many cuzqueños. The secularizing trends of a century (and lack of viable alternatives) made this route seem increasingly attractive to cuzqueños. After all, Spaniards themselves were sharpening the language and heightening the urgency of the call for agrarian reform. Jovellanos saw mortmain as the root of Spain's decline and reiterated Campomanes's demand that legal limits be imposed to halt alienation of land to the church.[110] Cuzco's ecclesiastical institutions were vulnerable to such criticism. They had, in fact, been amassing considerable property, though whether they could put it to good use was another matter. And nunneries looked more than ever like "houses of commerce" rather than houses of contemplation and prayer.

When the attack on mortmain began in earnest in Cuzco, early in the nineteenth century, the monastic institutions of Cuzco entered a new phase of their collective existence. Some would disappear altogether, and the rest would struggle for their institutional lives. Had the entrenched criollo aristocracy of the provincial city not suffered such heavy blows itself, perhaps a spirited resistence would have been mounted. But Cuzco in the wake of the Túpac Amaru rebellion was fundamentally not the same. Aristocracy, Inca pride, old-style prosperity—all were destabilized. The institutional terrain was different, with intendants and an audiencia in place, and the old institutions had all their rifts and tensions exposed. In the midst of the confusion, no one knew how the church should be endowed, but increasingly people thought they knew how it should not be.

7 Surviving Republicanism

The turmoil in her unquiet city could not keep the widow Doña Josefa Holgado from carrying out her pious project. She knew the nuns of Santa Catalina were counting on her. The Clares had recently installed a brilliant retablo of mirrors in their church, and Doña Josefa had promised to help make the Dominicans' church similarly glorious, something the nuns of Santa Catalina could not hope to do without her support. They could barely afford rented resplendence. Each year the sacristan of the beleaguered community had to spend two or three hundred pesos of her own to rent proper adornments for important ritual occasions, a burden "because of which all the nuns avoided the Office of Sacristan." The childless Holgado had survived two husbands and had inherited enough to make a generous donation to Santa Catalina possible. By 1791 she had spent more than 6,000 pesos keeping her promise to the nuns, embellishing the main altar of their church "in such fashion that now they need not rent mirrors or any other pieces to adorn it."[1]

So it was that, despite all, the nuns of Cuzco still managed to have the mass celebrated in their churches at a high level of magnificence. As far as they were concerned, the exuberance and splendor of the rituals in their churches was still a sign of their city's spiritual health, just as it had been for centuries. So long as enough faithful believers like Holgado were around to help, the nuns could uphold the old ways of worship at the accustomed standards. The Clares and Dominicans also continued (despite their embattled finances) to go about many of their usual practices inside the cloisters, such as taking in foundlings, raising and educating girls, and providing widows a place to board.[2] They still received prisoners from time to time by order of local authorities. Battered wives still came to the nuns, fleeing abusive partners. And because the common life in Santa Clara and Santa Catalina was a thing of the past, individual nuns continued to rely heavily on their servants to help them maintain themselves and the secular women and children living alongside them. Convents thus remained busy, populous places—perhaps even larger than before, if we are to believe Ignacio de Castro. In 1788 Castro wrote of Santa Clara: "Including the Nuns, Schoolgirls, maids, and servants, I am told that House encloses five hundred people. Its church is small . . . but its interior is very ornate, particularly the mirrors that are the dominant *gusto* in Cuzco."[3]

In short, the *siglo de las luces* had weakened but not destroyed the spiritual economy of Cuzco. Certainly the city's cloistered nuns were no longer reproducing the prosperous regional dynasties of previous years. But neither had the nuns' relationships and practices changed entirely beyond recognition. The nuns still went to their locutorios to discuss the terms of a woman's profession, a schoolgirl's entry, or a loan to some local borrower, doing business at the grille with women like Doña Josefa Holgado and men like Don Pascual Díaz Calisaya, a kuraka of Lampa who in 1790 arranged a censo from the Clares, agreeing to pay them in cheeses produced on his ranches.[4]

The initial decades of the nineteenth century would be a disaster for the convents, however. Not only would their local base of support diminish strikingly, as more cuzqueños questioned, revised, and even discarded the protocols of their relationships with the nuns, but the king, their Most Catholic King himself, began to betray their most basic expectations of him. The nuns expected their Catholic monarchs to protect them. (When they needed to fend off an aggressive bishop in 1795, for example, the Clares appealed to the queen, "confident that you are our dear Mother, and that because we are of your sex, we your Vassals will find clemency in your noble breast, as in remotest Peru we adore you. . . . Let Your Majesty, beautiful Sun, not disdain to be our *Mamita*, and help us defenseless criollas.")[5] Little did the nuns suspect that royal finances were in such a disastrous state that their desperate monarch was about to undermine monastic finances as never before. Around the turn of the new century, Charles IV and his advisors aggressively changed the rules and attacked long-standing expectations about dominio. Monks and nuns should continue to pray, but their monasteries and convents should be truly poor—and "poverty" meant no servants and no more good land.

When Spanish rule itself gave way in Peru and throughout South America, things only grew worse for the nuns. Simón Bolívar went about setting up republican institutions to perform much of what had been the nuns' daily business: the schooling of girls, the care of orphans, the sheltering of the poor and needy. The Liberator also liberated the convents from some of their most valuable assets, dedicating them instead to produce an income for the new entities he had called into existence. The nuns were thus double losers: much of their charitable and educational work had been redistributed to others and large chunks of their property taken away. Definitively their governors had broken faith with them. When nuns addressed the new governing authorities of the republic of Peru or the municipality of Cuzco, they tended to do so in angry, injured tones — usually to resist some new encroachment of the *gobierno de turno*. The convents still dominated Cuzco's center with their large churches, and many faithful cuzqueños still cultivated relationships with the nuns. But the meanings of these relationships had changed. New institutions and expectations had grown up around them. By the mid-nineteenth century the nuns no longer held the place of authority they once did, and the spiritual economy to which they had been central was a shambles.

Paying for Independence

The city of Cuzco that had kept its intendant Mata Linares on edge continued to produce restiveness and revolt. By the early 1800s, some criollos were ready to rebel and were looking for Incas to help them do it. Two men were hanged in 1805 for plotting to overthrow the Spanish regime and install an Inca monarch. Neither had roots in the Cuzco region; one was from Arequipa, the other from Huánuco. Their dreams of criollo independence were of a rather messianic cast. Because they took the contents for providence, they gave little attention to gathering mass support or to preserving secrecy and were thus discovered and thwarted while in the dreaming stage. However, they did manage to recruit two descendants of the Inca to their cause — Manuel Valverde y Ampuero and Mariano Campero — as well as an indio noble named Pablo Inca Roca, along with an assortment of other professionals and minor bureaucrats eager for advancement, a handful of whom were sentenced to be deported for their involvement.[6]

In 1814, a much more serious revolt broke out in Cuzco. This time rebel columns would get as far as Huamanga, Arequipa, and La Paz, where the movement ended in bloodshed.[7] The occasion around which a number of Cuzco's criollos rallied in revolt was the liberal Spanish constitution of 1812, which seemed to promise them an increased role in local affairs. The liberal spirit of 1812 ended up pitting self-proclaimed Cuzco constitutionalists against the audiencia, whose judges reacted by jailing the leading constitutionalists in February 1814. However, the prisoners escaped six months later and took the members of the audiencia prisoner (except for the lone criollo among them, the limeño Don Manuel Vidaurre).[8] The constitutionalists then called on the services of Don Mateo García Pumacahua, the kuraka of Chincheros who had played a crucial role in defeating Túpac Amaru, and he agreed to join the rebellion, leading a force against Arequipa. Within a matter of months the movement was defeated by the royal army. Cuzco returned to a loyalist stance in time to avoid the use of force against it. The audiencia's judges were released and restored to their places, complaining of the indignities they had suffered at the hands of "a handful of men of the lowest extraction."[9] The conflict was over, but once more the tensions among Cuzco's Spanish and criollo leaders were exacerbated, their fears of being overwhelmed by an "Indian horde" revived.[10]

All the while, conflict intensified on other fronts. In 1804, Charles IV, in a desperate attempt to avert fiscal disaster, decided to extend to Spain's colonies a policy that selectively confiscated church assets for state use. Known as *consolidación*, the policy captured the endowments of pious projects such as capellanías by ordering the sale of their land and the calling in of their loans. The resulting income was channeled toward Madrid, and the royal government promised to pay interest on the receipts.[11] For the colonies the measure's scope was widened to include repayment of all debt to clerical corporations.[12] Charles IV believed he was achieving two worthwhile goals at once: remedying his financial crisis and releasing good agricultural lands from mortmain, the increasingly dreaded and reviled "dead hand" of the church. Consolidación caused an immediate furor in Spanish America, however, for there church wealth did not depend primarily on land held in mortmain (as was the case in much of Spain), but on credit. Calling in the debt to ecclesiastical creditors would bring down the entire viceregal economy, argued a number of articulate Spanish American spokesmen.[13] How could the king possibly expect people to pay off all their censos at once?

The nuns hastened to evade this state-decreed confiscation of their assets.[14] In 1806 the abbess of Santa Clara, Sor Asencia Valer, was caught making a suspiciously large loan (mútuo) of 19,200 pesos to her administrator Don Martín Valer (probably a relative). She claimed the deal had not gone through. However, her actions occasioned a vehement denunciation to the local *junta de consolidación* about the shifty, fraudulent practices of the monastic orders and their devious administrators:

> They are lending out all the money they have in their coffers, in order that it not pass into the hands of the Sovereign. . . . It would be better if the convents were to impose obligations on some properties, rather than simply lend it out, for in this way the Crown would receive at least some benefit from the right to the Sales Tax and the fifteen percent of the latest tax; but at present they engage not only in violent breaking of the law, but in criminal usurpation of the rights and interests of the Sovereign.[15]

Sor Asencia Valer may have managed to place her community's assets beyond the reach of royal authorities in 1806. Yet the monastic houses of Cuzco would not long be able to fend off the importunate, cash-starved colonial regime, despite their most determined and ingenious efforts.

As Bourbon rule collapsed after Napoléon's invasion of Spain in 1808, South America began a fitful, costly transition to independence that would prove very expensive for the royalist stronghold of Peru.[16] The viceroyalty's ecclesiastical institutions, merchant guild, trade associations, and other corporations would see their funds drained away by one forced loan after another. Most of the fighting in Peru through 1821 took place along the coast. On July 28, 1821, the independent republic of Peru was proclaimed in Lima by the Argentine general José de San Martín. Viceroy José de La Serna decided to retreat into the highlands to regroup before trying to reassert royal control. Cuzco (a well-fortified bastion of Spanish officialdom in the wake of Túpac Amaru's rebellion) offered its services to the retreating viceroy, who accepted the offer and headed further into the southern sierra.[17]

Thus in 1822 Cuzco became the center of the rapidly failing viceroyalty of Peru. Belatedly, the city reclaimed the position of preeminence it had lost almost three centuries earlier.[18] But this privilege came at the price of numerous forced loans (euphemistically called "voluntary contributions") to support the royal war effort. In March 1823, Sor Asencia Valer, once again abbess of Santa Clara, wrote to the head of Cuzco's provincial deputation about the latest levy. She began by assuring him that were it not for the convent's current woes, she would be the first to come forward with funds "destined for a cause so sacred." Valer then explained that the government had already seized 50,000 pesos' worth of assets from the Clares ("some due to consolidación, others to voluntary contributions"), paying them nothing in return for two years, on account of which her convent was owed 5,000 pesos.[19] The amounts that the Clares were able to collect did not cover their basic needs. Tenants usually paid in maize, potatoes, and other foodstuffs rather than in cash, and the nuns felt obliged to admit their produce at a high price, often paying for it to be brought to Cuzco in pack animals as well.[20] "If to all this is added the fact that the convent pays half the tithe (medio diezmo), which the tenants discount from their payments, according to the Government's orders," Valer continued, "then Your Excellency will be easily persuaded that the current state of our finances is too miserable and insufficient . . . for further sacrifices." In closing, Valer made a "voluntary donation" of 1,000 pesos to the "sacred cause," but very much on her own terms: she discounted the amount from the 5,000 pesos the state treasury already owed Santa Clara! Whether or not the Spanish authorities admitted her cagey strategy, Valer again showed her resourcefulness at deflecting the government's demands.[21]

Meanwhile, in a secularizing move that must have struck the nuns as highly contradictory, the failing royal regime that depended on the monastic orders for emergency loans decided to make it easier for their members to leave the religious life. A viceregal decree (bando) of 1822 permitted regular clergy who wanted to gain release from their vows to appeal to the government to do so. Within four years, the republican government of Peru would reiterate the measure.[22] Whether this state-sponsored loosening of the solemn vows of the religious life had much effect on the monastic communities of Cuzco is hard to tell. One nun simply fled: Vicentina Rivas of Santa Clara was found in the company of two other women in nearby San Gerónimo in January 1823. The three women had tried to pass themselves off as beatas from San Blas, but one of Rivas's companions confessed to being the accomplice of a fugitive nun, whereupon Rivas was sent back to her cloisters.[23] At least one nun of Santa Catalina, Sor Rosa Vergara, did seek formal permission to be "secularized." Because she had fled her cloisters before doing so, however, her petition was never formally granted (as far as the record shows). Vergara's mother superior was completely unyielding, and utterly scornful of the government's attempt to interfere where it did not belong.[24]

Outside convent walls, many were eager to see this state-sponsored process of secularization go still further. Debtors began urging the government to intervene and cut the ties binding them to their ecclesiastical creditors. Some censuatarios were even emboldened to scold their ancestors for making censo bargains in the first place. In a remarkable collective protest of 1822, the censuatarios of Andahuaylas asked for a permanent reduction in the rate of their censos to 3 percent on grounds that the principals of censos "do not revolve, do not circulate, and are not employed."

> Either our elders wasted them [the principals], or they never existed, since *most censos were established in wills purely out of the old folks' devotion*; their expenses and liberality have been more than repaid by their posterity, and it may truthfully be said that the obligations have been repaid many times over; and still they are charged five percent, they are oppressed, stripped bare, and sent into the streets in recompense for the lavish ways of their ancestors.[25]

This was, of course, a very interested version of the past—a disavowal of the spiritual economy's complex workings, written as though virtually no one had ever approached a locutorio to ask nuns for a loan (or anything else of worth). Perhaps this generation of debtors had actually seen convents handle more hard-fought foreclosures than fresh loans. Perhaps they had also read the writings of Jovellanos and other advocates of reform. In any case, many censuatarios had come to see monastic houses as their adversaries, and censos as the burden of the past—the result of "lavish," misguided piety, rather than a factor in their ancestors' prosperity. By rendering the nuns' credit invisible, doubting debtors might more easily jettison a family tradition of supporting the nuns.[26]

The nuns must have been horrified by such brazenly impious assertions: these debts represented their dowry funds! If the government listened to such talk, their livelihoods would be in greater danger than ever. Church leaders reacted very defensively to such complaints, hurling their own heated rhetoric to insist that their censuatarios deserved no breaks. In response to the 1822 petition from Andahuaylas, for example, the Franciscan superior in Huamanga wrote scornfully of the "incomparable promises, admirable obsequiousness, and most humble beseechings" employed by censuatarios to coax their creditors into reducing their obligations, calling their excuses nothing more than "imaginative and preposterous lamentations." Intransigence was setting in on both sides of an increasingly great divide between debtors and their ecclesiastical creditors. The animosity and intensity would only increase after Cuzco became part of the new Peruvian republic.

Cuzco's brief stint as the loyal viceregal capital of Peru ended after the forces commanded by Viceroy La Serna were defeated in the crucial battle of Ayacucho in early December 1824. With the outcome at Ayacucho, Spain lost its last stronghold in South America. Within a matter of days, Cuzco gained a new governor and made the switch to republicanism. General Agustín Gamarra, a native of Cuzco sent to assume the office of prefect of the newly independent Department of Cuzco, made his entrance into the city on December 25, 1824. Recovering from the disorienting aftermath of Ayacucho, the city's leaders hastened to prepare a hearty welcome for the general with the requisite banquets, dances, and other festivities.[27]

The following year, in June 1825, Cuzco was paid a visit by the Liberator himself, Simón Bolívar. Once again the hard-hit local elite, or what remained of it, prepared to show its best face. The population witnessed one dazzling spectacle after another as banquets, feasting, and all manner of celebrations in honor of the victorious general went on for days. The wife of the prefect placed a jeweled crown upon Bolívar's head. Even the Incas were admitted to the festivities, albeit at a safe distance: in the pages of the local newspaper *El Sol del Cuzco*, Manco Cápac sent Bolívar his salutations "from the tomb."[28] The hero of South American independence would not make Cuzco his center of operations for long. Nevertheless, he would leave behind a number of measures of lasting impact.

While Bolívar was in Cuzco he undertook several founding acts on behalf of the new republic of Peru. In keeping with his staunch republicanism, and with his actions elsewhere, Bolívar decreed the establishment of several public institutions for the care and education of Cuzco's youth, to be funded with the expropriated resources of Cuzco's convents and monasteries. On July 8, 1825, he ordered the fusion of two formerly Jesuit schools, San Bernardo and San Francisco de Borja, into one school for boys: the Colegio de Ciencias y Artes. The move obliterated the distinction between the sons of the region's kurakas and those of its other elites. For Bolívar they were all citizens in the making; no such distinctions were needed. To endow the new republican Colegio de Ciencias, he applied the properties and funds of the Bethlemite Order, as well as the assets of the two extinguished Jesuit schools and funds from the local caja de censos.[29]

Then Bolívar went further, establishing on the same day a state-sponsored school for girls, the Colegio de Educandas. This initiative was justified on grounds that "the Education of Girls is the basis for family morality, and is entirely abandoned in this city." [30] Its endowment was likewise to consist of expropriated properties and income of the Bethlemites and Jesuits. The Colegio de Educandas (which still functions in Cuzco today, as does its counterpart the Colegio de Ciencias) is almost unique in Peru's early republican history: only in Lima did a similar public institution exist. [31] Elsewhere the education of girls remained in private hands, and was still overwhelmingly attended to by female religious. In Cuzco, however, an institutional alternative to the convents and beaterios had been established, and a precedent had been set for state involvement in the reproduction of local families through the education of girls as well as boys.

Finally, in a further encroachment on what had long been the socially reproductive work of Cuzco's clergy, Bolívar decreed the establishment of hospices for the care of orphans, the disabled, and the elderly, to be supported with the monastic houses' rents (including those of Santa Clara). [32] These measures apparently did not take effect as Bolívar had envisioned, however. By the occasion of the visit to Cuzco of President Luis José Orbegoso in 1834, several thousand pesos had been collected from the orders but no foundation had yet taken place. [33] Orbegoso himself decreed the establishment of the Beneficent Society of Cuzco (Sociedad de Beneficencia), charged with oversight of public charity and structured along the same lines as the newly created Beneficent Society of Lima. [34] Ecclesiastical institutions would not be stripped of their charitable functions; the new and heavily indebted republican state could hardly afford that. However, from the early nineteenth century, welfare activities would no longer operate out of an exclusively religious matrix: they would be given new institutional forms, and a secular stamp.

The nuns were dismayed: how dare anyone think that family morality and the education of girls had been "entirely abandoned" in Cuzco? Still, they took care to appear supportive of the new government— even the Clares, who, because their convent was considered Cuzco's richest, remained a primary target of expropriation. A draft of a letter from the Clares to the Supremo Consejo de Gobierno in November 1825 depicted the "deplorable situation" of Santa Clara's finances, so dilapidated by the "depredations of the enemy armies" that the nuns had been obliged to alienate and pawn properties to support themselves and to "avoid the excesses of violence threatened by the formidable rashness of despotism."[35] (The neat rhetorical about-face concerning the Spanish regime—the "sacred cause" of 1823 was characterized two years later as "despotism"—reflects perfectly the nuns' anxiety to curry favor with the new authorities, who had just taken away convent resources and might easily do more harm.) The letter's anonymous author repeated the litany of woes afflicting Santa Clara—forced loans, the half-tithe on convent properties, the loss of income from ruined properties—and summed up their impact on the convent's finances:

> Thus the twenty-five thousand pesos of imagined income are at present reduced to ~~twelve~~ nine thousand, destined for the support of a large community of fifty-three nuns of the black veil, five of the white veil, some donadas, and a considerable number of dependents indispensable for the maintenance of each one of them; the salary of an Administrator, Chaplains, a Doctor, Lawyer, Solicitor, Rent-collector, Scribes, Mayordomos of the haciendas, Sacristans, and other Subalterns.

Whatever the exact amount of her community's resources, the author's impassioned plea for clemency shows how frustrating "imagined income" was for meeting definite expenses. Reaching for maximum effect, she warned that the Clares might "perhaps be forced into the streets to prostitute themselves and break their vows."

Cuzqueños were not unmoved by the obvious decline of their city's convents. Many continued the ministrations of Doña Josefa Holgado: they loaned the nuns money to meet expenses, did legal, medical, and notarial tasks for them without charging, sent sewing and needlework to be done in the cloisters, and so forth.[36] Some were mystified by the conditions to which they saw the nuns reduced. In September 1825, a reader of the newspaper El Sol del Cuzco wrote in to ask the editor's help in clarifying what appeared to him to be an acute contradiction. "When the Convents of this City were established," he began, "they were without a doubt erected on a solid foundation capable of sustaining and nourishing in every sense those women who embraced the monastic life"—a foundation to which, he assumed, several hundred thousand pesos in dowry had been added over time as generations of nuns made their professions. Yet the convent could not provide for the nuns' most basic necessities. Each had to buy her own cell, repair it at her own expense, and pay for her own daily meals, wardrobe, and medicines, should any illnesses befall her. The prioresses were eternally complaining of shortfalls. What exactly had happened? "Whether owing to the corruption of our times or to some other cause I fail to understand," he mused, "something went wrong, since it is notoriously evident that these houses which should be sacred refuges of virtue . . . have turned into sinkholes into which enormous sums have disappeared . . . leaving the nuns to perish, having purchased their interment at a high price."[37]

Had the nuns responded, they probably would have blamed their debtors for neglect bordering on impiety, and their governors for impiety of the most brazen sort. The following year would be just as bad for the monastic orders of Cuzco. The new republic, needing cash as desperately as the regime it had replaced, began carrying out measures that under Bourbon rule had been discussed but not enacted. By decrees of September and October 1826, several monasteries and convents were suppressed, their resources confiscated by the government and directed toward educational and charitable purposes.[38] In Cuzco these measures closed one of the city's oldest monastic houses, San Agustín (founded in 1559): the friars were sent home and their resources seized. All three nunneries survived. The Clares, however, lost still more property. By 1826 the republican government had taken from them an hacienda called Chahuaytire, valued by the nuns at 30,000 pesos; five more estates worth an estimated 27,500 pesos, and several storefront properties in the city. The abbess calculated that Santa Clara had lost a total of 90,560 pesos of principal and 4,103 pesos in yields (réditos).[39] Whether the Dominicans and Carmelites had resources confiscated is unclear. In any event, they too were struggling, borrowing from local people to make ends meet in what the prioress of Santa Catalina termed "the present critical circumstances."[40]

In addition, the central government enacted a measure the clergy had long feared: a deep cut in the rate of censo returns. The Lima authorities (probably saddled with debts themselves) decided to favor those seeking relief from their debts at the church's expense. Censo rates were cut from 5 to 3 percent on urban properties, and down to only 2 percent on rural properties. The decree, issued from the Palacio de Gobierno in Lima on April 22, 1825, was meant to revive the Peruvian economy, and it cited as justification for the measure (characterized as "provisional," until such time as further study made it possible to draw up a general law regarding censos) the devastation caused by the wars of independence, the consequent deterioration of agriculture and industry, and the "unfortunate and inevitable" circumstances which made proprietors unable to bear the weight of their obligations while their creditors "collect the réditos without the least leniency."[41] The 1825 reduction in the rate of censo obligations turned out not to be provisional after all. It would remain in place as long as the censo economy survived, which meant that convents suddenly saw about half their investment income vanish for good.

Moreover, the government realized that the new measures could be made effective only if state-appointed mayordomos were put in charge of convent finances. The central government thus named ecónomos to oversee the finances of the regular orders and bring them fully in line with the new decrees.[42] The role of a convent's mayordomo was crucial. Mayordomos might turn out to be the nuns' worst enemy—in fact, Santa Catalina was tied up for years in the 1770s in judicial proceedings with its mayordomo Diego Galeano, who was accused by the nuns of embezzling resources and who was ultimately removed from office and ordered to keep away from the convent.[43] But these administrators might also prove to be the nuns' close collaborators, as exemplified by the cooperation of Martín Valer with the abbess Sor Asencia Valer in helping Santa Clara manage its funds in the wake of the 1804 decree of consolidation. Accordingly, the key post was captured by the central government for its own purposes, a canny move that helped ensure that convents would not continue to find ways around the new republican legislation.

Thus by the mid-1820s, the state had placed itself right in the middle of convent business, leaving the nuns of Cuzco little room to maneuver out of their difficulties. In late 1826, the abbess of Santa Clara produced an especially clear statement of the situation from her community's vantage point.[44] She drew up a table carefully divided into four parts: income, government confiscations, expenses, and a demonstration of the insufficiency of total annual income. Her table put the government literally in the middle of things. It showed Santa Clara coming out ahead—but the sum was not large enough for the support of the nuns, argued Abbess María Morales. Income (8,708 pesos, 5 reales), reduced under the terms of the 1825 decree, was about twice as much as expenses (4,305 pesos), most of which had to do with the upkeep of the church and the rituals performed there and the salaries of "dependents." That left just over 4,400 pesos to be distributed among fifty-five nuns, meaning each got less than 2 reales a day with which to support herself (and anyone else who lived with her), "which . . . is absolutely inadequate to cover the cost of their food and clothing. And given that this income must also satisfy additional new Government Exactions, and is paid almost in its totality by the tenants in foodstuffs at high prices, there is not the least doubt that this sum is but a figment."

The nuns bitterly resented the unprecedented intrusion of government in their affairs. By 1829, Santa Catalina's prioress was lodging vivid complaints with the bishop against her convent's state-appointed administrator, Don Mariano Arrambide. She called him immoral, saying he had provided the nuns with nothing but bread to eat for two months: "Can Your Grace believe we have subsisted this long on mere rations of bread? This is what is happening, and this impious man wants us to live by miracles, and all that our insistence and complaints about our miserable situation get for us is anger and scolding from the Ecónomo."[45] Apparently she was not alone in her complaints. In 1830, the government relented, agreeing to turn the management of the regular orders' affairs back over to the church.[46] By that time, however, the Peruvian state had become deeply involved in the workings of social reproduction in Cuzco, and the nuns were far from seeing the last of national and local officials' attempts to penetrate into and control their business affairs.

"Tráficos Indecorosos" and Redefined Relationships

Secularization was (and is) extremely complicated, full of ambiguities and seeming oppositions: rejection and attraction, indifference and great intensity, believers, unbelievers. Certainly its reflection in Cuzco can be seen in debtors' willingness to sever the close ties their ancestors had established with the city's monastic houses, as well as in the beginnings of new, state-sponsored institutions like the Colegio de Educandas and the Sociedad de Beneficencia. In Peru and elsewhere, processes of secularization and nation-building were profoundly connected, involving the deliberate attenuation of old practices and the creation of new symbols, allegiances, institutions, and practices— national anthems, icons, congresses, and much else besides. People of all kinds participated in a multifaceted project of reworking (not necessarily abandoning) the frameworks and language of their relationships. Secularization was perhaps most closely expressed in economic terms by those who, like the nuns, felt it most: they anatomized it in tables, summed it up in figures, tried to record its impact (in the hope of someday reversing it).

Secularization certainly had other aspects as well, harder to find committed to paper. That fewer people were sending their daughters to the convents reflects more than the nuns' state of penury. It bespeaks the nuns' loss of "autoridad," of local people's reverence and respect. Because the Clares and Dominicans in particular no longer seemed prayerful and pure, but worldly and grasping, cuzqueños saw reflected in them a convincing portrait of their own painful decline. Some, like Eustaquio de Rebolledo, reacted in anger. Perhaps the sharpest image of the strikingly diminished place the conventos grandes occupied by 1826 comes from Rebolledo's outraged letter of March 10 to the "Señores of the Illustrious Municipality" of Cuzco. He charged the Clares and Dominicans with running a vicious criminal conspiracy, a traffic in women:

> It has come to my attention that the Nuns of Santa Clara and Santa Catalina are holding servants from local Houses in their Monasteries on the pretext of correction, as well as others who are younger and bought from persons who steal them and sell them to the Nuns, who take advantage of their labor without paying them wages, supposing that the former are prisoners and the latter slaves. . . . The servants sent [to the convents] on the pretext of correction, are . . . condemned to be the victims of the Nuns' fury, and the torments they suffer—although they are not delinquents, nor were they tried and sentenced to such a hell—go unheard. The others are children who have been fooled and seduced by the heinous agents of the monasteries, who make the girls over to the Nuns at different prices as though they could be sold. These same criminals, if they fall out with the Nuns or do not settle on a price, look for outsiders, especially people from Arequipa, to whom they sell [the girls]. Humanity is outraged to see such horrendous crimes tolerated, and nature itself groans to see her children suffer. . . . [S]uch depraved behavior is as criminal as it is contrary to a free government like our own, which the Almighty has granted us.[47]

For Rebolledo, nuns had become the very source of corruption of Cuzco's young women, a locus of depravity. Under cover of the pretext of "vigilant conservation of the order of families," the nuns actually sold local girls into slavery! Who would want to send an innocent daughter to such a place? Rebolledo sought a remedy for this monstrous evil from a new source of authority: the municipal Cuzco government he saw as God-given and free. His charges were taken seriously enough that he succeeded in obtaining an inspection of Santa Clara and Santa Catalina by local authorities. In June 1826, the municipality and "Fathers of the Fatherland" received a report recommending "the expulsion of old, corrupt secular women, who exist in copious numbers, and are maintained for no good reason," as well as the expulsion of servants, "who with their children on their backs, full of worldly maxims, roil the precious harmony of the cloisters." The authors also recommended that only schoolgirls from ages seven to twelve be allowed to remain inside the cloisters.

This was hardly the nightmarish state depicted by Rebolledo. The inspectors decided it was the servants who were at fault, not the nuns. Rebolledo was not alone in his suspicions, however—nor was he the first to accuse the nuns of stealing servants. In 1800, Doña María Ana Fernández had complained that Ignacia, a "cholita" she had raised, had been stolen from Fernández's house and had somehow wound up inside Santa Catalina with the nun Martina Bejarano. Fernández had succeeded in getting the prioress to return Ignacia to her, but Ignacia had been stolen again and taken to live with the same nun as before.[48] By 1826 such charges had become sufficiently common to convince Rebolledo of a conspiracy. Allegations that the Clares and Dominicans stole women were repeated in subsequent years, and seem as good a reflection as any of the nuns' desperate need for labor and of their slipping status in the eyes of cuzqueños.

Fresh rumors of scandal in the cloisters must have spread in 1852 after the abbess of Santa Clara complained about a routine inspection. The presiding official reported in detail about his discovery: "the arbitrary imprisonment of nine girls, who were found shut inside an oven and some rooms." Although the abbess and other high-ranking nuns had tried to distract his attention, he and a fellow inspector had nevertheless heard denunciations of the girls' imprisonment and ordered the girls released. "Most of them," it turned out, "had been stolen from their pueblos, and from the houses of their parents, to be made to serve the nuns with hard labor as though they were prisoners, which moved us to decree their liberty." His companion added that "the nuns know that the periodic inspections of Monasteries are practiced to prevent those houses, exclusively dedicated to serving God, from forcibly holding women . . . converting said houses into workshops of forced labor that parody the old obrajes."[49]

Obrajes were hated colonial sweatshops, symbols of oppression and lack of liberty. That Santa Clara and Santa Catalina could be likened to obrajes shows how far the nuns had fallen in some people's esteem:

their convents might represent unfreedom. For centuries the nuns had represented (among other things) refuge from abuse, a place of safety for women fleeing violence. Now the nuns stood accused of committing abuse themselves. Convents had received female prisoners over the years, too, but before the nineteenth century no one seems to have suspected the nuns of deviously fabricating "prisoners" to serve them. They had been trusted to keep their categories of women straight without outside supervision.[50]

Were the nuns actually doing anything differently than they were before? Not if we attend to their version of what was happening. The 1856 case of a maid named Catalina Flores suggests that some "thefts" may have materialized when people used the convents strategically to resolve disputes over labor. The prioress of Santa Catalina, accused by a man named Quevedo of holding Catalina Flores improperly, claimed that Flores had fled to Santa Catalina after her mistress Doña María Fronio had reprimanded her, and that Fronio had asked the nuns to take Flores in until she could be returned to her mother. The matter had turned controversial (by the prioress's telling) only because Quevedo had decided to accuse the nuns of wrongdoing in order to acquire the girl as his servant instead.[51] To keep such incidents from occurring, diocesan authorities sent a circular to all Cuzco's convents and beaterios instructing them not to receive depositadas or to hold any women against their will without clear authorization from the Palacio Episcopal.[52]

One thing seems clear enough: by midcentury, struggling members of Cuzco's elite, its *gente decente*, were engaged in a fierce competition for the labor of servant girls. Certainly the Clares and Dominicans felt a pressing need for servants' labor to support them—something the authorities consistently failed to recognize or acknowledge. The "copious" numbers of secular women who in 1826 looked to inspectors like they were being "maintained for no good reason" were in all likelihood doing what beatas did: going and coming, rounding up small jobs to do, and assisting the nuns with their labor. Convent assets generated only a fraction of what a nun needed to support herself (much less anyone else). Thus the nuns strenuously resisted all attempts to take their servants away: when inspectors tried to remove the servants from Santa Catalina in 1826, the Dominicans successfully prevented them.

By midcentury, matters had reached an impasse. People criticized the nuns' handling of their servants, officially and unofficially, yet the nuns refused to do without them. So complaints—even full-blown conspiracy theories — kept surfacing regularly. All the while, the number of cloistered nuns began to dwindle as convent resources continued to shrink. Where once Contreras y Valverde had seen hundreds of people, now there were only dozens. By the 1860s, the number of professed nuns in Santa Clara had dropped from fifty-five to only twenty; Santa Catalina had seventeen professed nuns, and Santa Teresa eighteen.[53] Even the relatively austere Carmelites seem to have been relying heavily on the labor of servants; by this time, they had about as many servants as nuns.

The convents themselves began shrinking, too. By 1853 the city's managers had concluded that it would be in the public interest to demolish a large portion of the premises of Santa Catalina. They argued that the city's "comfort, beauty, and decency" would be best served by eliminating "the lower part" of the convent, because to do so would eliminate a narrow bend in the alley outside, which had become "a bin of filth and uninhabitable, and a regular gathering place for evildoers . . . [such that] no one will pass by there after seven o'clock at night, and people feel obliged to go two or three blocks out of their way, no matter how urgent or necessary their business." In short, city managers wanted a straight, clean street. "Moreover," they adduced on behalf of their proposed project, "this part of the Monastery is not its property but that of individuals who sell [it] to those who want to live as *Seglaras*; at present it is completely ruined and uninhabitable. Although one way or another it is private property," they noted, "nevertheless it should not be so respected as to say that as property of the Church it can only be changed after legal requisites are obeyed."[54]

Not surprisingly, the Dominicans were quick to denounce this plan as "an attack on the inviolability of sacred things," expressing their hope that the prefect would be pious enough to ignore it. Why should the nuns lose a large part of their convent to remove one offending bend in the street outside?

If it is so easy to demolish even convents for purposes of beautification, why do the City Managers not ask to demolish the San José inn, or the houses of Dr. Artajona, Don Mariano León Velasco, the Fernández family, or the countless other houses that are still private property, and whose alleyways are longer, narrower, and more filthy and dangerous? Doubtless because property should be respected; but as they allege, without proof, that the lower part of the Monastery belongs to particular people and is outside the requisites of the law regarding alienation of church property, we must inform them this is untrue. . . . As for the small alleyway being a gathering place for Evildoers, we have to say that most of the city is comprised of even longer, narrower, dirtier passageways; guards and gendarmes have been placed in the alley to prevent trouble, and the Monastery pays them two pesos a month.[55]

The Dominicans went on to cite the most recent legal codes on their own behalf. They warned that if the proposal were enacted they would be reduced to living "with their garbage inside their cells." Their convent was already smaller than all the others, they argued, and "with the infinite exactions since the time of the King" they had become too poor even to construct burial niches for themselves. The nuns even employed the same strategy used by their remote predecessors centuries earlier to gain a firm place for themselves in Cuzco, drawing on their convent's resonant connection to the Inca past: "[I]n the part they want to demolish stood the old temple of the Acllas." [56]

With this defensive barrage Santa Catalina seems to have won the battle of 1853 against city officials. The convent apparently lost ground at some point, however: it no longer extends south as far as the street that in 1853 marked one of its limits, the Pampa de Maruri. Years later the Clares would lose terrain to the city of Cuzco as well. The fruit orchard enclosed within their convent's walls would eventually become part of the municipal marketplace. When in 1922 the abbess of Santa Clara finally reached a negotiated settlement with municipal officials to prevent further "dismemberments" of her convent, she did not trust their word, and she immediately sought permission to build houses on convent property bordering the municipal market. Her object, she told diocesan authorities, was "to place a considerable barrier against new expropriations the city government intends to make on our land across from the Market." [57]

As mother superiors waged this kind of block-by-block battle against city authorities, their cloisters were literally falling apart. In 1860 the abbess of Santa Clara alerted the diocese that the dome of her convent's church needed reinforcement, as it was threatening to collapse. Cracks were opening in the buildings of the first interior patio, and "all the rest of the convent is crumbling." Income had fallen to 6,893 pesos a year.[58] This was clearly not enough to pay for the urgently needed repairs, and nine years later her successor wrote to inform the

A busy, narrow pedestrian street running alongside Santa Catalina, probably the one that concerned municipal officials in 1853. Photo by K. Burns.

diocese that the cloister surrounding the convent's second patio had collapsed.[59] Meanwhile, the income of the Dominican nuns had fallen to only 3,960 pesos annually.[60]

City government may have been the only expanding institution in Cuzco during these difficult years. The city itself was generally dwindling and crumbling like the convents. Decline was, by all accounts, increasingly serious and evident in Cuzco during the middle decades of the nineteenth century.[61] The city's population fell by almost half from the 1790s to the 1860s as many people migrated to the countryside in an effort to sustain themselves and their families.[62] Economically, the Cuzco region continued to stagnate. If Cuzco had possessed mines, guano, or some other major attraction, investors might have beaten a path over the mountains to it, but the region held few enticements by comparison with other, more accessible places. Arequipa, more conveniently located for internal and foreign markets, easily surpassed Cuzco in the nineteenth century as a center of commerce, and Cuzco shifted from being an economic satellite of Potosí to being a disgruntled dependent of Arequipan commercial houses, which sent in their representatives to do business.[63] Isolated and turned in upon itself, Cuzco struck observers as the picture of decay, merely a remnant of the grand, imperial Inca capital they had expected, a home to nostalgia and faded glory.

Still the encroachments of the resource-poor state continued. The final blow to the censos on which monastic houses had depended for centuries came in 1864. On December 15, President Juan Antonio Pezet proclaimed a law facilitating the cancellation of censos and capellanías, characterizing the law as a blow struck for "the absolute extinction of all kinds of entailment, opposed by their nature to the development of the nation's wealth," and on behalf of "the free alienation of property."[64] The new initiative was an adjusted version of the old consolidación. All censos could be paid off at a small fraction of their value: one-fourth in the case of urban properties, one-sixth for rural properties. Debtors were to pay the relevant amounts of cash directly to the government (in Cuzco, to the departmental treasury), which would assume annual payments to their creditors. In theory, creditors would not lose any income; they would simply get it from the government. But spokesmen for the church foresaw disaster and railed against the new law, calling it "unfair in its essence, unconstitutional in its provisions, and antieconomical in its results."[65]

This time no one thought (or ventured) to appeal to their governors' piety. So little remained of the spiritual economy—the densely meaningful, long-term relationships by which families and convents had once produced and reproduced themselves—that even church leaders had dropped their appeals to piety and argued solely on legal and economic grounds. But their protests were of no use. After the law went into effect, many propertied cuzqueños rushed to take advantage of its attractive terms. By 1867, the treasury of the Department of Cuzco had collected several thousand pesos and formally canceled numerous obligations cuzqueños had once paid to Cuzco's monasteries and convents. That year, four of Cuzco's monastic orders submitted detailed

Table 5 Report on canceled censos, 1867

	Value of Canceled Debts	Amount received by Cuzco Treasury	Interest Paid Out
Franciscans	17,121 soles	2,953 soles	0
Mercedarians	26,036 soles	5,025 soles	0
Carmelites	16,700 pesos (est.)	—	0
Clares	74,783 pesos	—	0

Sources: Archivo Arzobispal del Cuzco, C-XXIX, 1, 13, "Razón de los fundos que se han redimido pertenecientes al convento de San Francisco," March 15, 1867; C-XXIX, 1, 1, letter of March 15, 1867 (regarding the Mercedarians); C-XXIV, 1, 15, letters of March 12–15, 1867 (regarding the Carmelites and Clares).

Note: The sol was adopted as the republic's new unit of currency in 1863, replacing the peso at a rate of 80 to 100.

accounts of the canceled censos that had formerly brought them income.[66] They had yet to see a single payment from the government (see Table 5).

In 1867, the year Mexican politicians enacted a massive disentailment and sale of church property, news reached Cuzco that a similar proposal was making its way through the Peruvian Congress.[67] The archbishop of Lima, José Sebastián Goyeneche, alerted the bishop of Cuzco and urged him to write to Lima in protest. Seriously alarmed, Goyeneche warned his colleague that the proposed secularization of all church property, if enacted, would be "a mortal blow to the Church."[68] The archbishop himself wrote a lengthy and eloquent defense against those "modern reformers" who would "reduce the Church to slavery."[69] Unlike the situation in Mexico, however, the Peruvian conjuncture did not produce a decisive liberal victory over mortmain. The Peruvian church managed to keep its right to dominio. Still, the 1864 law regarding censos and capellanías was a serious setback for Cuzco's convents and monasteries, coming as it did after decades of falling income and general deterioration.

The old bonds of the spiritual economy were completely frayed. The nuns could no longer entertain the notion that things would revert to the way they had been once the crisis had passed and debtors had recovered. Local support had changed, dwindling to such an extent that the government could do almost what it liked to the convents, unopposed. People would still come to the church to pray, and perhaps stop by the locutorio occasionally to visit, but the old style of forging powerful, symbiotic alliances was gone. By the 1860s it appears that the nuns of Santa Clara and Santa Catalina were no longer in the business of raising and educating large numbers of children. Archival traces of girls, infants, and bustling households all but disappear. The nuns did still receive the occasional depositada; correction thus remained part of their socially reproductive role (even though the walls of Santa Clara were quite literally falling down and could hardly be expected to contain anyone). But convents had little to loan and were able to play only a very limited role where credit was concerned. The amounts they took in on their rentals, leases, and remaining censos yielded only a small fraction of former income. From time to time, in order to raise cash for operating expenses, the nuns resorted to selling the precious objects that adorned their churches and cells.[70] The nuns continued to live in private cells—attended by their servants, taking meals in their own quarters rather than in a common refectory—while their cloisters crumbled around them.

Given this grim context, the Clares and Dominicans began to examine measures they had long refused to consider. The Clares listened carefully when in 1859 a priest conducting spiritual exercises in the convent exhorted them to observe the common life—to live and eat together, drawing their sustenance from a common pool of resources and admitting no secular women into their cloisters. That year they took an initial step toward vida común, asking the diocese to remove two married women they had been ordered to detain.[71] Gradually the idea of reform gained adherents among the Dominicans as well. Elsewhere in Peru, in the late eighteenth century, the common life had been imposed on conventos grandes rather violently from the outside (with chaotic, mixed results). In Cuzco, however, the common life was pushed only sporadically, as in 1826, without the kind of serious campaigns waged by ecclesiastical authorities in Lima and Arequipa. Reform seems to have occurred gradually from within as the nuns contemplated their convents' slow, painful decline.[72] After significant midcentury turmoil over "stolen" servants, the nuns of Santa Clara and Santa Catalina had to face the obvious: not only did cuzqueños not support them as before, but many actually opposed, suspected, and accused them.

Penury (and the resulting bitterness over "stolen" servants) thus accomplished what earlier generations of critics and reformers had found impossible. In 1861, the abbess of Santa Clara indicated to Cuzco's ecclesiastical authorities that a majority of the nuns wanted to adopt the common life, a step that only a few of the most elderly nuns opposed.[73] A year later, the prioress of Santa Catalina wrote that all but two members of her community had also voted in favor of reorganization and reform. Prioress Dominga de la Encarnación observed with regret that "from time immemorial, the spirit of fraternity and Common life" had been absent in her community, whose members were living "dispersed and disunified, because of the necessity to provide ourselves with food to eat, neglecting the duties we vowed to uphold." Nevertheless, her convent still had enough assets to support its "diminutive personnel." The nuns wanted to fulfill their founders' intentions:

> [T]he monastery was founded with the pious intention that we observe the common life, since it is equipped with a refectory, dormitory, workroom, and other spaces destined exclusively for that purpose. Lately the rations we receive in rural produce, far from satisfying our natural necessities, work against us and distract us from the service of God, because we are obliged to conduct an indecorous traffic in these articles. Thus we want and desire promptly to reinstate [our rule] and reform ourselves, formally and materially, observing our rule as far as it is within our power to do so, with only the changes that present circumstances demand.[74]

For the nuns, spiritual and economic goals were still inextricably connected. They may well have seen their hard times as an admonishment from their divine bridegroom for neglecting their spiritual duties and the "primordial" rigor of their rules. The reform they had decided upon was carried out gradually over the next several years. In the case of Santa Catalina, the priest designated by the diocese to begin the reform laid out a detailed plan in 1862 for the removal of "obstacles" to the common life. His plan included everything from indemnifying the owners of private cells to walling up with adobes the windows overlooking streets along the convent's perimeter.[75] Whether any servants or other secular women were expelled from the cloisters is unclear. Since reform occurred gradually, the remaining secular women probably left when they could find a place for themselves in the city outside. Some servants may have taken simple vows and become lay sisters in order to stay within convent walls.

In the 1860s, then, the nuns of Cuzco not only rebuilt their walls as best they could, but reinforced their commitment to enclosure, deciding to renew the strictness of their religious observance and turn their backs on the importunateness and impiety of "el siglo." By the early 1870s, the Dominicans had reorganized their living arrangements to accord with the requirements of the common life. They ate meals together in the refectory and drew their sustenance from a common source, no longer depending on their own particular incomes and assistants. The Clares had completed their reform by the mid-1880s.[76] The common life presumably offered economies of scale, and the decline in the number of convent inhabitants made the day-to-day operations of Santa Clara and Santa Catalina more manageable. Now these communities held roughly the same number of women as Santa Teresa, where the common life had been observed all along (and which diocesan authorities had consistently praised as a "plantel de virtudes").

In short, the nuns of Cuzco became recognizably "modern" cloistered nuns, living communally, withdrawn from "el siglo." For the Clares and Dominicans, adopting the common life in the 1870s and 1880s meant coming full circle to the kind of life they imagined their distant predecessors had led: a life in accordance with the founders' prescribed rigor. Antonio Arbiol (author of *La religiosa instruida*) would have been delighted. For that matter, Saint Augustine would have been, too: fortifying the City of God was much more important than any mundane project.

Conclusions

As the nuns withdrew to concentrate on their prayers, convent locutorios and entryways that for centuries had been sites of busy activity began to see much less use. Servants no longer streamed out of the convent entryways on a multiplicity of errands; after the reforms of the 1870s and 1880s, those who remained in the nuns' service led much more rigorously cloistered lives. Nor did cuzqueños approach the convent grilles as frequently as before. Their daughters no longer spent their childhoods in the cloisters; their sisters, wives, and widowed mothers no longer boarded there. The government in Lima had made it almost irresistibly attractive for families to divest themselves of the censos they paid into the convents' coffers, and many had done so. People still came to the locutorio to satisfy what remained of their financial obligations to the nuns, and approached the torno to leave valuables for safekeeping or to buy sweets and pastries. They joined the nuns in praying for the republic to survive its wars, and in various other ways they supported them and participated with them in a common sphere of ritual observance.[77] But the amount of contact between the nuns of Cuzco and secular people was much reduced. So, too, was the convent's significance in the lives of the city's people.

Cuzqueños now looked elsewhere for many things they had once sought from the city's cloistered nuns. Between 1825 and 1860, the education of elite local girls had been entrusted to other women and institutions: the new republican girls' school; the Colegio de Educandas, founded by Bolívar; the schools opened by a number of new teaching orders, made up of active rather than contemplative nuns. Reform of Cuzco's convents meant that not only schoolgirls but all seglares were disallowed inside the cloisters: widows, prisoners, refugees, and visitors in general could enter only under special circumstances. Financially the convents had also been displaced from activities to which they had long been central. Most people now sought credit and a place to keep their cash from the merchant houses and the new banks that were starting to do business in Cuzco by the late nineteenth century.[78]

Moreover, the convents no longer offered cuzqueños a mirror in which to gauge their city's standing and authority. Like the widow Doña Josefa Holgado decades earlier, Cuzco's well-to-do citizens sought to make their city as glorious as possible, but the interiors of the city's churches were no longer as likely to be the focus of their energies and outlays. They looked elsewhere for a sense of their city's luster and importance: to the magnificence of municipal functions like the feting of the Great Liberator Bolívar, for example. They celebrated the adornment of their city's plazas with patriotic monuments, and saw convincing evidence of their municipality's modernity in the new marketplace rising from what had once been the orchard of Santa Clara. New values were expressed by cuzqueños in new keywords: hygiene, order, and progress. Municipal authorities did what they could to help the city and its citizens achieve the goal of becoming modern.

Emblematic of this historic shift in beliefs and priorities—a product, as we have seen, of several decades' worth of changes, from the streets and salons of Europe to those of Cuzco—was the 1853 move by city officials to demolish half of Santa Catalina in order to straighten a street. Their proposal succinctly conveys an attitude toward church property that would have been unthinkable in earlier centuries: the inside of a convent mattered far less than the hygiene of the alleyway outside. Seizing church property seemed to these citizens only a minor obstacle. Little wonder local officials were particularly unwelcome in the nuns' visiting parlors. When a city inspector came around to Santa Clara in 1889, intent on determining the degree of good order and hygiene ("policia y aseo") within the cloisters, the abbess refused to reveal anything and curtly dismissed him: "I need not respond when there are canonical laws and conciliar dispositions to uphold and respect."[79]

Ironically, at a material level the nuns survived republicanism by becoming pensioners of the very government they were trying so hard to ignore. The Peruvian state which had so aggressively disrupted the nuns' long-term financial arrangements, wresting away the principals of their censos and capellanías, provided (albeit with irregularity) much of the convents' income. In 1872, for example, Santa Clara received almost half its total income from the National Credit Bureau in Lima.[80] The nuns had no choice but to accept this arrangement—but that did not mean they had to receive government officials or honor all their importunate demands.[81]

Instead, the nuns concentrated on leading stainless lives of prayer. More and more, the cloistered women of Cuzco led lives in accordance with the dictum that a nun should be "in this world but not of it." They embraced the common life, embraced their rule, and withdrew deep into their cloisters. And to this day, when they appear before the grilles of their locutorios, they see whom they want to see.

Epilogue

By the time I arrived in Cuzco to do research on the city's cloistered convents, just over a century had elapsed since the Clares and the Dominicans had decided to adopt vida común, the common life many people now assume the nuns always lived. In 1989 the communities of Santa Clara, Santa Catalina, and Santa Teresa still held around two dozen professed women apiece—roughly the same number they had reached a century earlier after many decades of decline. The way to speak to the nuns at any length in 1989 was still the same as it was a century (or more) earlier: to sit before the grilles of their locutorios.[1] And the nuns were still wary of outsiders, especially those attempting to gain access to their cloisters or detailed knowledge of their affairs.

The Clares' attitude toward outsiders had hardened into an almost insuperable defensiveness. The nineteenth-century reform movement that had led the nuns to stop up even their highest windows with adobes had also reinforced their reserve with anyone unfamiliar to them, anyone not related by kinship, long proximity, or ecclesiastical connections. A 1945 petition I came across in the diocesan archive showed me clearly enough that at midcentury Cuzco's municipal inspectors were still faring poorly in their approaches to the nuns. Abbess María Jesús de la Cruz Urquizo, convinced that a Communist mayor wanted to spy on her community, asked her prelate to deceive the mayor on her behalf. In Urquizo's prose the verb "to inspect"— inspeccionarse—became almost an epithet, and the mayor a threatening Cold Warrior intent on deceitful penetration:

> [T]he Mayor desires to enter our cloisters for the purpose of inspecting whether we are really doing construction in the

section of the sheds which belongs to the Monastery, and to impede the entry of these Communist gentlemen, who under the pretext of informing themselves about construction work inspect the limited space that remains to us. . . . I beg of your paternal kindness that you dissemble for us if you can, telling the Mayor that to enter these cloisters requires license from the Papal Legation; that should discourage him and stop his demands.[2]

I had other things in mind and hoped to do better, but before long my own worldly proposal to the Clares would be rejected (in terms another researcher may one day come across in the diocesan archive). In the locutorio of Santa Clara I told Abbess Juana Marín Farfán that I wanted to write a history of the Clares' institutional past, offering to organize and microfilm old records and generally to set the record straight. At first she was interested: she needed someone who could read the convent's old papers, since she was in the midst of trying to prove Santa Clara held valid title to a property on the city's central plaza. On my next visit to the locutorio I brought historian Antonio Acosta to help me. The abbess produced the document she wanted us to transcribe so that she could enter it at the municipal registry of deeds: a sixteenth-century act of donation. In our astonishment we set about writing down its contents for her. After more conversations, however, the abbess decided not to grant me any further access to her community's archives, telling me that it did not matter what people wrote or said about her convent. She and the other nuns, she said, cared only about "doing God's work."

What was a historian to do? I went to Santa Catalina, this time on an errand for a friend who needed a document delivered to the nuns. In the Dominicans' locutorio in 1990 and 1991, as I gradually got to know the entire community, I began bringing a laptop computer and transcribing old, fading records (most of which I could also have consulted in the public archives, had I known in which notary's papers I should find them): the founders' wills, a list of schoolgirls, and countless censos al quitar. I made an index for the nuns of the contents of their calfskin-bound volumes of documents. My small computer and the prioress's good-humored interest in the ways it might serve her community gave us something around which to form a friendly relationship in the locutorio. I saw others doing so as well: people whose relatives were in the cloisters, or who came to the torno to bring the nuns gifts of food at harvesttime or to purchase the wafers the nuns made in their sala de labores or the tiny marzipan figures they fashioned in their kitchen.

Over time, our exchanges grew more elaborate. When I traveled to Texas, the nuns gave me astounding quantities of carefully packaged *animalitos* of marzipan, along with the address of cloistered Dominican nuns in Lufkin whom they wanted me to contact, and I returned to Cuzco bearing them news and a box of various items from the nuns of Lufkin. One day the prioress jokingly asked me if I could arrange to get her convent a small car. Instead, along with a friend, I accompanied a nun from Arequipa on a specially arranged tour of the Inca ruins overlooking the city: the prioress knew that the nun was homesick and needed some refreshment, and she arranged for a local priest to drive us to one of the city's most beautiful vantage points. Some time later, we arranged a showing inside the locutorio of videotaped images of the Corpus Christi procession as it wound its way through the thronged and petal-strewn streets outside the convent. The nuns were rapt as they watched the saint of each parish borne laboriously by faithful cuzqueños on its centuries-old way: each year the nuns could hear but not see this elaborate and fervent spiritual event. Now the saints were processing through their locutorio.

Had I gone to study the convents of Mexico or Spain instead, I might never have entered a locutorio. Because of the massive liberal expropriations of church property carried out during the nineteenth century in those countries, their national archives contain reams of church papers of all kinds, including many convent archives. In Cuzco, however, necessarily more elaborate, unpredictable transactions are required of anyone wanting to research the church, and these have their benefits as well as their drawbacks. As I made my way slowly through various kinds of records and learned to have a comfortable conversation before the grille, I realized I was participating in very old kinds of exchanges. And I gradually realized that the stakes (so easily trivialized in 1990) were very small, relative to what they had once been.

In short, I had entered a habitus—not a timeless place (as I had known), but a product of historically specific actors, dispositions, and actions. Gradually I started to be able to imagine why these exchanges had over time lost their charge, to imagine the rich multiplicity of meanings they had held for cuzqueños and why the cloistered nuns of Cuzco had become so withdrawn. For centuries their aristocratic predecessors had been leading actors at the center of Peru's colonial stage. Yet shifting practices—indissociably spiritual and economic, involving beliefs and investments of various kinds—had displaced and decentered them and their institutions almost to the point of disappearance. In Cuzco, the years from 1720 to 1880 were a time of almost uninterrupted decline for the city's cloistered convents, with especially painful jolts around 1780–82, 1804–6, 1825–26, and 1864–65. About the time the exquisitely ironic *costumbrista* Ricardo Palma had started to embalm cloistered nuns in his *Tradiciones peruanas* as part of a quaint colonial past, the nuns and their male monastic counterparts were contemplating the very real prospect that the Peruvian government would close their monastic houses entirely. It did not happen that way, but by around 1860 decades of growing criticism had made their monastic extinction appear distinctly possible. The nuns of Cuzco decided on the solution of reform and withdrawal: a determination that can been seen as a flight backward into archaic monastic practices—or, alternatively, as their own declaration of independence from "el siglo."

Yet I found it impossible to mark the "end" of the spiritual economy of Cuzco. The city's most prosperous families still cultivate good relations with the city's cloistered nuns, even though the spiritual and economic goals of cuzqueños have long since been split apart, and the means for satisfying them greatly diversified. Many of the practices most basic to the old spiritual economy of Cuzco still exist, or did until very recently. Until the 1940s, the convents continued to collect income on a few outstanding censos and to loan money: in 1943, for example, a woman named Cleofé Tisoc borrowed 10,000 soles from the Carmelites because they offered her a better interest rate than her bank.[3] As late as the 1950s, local women were still expected to bring dowry on professing their solemn vows.[4] And the nuns continue to draw much of their income from renting and leasing properties over which their convents have exercised dominio for decades, even centuries. In these and in countless other small ways, the cloistered nuns of Santa Clara, Santa Catalina, and Santa Teresa still play a role in the lives of the families and society around them.

The spiritual economy of Cuzco did not simply end. Rather, cuzqueños themselves gradually marginalized it, while still participating in its workings, as they do to this day. Perhaps soon, like some of their monastic counterparts elsewhere, the cloistered nuns of Cuzco will themselves take up computers and take an interest in writing their own versions of this story. They do not lack for rich material.[5] The distinctions they draw will of course differ from mine. In the meantime, I offer my version and my part in a story that continues in the now quiet spaces of Cuzco's locutorios.

Appendix 1

Santa Clara's First Entrants

Name	Parents	Father's Rank or Occupation	Date of Entry	Board (pesos/yr.)	Dowry	Outcome
Isabel Clara	[Alonso Díaz]	Encomendero	?	130 p. corrientes	950 p. and 170 cattle	Professed (1562) as Isabel de Santa Clara
Francisca de la Concepción	[Alonso Díaz]	Encomendero	?	130 p. corrientes	—	Removed
Doña María de Betanzos	Juan de Betanzos; Angelina Yupanqui	Encomendero	1560	** 11 milk cows	—	Married
*Ana	[Diego Fernández]	?	1560	20 p. ensayados	200 p. ensayados	Professed (1564) as Ana de San Joaquín
*Inés de Casalla	[?]	?	1560	33 p., 2 tomines, 8 granos	400 p. ensayados	?
*Luisa de Narváez	[Pedro Narváez]	"Vecino"; encomendero?	1556?	40 p. ensayados and 18 fanegas corn	—	Married
Ana del Puerto	Juan del Puerto	?	1560	50 p. ensayados	750 p. ensayados	Professed (1564)
Juana del Puerto	Juan del Puerto	?	1560	50 p. ensayados	750 p. ensayados	Professed (1564)
Leonor	Antonio García	?	1560	40 p. corrientes	—	Died (1562)
Beatriz Muñoz	Muñoz	"Criado de Garcilaso de la Vega"	1560	60 p. corrientes	?	?
Beatriz Hernández	Antonio Hernández	"Trata en Potosí" (merchant)	1560	80 p. corrientes	?	?

Name	Parents	Father's Rank or Occupation	Date of Entry	Board (pesos/yr.)	Dowry	Outcome
Juana Pérez	Antonio Pérez	"Criado de dho. Monesterio"	1560	70 p.	?	?
Catalina de San José	?	?	1560	**350 p. ensayados	—	Married
*Beatriz ("morena pobre")	[?]	?	1560	None	—	Given to Doña Petronila de Cáceres
*Ana	[?]	?	1560	None	None	?
Luisa Pizarro	Mateo Pizarro	"Está en Chile"	1560?	None	—	Given to Catalina Maldonado
Beatriz Arias	[Bernardino Arias]	Died at battle of Villacurí	1560	None	None	Professed (1570) as Beatriz de la Encarnación
María de Medina	[Medina]	Died at battle of Guarina	1560	None	—	Given to Doña Beatriz Retes, abbess's daughter
Ana de Medina	[Medina]	Died at battle of Guarina	1560	None	—	Given to Doña Beatriz Retes, abbess's daughter
Ana Téllez	Bernabé Picón	"Vecino"; encomendero?	?	None	—	Married

Name	Parents	Father's Rank or Occupation	Date of Entry	Board (pesos/yr.)	Dowry	Outcome
Elvira de Figueroa	[Gonzalo Picón]	?	?	None	—	Removed by Tinoco, her brother-in-law
Francisca de Balda	Antonio de Balda	"Está en los Charcas"	1561	None	—	Removed by her father
Isabel de Escobar	Escobar	"Un antiguo"	1561	None	—	Removed by her father
Queteria de Molina	Molina	"Pobre"	1561	None	—	Removed by her father
Catalina de Molina	Molina	"Pobre"	1561	None	—	Removed by her father
Gerónima	[?]	?	1561	None	—	Removed by Isabel de Porras
Francisca	[?]	?	1561	None	None	?
*Juana	[?]	?	1561	None	—	Removed by Francisca de Riveros
Ana de San Joaquín	Hernán González; [Spanish mother]	Smith	1561	None	—	Removed by parents
Ana de Alvarado	?	?	1561	**205 p. corrientes and 127 p. ensayados	?	?

Name	Parents	Father's Rank or Occupation	Date of Entry	Board (pesos/yr.)	Dowry	Outcome
Constanza García	Gerónimo García	Merchant	1560	40 p.	—	Removed by her father (1562)
Ana de Castro	[Antonio de Castro]	?	1561	**600 p.	—	Married to Francisco Manso, Spaniard (1562)
Isabel de Góngora	Góngora	Tailor	1560	100 p.	—	Married (ca. 1568)
Isabel de Béjar	Velasco de Béjar	?	1561	**100 sheep	100 sheep and 1 silver ingot	Professed as Gerónima de la Purificación
Isabel de Lemos	Gómez González	?	1561	35 p. ensayados	440 p. ensayados	Professed (1564) as Inés de Santa Clara
*Francisca Arias	[Bernardino Arias]	Died at battle of Villacurí	1561	None	—	Died in house of Pedro López
*María de Chávez	Francisco de Chávez	Encomendero?	1561	None	—	Married to Gaspar de Escobar, Spaniard (1561)
Catalina de Torres	Roberto Torres	Priest	1561	40 p. corrientes	—	Removed by her father
Isabel de Figueroa	García de Figueroa	?	1561	50 p. corrientes	—	Removed by her father

Name	Parents	Father's Rank or Occupation	Date of Entry	Board (pesos/yr.)	Dowry	Outcome
Doña Ana de Uceda	Diego de Uceda	Encomendero, La Paz	1562	**1,000 p. ensayados	1,000 p. ensayados	Professed (1564) as Doña Ana de la Concepción
Doña Luisa de Berrio	Diego de Uceda	Encomendero, La Paz	1562	**1,000 p. ensayados	1,000 p. ensayados	Professed (1564) as Doña Luisa de San Francisco
*Francisca de Marchena	"Un fulano Marchena"; Catalina, "natural de Guanico"	Encomendero?	1562	**400 p. ensayados	400 p. ensayados	Professed (1564) as Francisca de Santiago
*María de Hermosa	[Juan Rodríguez de Villalobos]	Encomendero	1562	100 p. corrientes	—	Married
Isabel González	García González	"El antiguo"	1563	**50 varas of cloth, 34 sheep, 102 fanegas of wheat	—	Removed by her father
*Catalina de los Angeles	?	?	1561	50 p.	500 p. ensayados	Professed (1564)
*Doña Beatriz Clara Coya	[Sayri Túpac]; Cusi Huarcay	El Inca	1563	?	—	Married to Martín García de Loyola
*Isabel de Tordesillas	[Tordesillas "de Arequipa"]	Died at battle of Guarina	1561	None	None	Professed as Isabel de los Angeles

Name	Parents	Father's Rank or Occupation	Date of Entry	Board (pesos/yr.)	Dowry	Outcome
Catalina Marcos	Marcos Alfonso	"Conquistador y pobre"	1563	30 p. and 12 fanegas of wheat	—	Removed by the chantre, her tutor
Ana Rodríguez	Alejo Rodríguez	Encomendero?	1562	None	—	Given to Doña Catalina de Retes, abbess's daughter
Beatriz Muñoz	Francisco Muñoz	Merchant	1563	50 p. corrientes	—	Removed by her father
Isabel Muñoz	Francisco Muñoz	Merchant	1563	50 p. corrientes	—	Removed by her father
*Luisa de Vargas	Hernando de Vargas	Encomendero, La Paz	1562	** 500 p. ensayados	500 p. ensayados	Professed
*Catalina de Santa Clara	"Un hombre portugués" en Abancay	?	1561	200 p. corrientes	?	?
Isabel Farel	Francisco Farel	?	1564	50 p. ensayados	—	Married (1571)
*Leonor Domínguez	Simón Godines	?	1564	60 p. ensayados	—	Removed by her father
María Orué	Pedro de Orué	Encomendero	1564	100 p. corrientes	100 cattle and 500 sheep	Professed

Name	Parents	Father's Rank or Occupation	Date of Entry	Board (pesos/yr.)	Dowry	Outcome
Leonor de la Trinidad ("española")	?	?	?	None	None	Professed
Magdalena de la Trinidad	Juan de San Miguel	Encomendero	?	**600 p. ensayados	600 p. ensayados	Professed
Clara de San Francisco ("española")	?	?	?	None	None	Professed
Doña María de la Visitación	Mancio Sierra de Leguizamo	Encomendero	?	** 300+ cattle	300+ cattle	Professed

Sources: "Libro original que contiene la fundación del monesterio de monxas de señora Sta. Clara desta cibdad del Cuzco; por el qual consta ser su patrono el insigne Cabildo, Justicia y Reximiento desta dicha cibdad: Año de 1560," ed. Domingo Angulo, Revista del Archivo Nacional del Perú 11 (1939), 55–95, 157–84; Archivo Departamental del Cusco, Protocolos Notariales, Juan de Pineda, 1656, ms. copy of the foundation book.

Note: Parents whose names are shown within square brackets were deceased; p. = pesos.

* = Brought to Santa Clara by someone other than parents.

** = Lump sum or quantity provided toward entrant's board in lieu of annual stipend (and which might become her dowry if she professed).

Appendix 2

Santa Clara's Holdings in 1582–86

Listed for 1582:

A lien (*censo*) on the store and house of Juan Arias Maldonado, for 142 pesos, 2 tomines ensayados annually;

A lien on the store and house of Francisco Mexía, for 71 pesos, 2 tomines ensayados annually;

A lien on the house of the priest Pedro Arias, for 57 pesos corrientes annually;

A lien payable by Don Francisco de Acuña, for 50 pesos ensayados annually;

A lien payable by the sons of Pedro de Urea, for 57 pesos corrientes annually;

A lien on the farm (*chácaras*) of Guancaro belonging to Juan Fernández Coronel, for 100 pesos ensayados;

A lien payable by Juan Alvarez Maldonado, for 107 pesos ensayados annually;

A second lien payable by Don Francisco de Acuña, for the principal of 1,000 pesos;

A lien on the house of Rodrigo de Esquivel, for 214 pesos, 2 tomines, payable in pesos corrientes;

A lien on the house of the "Comendador" Gerónimo Costilla, for 200 pesos corrientes;

A lien payable by Gerónimo Bote, for 50 pesos ensayados annually;

Income (*renta*) of 250 pesos ensayados annually, payable by the Indians of Juliaca;

Income of 284 pesos ensayados, 100 fanegas of maize, 80 fanegas of wheat, and 130 "birds" (*aves*) annually, payable by the Indians of "Suti" and "Cucuchiray";

Income of 130 pesos ensayados, 30 fanegas of maize, and 102 chickens and hens annually, payable by the Indians of "Corca";

A store that Alonso de Hinojosa left the convent, rented for 70 pesos corrientes annually;

Added to the 1582 list in 1586:

A lien on the property (*hacienda*) of "what's-his-name" (*fulano*) Porras, for 214 pesos, 2 tomines ensayados annually, payable in pesos corrientes;

A lien payable by Juan Gómez Ynga, for 200 pesos [corrientes] annually;

A lien on the farm (*chácara*) of Lamay, payable in 50 fanegas of flour annually;

A silver ingot (*barra de plata ensayada*) annually, in accordance with the will of Rodrigo de León;

A lien on the property (*haciendas*) of Pedro Vásquez, for 54 pesos ensayados annually;

A lien on the property that belonged to Hinojosa and became the city jail, for 18 pesos corrientes annually;

1 *topo* of alfalfa-growing land in Guancaro belonging to Alonso de Hinojosa;

A lien corresponding to the dowry of Ana de Vega, for 214 pesos, 2 tomines ensayados annually, payable in pesos corrientes;

A house in San Blas where the servants (*yanaconas*) of Santa Clara live;

A lien payable by Diego Quijano, for 107 pesos, 2 tomines ensayados annually;

A lien payable by Juan Gómez, for 200 pesos corrientes annually;

10,000 sheep and 199 head of cattle pastured in "el Collao" near Pucara;

A ranch (*estancia*) in Jaquijaguana with 152 head of cattle;

50 fanegas of wheat annually from the *chácara* of Lamay;

80 fanegas of wheat and 130 fanegas of maize, payable by the Indians of "Tambo" and "Corcora";

240 "birds";

A gristmill at "Sape";

Houses alongside the convent where the mayordomo lives.

Source: "Libro original," ed. Angulo, 176–81.

Appendix 3

The Founders

My lady Doña Lucía de Padilla, the founder of this monastery of Our Lady of the Remedies, advocation of our mother Saint Catherine of Siena, was from Antequera and of the Padillas, cousin of the *adelantado* Don Martín de Padilla, Count of Santa Gadea, his surnames Casillas, Chacones, O[−]ocones, Narváez and Ahumadas. She came to the city of Arequipa with her father or brother and a sister named Doña Beatriz de Casillas y Padilla along with the conquistador Juan de la Torre, *vecino de indios*. My lady Doña Lucía married Don Fernando de Ribera de los Perafanes, a conquistador and encomendero. In this marriage she had two children, Friar Antonio de Ribera of the Dominican Order and my lady the prioress, Doña Isabel de Padilla, our patron and founder. She married a second time to a Basque gentleman named Juan de San Juan. Her third marriage was to another gentleman named Pedro de Ahedo, with whom she had a son named Don Pedro de Ahedo whom she loved exceedingly well, and because of his death and her not having had any children with our founder Captain Gerónimo Pacheco, she decided to found this monastery. Her fourth husband, our founder, was a person of great authority and Christianity, as would be experienced in this city of Cuzco when he became its *corregidor*. My lady Doña Lucía was highly esteemed in the city of Arequipa, a lady of great pomp, jewels, and riches, with which she endowed the monastery. Living very austerely and dressing simply, she always attended matins because by day she attended to her business affairs. She did not take the habit until she was near death so that the King would not take her Indians, and thus she died a novice. Trusting God would give her life and so as not to lose the Indians, she died a novice like a saint, with great acts of contrition. She was very zealous of God's honor and was always an extremely Christian lady even while living in the world in the midst of such pomp and splendor. She did everything she could for the nuns, adorning the altars, and it could be seen long afterward how much she did for the churches. She was very devoted to the Company of Jesus and greatly assisted in its foundation in Arequipa, and after founding this monastery she gave the Jesuit school in Arequipa a vineyard in the valley of Churunga. Her death was deeply felt and mourned; she died in the year 1608.

She married her daughter, our prioress Doña Isabel de Padilla, in the city of La Paz to an elderly Basque gentleman and conquistador named Pedro Basáez, and they had a daughter who died young. Pedro Basáez also died, and because of his death her parents brought her back to their house in Arequipa. Then her stepfather Captain Gerónimo Pacheco was given the opportunity to become corregidor of this city of Cuzco, whereupon he and his wife, my lady Doña Lucía de Padilla, brought her to this city, where she decided to become a nun, and during the interim of his term as corregidor they sent for a bull and brief from the Pope so that she might take the habit and profess in one day, which His Holiness granted her. [Doña Isabel de Padilla] took the habit in the monastery of Santa Catalina de Sena in the city of Arequipa on the fifteenth of July in the year 1582 at the age of twenty-five. Later her prelates made her reformer of the monastery, and of the seventeen years she was there, she was prioress for ten. She did much to increase the monastery both spiritually and temporally, and was greatly loved and esteemed by all of the nuns. This was clear from the extremes to which they reportedly went when she left to found this monastery, as all of them wrote her letters full of love and affection, sending them all the way to this city. Because of the death of Don Pedro de Ahedo her mother, my lady Doña Lucía, decided to found this monastery and to give what she would have given her son and daughter-in-law to Our Lady of the Remedies. She started the monastery in her own house with the name of Our Lady of the Remedies because her son Don Pedro had died calling out to Our Lady of the Remedies, and this was the image [venerated] in Antequera. He died in Pichigua on his way to do business in this city. [Doña Lucía] obtained permission and made arrangements to remove her daughter, my lady Doña Isabel de Padilla [from Santa Catalina de Sena in Arequipa]. She proposed to her that the nuns be of the Immaculate Conception or discalced Franciscans. My lady the prioress told her mother that if she had to change her habit she would not leave to undertake the new foundation, as she was very devoted to Saint Dominic and to Saint Catherine of Siena. Given the resistance of her daughter, [Doña Lucía] conceded that it should be as she wished, and so there were two monasteries in Arequipa of the same habit.

[Doña Isabel de Padilla] left to found this monastery and it was founded the first of August in the year 1599. Because our prioress did not want to change her habit, there were two monasteries in Arequipa of the same Order. Six or seven years after that was the ruinous calamity of the volcanic ashes that burst out from Ubinas in the province of Tambo, Moquegua, which although distant from Arequipa rained in the city as though the volcano of Arequipa had erupted. There was great sterility, and for seven years no maize grew and all of the food was carted in from elsewhere and very expensive, and all of the vineyards were so damaged that for many years they produced nothing, and all was in a pitiful state. Thus has that city been made so poor and needy, and all that the founders gave to this house was diminished. In the floods that came afterward an entire vineyard was washed away.

The reason this monastery was moved to the city of Cuzco was the earthquake that struck on the twenty-fourth of December in the year 1604. Our founders were afraid that all the disasters that kept occurring in that city would diminish the virtue and saintliness they wanted to foment in the monastery. What they most wanted was for there to be great religiosity in this monastery and no need of doing business with the outside world. Extreme poverty had been caused by such calamities, one after another, and our founder Captain Gerónimo Pacheco had died; he did not live more than a month after the new foundation. Thus, right after the earthquake Doña Lucía and Doña Isabel sent a proposal to the city of Cuzco to Bishop Don Antonio de Raya, telling him of their intention to move to this city and the reasons that impelled them to take action with His Excellency's permission and licence. He gave it very gladly, sending Bautista de Solórzano and the factor Don Fernando de Cartagena, and because on the same day they were to leave he became very ill, he could not go, and elected Licenciate Juan Guerrero de Vargas, a very authoritative and capable person. He also sent Don Fernando de Salazar, who later became treasurer in this cathedral chapter and *provisor*, and another very virtuous clergyman named Gabriel de Herrera. His Excellency provided everything that was needed in the way of mules, saddles, tents, and miscellaneous gear, and ordered all the priests along our route to make preparations to attend us, seeing to our reception as well as our care and lodging in the parishes of the countryside. This was done with singular attentiveness because of his promise to reward whoever might attend us the best, and his admonitions that he who failed would cause His Excellency great disappointment in not doing what the other priests did with festivities and presents.

We left Arequipa on the first of January in the year 1605, to that city's great sorrow, and with such clamor, tears, and sobs that it seemed like Judgment Day; it was necessary for Juan Guerrero de Vargas, whom His Excellency had sent to escort us, to order on pain of excommunication that they calm themselves and allow us to leave. Twenty-five of us were nuns, and as it was a new foundation there were no more. There were also two secular girls who were nieces of the founders, Doña María de San José, who took the habit here in 1607, and Doña Costanza de Padilla, who took the habit some years later when she came of age. We walked in such religiosity, composure, and silence that whenever a reception party approached us we covered our faces with our veils, not allowing anyone to see us. The priests put on great festivities, the caciques gave us many gifts, and the rest of the people went out to receive us on their knees, with dancing and much music, and they kissed our habits and scapulars. In some places the priests lodged us in their houses, where they were able, and in others we stayed in churches, inns, and houses of corregidores. Once when it was necessary to camp outdoors, the priest was so attentive that he ordered a place to be dug out so that we might fit snugly inside; today travelers lodge there and it is called the Cave of the Nuns. He ordered that makeshift kitchens be made to treat us, and they hunted and prepared game for us to eat. We remained three or four days in that place because it began to snow. We arrived here on the eve of the Purification of Our Lady and were very well received. His Excellency [the Bishop of Cuzco] Don Antonio de Raya had arranged for us to go to the *plazuela* of Santo Domingo, and the nuns of Santa Clara had begged him to allow them to receive us that day and welcome us; they welcomed us, but did not take us into their cloisters, which His Excellency much regretted. We ate there, and in the afternoon were accompanied by His Excellency and the two cabildos (the corregidor at that time being Don Pedro de Córdoba Mejía) and all of the important people of the city, both gentlemen and ladies, as well as a great many others—many from out of town, and a multitude of Indians—so that we could barely walk, and there was much music and dancing and fireworks. They escorted us to the principal church, where we were received by the cantors, who sang *aynos*. Then they had us enter the church of the Company of Jesus, which had been specially decorated, and from there we went into the church they had prepared for us in the house of Captain Martín de Olmos, which later belonged to Don Gerónimo [Costilla] Gallinato. There was a door in the church leading to the cloister and we entered it, and His Excellency waited inside the church until they had finished sealing it up. We went inside the bedrooms and found by the doors cots and mattresses and blankets for those who needed them, all very neat and clean; the refectory was also very orderly. As long as our sainted father lived [Bishop de la Raya, d. 1606], he sent money for our monthly expenses along with some of the gifts he received, and did this with such love and charity that had he lived longer he would have left us very well cared-for indeed. He used to say that as soon as he paid what he owed for the foundation of the school in Huamanga, all the rest would go to this monastery.* God soon took him from us. My lady Doña Lucía de Padilla, our secular founder, went out into the streets from house to house to ask for alms, along with the wife of the corregidor, Doña María de Peñalosa, a very saintly lady. They were joined by Doña Catalina Duarte, who also gave us an annuity that the monastery still receives. People promised much but gave almost nothing, which was a great pity. It was hard for us after the death of His Excellency, until money was brought from the sale of houses and other properties in Arequipa so that we might buy these houses which the monastery occupies today. To turn them into cloisters it was necessary to make and unmake many things, and those who entered did not bring the dowry they now do, but less: for one thing, because of the urgent need for money to complete the cloisters, and for another, so that [local women] would become nuns, because since we were outsiders (forasteras) and they had their monastery here, there were difficulties. In order to populate the cloisters and remake them and fund construction, the dowries were lowered, and for these reasons the dowries could not be invested.

Source: Archivo de Santa Catalina de Sena (ASCS), Cuzco, "Inventario de la funda- ción," doc. 3.

*Contreras y Valverde, in Relación de la ciudad del Cuzco, 119, lists among the charitable works of Bishop de la Raya the founding of a Jesuit school in the city of Huamanga (today Ayacucho).

Appendix 4

Partial Genealogy of the Costilla Family

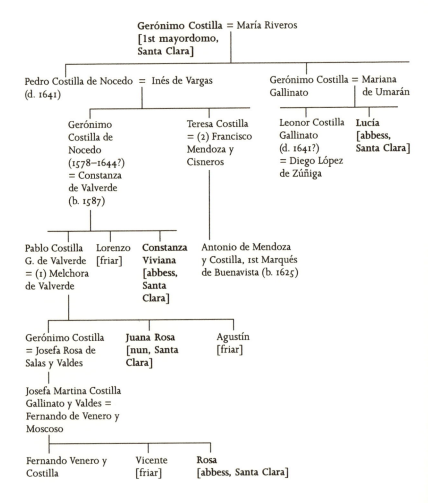

Gerónimo Costilla = María Riveros
[1st mayordomo,
Santa Clara]

Pedro Costilla de Nocedo = Inés de Vargas
(d. 1641)

Gerónimo Costilla = Mariana
Gallinato | de Umarán

Gerónimo
Costilla de
Nocedo
(1578–1644?)
= Constanza
de Valverde
(b. 1587)

Teresa Costilla
= (2) Francisco
Mendoza y
Cisneros

Leonor Costilla
Gallinato
(d. 1641?)
= Diego López
de Zúñiga

Lucía
[abbess,
Santa Clara]

Pablo Costilla
G. de Valverde
= (1) Melchora
de Valverde

Lorenzo
[friar]

Constanza
Viviana
[abbess,
Santa
Clara]

Antonio de Mendoza
y Costilla, 1st Marqués
de Buenavista (b. 1625)

Gerónimo Costilla
= Josefa Rosa de
Salas y Valdes

Juana Rosa
[nun, Santa
Clara]

Agustín
[friar]

Josefa Martina Costilla
Gallinato y Valdes =
Fernando de Venero y
Moscoso

Fernando Venero y
Costilla

Vicente
[friar]

Rosa
[abbess, Santa Clara]

Appendix 5

Nuns Professing in Santa Catalina, 1654–79

Year	Velo Negro	Velo Blanco	Donada	Not Specified	Total
1654	1	0	0	0	1
1655	2	0	0	0	2
1656	1	2	0	0	3
1657	1	1	0	0	2
1658	2	0	0	1	3
1659	4	2	0	0	6
1660	5	2	0	0	7
1661	6	1	0	0	7
1662	5	1	0	0	6
1663	1	1	0	0	2
1664	4	6	0	0	10
1665	4	0	0	1	5
1666	5	0	0	1	6
1667	3	3	0	0	6
1668	1	0	0	0	1
1669	6	2	4	1	13
1670	1	0	0	0	1
1671	0	0	0	0	0
1672	0	0	0	0	0
1673	1	0	0	0	1
1674	*1	0	0	0	*1
1675	0	0	0	4	4
1676	0	0	0	3	3
1677	0	0	0	4	4
1678	0	0	0	2	2
1679	0	0	0	11	11
Total	54	21	4	28	107

Source: ASCS, "Libro de profesiones."

* = Undated profession, velo negro; appears to correspond to 1673 or 1674.

Notes

All translations are mine unless otherwise indicated. References correspond to documents' locations in 1989–95.

Introduction

1. Even ecclesiastical historians have had little to say about Peru's convents and nuns. Antonine Tibesar, for example, in *Franciscan Beginnings in Colonial Peru* (Washington, D.C.: Academy of American Franciscan History, 1953), does not mention the Franciscans' "sister" order, the Poor Clares.

2. See, for example, the encomiums Ismael Portal dedicates to the nuns of Lima in *Lima religiosa (1535–1924)* (Lima: Librería e Imprenta Gil, 1924).

3. See Irene Silverblatt, *Moon, Sun, and Witches: Gender Ideologies and Class in Inca and Colonial Peru* (Princeton: Princeton University Press, 1987), 81–108, for an insightful analysis of *acllas* and the gender politics of Inca statecraft.

4. Antonio Vázquez de Espinosa, *Compendio y descripción de las Indias occidentales*, ed. B. Velasco Bayón, Biblioteca de Autores Españoles 231 (Madrid: Ediciones Atlas, 1969), 302, writing of La Encarnación.

5. Archivo Departamental del Cusco (hereafter ADC), Asuntos Eclesiásticos, leg. 7, "Autos que siguen contra las haciendas nombradas Cayllacalle," fol. 21.

6. Pierre Bourdieu, *Outline of a Theory of Practice*, trans. Richard Nice (New York: Cambridge University Press, 1977), esp. 78–87. See also Steven Feierman's valuable discussion of the issues at stake in the study of habitus, practice, and discourse: *Peasant Intellectuals: Anthropology and History in Tanzania* (Madison: University of Wisconsin Press, 1990), 27–39.

7. Benedict Anderson's insight into the selective negation involved in creole nation-building—see his *Imagined Communities: Reflections on the Origins and Spread of Nationalism* (New York: Verso, 1991)—can be extended to the spiritual economy, from whose workings many "creole pioneers" were vigorously trying to extricate themselves during the nineteenth century.

8. In the Philippines, for example: Carmen Yuste suggests that Mexican merchants transferred capital to create *obras pías* there to ensure not only their salvation but their liquidity ("Los comerciantes de la Ciudad de México en la

negociación transpacífica," in Leonor Ludlow and Jorge Silva Riquer, eds., *Los negocios y las ganancias de la colonia al México moderno* [Mexico City: Instituto Mora and UNAM, 1993], 211–24).

9. See Electa Arenal and Stacey Schlau, *Untold Sisters: Hispanic Nuns in Their Own Works* (Albuquerque: University of New Mexico Press, 1989); Jean Franco, *Plotting Women: Gender and Representation in Mexico* (New York: Columbia University Press, 1989), 3–54; Kathleen Myers, *Word from New Spain: The Spiritual Autobiography of Madre María de San José (1656–1719)* (Liverpool: Liverpool University Press, 1993); and Kathryn Joy McKnight, *The Mystic of Tunja: The Writings of Madre Castillo, 1671–1742* (Amherst: University of Massachusetts Press, 1997).

10. For historians of the Andes this will come as no surprise: the accumulated weight of centuries of notarial scribbling has been the ballast of the Peruvian ethnohistorical project of recent decades. The methodological and theoretical implications of reliance on *escribanos* have rarely been drawn out, however. Meeting historical actors through notarial mediations means we cannot simply recover their "authentic voices"; it requires that we problematize overly simple notions of agency to account for such indirection. To recognize notarial procedures and formulas, I relied on Gabriel de Monterroso y Alvarado, *Prática civil y criminal e instructión de scrivanos* (Valladolid: Francisco Fernández de Córdova, 1563).

11. Because of the perspective the sources afforded me, I was able to tell little about the nuns' prayers and devotions. No architectural plans turned up; no logs of confraternities' business; very little about confessors, and relatively little about *mayordomos*, the stewards of convent affairs who served as the nuns' proxies. I hope others may be able to locate such sources in the future.

12. Octavio Paz, *Sor Juana; or, The Traps of Faith*, trans. Margaret Sayers Peden (Cambridge: Harvard University Press, 1988), 271, citing Dorothy Schons.

13. Early results of Lavrin's extensive scholarship include "The Role of Nunneries in the Economy of New Spain in the Eighteenth Century," *Hispanic American Historical Review* 46:4 (1966), 371–93, and "Ecclesiastical Reform of Nunneries in New Spain in the Eighteenth Century," *The Americas* 22 (1965), 182–203.

14. Michel de Certeau, *The Practice of Everyday Life*, trans. Steven Rendall (Berkeley and Los Angeles: University of California Press, 1984).

15. Marisol de la Cadena, "Race, Ethnicity, and the Struggle for Indigenous Self-representation: De-indianization in Cuzco, Peru (1919–1992)" (Ph.D. diss., University of Wisconsin, 1996).

Chapter 1   *Gender and the Politics of Mestizaje*

1. ADC, Libro de Actas del Cabildo 1 (1545–52), fols. 152v–53v.

2. "Libro original que contiene la fundación del monesterio de monxas de señora Sta. Clara desta cibdad del Cuzco; por el qual consta ser su patrono el insigne Cabildo, Justicia y Reximiento desta dicha cibdad: Año de 1560," ed. Domingo Angulo, *Revista del Archivo Nacional del Perú* 11 (1939), 55–56, 64.

3. ADC, Libro de Actas del Cabildo 1 (1545–52), fol. 153.

4. "Libro original," ed. Angulo, 59–60.

5. Ibid., 60 (emphasis mine).

6. Ibid., 61.

7. Evangelization has long been figured as (Spanish male) conquest and penetration of the Andes, a story in which women played little part. See Fernando de Armas Medina, *Cristianización del Perú (1532–1600)* (Seville: Escuela de Estudios Hispano-Americanos, 1953) and Rubén Vargas Ugarte, *Historia de la Iglesia en el Perú*, 5 vols. (Lima and Burgos: Editorial Santa María et al., 1953–62), vols. 1 and 2. Recent work emphasizes women's part in Andean efforts both to resist Christianity and to harness its powers in ways missionaries never intended. See Steve J. Stern, *Peru's Indian Peoples and the Challenge of Spanish Conquest* (Madison: University of Wisconsin Press, 1982), 51–67; María Emma Mannarelli, "Inquisición y mujeres: Las hechiceras en el Perú durante el siglo XVII," *Revista Andina* 3:1 (1985), 141–55; and Silverblatt, *Moon, Sun, and Witches*, 197–210. But the gendered metaphor of penetration is far from being revised out of existence, and thus Polo can still surprise us: he can envision evangelization otherwise, as a reproductive process counting Spanish women among its agents.

8. "Libro original," ed. Angulo, 61–62, 80.

9. Ibid., 55–95, 157–84. Angulo worked from a copy of the book which may be found in ADC, Juan de Pineda, 1656, fols. 621–74.

10. Given the scarce sources, it is impossible to determine the number of culturally "Spanish" women living in Cuzco circa 1560. Thus my argument turns on the significance of the mestizas as cultural capital, and on that of the convent as a gendered response to the crisis of encomendero authority.

11. My approach has been inspired by the work of Joan Wallach Scott, whose *Gender and the Politics of History* (New York: Columbia University Press, 1988) is acknowledged in the title of this chapter.

12. See Patricia Seed, " 'Failing to Marvel': Atahualpa's Encounter with the Word," *Latin American Research Review* 26 (1991), 7–32.

13. James Lockhart, *The Men of Cajamarca* (Austin: University of Texas Press, 1972), 97, specifies the amount of treasure Maldonado received. John Hemming, *The Conquest of the Incas* (New York: Harcourt Brace Jovanovich, 1970), mentions Atahualpa's sister in footnotes (79n and 597n).

14. Pero Sancho, *La relación de Pero Sancho*, trans. Luis A. Arocena (Buenos Aires: Editorial Plus Ultra, 1986), 135.

15. Pedro de Cieza de León, *Crónica del Perú, Primera Parte*, 2d ed., ed. Franklin Pease G. Y. (Lima: Pontificia Universidad Católica, 1986), 258.

16. Noble David Cook, *Demographic Collapse: Indian Peru, 1520–1620* (New York: Cambridge University Press, 1981), 38–40 and 211–19, estimates that by 1530 the "population cluster" of Cuzco held 150,000 to 200,000 people.

17. Raúl Porras Barrenechea provides records of Cuzco's Spanish foundation in "Dos documentos esenciales sobre Francisco Pizarro y la conquista del Perú," *Revista Histórica* 17 (1948), 74–95.

18. The earliest published accounts of the Incas—one anonymous, another by Francisco de Xerez—appeared in Seville in 1534; see Xerez, *Verdadera relación de la conquista del Perú*, ed. Concepción Bravo (Madrid: Historia 16, 1985), 28–29.

19. The *kurakazgo* was a kinship-based unit of labor mobilization and tribute collection with deep Andean roots, predating the Inca empire. See Karen Spalding, *Huarochirí: An Andean Society under Inca and Spanish Rule* (Stanford: Stanford University Press, 1984), and Stern, *Peru's Indian Peoples*.

20. As disease ravaged the indigenous population and tribute shrank, encomiendas finally were not worth fighting for in Peru. Still, encomiendas survived in one form or another until the eighteenth century: Silvio Zavala, *La encomienda indiana*, 2d ed. (Mexico City: Editorial Porrúa, 1973), 244–55, and José de la Puente Brunke, *Encomienda y encomenderos en el Perú* (Seville: Diputación Provincial de Sevilla, 1992).

21. Cook, *Demographic Collapse*, 211–19, discusses the impact of war, disease, migration, and exploitative labor arrangements on the population of Cuzco. By comparison with the coast, "Cuzco was a healthier place for the Indian to live" (217).

22. De la Puente, *Encomienda y encomenderos*, 337–82, gives details on the value of Cuzco's encomiendas; see also Zavala, *La encomienda indiana*, 238–39.

23. Stern, *Peru's Indian Peoples*, 31–33, 41–42, gives fascinating glimpses of the means Diego Maldonado used to become "el Rico" in these years, cultivating kurakas with gifts and favors. José Antonio del Busto Duthurburu, in "Maldonado, el Rico, Señor de los Andahuaylas," *Revista Histórica* 26 (1962–63), 130, indicates that Maldonado could be abusive as well.

24. Fray Vicente de Valverde v. Francisco González, January 22, 1539, and v. Juan Begines, February 8, 1539, Archivo General de Indias (hereafter AGI), Seville, Audiencia de Lima, 305. The Crown responded to Valverde's reports with a 1541 decree that Indian women held by Spaniards be placed in the care of married Spanish women; see *Colección de documentos para la historia de la formación social de Hispanoamérica, 1493–1810* (hereafter CDFS), 3 vols., ed. Richard Konetzke (Madrid: Consejo Superior de Investigaciones Científicas, 1953–62), 1:208–9.

25. CDFS, 1:12–13.

26. CDFS, 1:182, 187, 193, for measures imposing this requirement on encomenderos in various parts of the Americas.

27. Garcilaso states in his *Royal Commentaries of the Incas and General History of Peru, Part Two*, trans. Harold V. Livermore (Austin: University of Texas Press, 1966), 734, that "in the early days, when an Indian woman bore a child to a Spaniard, all her relatives respected and served the Spaniard like an idol, since he had joined their family. This was of great help in pushing forward the conquest of the Indies."

28. Encomenderos aspired to noble status, and the growing Spanish obsession with "purity of blood"—i.e., "old Christian" ancestry, with no recent converts from Judaism or Islam in one's family tree—may have made them averse to marrying Incas, who were themselves new converts. But the chance to marry into Inca wealth could override all obstacles, as the case of Doña Beatriz Clara Coya shows.

29. Garcilaso's account of an Inca "princess" obliged to marry a plebeian Spaniard (*Royal Commentaries*, 1229–30) suggests Inca women's anger at such treatment—and Garcilaso's own. His father had left his mother in this fash-

ion, arranging her marriage to an undistinguished Spaniard and taking as his wife Doña Luisa Martel de los Ríos.

30. Ibid., 607.

31. James Lockhart, in *Spanish Peru 1532–1560: A Colonial Society* (Madison: University of Wisconsin Press, 1968), 167, states that "ninety-five per cent of the first generation of mestizos were illegitimate." Because "the few legitimate mestizos . . . were accepted fully as equals," he continues, "the Spanish may have considered illegitimacy to be a more serious blemish than mixture with Indians."

32. Vargas Ugarte, *Historia de la Iglesia*, 1:310, cites the Dominican friar Domingo de Santo Tomás, who wrote from Lima to the Council of the Indies in 1550 making such recommendations. For mestizas, he clearly had in mind the Spanish model of the *recogimiento*, a place where women might live secluded from the secular world, though not under solemn monastic vows.

33. According to del Busto, "Maldonado, el Rico," 127–28, 142n, Juan Arias Maldonado fought in several major battles and saved his father's life in 1554 during the battle of Chuquingua.

34. Diego de Esquivel y Navia, *Noticias cronológicas de la gran ciudad del Cuzco*, 2 vols. (Lima: Banco Wiese, 1980), 1:157. The minutes of the cabildo do not say that this *provisión* was the stimulus for the creation of Santa Clara, but the timing suggests it was.

35. ADC, Libro de Actas del Cabildo 1 (1545–52), fols. 153–54. The purchased and donated properties are described as being near the outskirts of Cuzco, by the road leading out of the city, "junto a do dizen chaquylchaca."

36. Armas Medina, *Cristianización del Perú*, 135–72.

37. "Libro original," ed. Angulo, 55. Little is known about Ortiz, widow of Juan de Retes, an even more obscure figure. According to Diego de Mendoza, *Chrónica de la provincia de S. Antonio de los Charcas* (La Paz: Editorial Casa Municipal de la Cultura "Franz Tamayo," 1976), 377, Ortiz attended the poor in the hospital of Espíritu Santo dressed as a Franciscan tertiary.

38. The "Libro original," ed. Angulo, 56, gives March 16, 1557, as the date the cabildo decided to request authorization from the Crown. Meanwhile, the cabildo performed its own formal founding acts in 1558. When royal authorization was obtained, additional founding acts were performed in the early 1560s.

39. La Encarnación was formed as a recogimiento under Augustinian auspices in 1557 and raised to the rank of monastery in 1561, becoming Lima's first convent for women. Antonio de la Calancha, *Crónica moralizada de Antonio de Calancha*, ed. Ignacio Prado Pastor, 6 vols. (Lima: Universidad Nacional Mayor de San Marcos, 1976), 3:969–73; see also Lourdes Leiva Viacava, "En torno al primer monasterio limeño en el Virreinato del Perú, 1550–1650," in Manuel Ramos Medina, ed., *El monacato femenino en el imperio español* (Mexico City: Condumex, 1995), 319–30.

40. San Juan de la Penitencia was founded in 1553 by three propertied residents of Lima specifically to care for orphaned mestizas. See Nancy van Deusen, "Los primeros recogimientos para doncellas mestizas en Lima y Cusco, 1550–1580," *Allpanchis* 35/36:1 (1990), 249–91.

41. Calancha, *Crónica moralizada*, 3:970–72; Leiva, "En torno al primer monasterio limeño," 322.

42. On the concept and practice of recogimiento, see Nancy van Deusen, *Dentro del cerco de los muros: El recogimiento en la época colonial* (Lima: CENDOC, 1988).

43. See, for example, the work of Elizabeth Lehfeldt, "Sacred and Secular Spaces: The Role of Religious Women in Golden-Age Valladolid" (Ph.D. diss., Indiana University, 1995).

44. The cabildo of Arequipa is quite explicit in its support of the foundation of Santa Catalina, for example: Dante E. Zegarra López, *Monasterio de Santa Catalina de Sena de Arequipa y Doña Ana de Monteagudo, priora* (Arequipa: Corporación Departamental de Desarrollo de Arequipa, 1985), 24.

45. *Colección de documentos inéditos relativos al descubrimiento, conquista y colonización de las posesiones españolas en América y Oceanía* (hereafter CDIAO), ed. Luis Torres de Mendoza, 48 vols. (Madrid: Imprenta de Manuel G. Hernández, 1864–84), 18:16–18, *real cédula* of November 19, 1551, giving encomenderos three years in which to marry and take their wives to Peru.

46. Del Busto, "Maldonado, el Rico," 128.

47. According to Lockhart, *Spanish Peru*, 167, Maldonado "married his daughter to a Spanish don, with a dowry of 20,000 pesos." Possibly she was educated by Ortiz before the founding of Santa Clara, but she does not appear in the list of mestiza residents in the "Libro original."

48. "Libro original," ed. Angulo (see note 2 above).

49. Ibid., 161.

50. This conclusion can be reached by reading between the lines of the foundation book. Whoever kept it, probably Francisca de Ortiz, registered Spaniards' identity saliently; see the three entries of Spaniards, ibid., 89, 160–61. In December 1565, the cabildo noted that all the Spaniards who had professed had brought no dowry (72). Only four of the eighteen professed nuns are listed as having brought no dowry, and two of these four are clearly marked "Spaniards," suggesting that sixteen of the nuns were mestizas.

51. Ibid., 89.

52. The information about Doña Beatriz that follows is drawn primarily from María Rostworowski de Diez Canseco, "El repartimiento de Doña Beatriz Clara Coya en el valle de Yucay," *Historia y Cultura* 4 (1970), 153–58; Hemming, *Conquest of the Incas*, 297–300, 311–14, 459–61; and official correspondence in *Gobernantes del Perú: Cartas y papeles, siglo XVI*, ed. Roberto Levillier, 14 vols. (Madrid: Sucesores de Rivadeneyra et al., 1921–26), vol. 3.

53. "Libro original," ed. Angulo, 158.

54. Sons of "doctor buendía" (*Gobernantes del Perú*, ed. Levillier, 3:156, 162, 229), the brothers are also called "relatives" of Diego Maldonado's mestizo son Juan Arias Maldonado, but the kinship connection is unclear. As all three were implicated in the 1567 "mestizo mutiny" described below, it is often assumed the brothers were mestizos, but they do not appear as such in official reports, as Juan Arias Maldonado does.

55. Hemming's translation in *Conquest of the Incas*, 312, citing García de Castro's letter to the Crown in *Gobernantes del Perú*, ed. Levillier, 3:156.

56. Maldonado was forcibly returned to Spain, and Beatriz went to Chile with her husband, who had been made governor. In Concepción they had a daughter, Doña Ana María. Loyola was killed in 1598 and his wife lived thereafter in Lima, where she died in 1600; her descendants became Marqueses of Oropesa. See Rostworowski, "El repartimiento de Doña Beatriz Clara Coya," 157–58, and Hemming, *Conquest of the Incas*, 459–61.

57. No reliable figures exist on the number of Spanish women in Cuzco, but Lockhart estimates (*Spanish Peru*, 152) that in the entire viceroyalty there may have been only 150–200 Spanish women by 1541, 300–400 by 1543, and about 1,000 by 1555. This population was concentrated in coastal cities, but by midcentury some *españolas* had made it to Cuzco despite the ongoing warfare, most no doubt wives and relatives of encomenderos. See Garcilaso's dramatic account (*Royal Commentaries*, 1318–21) of an encomendero's wedding banquet in 1553, interrupted by a major rebellion that sent guests clambering for the rooftops.

58. Armas Medina, *Cristianización del Perú*, 396–98; Vargas Ugarte, *Historia de la Iglesia*, 1:311–13.

59. According to Hemming, *Conquest of the Incas*, 312n, María was "seduced and abducted by one Juan Baptista de Vitoria while a novice in the convent," married the obscure Vitoria, and was disinherited by her father. Hemming indicates that a second marriage followed, to Gaspar Hernández (209). I am grateful to John H. Rowe for referring me to ms. A155 in the Biblioteca Nacional (BN), Lima, which indicates that Betanzos forgave his daughter and gave her back her inheritance in July 1566. The case of Francisco Pizarro's daughter by Quispe Sisa makes a fascinating comparison; see María Rostworowski de Diez Canseco, *Doña Francisca Pizarro: Una ilustre mestiza, 1534–1598* (Lima: Instituto de Estudios Peruanos, 1989).

60. This may have been the case with "Ana," who figures in the "Libro original," ed. Angulo, merely as the orphan daughter of "Diego Fernández" (82). Since this surname is easily confused with "Hernández" in sixteenth-century documents and in transcriptions of them (and Angulo made his share of mistakes), Ana's father may have been Diego Hernández; if so, Ana may have been the daughter of a very high-ranking Inca, Beatriz Huayllas Ñusta. Or she may have been the child of another encomendero of the same name: de la Puente, *Encomienda y encomenderos*, 423.

61. "Libro original," ed. Angulo, 69.

62. *Constituciones generales para todas las monjas, y religiosas sujetas a la obediencia de la orden de N. P. S. Francisco, en toda esta familia cismontana* (Mexico City: Imprenta de la Viuda de Francisco Rodríguez Lupercio, 1689), fol. 58, prohibits servants ("freylas donadas") from wearing the black veil.

63. I allude here to the intellectual contests then coming to a head on the other side of the Atlantic, between Bartolomé de Las Casas and Juan Ginés de Sepúlveda, over the proposition that "Indians" were, in Aristotelian terms, "natural slaves," hence fit to be conquered and distributed in encomienda. Anthony Pagden, in *The Fall of Natural Man* (New York: Cambridge University Press, 1982), gives the coordinates of various debaters' positions.

64. "Libro original," ed. Angulo, 160–61.

65. I am not suggesting that Francisca de Jesús and her companions acted in accordance with racialized practices of today, but pointing to an especially fluid moment in the South American prehistory of "race" which still needs to be investigated. Here legitimacy appears to be relativized, and other things (new conversion to the faith?) may have made mestizas seem less than "authoritative" in Spaniards' eyes. This rhetoric of *autoridad* is far from clear; likewise the role physical appearance played in late-sixteenth-century acts of discrimination.

66. Ibid., 71.

67. Ibid. It is not clear whether the protest originated within Santa Clara, from the demoted mestizas, or from their fathers, who were certainly in a state of heightened anxiety about their own status and that of their mestizo children.

68. The cabildo prevailed upon the Franciscan provincial to decree that nuns wearing the white veil be allowed to take the black veil (ibid., 72–73). Whether the cabildo's pressure succeeded in promoting any wearers of the white veil to the black veil is unclear from available sources.

69. The Third Council of Peruvian bishops in Lima (1582–83) also decided in favor of mestizas' equality, but to little avail. See *Concilios limenses (1551–1772)*, ed. Rubén Vargas Ugarte, 3 vols. (Lima: Tipografía Peruana, 1951–54), 1:358.

70. Marvin Goldwert recounts this crucial contest in "La lucha por la perpetuidad de las encomiendas en el Perú virreinal, 1550–1600," *Revista Histórica* 22 (1955–56), 350–60, continued in 23 (1957–58), 207–20. See also de la Puente, *Encomienda y encomenderos*, 78–95.

71. For an idea of the extreme complexity of the issues they were trying to resolve, and the centrality of marriage and reproduction, see CDFS, 1:340–60.

72. John V. Murra gives interesting details in "'Nos Hazen Mucha Ventaja': The Early European Perception of Andean Achievement," in Kenneth J. Andrien and Rolena Adorno, eds., *Transatlantic Encounters: Europeans and Andeans in the Sixteenth Century* (Berkeley and Los Angeles: University of California Press, 1991), 79–83.

73. A judge (*oidor*) from the Audiencia de Lima, Dr. Cuenca, was sent to Cuzco when a mutiny against the encomenderos threatened to break out in 1561; see his report in *Audiencia de Lima: Correspondencia de presidentes y oidores*, ed. Roberto Levillier (Madrid: Imprenta de Juan Pueyo, 1922), 294–99. An October 1563 petition to the king by the cabildo of Cuzco (AGI, Audiencia de Lima 110) shows that agitation over *perpetuidad* was far from over.

74. *Gobernantes del Perú*, ed. Levillier, 1:422.

75. Letter of Lic. Monzón to the Crown, Lima, February 10, 1563, in *Audiencia de Lima*, ed. Levillier, 285.

76. *Gobernantes del Perú*, ed. Levillier, 1:521. The viceroy Conde de Nieva noted that encomenderos had not been interested in individual dealmaking so long as the prospect of perpetuity existed, but had begun changing their minds.

77. Documentation of the incident is contained in AGI, Justicia, 1086; see

Héctor López Martínez, "Un motín de mestizos en el Perú (1567)," *Revista de Indias* 24 (1964), 367–81.

78. According to Del Busto, "Maldonado, el Rico," 131–32, Maldonado was able to obtain his son's release, but López Martínez, "Un motín de mestizos," 380–81, indicates that Juan Arias Maldonado was exiled to Spain, where in 1578 he petitioned the Crown to be allowed to return to Peru. ADC, Testimonios Compulsos, leg. 1, contains testimony that Juan Arias Maldonado made a will in Panama in 1583 during his return from exile. Garcilaso records in his *Royal Commentaries* that his mestizo contemporary died within three days of arriving in Peru "of pure joy and pleasure at being back in his own country" (1476).

79. *Gobernantes del Perú*, ed. Levillier, 3:235. In this letter of February 1567, García de Castro complains about mestizos and mulattoes; in other letters, mestizos and criollos, or simply "those born in these lands."

80. *Gobernantes del Perú*, ed. Levillier, 3:267. García de Castro begins this passage of his September 1567 letter by referring to mestizos and mulattoes, but the context makes it clear that he regards mestizos as an especially potent threat. Philip II responded with a 1568 decree (cited in CDFS, 436–37) that mestizos and mulattoes not be allowed to bear arms.

81. AGI, Audiencia de Lima, 110, records of the cabildo sessions of April 1571 to January 1, 1572.

82. Nevertheless, as de la Puente shows in *Encomienda y encomenderos*, 85–94, the encomenderos of Cuzco made efforts to reopen the case for perpetuity well into the seventeenth century.

83. ADC, Protocolos Notariales, Antonio Sánchez, leg. 19 (1571–72), fols. 538–49v, contains Diego Maldonado's *poder para testar* in which he names Juan Arias as his natural son by Doña Lucía and makes him heir to an extensive entail. ADC, Testimonios Compulsos, leg. 1, contains incomplete records of a 1583 suit between Juan Arias's children over succession in the entail. Maldonado heirs to this entail continued to play a salient role in Cuzco's affairs for generations.

84. By the seventeenth century the categories of *velo negro* and *velo blanco* were firmly inscribed in conventual practice not only in Cuzco but elsewhere. For Lima, see Luis Martín, *Daughters of the Conquistadores: Women of the Viceroyalty of Peru* (Albuquerque: University of New Mexico Press, 1983), 179–92. Comparative work is needed to show what kinds of historically specific boundaries these categories reinforced.

85. Both describe Santa Clara's early entrants as *doncellas nobles* and daughters of conquistadores. Mendoza, *Chrónica de la provincia de S. Antonio de los Charcas*, 68–72, 377–474; Diego de Córdova Salinas, *Crónica Franciscana de las provincias del Perú*, ed. Lino G. Canedo (Washington, D.C.: Academy of American Franciscan History, 1957), 890–94.

86. "Libro original," ed. Angulo, 168. After Francisca de Jesús, the next two abbesses of Santa Clara were Spaniards: Clara de San Francisco served two terms (1576–79, 1579–82), then was succeeded by Bernardina de Jesús (1582–

85). While the foundation book is unclear on the identity of the twenty-five women professing during their tenure (and the list is truncated at 1583), ten are "doñas" and may well have been criolla daughters of important Spaniards. This was certainly the case with Doña Mencía, and it appears to be true of the two Villafuerte sisters and the two Sotelo sisters (166–67).

87. See Elizabeth Anne Kuznesof, "Ethnic and Gender Influences on 'Spanish' Creole Society in Colonial Spanish America," *Colonial Latin American Review* 4 (1995), 153–76, who seeks to historicize race by investigating the category of "creole." Kuznesof uses "race" in confusing ways that reveal the difficulty of setting aside modern usage; for example, she indicates Spanish colonial usage associated "race" (for which no Spanish keyword is provided) with "civilization" and "genetic characteristics" (164), a set of discursive connections that sounds altogether modern. Yet she is among the first historians of colonial Spanish America to treat race as "a social category" (165) rather than as a self-evident, transhistorical category, and to use gender analysis in the process.

Chapter 2   The Dilemmas of Dominio: Reconciling Poverty and Property

1. *Constituciones generales*, fol. 3.

2. Mendoza, *Chrónica de la provincia de S. Antonio de los Charcas*, 380.

3. Ibid., 408.

4. Antonio Arbiol, *La religiosa instruida* (Madrid: Imprenta Real de la Gazeta, 1776), 158.

5. All monastic orders struggled with the dilemmas of pursuing religious poverty in the midst of profit-oriented economies, as Lester K. Little shows in *Religious Poverty and the Profit Economy in Medieval Europe* (Ithaca: Cornell University Press, 1978). Trying to resolve such dilemmas, the Council of Trent granted all monasteries (with certain exceptions) the right to possess immovable property; see *Canons and Decrees of the Council of Trent*, ed. H. J. Schroeder (Rockford, Ill.: TAN Books & Publishers, 1978), 218–19.

6. Santa Teresa de Jesús, *Libro de las fundaciones*, 3d ed., ed. Antonio Comas (Madrid: Alianza Editorial, 1984), 87–88.

7. Ibid., 144.

8. "Libro original," ed. Angulo, 75; *Constituciones generales*, fol. 62v. Garcilaso describes the scarcity and value of Spanish animals, crops, and so forth in his *Royal Commentaries*, 579–606.

9. Mendoza, *Chrónica de la provincia de S. Antonio de los Charcas*, 68.

10. On lay patronage of monastic foundations and concern for lineage, see Jodi Bilinkoff, *The Avila of Saint Teresa: Religious Reform in a Sixteenth-Century City* (Ithaca: Cornell University Press, 1989), esp. 35–52.

11. Nuns could hardly be expected to keep horses and arms and rush into battle to defend the king's interests. But then, neither could an unbaptized Inca be expected to see to the effective Christianization of "his" Indians. In short, the assignment of this encomienda thoroughly defied the usual logic.

12. The Franciscan friars of Cuzco also exercised rather vaguely defined

stewardship on behalf of the nuns from the time of Santa Clara's foundation, as indicated in the "Libro original," ed. Angulo, 66. However, the cabildo reserved for itself "el patronazgo y administración, quanto a lo temporal."

13. Archivo de Santa Clara (hereafter ASC), Cuzco, "Volumen de varias escrituras que pueden servir de títulos," fols. 41–56.

14. I am grateful to John Rowe for taking me to visit the ruins of Quespiguanca, a royal estate of Huayna Capac, near the town of Urubamba in July 1989. These included a majestic Inca gateway, some three stories high, standing in a modern farmer's field. The site of a colonial obraje may be seen nearby.

15. Cieza, *Crónica del Perú, Primera Parte*, 261. Esquivel y Navia, in *Noticias cronológicas*, 1:156, records that Cuzco's cabildo was prohibited by the Audiencia of Lima in 1550 from moving the city to Yucay.

16. Luis Miguel Glave and María Isabel Remy, *Estructura agraria y vida rural en una región andina: Ollantaytambo entre los siglos XVI y XIX*, Archivos de Historia Andina 3 (Cuzco: Centro de Estudios Rurales Andinos "Bartolomé de Las Casas," 1983), 524, cite the standard reckoning of the fanegada's area, about 2.9 hectares.

17. Archivo Histórico Nacional (hereafter AHN), Madrid, Sección de Ordenes Militares: Santiago, exp. 5170, Don Antonio de Mendoza y Costilla, Cuzco, 1672.

18. Ibid. Antonio established a *mayorazgo* and made out his will in 1559; he was buried in the chapel that his parents had founded.

19. Archivo de San Francisco (hereafter ASF), Lima, Registro 15, June 3, 1577, concerning Gerónimo Costilla's desire to be buried in the *capilla mayor* of the church of Santa Clara and to secure his descendants' right to burial there. See also BN, Sala de Investigaciones, ms. B457 (1623), regarding the dispute between Pedro Costilla and Santa Clara.

20. Costilla was more noble, but Maldonado had outstripped his *compatriota* in the pursuit of Andean wealth; see Stern, *Peru's Indian Peoples*, 31–33, 41–42. From La Gasca in 1548 Costilla got only a share in the mediocre encomienda of Asillo.

21. ASC, "Volúmen de varias escrituras," fols. 41–56.

22. Spanish records usually specify these types of tenure in tandem. See César Antonio Ugarte, *Los antecedentes históricos del régimen agrario peruano* (Lima: Librería e Imprenta Gil, 1918), 72–78. See Susan Elizabeth Ramírez on tenure changes along the north coast: *The World Upside Down: Cross-cultural Contact and Conflict in Sixteenth-Century Peru* (Stanford: Stanford University Press, 1996).

23. Archivo General de la Nación (hereafter AGN), Lima, Campesinado: Derecho Indígena, leg. 31 (suplementario), cuaderno 614 (1559), "Autos que siguió Juan de Arrendolaza en nombre del Convento de la Merced del Cuzco contra D. Francisco Mayontopa, cacique principal del repartimiento de Collatambo en el valle de Tambo"; AGN, Superior Gobierno, leg. 1, cuaderno 10 (1586), for the town of Maras v. the Jesuits. Regarding the Augustinians of Cuzco, see ADC, Beneficencia, Libro Becerro 7, fols. 675–78.

24. *Los virreyes españoles en América durante el gobierno de la Casa de Austria: Perú*, ed. Lewis Hanke, 7 vols. (Madrid: Atlas, 1978–80), 1:34.

25. AGN, Superior Gobierno, leg. 1, cuaderno 10 (1586). The Jesuits sought 150 fanegadas to grow wheat. The indigenous leaders of Maras declared "que en toda la comarca . . . no ay tierras nyngunas vacas ny que ayan sido de los yngas ny de guacas . . . [y] que si algunas tierras a avido de los dichos yngas las poseen y tienen españoles de manera que no ay tierras nyngunas baldias ni heriazas que poder dar."

26. See Juan Polo de Ondegardo, *El mundo de los incas*, ed. Laura González and Alicia Alonso, Crónicas de América 58 (Madrid: Historia 16, 1990), 66–69. For an interesting new analysis of Polo de Ondegardo's stance regarding "lands of the Inca and the Sun," see Carlos Sempat Assadourian, *Transiciones hacia el sistema colonial andino* (Lima: Instituto de Estudios Peruanos, 1994), 92–150.

27. See Stern, *Peru's Indian Peoples*, 114–37, on kurakas' use of Spanish justice to defend themselves, albeit at high cost both to themselves and to their communities.

28. AGN, Campesinado: Derecho Indígena, leg. 31, cuaderno 614, año 1559, "Autos que siguió Juan de Arrendolaza," fols. 17v–18, 26v. The *mitimaes* were part of Ollantaytambo's preconquest labor regime, presumably assigned there by the Inca.

29. Some local land would have been assigned to produce for the huacas. Cuzco's corregidor Polo de Ondegardo, before whom this case was heard, was engaged in a determined pursuit of information about the sacred sites of the Incas, the better to eradicate them and further Christian evangelization.

30. AGN, Campesinado: Derecho Indígena, leg. 31, cuaderno 614, "Autos que siguió Juan de Arrendolaza," fols. 4v–5, 20.

31. One source on neighboring Yucay from 1552 indicates that its native population had by that time decreased from more than 3,000 to only 700: ADC, Beneficencia, vol. 4, fols. 14–15v. See also Cook, *Demographic Collapse*, 219–22. Ann M. Wightman, in *Indigenous Migration and Social Change: The Forasteros of Cuzco, 1570–1720* (Durham: Duke University Press, 1990), 68–69, discusses the gap between official and actual indigenous populations.

32. It is hard to analyze the growth of a regional land market in detail, since notarial records from the sixteenth century are scarce, but the high turnover rate of certain pieces suggests that a good deal of speculative buying occurred.

33. Glave and Remy, *Estructura agraria y vida rural*, 107–21, 138–46. In 1562 caciques were prohibited to sell land: Esquivel y Navia, *Noticias cronológicas*, 1:208. See Franklin Pease, *Curacas, reciprocidad y riqueza* (Lima: Pontificia Universidad Católica del Perú, 1992) for more on kurakas' paths to wealth.

34. Polo de Ondegardo, in *El mundo de los incas*, 49, writes: "[E]sta parte del Inca no hay duda sino de todas tres era la mayor." However, he has just observed that the portion dedicated to the Sun was so great that even if the Inca had had nothing else to do but distribute it for ritual purposes, he would have been very busy (46).

35. Ibid., 67.

36. In the early decades of Spanish settlement, cabildos held far-reaching powers and they routinely made land grants. Toledo would restrict these

powers on his visit to Cuzco in 1572; see *Fundación española del Cusco y ordenanzas para su gobierno*, ed. Horacio H. Urteaga and Carlos A. Romero (Lima: Talleres Gráficos Sanmartí, 1926), 70.

37. On the Andean logic of access to land through kinship and reciprocity, see Spalding, *Huarochirí*, 9–41, and Ramírez, *The World Upside Down*, 42–63.

38. Polo de Ondegardo, *El mundo de los Incas*, 50 (emphasis mine).

39. Ibid., 38–39. Polo states that the natives have been obliged to adopt dubious practices ("hacer emulaciones malas y reprobadas") to get what they want.

40. Glave and Remy, *Estructura agraria y vida rural*, 81; ADC, Colegio de Ciencias, leg. 33.

41. According to Garcilaso, *Royal Commentaries*, 245–46, "A tupu of land was enough to maintain a peasant and his wife without family. As soon as they had children, each boy was given a tupu and each girl half a tupu. . . . [N]o one could buy it or sell it."

42. See the New Laws of 1542–43 in CDFS, 1:218. Violations were frequent, however; see Lockhart, *Spanish Peru*, 56.

43. ASC, "Volúmen de varias escrituras."

44. ADC, Colegio de Ciencias, leg. 33, doc. 9, fols. 181–82.

45. For both the 1589 and the 1592 sale, see ibid., fols. 173–78.

46. "Libro original," ed. Angulo, 76.

47. ASF, Registro 15, no. 6, fol. 991.

48. The Indians of Corcora were to be assessed an appropriate amount, payable directly to royal officials in Cuzco, who would then be responsible for getting it to Santa Clara. The convent's 1582–86 and 1602 inventories show that the nuns received pesos, grain, and chickens annually from Corcora. See "Libro original," ed. Angulo, 174, 178.

49. Suriguaylla would remain in the family for several generations; see ADC, Corregimiento, Causas Ordinarias, leg. 49 (1768), exp. 1096, "Autos que sigue el monasterio de Santa Clara contra las haciendas nombradas Suriguailla."

50. Both Santa Clara and Costilla had interests well to the south of Cuzco too, in the area the Spaniards called "el Collao." Costilla held his principal encomienda at Asillo. By the 1580s, the nuns had acquired a livestock ranch called Caco, located near Pucará. The coincidence points again to the close relationship between the convent and its mayordomo.

51. The cabildo set the purchase price of the chapel at 3,000 pesos ensayados ("Libro original," ed. Angulo, 74–75). According to Mendoza, *Chrónica de la provincia de S. Antonio de los Charcas*, 69, Costilla paid an equivalent amount of pesos corrientes (4,770 pesos) to reserve the chapel for himself and his descendants. A copy of the notarial record to this effect (ASF, Registro 15, no. 6, fols. 1096–1111) indicates that Costilla took possession of the chapel on June 3, 1577. The old conquistador died around 1581.

52. ASC, "Volúmen de varias escrituras," fol. 95.

53. "Libro original," ed. Angulo, 73. Thomas M. Kealy notes, in *Dowry of Women Religious*, Canon Law Studies 134 (Washington, D.C.: Catholic University

of America Press, 1941), 19 and 29–31, that dowry was generally set by local ecclesiastical authorities. In Lima it remained fixed for most of the colonial period at 3,177 pesos corrientes (2,000 pesos ensayados).

54. For example: ADC, Antonio Sánchez, 1582, *censo-gravamen* on property of Rodrigo de Esquivel to pay his daughter's dowry to Santa Clara.

55. The thirteenth-century Iberian legal code illustrates such censos with a sample that suggests the clergy's reliance on such dealings: "Be it known to all who read this contract that I, *fulan*, abbott of thus-and-such monastery . . . do give in censo . . . such-and-such a property in such-and-such place." Partida 3, Title 18, Law 69 in *Las Siete Partidas del Rey Alfonso el Sabio, cotejadas con varios códices antiguos por la Real Academia de la Historia*, 3 vols. (Madrid: Imprenta Real, 1807), 2:593–94.

56. Both Pachar and Caco figure in Santa Clara's foundation records: "Libro original," ed. Angulo, 76, 174, 181. Pachar was not sold until the eighteenth century, and Caco still shows up in an 1872 list of Santa Clara's productive assets: Archivo Arzobispal del Cuzco (hereafter AAC), C-LVIII, 4, 47, inventory of September 27, 1872.

57. Tomás de Mercado, *Summa de tratos y contratos de mercaderes* (Seville: Hernando Díaz, 1571), fol. 79.

58. However, unlike the "abominable sin" of homosexuality (*pecado nefando*), usury was not punishable by death.

59. Moreover, to lend at interest was to violate the commandment of Deuteronomy 23:19, "Thou shalt not lend upon usury to thy brother." However, according to Deuteronomy 23:20, it was permissible to lend to strangers at usury; see Benjamin Nelson, *The Idea of Usury: From Tribal Brotherhood to Universal Otherhood*, 2d ed. (Chicago: University of Chicago Press, 1969).

60. Luis Alfredo Tapia Franco, "Análisis histórico institucional del censo consignativo en el derecho peruano" (B.A. thesis, Pontificia Universidad Católica del Perú, Lima, 1991), chap. 2, provides some examples.

61. In sixteenth-century manuals for notaries, the relevant document is often referred to as an *imposición de censo*. See, for example, Hernando Díaz de Valdepeñas, *Suma de notas copiosas y muy sustanciales y compendiosas* (Toledo: Hernando Díaz and Juan de Medina, 1544), fols. 11–12, and Monterroso y Alvarado, *Pratica civil y criminal*, fol. 135.

62. ADC, Luis de Quesada, 1571–81, fols. 521–23v, censo al quitar of November 13, 1581.

63. Book 5, Title 15, Laws 4, 12, and 13 in *Recopilación de las leyes destos reynos*, 3 vols. (Madrid: Catalina de Barrio y Angulo and Diego Díaz de la Carrera, 1640), vol. 2, fols. 42v, 44v.

64. Tapia, in "Análisis histórico," chap. 2, cites a case that came before the authorities in Lima in the early 1640s. A woman contracted to lend a man 4,400 pesos but only gave him 4,000 pesos, whereupon he denounced her for charging interest (10 percent).

65. In the 1620s, de la Torre's heirs argued that a censo could not have been placed on mines "since they all belong to His Majesty." ADC, Cristóbal de Luzero, 1627–28, fols. 521–521v, December 19, 1628.

66. The censo al quitar looked so much like usury that Mercado felt the need to be quite clear, adding several pages on the subject to his 1569 manual, *Tratos y contratos de mercaderes y tratantes* (Salamanca: Matías Gast), when it was reprinted in 1571.

67. Bartolomé de Albornoz, in *Arte de los contractos* (Valencia: Pedro de Huete, 1573), fol. 108, notes that the censo al quitar "was introduced in this kingdom after the year 1500 and as it was a new practice, not yet made orderly . . . there was no agreement as to the interest that should be charged . . . [and] there were great disparities." He recalled that when he was a boy the rate of return on censos ranged as high as 11 percent annually, and that the friars would reprehend those who contracted for such rates (fol. 109).

68. A property given at censo could be repossessed by its owner, however, if the recipient failed to meet his payments on it for two consecutive years (three years if the property's owner was a layman rather than an ecclesiastical institution). Ibid., fol. 100v.

69. Albornoz (ibid., fols. 107v–9) notes that widespread use of the censo al quitar in Spain followed closely after the 1492 expulsion of the Jews, who had played a key lending role in the Spanish economy. He implies that Catholics were assuming a dangerously tainted activity. The danger of losing one's collateral property for nonpayment was real, in any case. In the Leyes de Toro of 1505, Law 68, cited by Diego de Espino y Cáceres, *Quaderno de las Leyes de Toro y nuevas decisiones, hechas y ordenadas en la ciudad de Toro, sobre las dudas de derecho que continuamente solian, y suelen occurrir en estos reynos* (Salamanca: Diego Cussio, 1599), 25–26, states that anyone who imposes a censo on his property and fails to pay according to the stipulated deadlines shall have his property seized in accordance with the terms of the contract. According to Albornoz, *Arte de los contractos*, fol. 109, this is the earliest reference in Castilian law to the censo al quitar.

70. Albornoz, *Arte de los contractos*, fol. 109, notes that the contract of *enfitéusis* is not redeemable, whereas the censo al quitar is—and that both are commonly called "censos."

71. This was an important development in the history of credit, albeit an unsettling one for Iberians. Even though Popes Martin V (in 1428) and Calixtus III (in 1455) had approved the practice, to many contemporary observers it still looked suspiciously like usury. For historical perspective on censos, see Raymond de Roover, *Business, Banking, and Economic Thought in Late Medieval and Early Modern Europe*, ed. Julius Kirshner (Chicago: University of Chicago Press, 1974); John T. Noonan Jr., *The Scholastic Analysis of Usury* (Cambridge: Harvard University Press, 1957); Marjorie Grice-Hutchinson, *The School of Salamanca: Readings in Spanish Monetary Theory, 1544–1605* (Oxford: Clarendon Press, Oxford University, 1952); and William Chester Jordan, *Women and Credit in Pre-Industrial and Developing Societies* (Philadelphia: University of Pennsylvania Press, 1993). For Peru, see Alfonso W. Quiroz, "Reassessing the Role of Credit in Late Colonial Peru: Censos, Escrituras, and Imposiciones," *Hispanic American Historical Review* 74 (1994), 193–230, and *Deudas olvidadas: Instrumentos de crédito en la economía colonial peruana 1750–1820* (Lima: Pontificia Universidad Católica del Perú, 1993).

72. Albornoz, *Arte de los contractos*, fol. 115v.

73. *Ordenanza hecha por el muy reverendo señor prior del monesterio de Nuestra Señora Santa María de Guadalupe, en la qual se contienen las condiciones conque se deven hazer los contratos del censso al quitar para que sean sin offensa de Nuestro Señor* (Guadalupe: Francisco Díaz, 1548). The anonymous author recommends that Christians abstain from living off the proceeds of censos al quitar.

74. The credit "landscape" of colonial Cuzco is examined in more detail below, in Chapter 5. María del Pilar Martínez López-Cano notes that ecclesiastical lenders assumed a dominant credit-giving role gradually, as incomes accumulated over time. During the sixteenth century, individual lending predominated in Mexico City credit; see Martínez López-Cano, *El crédito a largo plazo en el siglo XVI: Ciudad de México (1550–1620)* (Mexico City: UNAM, 1995).

75. *Constituciones generales*, fol. 62v: "Los dotes se emplearán todos en renta, por escusar el inconveniente grande que ay, en que crezca el numero de las Religiosas, y no se vaya aumentando la renta; y la Abadessa que consumiere algun dote . . . será privada de su oficio."

76. Most of the 1602 dealings called "censos" in the foundation records of Santa Clara were probably liens placed on property to cover dowries. However, some clearly correspond to loans of particular nuns' dowry funds. Arnold J. Bauer has made the valuable point that a lien transaction is not the same thing as a loan, even though the contractual instrument used is the same (the censo al quitar, or censo consignativo); see his important article "The Church in the Economy of Spanish America: *Censos* and *Depósitos* in the Eighteenth and Nineteenth Centuries," *Hispanic American Historical Review* 63 (1983), 707–33. Both kinds of transactions can be seen as economically "productive," however, in that both involved an advance of credit by Santa Clara.

77. Polo de Ondegardo, *El mundo de los incas*, 66.

78. *Tasa de la visita general de Francisco de Toledo*, ed. Noble David Cook (Lima: Universidad Nacional Mayor de San Marcos, 1975), 194.

Chapter 3 Forasteras Become Cuzqueñas

1. Esquivel y Navia, *Noticias cronológicas*, 1:279–80.

2. Keith A. Davies, *Landowners in Colonial Peru* (Austin: University of Texas Press, 1984), 94–97.

3. Archivo de Santa Catalina de Sena (hereafter ASCS), Cuzco, "Inventario de la fundación," doc. 3, fol. 59.

4. Wightman, *Indigenous Migration and Social Change*, is indispensable for a full view of the contemporary significance of the term "forastero/forastera," generally used to refer to indigenous migrants who had severed ties with their ayllus.

5. Vasco de Contreras y Valverde, *Relación de la ciudad del Cuzco*, ed. María del Carmen Martín Rubio (Cuzco: Imprenta Amauta, 1983), 187–88.

6. Ibid., 188.

7. ASCS, "Inventario de la fundación," doc. 3, fol. 57.

8. The information on Padilla is drawn from ASCS, "Inventario de la fundación," doc. 3. On the importance of the widows of encomenderos, who (like

Padilla) might retain their deceased husbands' privileges through several marriages and exercise considerable power, see Lockhart, *Spanish Peru*, 177–78, and Garcilaso, *Royal Commentaries*, 1230.

9. De la Puente, *Encomienda y encomenderos*, 412n4.

10. ASCS, "Inventario de la fundación," doc. 3, *carta de dote* of August 30, 1575. Viceroy Toledo may well have arranged Padilla's marriage to Pacheco, his compatriot and *hombre de confianza*. An inventory of Padilla's dowry (*bienes dotales*), drawn up in Arequipa on August 30, 1575, is contained in fols. 90–93.

11. For a detailed account of the growth of Arequipa's wine economy, see Davies, *Landowners in Colonial Peru*.

12. *Tasa de la visita general*, ed. Cook, 228–30. Somewhat different figures are provided in de la Puente, *Encomienda y encomenderos*, 412, 415, and 421, which add up to 2,262 pesos, 4 tomines ensayados in tribute ("libre de costas").

13. The *Tasa de la visita general*, ed. Cook, 58, reflects that Padilla was dispossessed of the encomienda "por delito que dicen que cometió en matar al dicho su marido."

14. Esquivel y Navia, *Noticias cronológicas*, 1:239–43.

15. That some urgency was involved is suggested by the fact that a papal bull was obtained, allowing her to profess without serving the standard yearlong novitiate: ASCS, "Inventario de la fundación," doc. 4, fol. 60.

16. ASCS, "Inventario de la fundación," doc. 3, fol. 57v; doc. 8, fols. 94–131.

17. ASCS, "Inventario de la fundación," doc. 3, fol. 58.

18. ASCS, "Inventario de la fundación," doc. 1, fols. 1–55, July 28, 1599.

19. ASCS, "Inventario de la fundación," doc. 3, fols. 57–57v. In 1556, for example, Padilla sought and obtained an inquest into Ginesa Guillén's mismanagement of her portion of the Arones encomienda; see *Documentos para la historia de Arequipa*, ed. Víctor M. Barriga, 3 vols. (Arequipa: Editorial "La Colmena," 1939–55), 3:274–98.

20. ASCS, "Inventario de la fundación," doc. 3, fol. 58v.

21. Ibid., fols. 58v–59.

22. See Harold Wethey, *Colonial Architecture and Sculpture in Peru* (Cambridge: Harvard University Press, 1949), and Valerie Fraser, *The Architecture of Conquest: Building in the Viceroyalty of Peru, 1535–1635* (Cambridge: Cambridge University Press, 1990).

23. The population of the city can be estimated only roughly. Wightman, *Indigenous Migration and Social Change*, 268, suggests that "the city's population, sustained by a steady influx of migrants, probably hovered in the 10,000 range throughout the mid-colonial period."

24. Félix Denegri Luna, in his prologue to Esquivel y Navia, *Noticias cronológicas*, 1:xiii–xv, emphasizes cultural fusion and artistic achievement. Using different criteria, David P. Cahill, in "Repartos ilícitos y familias principales en el sur andino: 1780–1824," *Revista de Indias* 48 (1988), 459, considers that the second half of the seventeenth century and first two-thirds of the eighteenth represented the "golden age" of Cuzco's elite families, especially those involved in textile production. Kenneth Andrien, in *Crisis and Decline: The Viceroyalty of Peru in the Seventeenth Century* (Albuquerque: University of New Mexico Press, 1985),

views the century as a period of fiscal crisis, yet notes the rise of "vibrant regional centers" like Cuzco which "acquired a buoyancy of their own and produced a wide variety of agricultural and manufactured goods" (18).

25. Richard L. Garner, "Long-Term Silver Mining Trends in Spanish America: A Comparative Analysis of Peru and Mexico," *American Historical Review* 93 (1988), 898–935. On the regional impact of mining, see the influential work of Carlos Sempat Assadourian, *El sistema de la economía colonial: Mercado interno, regiones y espacio económico* (Lima: Instituto de Estudios Peruanos, 1982) and Enrique Tandeter, *Coercion and Market: Silver Mining in Colonial Potosí, 1692–1826* (Albuquerque: University of New Mexico Press, 1993).

26. Luis Miguel Glave, *Trajinantes: Caminos indígenas en la sociedad colonial, siglos XVI–XVII* (Lima: Instituto de Apoyo Agrario, 1989), 181–362, undertakes a detailed analysis of the effects of Potosí's economic circuitry on Andean society during the seventeenth century.

27. Bartolomé Arzáns de Orsúa y Vela, in his *Historia de la villa imperial de Potosí*, mentions Cuzco as a source of sugar and cloth; curiously, he leaves out coca. The earliest Cuzco notarial records, from the 1560s and 1570s, are full of contracts for shipping coca to Potosí. Sugar production was also getting under way, as indicated by ADC, Luis de Quesada, 1571–81, fol. 376, the 1581 hiring of "Francisco Amao yndio" to make sugar in Juan Flores's ingenio and teach the skills to a slave and three *yanaconas* (indigenous servants not attached to ayllus). Regarding Cuzco's obrajes, see Neus Escandell-Tur, "Producción y comercio de tejidos coloniales: Cusco, 1570–1820" (Ph.D. diss., University of California–San Diego, 1993).

28. Research and documentation are scarce on the infamous Spanish programs of *reducción* and *composición*, but for a good idea of the impact of *composición* on Ollantaytambo after 1594, see Glave and Remy, *Estructura agraria y vida rural*, 87–92.

29. Cook, *Demographic Collapse*, 246.

30. Wightman, *Indigenous Migration and Social Change*, 63–67, argues that "the official Indian population of the bishopric of Cuzco reached its lowpoint much earlier than has been believed," around 1690, when a maximum of 82,367 *originarios* inhabited the bishopric.

31. See Carolyn S. Dean's study of Corpus Christi as a staging ground for both fixing and destabilizing Inca precedence over the city's Cañaris and Chachapoyas: "Ethnic Conflict and Corpus Christi in Colonial Cuzco," *Colonial Latin American Review* 2 (1993), 93–120.

32. Hemming, drawing on the pioneering work of Ella Dunbar Temple, portrays this great-grandson of Huayna Cápac as having been raised "a perfect Spanish gentleman" (*Conquest of the Incas*, 461–66). Don Melchor Carlos languished in Spain, where he petitioned to enter the knighthood of Santiago; see Guillermo Lohmann Villena, *Los americanos en las órdenes nobiliarias (1529–1900)*, 2 vols. (Madrid: Consejo Superior de Investigaciones Científicas, 1947), 1:199–201.

33. See Stern, *Peru's Indian Peoples*; Spalding, *Huarochirí*.

34. During the late sixteenth century Philip II had granted the privileges

of *hidalguía*, or nobility, to the legitimate descendants of conquerors and first settlers: *Recopilación de leyes de los reynos de las Indias*, 3d ed., 4 vols. (Madrid: Andrés Ortega, 1774), 2:90, Book 4, Title 6, Law 6.

35. Glave, *Trajinantes*, 289–92.

36. ADC, Libro de Actas del Cabildo 14, censos de indios, fols. 3–3v.

37. For examples see AAC, Parroquia del Sagrario, Matrimonios, 1628–86, fols. 180–80v; Matrimonios, 1692–1728, fol. 93v.

38. ADC, Colegio de Ciencias, leg. 5 (1648–1736), cuaderno 1, año 1648.

39. The diocese of Cuzco was subdivided soon thereafter: Contreras y Valverde, *Relación*, 124.

40. ASCS, "Inventario de agosto," fol. 32, August 29, 1606.

41. ASCS, "Inventario de la fundación," document 3, fol. 59.

42. Contreras y Valverde (*Relación*, 123–24) indicates that the next bishop, Don Fernando de Mendoza, did not arrive until late 1611.

43. ASCS, "Inventario de la fundación," doc. 3, fol. 59.

44. Ibid., fols. 57–57v.

45. ASCS, "Inventario de junio," fols. 137–49, censos on Arequipan vineyards of Tintin and Sondor.

46. One of the couple's daughters, Isabel de Tapia y Padilla, would later become a nun in Cuzco and serve as prioress of Santa Catalina in the 1650s and 1660s.

47. The problem of administering property at a distance was also being faced by the nuns of Santa Clara in Lima; see BN, ms. B702 (1610).

48. ASCS, "Inventario de los meses de agosto, setiembre, octubre, noviembre y diciembre," following fol. 137, letter of October 2, 1668.

49. Running the convent was largely a Padilla family matter during the community's initial decades in Cuzco. Andrea de Padilla became the convent's subprioress by 1611. Her brother Juan de Vargas served for many years as Santa Catalina's chaplain, handled convent business, and left the nuns his estate when he died. ASCS, "Inventario de junio," fol. 95, June 18, 1627, indicates that Vargas and Andrea de Padilla made the convent loans to help it meet expenses.

50. Ibid., fol. 32, May 6, 1617.

51. ADC, Francisco Hurtado, 1623, fols. 1580–84v, December 3, 1623.

52. ADC, Francisco Hurtado, 1620, fols. 104–10, January 4, 1620.

53. ASCS, "Inventario de octubre," fol. 57, October 17, 1608; ASCS, "Inventario de noviembre," fol. 42, November 27, 1619.

54. ASCS, "Inventario de junio," fol. 32, May 6, 1617.

55. ASCS, "Inventario de agosto, setiembre, octubre, noviembre y diciembre," fol. 14; unfortunately, the document is missing. According to the table of contents, the provisión was issued at Lima on September 9, 1639.

56. Ibid., fol. 137, October 2, 1668. According to the prioress, the kurakas and local officials were using the laborers in their own fields instead. About the same time, according to ASCS, "Inventario de abril," fol. 236, May 20, 1665, Santa Catalina was trying to hold onto yanaconas living and working on its estancia Acanuco in Paucartambo.

57. ASCS, "Inventario de la fundación," doc. 3, fol. 59.

58. ASCS, "Inventario de la fundación," doc. 13, fols. 155–57.

59. ASCS, "Inventario de marzo," fol. 283, March 2, 1684.

60. On the crucial role of acllas in Inca culture and state-building, see Silverblatt, *Moon, Sun, and Witches*, 81–108.

61. ASCS, "Inventario de la fundación," doc. 18, fol. 174, proxy given by Isabel de Padilla to Agustín de Tapia to collect the remainder of the dowry of "Doña Leonor de Esquivel, hija de Don Melchor Carlos Ynga," dated July 5, 1614. See also Lohmann Villena, *Los americanos en las órdenes nobiliarias*, 1:199–200.

62. ASCS, "Inventario de la fundación," doc. 19, fols. 179–79v.

63. Villegas lived in Cuzco by 1547, married a captain named Francisco de Boloña with whom she had at least one child, and became a widow sometime after 1576: ADC, Libro de Actas del Cabildo (1545–48); ADC, Juan de Quiroz, 1576–77, December 27, 1576.

64. ASF, Registro 15, parte no. 5, fol. 724v, codicil of April 17, 1600, citing the original donation of September 6, 1594, before the Cuzco notary Andrés de Quesada.

65. Ibid., f. 716, April 20, 1600.

66. ASF, Registro 15, no. 6, fols. 1096–1111, June 3, 1577.

67. Ministerio de Relaciones Exteriores (RR. EE.), Lima, Archivo de Límites, Signatura CSG-2 (1559–1613), fols. 147–49, provisión del virrey D. Luis de Velasco, August 23, 1603.

68. Esquivel y Navia, *Noticias cronológicas*, 2:47–48.

69. ADC, Cristóbal de Luzero, 1625–26, fols. 314–58v, June 26–30, 1625.

70. BN, ms. B457 (1623). The case was appealed before the Audiencia de Lima, and when Don Pedro died in 1641 it had still not been settled.

71. ADC, Cristóbal de Luzero, 1623–24, fols. 278–86v, July 16–18, 1624.

72. Consider, for example, the first convent in Huamanga (Ayacucho), founded by the Oré family for its daughters; the sons of the family were sent to Lima to take religious orders.

73. Esquivel y Navia, *Noticias cronológicas*, 2:90–97.

Chapter 4 Reproducing Colonial Cuzco

1. The grille was (and in many convents still is) double, in accordance with the wishes of Clement VIII, who ordered that "at least two strong, thick grilles be placed, one on the interior, the other at least a little over half a *vara* away, and the iron bars should be close enough that a hand cannot reach through, even a slender hand" (Arbiol, *La religiosa instruida*, 474). The rule of the Clares specified that the grille be made of "subtly punctured sheets of iron," the better to limit visibility (*Constituciones generales*, fol. 11v).

2. Arbiol, *La religiosa instruida*, 467, 491.

3. *Constituciones generales*, fol. 11v.

4. See, for example, a 1787 conflict over property between Doña María Dominga Almiron y Villegas and a nun of Santa Catalina: AAC, LXXIII, 2, 40 (año 1787), fol. 2.

5. ADC, Cabildo, Justicia Ordinaria, Causas Civiles, leg. 11 (1683–89); Esquivel y Navia, *Noticias cronológicas*, 2:294.

6. AAC, XXXVIII, 2, 22 (año 1682). Don Agustín Jara de la Cerda, a prominent criollo and regidor, was accused of violating Tapia's right to ecclesiastical immunity. He argued that he had removed Tapia from a patio not covered by ecclesiastical immunity "because it is a place where Indians and other servants of the Monastery live" (fols. 9–9v).

7. Archivo Arzobispal de Lima (hereafter AAL), Apelaciones del Cuzco, leg. 24 (1676–78), documents regarding the infraction of *violación de clausura* by Losada y Novoa; see also Martín, *Daughters of the Conquistadores*, 223–28.

8. Mary Elizabeth Perry, *Gender and Disorder in Early Modern Seville* (Princeton: Princeton University Press, 1990), 80, notes that such attachments, known as *devociones de monjas*, were commonplace in Spain and were satirized by Quevedo and Góngora.

9. See, for example, Martín, *Daughters of the Conquistadores*, 201–2, 215, 234.

10. AAL, Apelaciones del Cuzco, leg. 16 (1659–60), appeal from Santa Catalina, 1660.

11. On April 26, 1664, for example, Tomás de Herrera Guzmán agreed to provide two years' worth of daily music lessons in harp and organ to the nuns and novices of Santa Clara: ADC, Lorenzo de Messa Andueza, año 1664, fols. 418–18v. Convent communities often discounted or waived the full dowry to encourage good musicians and singers to profess.

12. ADC, Lorenzo de Messa Andueza, año 1655, fols. 1707–16, August 4, 1655.

13. ASCS, "Inventario de noviembre," fol. 275, 1683 permission for Santa Catalina to enclose three houses the nuns had purchased.

14. In AAC, XVII, 2, 24 (año 1862), the nuns of Santa Catalina mention that their convent contains these spaces for the observance of the common life, or *vida común*. However, many nuns did not use these spaces, like Doña Juana de los Reyes Guzmán y de Quiros, a Dominican nun who petitioned to be excused from taking her meals in the refectory on account of illness: ADC, Alonso Beltrán Luzero, 1640–41, fols. 202–202v, March 21, 1640.

15. Arbiol, *La religiosa instruida*, 597.

16. Martín, *Daughters of the Conquistadores*, 175, 181, 196–98.

17. AAC, LXI, 3, 53, describes "una Casa bastante comoda con ocho quartos, y su respectivo oratorio," donated to Santa Catalina in 1806 by a nun desiring to profess. Another cell, described in a 1656 sale, had its own "despencita, un hornito y una alacena," and a door with a lock was to be installed: ADC, Lorenzo de Messa Andueza, 1656, fols. 101–2, January 10, 1656.

18. *Constituciones generales*, fols. 34, 39.

19. Ibid., fol. 37.

20. *Regla de N. P. S. Agustín, águila de los doctores, luz de la Iglesia. Manual, y espejo espiritual de sus hijas*, ed. Tomás de Espinosa (Granada: Imprenta Real de Francisco de Ochoa, 1677), fols. 29v–30.

21. Mendoza, *Chrónica de la provincia de S. Antonio de los Charcas*, 440.

22. *Constituciones generales*, fols. 22v–23.

23. See ADC, Francisco Hurtado 1616, fols. 1115–15v, regarding the profession of Isabel Arias, August 9, 1616.

24. *Constituciones generales*, fol. 38v.

25. On convent jails, infractions, and punishments, see *Regla de N. P. S. Agustín*, ed. Espinosa, fols. 40v–42, and *Constituciones generales*, fol. 41.

26. *Constituciones generales*, fol. 15v.

27. These advisors were called *madres de consejo* by the Clares, *discretas* by the Dominicans, and *clavarias* by the Carmelites.

28. *Constituciones generales*, fol. 59.

29. Alternatively, the community might admit up to one servant (*criada*) for every ten nuns. The *Constituciones generales*, fols. 59v–61, make it clear that servants were to be allowed only in convents having no lay sisters to do the heavy tasks.

30. In their terms, *legas*: *Regla de N. P. S. Agustín*, ed. Espinosa, fol. 30.

31. *Constituciones generales*, fol. 61.

32. Contreras y Valverde, *Relación*, 178, 188. The same was true of several of Lima's convents; a detailed December 1783 census may be found in AAL, Papeles Importantes, leg. 18, exp. 20.

33. Board was set at 150 pesos a year; see ADC, Lorenzo de Messa Andueza, año 1655, fol. 2220–20v, November 23, 1655. Women and girls of all ages might be boarded by a parent or husband. Marcos de la Cuba, for example, agreed to pay the clarisas 150 pesos a year to board his wife and daughter: ibid., año 1656, fols. 537–38, March 4, 1656.

34. AAL, Apelaciones del Cuzco, leg. 24 (1676–78), *expediente* against Don Antonio de Losada y Novoa for violación de clausura.

35. ASCS, "Inventario de los instrumentos respectivos a la fundación," doc. 27. For examples of such contracts, see Lorenzo de Messa Andueza, 1655, fol. 599, April 5, 1655, concerning the boarding and schooling of the ten-year-old Melchora de Claves inside Santa Clara, and fols. 884–85, May 13, 1655, regarding that of Juana de Gaona. In each case the cost was 50 pesos a year.

36. Such acts were recorded only rarely—for example, in the testimony of Tomasa de San José against a resident of Santa Catalina named Pascuala Tito. Sor Tomasa testified that Pascuala Tito had screamed insults at her, saying among other things "that I was abandoned at the torno, and raised in a dirty crib" (AAC, XXXVII, 1, 10 [1795]).

37. At the time of her profession, for example, Doña Juana de Tapia was described as the *expuesta* of the nun who had raised her in Santa Catalina ("su expuesta"); see ADC, José Tapia Sarmiento, años 1769–71, fols. 170v–71, July 30, 1770. See also Martín, *Daughters of the Conquistadores*, 79–85.

38. AAC, LXXXII, 1, 9 (1823): the nun Victoria de San Gabriel of Santa Clara, describing her goddaughter Lorenza Cabrera as "una cholita Ahijadita mia . . . a q[uie]n la crié y la eduqué desde sus primeros pañales." From the mid-seventeenth century on, countless documents mention girls raised by nuns "from the time they were born," "from a tender age," "from childhood."

39. There is almost no mention of *seglarados* in the records I have seen. However, in ASCS, "Inventario de los instrumentos respectivos a la fundación,"

doc. 19, a report dated July 27, 1618, mentions that Santa Catalina has gone into debt to build two *cuartos*, or rooms: "one for the education and raising of girls . . . the other for married women who want to enclose themselves while their husbands are absent."

40. E.g.: a nun of Santa Catalina named Rosa Vergara y Cárdenas, who wrote that the nun who raised her taught her "to read and write, and also to sing" (AAC, paquete no. 45 (319–20), años 1692–1922, exp. 5 [1827]). The same nun had also raised Rosa's mother inside Santa Catalina.

41. See, for example, ADC, Gregorio Básquez Serrano, 1708–9, fols. 363–65v, July 14, 1709, in which a Dominican nun receives her prioress's permission to donate a cell to each of the two orphans she has raised.

42. Doña María Dominga Almirón y Villegas left Santa Catalina, married, and left the city. Years later she tried to reclaim the cell that had been left to her by the nun who had raised her, but it had been taken over by a different nun, Josefa de la O, who became angry at Almirón y Villegas and left her standing at the grille unsatisfied: AAC, LXXIII, 2, 40 (1787).

43. AAC, LXXIII, 3, 55 (1646), fols. 2–2v, February 20, 1646, testimony of the nun Doña Feliciana de San Nicolás.

44. ADC, Alonso Beltrán Luzero, 1642–43, fols. 105–7v, January 13, 1642.

45. ADC, Lorenzo de Messa Andueza, 1661, fols. 138–138v, February 4, 1661, *asiento de aprendiz*. Some nuns inherited slaves when family members died; see, for example, ADC, Pedro José Gamarra, 1762–63, fols. 4–5v, regarding a Clare who inherited two slaves from her sister.

46. ASCS, "Inventario de los instrumentos respectivos a la fundación," doc. 27, fol. 250, April 20, 1652. Martín, in *Daughters of the Conquistadores*, 185, describes Lima's donadas as "a buffer" between professed and unprofessed women, and as "exalted maids" who were "segregated from maids and slaves and placed socially a notch above them in the complex hierarchical structure of the nunnery." This may well have been the donadas' place in Cuzco.

47. ADC, Asuntos Eclesiásticos, leg. 3 (1739–50), requests granted April 2, 1743, and October 5, 1742. Not all orphans were raised to become maids, however. Doña Manuela de San Martín of Santa Catalina clearly raised two orphans to become nuns, and she received permission from her prioress to leave a cell to each of them: ADC, Gregorio Básquez Serrano, 1708–9, fols. 363–65v, July 14, 1709.

48. Donald L. Gibbs, in "The Economic Activities of Nuns, Friars, and their Convents in Mid-Colonial Cuzco," *The Americas* 45 (1989), 343–62, has drawn attention to cuzqueños' purchase of cells within Cuzco's convents. See also Martín, *Daughters of the Conquistadores*, 192–200, on the formation of "family clusters" in Lima's convents.

49. ADC, Alonso Beltrán Luzero, 1630–31, fols. 580–81v, December 9, 1630, and 57–58v, January 18, 1631.

50. AAC, XXV, 1, 13 (1741), September 13, 1741.

51. ASCS, "Inventario de las escrituras del mes de octubre," doc. 20, February 26, 1633.

52. ADC, Lorenzo de Messa Andueza, 1655, fols. 1707–17v, August 22, 1655.

53. AAL, Apelaciones del Cuzco, leg. 24 (1676–78), 1678 expediente against Losada y Novoa.

54. AAL, Apelaciones del Cuzco, leg. 36 (1704–6). See also ADC, Asuntos Eclesiásticos, leg. 5 (1768–70), which contains the 1770 case of Angela Angulo, whose husband had her committed to Las Nazarenas for adultery despite her denial of the charges; and AAC, XXVI, 3, 44, regarding Jacoba Oquendo, committed to Santa Catalina by her mother in 1831 for disobedience.

55. A decision in the case of Cipriana Villalba, *ropavejera*, does not figure in the available documents, however; see AAC, XII, 5, 84 (1773).

56. On Aymulo's apparent attempt to kill her husband, Eusebio Pérez, by throwing him into a river, see AAC, XLIII, 4, 68 (1771).

57. Cuzco's convents absorbed functions that in larger cities were apportioned among a wider range of institutions. Florence, for example, had a specific place for the "badly married"; see Sherrill Cohen, *The Evolution of Women's Asylums since 1500: From Refuges for Ex-Prostitutes to Shelters for Battered Women* (New York: Oxford University Press, 1992).

58. "Libro original," ed. Angulo, 71.

59. ASCS, "Libro de profesiones," indicates that these amounts remained stable into the early nineteenth century.

60. In a contested election for prioress of Santa Catalina in 1644, appealed to Lima in an expediente in AAL, Apelaciones del Cuzco, leg. 6 (1644–45), thirty-nine women voted, too few to have included nuns of the white veil.

61. AAC, LXXVI, 2, 24, *auto* regarding three houses and a *callejón* added to Santa Clara, November 19, 1683.

62. Note that the nuns of Cuzco thus reworked two categories that their constitutions treated as alternatives—lay sister (donada) and servant (criada)—into complements. Rather than two categories of cloistered women, then, Cuzco's convents had five: nun of the black veil; nun of the white veil; donada; servant; slave.

63. AAC, LXI, 3, 53, expediente of June 19, 1806, containing papers concerning the December 20, 1735, donation (fols. 11–14v).

64. Martín, *Daughters of the Conquistadores*, 179, 183.

65. In another passage, the clergyman adds that he is assisting Ugarte "in view of her Humility, Virtue, and good blood" (ADC, Alejo González Peñaloza, 1732–35, December 5, 1733).

66. See for example ADC, Alejo Fernández Escudero, 1721, fols. 620–21v, September 1, 1721: two local priests arrange to pay the dowries of their nieces. Years later the women, Magdalena and Bernarda de Esquivel, would assume a dominant role inside Santa Clara, each serving as abbess several times.

67. On the varieties of illegitimacy in this period, see María Emma Mannarelli, *Pecados públicos: La ilegitimidad en Lima, siglo XVII* (Lima: Ediciones Flora Tristán, 1993).

68. AAL, Apelaciones del Cuzco, leg. 6 (1644–45).

69. Doña María was the hija natural of Don Gerónimo Costilla Gallinato: ADC, Gregorio Básquez Serrano, 1708–9, fols. 455–55v, December 12, 1709.

70. ADC, Corregimiento, Causas Ordinarias, leg. 25 (1689–90), exp. 517, año 1690.

71. José de Rezabal y Ugarte, *Tratado del real derecho de las medias-anatas seculares y del servicio de lanzas a que están obligados los títulos de Castilla* (Madrid: Don Benito Cano, 1792), 157, 168.

72. See John H. Rowe, "The Incas under Spanish Colonial Institutions," *Hispanic American Historical Review* 37 (1957), 155–58.

73. AGI, Audiencia de Lima, 306.

74. Numerous contracts for wet nurses may be found in the ADC, and Glave has drawn attention to them in *Trajinantes*, 358–61.

75. See, for example, the case of a Spanish merchant who crossed the powerful, haughty Marqués de Valleumbroso: Bernard Lavallé, *El mercader y el marqués: Las luchas de poder en el Cusco (1700–1730)* (Lima: Banco Central de Reserva del Perú, 1988).

76. AGI, Audiencia de Lima, 492, as cited by Michèle Colin, *Le Cuzco à la fin du XVIIe et au début du XVIIIe siècle* (Paris: Institut des Hautes Etudes de l'Amérique Latine, 1966), 144.

77. ASCS, Inventario de noviembre, doc. 6, fol. 44, Lima, November 27, 1619.

78. Doña Feliciana was thus a great-granddaughter of the Inca Túpac Amaru (father of Doña Magdalena); see Hemming, *Conquest of the Incas*, 507. She figured among the *madres de consejo* by 1677, according to AAC, XLIX, 1, 16 (December 23, 1677).

79. ASCS, Inventario de diciembre, doc. 13, fol. 90, December 16, 1660.

80. ADC, Gregorio Básquez Serrano, 1708–9, fol. 201v, June 15, 1708. Don Gaspar imposed a censo of 2,000 pesos on his land in Paucartambo in order to support Doña Antonia in Santa Clara. She received a discount by "enseñando a otras de bajonera por que no ayga falta en este dho combento" (fols. 210–12v).

81. ADC, Francisco Maldonado, 1713, fols. 587–88v, November 25, 1713; ASCS, "Inventario de mayo," doc. 80, May 1, 1717.

82. ADC, Matías Ximénez Ortega, 1717–18, fols. 325–28v, July 1, 1717. Thirty years later Doña Agustina Suta, ñusta, daughter of Don José Tamboguaso, "Ynga alferez real" and *gobernador* of the pueblo of Taray in Calca y Lares, was also received as a nun of the white veil in Santa Catalina, according to ADC, Alejo González Peñaloza, 1744–50, August 26, 1747.

83. ADC, Matías Ximénez Ortega, 1717–18, fols. 325–28v, July 1, 1717; Pedro José Gamarra, 1739, fols. 152–55v, May 14, 1739.

84. This limitation may have reflected the overall impoverishment of the noble Indians of Cuzco, but further research is needed to clarify this point.

85. Las Nazarenas nearly succeeded in becoming a convent in the eighteenth century. AGI, Audiencia de Cuzco, 64, contains relevant papers.

86. *Cuzco 1689: Economía y sociedad en el sur andino*, ed. Horacio Villanueva Urteaga (Cuzco: Centro de Estudios Rurales Andinos "Bartolomé de Las Casas," 1982), 230–33.

87. AAC, XXXI, 1, 18.

88. ADC, Corregimiento, Causas Ordinarias, leg. 25 (1689–90), exp. 505, October 31, 1689.

89. AAL, Apelaciones del Cuzco, leg. 36 (1704–6), *petición* of 1704.

90. Perhaps Cuzco's convents served to shelter and discipline secular women who were "Spanish" (i.e., Spanish, criolla, and/or well-to-do), while the beaterios took in secular penitenciadas and *refugiadas* who were "Indian" and/or poor.

91. As we shall see, caciques gained more than enhanced status by associating themselves closely with Cuzco's convents: they might also obtain credit and spiritual benefits.

92. Forthcoming studies by Manuel Burga, Carolyn Dean, David Garrett, and Ann Wightman will contribute significantly to our understanding of this segmented elite and this critical midcolonial *coyuntura*.

93. See ADC, Asuntos Eclesiásticos, leg. 1 (1713–34), exp. 6, an ecclesiastical order that the nuns of Santa Catalina remove the adornments (ribetes) from their habits.

94. Mendoza, *Chrónica de la provincia de S. Antonio de los Charcas*, 386, 398, 453–54.

95. See Martín, *Daughters of the Conquistadores*, 201–42, and AAL, Papeles Importantes, leg. 18, exp. 3–7, 10–12, 14, 21, 22.

96. See AGI, Audiencia de Lima, 333, report of Don Fernando de Castilla Altamirano, Cuzco, June 16, 1647, who informs the Crown that he has seen "in this city particular devotion to Nuestra Señora del Carmen."

97. *The Collected Works of St. Teresa of Avila*, vol. 1: *The Book of Her Life, Spiritual Testimonies, Soliloquies*, 2d rev. ed., trans. Kieran Kavanaugh, O.C.D. and Otilio Rodríguez, O.C.D. (Washington, D.C.: Institute of Carmelite Studies, ICS Publications, 1987), 84–85.

98. Esquivel y Navia, *Noticias cronológicas*, 2:131–33.

99. An intriguing possibility is raised by a contract in ADC, Pedro José Gamarra, 1741, fols. 357–59v, February 28, 1741, in which the widow of Don Alonso Guampu Tupa and her daughter sell an asset using a Quechua interpreter. Perhaps in Santa Teresa indias nobles were allowed to take the black veil in the eighteenth century. That prominent criollas also entered the convent is plain from ADC, Pedro José Gamarra, 1749, fols. 337–37v, July 14, 1749.

100. To the contrary, their austerity spared them considerable expense and, because they were a smaller community, their endowment went further.

101. ADC, Alejo Fernández Escudero, 1711, fol. 485, July 7, 1711, indicates that Santa Teresa received the professions of nuns of the white veil at the standard local rate: 1,165 pesos, 2 reales corrientes.

102. Casuistry's root is the Latin *casus*, "case" or "chance." For some idea of how a scholastic legal mind worked, see Arbiol, *La religiosa instruida*, 162, on the categories of license that nuns might receive from their superiors: "Hay licencia general, y particular, clara, expresa, tacita, interpretativa, o presunta." He defined each with care; the last, "licencia tacita, interpretativa, o presunta," was so called because "aunque no está concedida en terminos expresos, claros, y formales . . . se tiene por cierto, con bastante fundamento, que el Prelado, y la Prelada la concederian, si se les pidiese."

1. Covarrubias elaborates on possible entanglements under *grada*, "grille," telling of frustrated male desire: "El italiano la llama *grata*, y cuentan de un galán que, viendo a su dama en una reja, y estando desfavorecido della, le dixo: '¡O ingrata ingrata!'; la primera voz sinifica ser ingrata, y la segunda estar en la reja, o detrás de la red, como loca." See *Tesoro de la lengua castellana o española*, ed. Martín de Riquer (Barcelona: Editorial Alta Fulla, 1987), 653.

2. ADC, Cabildo, Justicia Ordinaria, Causas Civiles, leg. 11 (1683–89). Such lending and pawning of jewelry was clearly part of the colonial circuitry of credit and alliance.

3. In his will (ADC, Antonio Pérez de Vargas, 1689–92, fols. 172–80) Costilla's son Don Gerónimo Costilla Gallinato indicated that Suriguaylla belonged to him and was the subject of a dispute with Santa Clara over censo payments. Apparently a settlement was reached, since the hacienda stayed in the family and continued to be used to secure loans from the Clares. See ADC, Corregimiento, Causas Ordinarias, leg. 49 (1768), exp. 1096, "Autos que sigue el monasterio de Santa Clara contra las haciendas nombradas Suriguailla."

4. The Costillas diversified by cultivating other potential lenders as well: the Augustinians, for example.

5. For recent contributions and an overview of the dynamics of regional Andean economies, see Brooke Larson and Olivia Harris, eds., *Ethnicity, Markets, and Migration in the Andes* (Durham: Duke University Press, 1995); Glave, *Trajinantes*.

6. María del Pilar Martínez López-Cano notes the relative archival invisibility of "private" credit: "El crédito particular en España: Formas y controversias," in Leonor Ludlow and Jorge Silva Riquer, eds., *Los negocios y las ganancias de la colonia al México moderno* (Mexico City: Instituto Mora and UNAM, 1993), 38. A 1696 case of an oral contract is mentioned in ADC, Pedro de Cáceres, 1696, fols. 285–88, September 7, 1696.

7. Credit has until recently been most visible from the vantage point of the hacienda; see Glave and Remy, *Estructura agraria y vida rural*, and Jorge A. Guevara Gil, *Propiedad agraria y derecho colonial* (Lima: Pontificia Universidad Católica del Perú, 1993).

8. Victoria Hennessey Cummins illuminates its elaborate subterfuges: "The Church and Business Practices in Late Sixteenth-Century Mexico," *The Americas* 44 (1988), 431–40. See also María del Pilar Martínez López-Cano, ed., *Iglesia, estado y economía, siglos XVI al XIX* (Mexico City: Instituto Mora and UNAM, 1995). New Peruvian research has brought Lima merchants into focus: Margarita Suárez, *Comercio y fraude en el Perú colonial: Las estrategias mercantiles de un banquero* (Lima: Banco Central de la Reserva and Instituto de Estudios Peruanos, 1995).

9. Brian R. Hamnett drew attention to this trend in "Church Wealth in Peru: Estates and Loans in the Archdiocese of Lima in the Seventeenth Century," *Jahrbuch für Geschichte von Staat, Wirtschaft und Gesellschaft Lateinamerikas* 10 (1973), 113–32. Quiroz, in "Reassessing the Role of Credit," 202–5, notes that the Inquisition became one of Lima's largest ecclesiastical creditors.

10. Stern (*Peru's Indian Peoples*, 81, 97–100) notes the workings of these cajas under Viceroy Toledo's "grand design" for Spanish colonial rule.

11. See Quiroz, "Reassessing the Role of Credit," 206–9, for more on Lima's caja de censos de indios.

12. ASCS, "Inventario de agosto," doc. 1, fols. 5v–8, June 28, 1599.

13. Don Diego's complaints appear in AAC, II, 1, 12 (1657). See also Vilma Ceballos López, "La Caja de Censos de Indios y su aporte a la economía colonial (1565–1613)," *Revista del Archivo Nacional del Perú* 26 (1962), 269–352; María del Carmen Martín Rubio, "La Caja de Censos de Indios en el Cuzco," *Revista de Indias* 39 (1979), 187–208.

14. Donald L. Gibbs first called attention to this in "Cuzco, 1680–1710: An Andean City Seen through Its Economic Activities" (Ph.D. diss., University of Texas–Austin, 1979).

15. Bauer, "The Church in the Economy of Spanish America." On censos consignativos, their history and variations, see Gisela von Wobeser, "Mecanismos crediticios en la Nueva España: El uso del censo consignativo," *Mexican Studies/Estudios Mexicanos* 5 (1989), 1–23.

16. ADC, Alonso Beltrán Luzero, 1630–31, fols. 145–53v, February 14, 1631.

17. Agustín went on to become a member of the regular clergy himself, but joined the Franciscans of Cuzco.

18. Cuzco's archives contain extensive records on the finances of these monastic houses, including many censos of various kinds. The men's orders both extended and received credit locally. The Franciscans, by contrast, appear to have been relatively uninvolved in such dealings.

19. In 1715, for example, the Dominican nuns loaned 1,000 pesos, half of which belonged to the Cofradía de las Animas "fundada en este Monasterio" (ASCS, "Inventario de agosto," doc. 49, August 9, 1715).

20. The hacienda Santotis, for example; see Guevara Gil, *Propiedad agraria y derecho colonial*. The Augustinians and Bethlemites held several haciendas of the Ollantaytambo region, as did members of the secular clergy; see Glave and Remy, *Estructura agraria y vida rural*.

21. More research will be needed for the credit panorama of Cuzco to become clear. Cuzco's Jesuits were probably credit-hungry borrowers more often than they were lenders, since they had large enterprises to maintain and schools to run. On merchants' role in credit, see Escandell-Tur, "Producción y comercio de tejidos coloniales," 51–128.

22. ASCS, "Inventario de marzo," doc. 31, list entitled "Memoria de las escrituras cobrables, que entregó la señora María de los Remedios, priora que fue, a la señora Catalina de San Ambrosio y Mendoza, priora actual," March 2, 1684. The amount of principal cannot be ascertained for 23 of the 166 entries. Since the average transaction was more than 2,000 pesos, the missing principal might have come to 46,000 pesos, raising the total principal to 343,433 pesos and the convent's annual income to as much as 17,172 pesos.

23. ADC, handwritten list of 78 items entitled "Memoria de los censos que al presente pagan los censuatarios del Cuzco, que se hizo en 29 de febrero de 1676," inserted into the back of a hand-copied volume from the library of the monastery of San Agustín: Lorenzo de Niebla, *Summa del estilo de escribanos*

y de herencias y particiones y escripturas y avisos de jueces (Seville: Pedro Martínez de Bañares, 1565).

24. ASCS, "Inventario de febrero," doc. 28, February 7, 1668.

25. ASCS, "Inventario de junio," doc. 46, inventory of the bienes of Madre Juana del Carmen, who died on June 5, 1688.

26. ASCS, "Inventario de diciembre," doc. 30, December 20, 1700.

27. Examples of this kind of "tracking" of particular women's dowries are numerous; see, for example, ADC, Pedro de Cáceres, 1697, fols. 450–57v.

28. Philip T. Hoffman, in "Confidence in Your Notary: The Business of Intermediation in Eighteenth-Century Parisian Credit Markets," a paper presented at the Shelby Cullom Davis Center for Historical Studies, Princeton University, January 26, 1996, shows how Parisian notaries often acted as brokers for their clients. Cuzco's notaries, privy to valuable business information, probably did the same. This would explain the rapidity with which people made their way to the locutorio once a censo had been repaid to the nuns.

29. Martín López de Paredes, a notary who handled much of Santa Catalina's business in the late seventeenth century, contracted to receive 1,000 pesos from the nuns in a censo of June 23, 1663: ASCS, "Inventario de las escrituras del mes de junio," doc. 30.

30. ADC, Lorenzo de Messa Andueza, 1670, fols. 805–9v. This appears to be the initial phase of consolidation of the well-known obraje-hacienda complex of Lucre. See Escandell-Tur, "Producción y comercio de tejidos coloniales," 86–119.

31. They engaged in a standard transaction of the day: the composición de tierras. See ADC, Lorenzo de Messa Andueza, 1645–47, fols. 2137–46v. See also Glave and Remy, *Estructura agraria y vida rural*, 87–92, and Guevara Gil, *Propiedad agraria y derecho colonial*, 174–86.

32. ADC, Lorenzo de Messa Andueza, 1670, fols. 1062–69v, November 11, 1670; ASCS, "Inventario de junio," doc. 38, June 25, 1675; ADC, Gregorio Básquez Serrano, 1708–9, fols. 119–27, March 15, 1708.

33. Doña Antonia Siclla secured the loan with her houses in the city of Cuzco ("barrio de la Calle Nueva") and her house and orchard in the valley of Guancaro; see ASCS, "Inventario de marzo," doc. 29, March 14, 1673.

34. ASCS, "Inventario del mes de henero," doc. 38, January 7, 1679.

35. ADC, Pedro José Gamarra, 1747, fols. 151–57v, June 2, 1747, obligación in the amount of 10,000 pesos for three years with annual payments of 500 pesos (5%). See Antonine Tibesar, "The *Alternativa*: A Study in Spanish–Creole Relations in Seventeenth-Century Peru," *The Americas* 11 (1955), 229–83.

36. ADC, Lorenzo de Messa Andueza, 1676, fols. 1159–68v, censo dated November 3, 1676.

37. ASCS, "Inventario de noviembre," doc. 37, November 9, 1718.

38. ASCS, "Inventario de diciembre," doc. 9, December 10, 1647.

39. ADC, Gregorio Básquez Serrano, 1709, leg. 53, fols. 6–12, January 9, 1709. Their grandmother had left them the hacienda Ancaypava on condition that they borrow 1,000 pesos to improve it.

40. ADC, Pedro de Cáceres, 1696, fols. 397–432v.

41. The records on Santa Catalina and Santa Teresa also reflect active investing by the nuns in many sugar ingenios of the Cuzco region.

42. During the sixteenth century these transactions had brought the convent a return of 7.14 percent annually, as did the censos al quitar. After the rate was adjusted downward by the Crown in the early seventeenth century, the contracts specified an annual payment of 5 percent of each property's value.

43. ADC, Pedro de Cáceres, 1697, fols. 236–43v. See AAC, XIX, 3, 47, petition of October 3, 1778, for an explicit statement of the disadvantages of renting convent property.

44. ADC, Alonso Beltrán Luzero, 1630–31, fols. 745–54v, November 26, 1631.

45. The administrator and additional witnesses also affirmed that leasing was preferable to hiring costly mayordomos, because "often no trustworthy mayordomo can be found" (ASCS, "Inventario de julio," doc. 19, fols. 134–36, July 30, 1648).

46. Caco appears on a list of Santa Clara's assets in 1872; see AAC, C-LVIII, 4, 47, Abbess Luisa La Torre to the bishop of Cuzco, September 27, 1872.

47. For eighteenth-century contracts concerning Caco, see ADC: Matías Ximénez Ortega, 1717–18, fols. 149–54; Alejo Fernández Escudero, 1724, fols. 464–72; Pedro José Gamarra, 1729–31, fols. 268–70; 1743, fols. 101–4, 148–50; 1755, fols. 106–10; 1762–63, fols. 248–50; 1766, fols. 420–22; 1767, fol. 48; Juan Bautista Gamarra, 1774–76, fols. 174–75; Anselmo Vargas, 1797–98, fol. 615.

48. The nuns used rental contracts as well as leases to manage Yllanya (rent was payable in sugar and "melados"). In 1710 the nuns leased the ingenio to Don Miguel de Mendoza y Valdes for 5,000 pesos a year in a *venta de por vidas;* see ASCS, "Inventario de junio," doc. 48, June 14, 1710. Santa Catalina still held Guambutio and Yllanya well into the twentieth century.

49. ADC, Cristóbal de Lucero, 1621–22, fols. 281–89v. The land in question, located alongside the Urubamba River, was sold to Hernando Mejía Durán, who paid 7,200 pesos in two bars of silver and four bags of coins. The nuns intended to use the money to expand Pachar.

50. ADC, Colegio de Ciencias, leg. 33, fols. 89–94. By the early eighteenth century, Pachar had been further enlarged, and the nuns were able to lease the entire hacienda for 5 percent of its value, or 2,000 pesos annually: ADC, Gregorio Básquez Serrano, 1711, fols. 20–25, January 15, 1711; Matías Ximénez Ortega, 1715, August 14, 1715. Pachar's importance is reflected in the unusually detailed contract, which specified that if the lessee failed to bring the stipulated grain to the convent on time, the nuns could charge him or her the cost of an equivalent amount of grain at market prices.

51. In 1658, for example, the merchant Diego de Molina bought a small quantity of maize: ADC, Lorenzo de Messa Andueza, 1658, fols. 1056–56v, September 3, 1658. The constitutions of the Clares explicitly provided for such sales: *Constituciones generales,* fol. 68.

52. ASF, Registro 10, exp. 22.

53. Ibid., exp. 5, "Razón de la entrada y gasto que tiene el obrage de Poma-

cocha del monasterio de Santa Clara de esta ciudad de Guamanga." According to this undated document, in one year the obraje of Pomacocha produced 30,000 varas of cloth, sold at 4 reales each. Of the resulting income of 15,000 pesos, 4,727 pesos were paid to Indian laborers and 3,100 pesos were distributed among the nuns, donadas, and servants.

54. Magnus Mörner, in *Perfil de la sociedad rural del Cuzco a fines de la colonia* (Lima: Universidad del Pacífico, 1978), 82, mentions in passing that the owners of Cuzco obrajes included "uno que otro convento."

55. See, for example, Enrique Llopis Agelán's detailed account of sales of surplus grain, olive oil, and other agricultural products by the Dominican nuns of Regina Coeli in Zafra from the 1770s to the 1830s: "Las economías monásticas al final del antiguo régimen en Extremadura" (Ph.D. diss., Universidad Complutense de Madrid, 1980), 809–40.

56. Tapia Franco, "Análisis histórico," chap. 2, cites a case that came before the authorities in Lima in the early 1640s. A woman contracted to lend a man 4,400 pesos but gave him only 4,000 pesos, whereupon he denounced her for charging interest (10%).

57. Some extreme cases may represent neglect or difficulty producing relevant legal documentation rather than generosity or forbearance on the part of the nuns—for example, a censo in the amount of 3,000 pesos which went unpaid for thirty-eight years and eight months. By the time the nuns of Santa Clara initiated a suit to recover on the censo, the arrears came to 5,800 pesos. See ADC, Pedro José Gamarra, 1769, fols. 269–75v, August 1, 1769. A few years later, the Clares entered a claim in a legal action that had been initiated by a different creditor against the hacienda of Aguacata in Abancay. The nuns claimed that the property carried two censos payable to them, and joined the suit to recover 3,400 pesos in principal and 13,428 pesos, 1 real in back payments—almost seventy-nine years' worth.

58. ADC, Gregorio Básquez Serrano, 1707, fol. 32, January 3, 1707; 1708–9, fols. 119–27v, March 17, 1708. The Marqués offered as security his hacienda Chinicara, which already carried 6,000 pesos' worth of principal in censos payable to the nuns of Santa Catalina.

59. Martín, for example, writes in *Daughters of the Conquistadores*, 178, that "through dowries and donations, some of the convents [of Lima] had accumulated a large amount of capital and a great deal of prime, urban real estate. All those assets were frozen in the hands of a religious community, [and] did not contribute to the normal flow of wealth within viceroyal society."

60. To take a representative example, María del Carmen Reyna in her study of Mexican convent finances, *El convento de San Jerónimo: Vida conventual y finanzas* (Mexico City: Instituto Nacional de Antropología e Historia, 1990), 33, states: "En principio, las familias económicamente poderosas procuraban que sus hijas contrajeran matrimonio ventajoso; sin embargo, cuando éstos no se llevaban a cabo, el ingreso al convento era lo mejor para la buena reputación y conservación de la fortuna de la familia." See, however, Susan A. Soeiro, who does a convincing job of explaining (rather than assuming) the usefulness of the convent as a fallback option for elites when times were hard: "The Femi-

nine Orders in Colonial Bahia, Brazil: Economic, Social, and Demographic Implications, 1677–1800," in Asunción Lavrin, ed., *Latin American Women: Historical Perspectives* (Westport, Conn.: Greenwood Press, 1978), 173–97.

61. This was known as the child's *legítima*. A family could also create a mayorazgo, a strategy that seems to have been used more often in the sixteenth century than thereafter.

62. Before taking their vows, novices typically renounced their worldly property, designating those who would inherit in their stead; hence the frequency in the archival record of women's renunciations of their legítimas. In an interesting case of 1677, a nun of Santa Catalina charged that her father had pressured her to give him full control over her inheritance, and she received permission to rewrite the terms of her *renuncia*; see AAC, XLIX, 1, 16 (1677), December 23, 1677.

63. ADC, Gregorio Básquez Serrano, 1708–9, fols. 195–200v, 232v–36, November 7 and December 29, 1708. Thereafter, her brother struggled to maintain the family's estate, and matters seem to have deteriorated rapidly. By the time he died in 1727, leaving no heir, the second Conde de la Laguna was overwhelmed by debt.

64. Since the Middle Ages, as Penelope D. Johnson shows in *Equal in Monastic Profession: Religious Women in Medieval France* (Chicago: University of Chicago Press, 1991), 13–34, religious profession was individual, but heavily influenced by family considerations.

65. Nor could a woman be kept out, if she was of sufficient age and understanding; see *Canons and Decrees of the Council of Trent*, ed. Schroeder, 228–29.

66. AAC, XLIX, 1, 16, doc. of December 23, 1677, regarding the profession of Doña María Juana de Guemes in Santa Catalina.

67. ADC, Pedro José Gamarra, 1753–54, fols. 425–27v, October 3, 1754. Rafaela's sister Francisca also entered Santa Clara. According to Rafaela, she and Francisca had each been left 10,000 pesos in their father's will, but Luciana and an accomplice had hidden the will and stolen the inheritance.

68. ADC, Pedro de Cáceres, 1697, fol. 105, March 5, 1697.

69. ADC, Matías Ximénez Ortega, 1711–14, fols. 106v–8v, October 6, 1713. The price was 580 pesos.

70. ADC, Pedro José Gamarra, 1741, fols. 369–70v, September 19, 1741.

71. ADC, Alejo González Peñaloza, 1744–50, July 1, 1745.

72. In 1741, for example, Juana Francisca de Jesús, widow of Don Alonso Guampu Tupa, and her daughter Pascuala Magdalena Teresa de Jesús, both cloistered nuns in Santa Teresa, sold a house in the city to a merchant named Don Eusebio de Betancur for 400 pesos. See ADC, Pedro José Gamarra, 1741, fols. 357–59v, February 28, 1741.

73. ADC, Alonso Beltrán Luzero, 1642–43, fols. 105–7v, January 13, 1642. This donation by María Panti, identified by the notary as an "yndia," was to last for the duration of her granddaughter's life.

74. ADC, Alejo González Peñaloza, March 22, 1741, for the first censo (200 pesos); for the embargo, see ADC, Corregimiento, Causas Ordinarias, leg. 46

(1763–65), exp. 1002, Santa Teresa v. Don Melchor Queso Yupanqui and Doña Josefa Pillco Sisa, 1764.

75. ADC, Alejo González Peñaloza, 1744–50, September 15, 1746.

76. ADC, Pedro José Gamarra, 1743, fols. 486–87v, July 1, 1743.

77. See Scarlett O'Phelan Godoy, *Rebellions and Revolts in Eighteenth-Century Peru and Upper Peru* (Cologne: Böhlau Verlag, 1985), and Steve J. Stern, "The Age of Andean Insurrection, 1742–1782," in Stern, ed., *Resistance, Rebellion, and Consciousness in the Andean Peasant World, Eighteenth to Twentieth Centuries* (Madison: University of Wisconsin Press, 1987), 34–93. Stern underscores the importance of the Juan Santos Atahualpa rebellion, which began in the central Andes in 1742.

78. This characterization depends on how one periodizes the city's middle to late colonial past, an issue on which historians are still far from reaching consensus. For David P. Cahill, the "golden age" of Cuzco's elite criollo families continued throughout the eighteenth century, up until 1780; in "Repartos ilícitos," 473, he focuses his analysis on the *repartos*. Studies by Luis Miguel Glave and Neus Escandell-Tur tend to confirm this impression, at least where the largest, most powerful elite clans are concerned. Of course, no historian yet has argued the existence of a golden age for the region's indigenous majority; if, as Ann Wightman suggests, the Andean tributary population was recovering demographically by the eighteenth century, it was still far from experiencing anything "golden." Kurakas and principales are a different matter; forthcoming studies should soon tell us more about their experiences and allegiances.

Chapter 6 Breaking Faith

1. By 1689 Goizueta's property included at least one estancia in the *doctrina* of Lampa and two in the doctrina of San Juan Bautista de Cabanilla. See *Cuzco 1689*, ed. Villanueva Urteaga, 59, 70–71.

2. AGI, Audiencia de Lima, 526, "Autos hechos por el Yllmo. Sr. Dn. fray Bernardo Serrada," October 17, 1730.

3. AGI, Audiencia de Cuzco, 64. This detail is contained in the papers concerning the Beaterio de Nazarenas.

4. AGI, Audiencia de Lima, 526, letter from "Fray Gabriel obispo del Cuzco" to the Crown, December 6, 1718.

5. "Autos hechos por el Yllmo. Sr. Dn. fray Bernardo Serrada"; Esquivel y Navia, *Noticias cronológicas*, 2:252.

6. "Autos hechos por el Yllmo. Sr. Dn. fray Bernardo Serrada."

7. AAC, XII, 3, 44, "Sumaria información," 1735.

8. As quoted by Richard Herr, *Rural Change and Royal Finances in Spain at the End of the Old Regime* (Berkeley and Los Angeles: University of California Press, 1989), 58–59; see also Herr, *The Eighteenth-Century Revolution in Spain* (Princeton: Princeton University Press, 1958), 18–19.

9. ADC, Corregimiento, Causas Ordinarias, Provincias, leg. 63 (1719–30), exp. of September 1720.

10. Esquivel y Navia, *Noticias cronológicas*, 2:220–23; Wightman, *Indigenous Migration and Social Change*, 42–43.

11. Garner, "Long-Term Silver Mining Trends," 910. Escandell-Tur shows a decline in textiles sent to Alto Perú in 1725–49: "Producción y comercio de tejidos coloniales," 309–10.

12. ASCS, "Inventario de agosto," doc. 68, regarding the sale of the hacienda of Guandar in 1721. The purchaser was granted a discount in his annual payments and a five-year grace period.

13. Lavallé, *El mercader y el marqués*, 142–47.

14. See, for example, a censo for the amount of 8,500 pesos, which Don Diego de Esquivel y Navia borrowed from Santa Clara in 1708: ADC, Gregorio Básquez Serrano, 1708–9, fols. 119–27, March 15, 1708.

15. ADC, Alejo González Peñalosa, 1732–35, August 29, 1733.

16. ASCS, "Legajo 5 de Varias escripturas y quentas ajustadas," doc. 12, "Extracto de los cargos de principales y réditos que hace el monasterio de Santa Catalina impuestos en las fincas del Marqués de Valleumbroso," fols. 23–29.

17. AGN, Juzgado de Aguas, cuaderno 3.3.4.14, año 1727; ADC, Pedro José Gamarra, 1744, fol. 493, December 3, 1744. When the estate was auctioned off, Santa Clara managed to obtain only seventeenth place in the ranking of creditors.

18. After Don Gerónimo Costilla Gallinato y Valverde died in 1692, his wife gave birth to an heir, Josefa Martina: ADC, Antonio Pérez de Vargas, 1689–92, fols. 172–80, September 5, 1692. Thereafter the Costilla surname was subsumed into a powerful criollo network of Venero y Moscosos and Jiménez de Lobatones.

19. In 1742, Santa Clara joined a suit another creditor brought against the couple's obraje, Paropuquio, for their failure to service their debts; see AAC, XXII, 3, 42 (1742–46). The nuns did not initiate the lawsuit, perhaps because the couple's daughter Rosa was a Clare. Sor Rosa Venero later served at least two terms as abbess (1767–70 and ca. 1780).

20. AGN, Superior Gobierno, leg. 13, cuaderno 281, año 1765.

21. Don Diego was the last legitimate son in the Esquivel line, and his heir Doña Petronila married a limeño in 1736. After the couple's grandson Don Pedro Nolasco de Zavala married a Lima criolla, the title of Marqués de Valleumbroso migrated to Lima. See Lohmann Villena, *Los americanos en las órdenes nobiliarias*, 2:160–61.

22. ADC, Alejo Fernández Escudero, 1721, fols. 620–21v, September 1, 1721.

23. The Ugartes held the mayorazgo founded by one of Cuzco's earliest Spanish settlers, Juan de Pancorbo. On the "vain, high-handed, and proud" Ugartes, see Luis Cúneo Harrison, "Descendientes y herederos del conquistador Don Juan de Pancorvo," *Revista del Instituto Peruano de Investigaciones Genealógicas* 11 (1958), 190–92; also see Lohmann Villena, *Los americanos en las órdenes nobiliarias*, 2:39.

24. According to Cúneo Harrison, "Descendientes y herederos," 191, the Inca connection derived from a seventeenth-century marriage between a Celiorigo and an Avendaño.

25. The Ugartes allied through marriage with the Jaras early in the eighteenth century: Lohmann Villena, *Los americanos en las órdenes nobiliarias*, 2:311–12. Don Agustín Jara de la Cerda was made Marqués de Casa Jara in 1744 (Esquivel y Navia noted laconically, "He gave 25,000 pesos"). See Rezabal y Ugarte, *Tratado del real derecho de las medias-anatas*, 152–53; Esquivel y Navia, *Noticias cronológicas*, 2:349.

26. Cahill, "Repartos ilícitos," 454–55; ADC, Bernardo José Gamarra, 1786, fols. 204–5, June 14, 1786.

27. ADC, Pedro de Cáceres, 1697, insert between fols. 39 and 40, indicates that Sor Rosalia de Ugarte was abbess of Santa Clara in 1757; and AAL, Apelaciones del Cuzco, leg. 51, 1782–89, indicates that Sor Bernardina de Ugarte was abbess in 1782. María de la O y Ugarte was prioress of Santa Catalina from 1724 to 1727 and from 1730 to 1733, according to records contained in ADC, Alejo Fernández Escudero, 1724, 1726, and 1727, and in ADC, Alejo González Peñalosa, 1732–35; Don Antonio de Ugarte was the convent's administrator by 1780, according to AAC, I, 2, 32.

28. ASC, "Volúmen de varias escrituras."

29. ADC, Alejo Gonzáles Peñalosa, August 7, 1744.

30. ADC, Asuntos Eclesiásticos, leg. 3 (1739–50). The ex-prioress mentions that a new tax (*impuesto*) has contributed to the rising cost of foodstuffs.

31. Some, like the obraje of Lucre, were thriving in these years. Escandell-Tur, "Producción y comercio de tejidos coloniales," 86–118, examines the case of the interrelated Ugarte-Arvisa-Arriola-Picoaga families who controlled Lucre.

32. Mörner, *Perfil de la sociedad rural del Cuzco*, 63–101; idem, *Compraventas de tierras en el Cuzco, 1825–1869* (Stockholm: Instituto de Estudios Latinoamericanos de Estocolmo, 1984), 51.

33. See, for example, ADC, Asuntos Eclesiásticos, leg. 3 (1739–50), 1739 doc. regarding the hacienda Oscollopampa, returned to Santa Catalina by a leaser unable to maintain his payments.

34. The Leyes de Toro of 1505 had mentioned the censo al quitar for the first time in order to make clear that the mechanism could lead to property seizure, even in cases in which the amount of principal was small in proportion to the property's value. An early Cuzco example may be found in ASCS, "Inventario de octubre," fol. 15, *causa ejecutiva* brought against the estate of Pedro Herquinigo in 1615.

35. Glave and Remy, in *Estructura agraria y vida rural*, 429–521, describe the crisis of maize production in Ollantaytambo after the 1770s, including the role played by debt. From the angle of observation of convent finances, the debt problem appears regionwide.

36. AAC, XII, 3, 44, "Sumaria información," 1735.

37. To take but one example, Guambutio, a valuable maize hacienda near Oropesa, was sold at auction for 23,000 pesos in 1708, at which point it carried 22,000 pesos' worth of censo obligations to Santa Catalina. The purchaser paid only 1,000 pesos in cash and agreed to assume annual payments to the convent on the censos. ADC, Cabildo, Pedimentos, leg. 109, 1571–1732.

38. ADC, Pedro José Gamarra, 1753–54, fols. 274v–83v, June 22, 1754.

39. Isidoro Alcaraz y Castro, *Breve instrucción del método, y práctica de los quatro juicios, civil ordinario, sumario de partición, executivo, y general de concurso de acreedores*, 4th ed. (Madrid: Imprenta de la Viuda e Hijo de Marín, 1794), 82.

40. ADC, Pedro José Gamarra, 1762–63, fols. 19–22v, January 15, 1762.

41. ADC, Pedro José Gamarra, 1751, fols. 234–35v, June 12, 1751.

42. ADC, Pedro José Gamarra, 1755, fols. 377–78v, October 10, 1755.

43. In 1754, for example, the Clares insisted on a perpetual leasing agreement ("Cenzo perpetuo irredimible") for the hacienda Callapuquio, expressing their concern that "all the haciendas in this bishopric are weighted down in censos" (ADC, Pedro José Gamarra, 1753–54, fols. 274v–83v, June 22, 1754).

44. ADC, Juan Bautista Gamarra, 1776–80, fols. 24–25v, December 17, 1776.

45. Carlos Daniel Valcárcel, ed., *La rebelión de Túpac Amaru*, vol. 2, pts. 1–4 of *Colección documental de la independencia del Perú* (Lima: Comisión Nacional del Sesquicentenario de la Independencia del Perú, 1971), 3:68.

46. More than a hundred seventy years had passed since the last Lima council. See *Concilios limenses*, ed. Vargas Ugarte, 2:103–10.

47. Mörner, *Perfil de la sociedad rural del Cuzco*, 42–44; Jorge Polo y La Borda, "La hacienda Pachachaca (segunda mital del siglo XVIII)," *Histórica* 1 (1977), 227.

48. John Lynch, *The Spanish-American Revolutions, 1808–1826* (New York: W. W. Norton & Co., 1973), 7.

49. O'Phelan (*Rebellions and Revolts*, 161–207) argues that "changes in the alcabala tax as well as the establishment of the Customs Houses . . . provided the initial impetus which culminated in the outbreak of the Great Rebellion" (161).

50. Jorge Juan and Antonio de Ulloa, *Discourse and Political Reflections on the Kingdoms of Peru*, ed. John J. TePaske (Norman: University of Oklahoma Press, 1978), 220.

51. The indispensable work of John H. Rowe shows that Inca nobles were plotting against the Crown by the 1660s. Many archival bits and pieces reflect the Incas' grievances. See, for example, AGI, Audiencia del Cuzco, 64, 1758 *representación* to the king by Don Gabriel Christan Reynoso Ynga of Cuzco, who had been denied the position of *racionero* in the cathedral chapter of Cuzco by the ecclesiastical cabildo; and Ministerio de RR. EE., Lima, Archivo de Límites, "Libro de actas del cabildo del Cuzco," 1725–35, fols. 174–92, regarding Don Pedro Arias de Miranda Ynga's demand that his privileges be respected. Both men claimed descent from Inca rulers.

52. O'Phelan, *Rebellions and Revolts*, 99–109; see also Alfredo Moreno Cebrián, *El corregidor de Indias y la economía peruana del siglo XVIII (los repartos forzosos de mercancías)* (Madrid: Consejo Superior de Investigaciones Científicas, 1977).

53. O'Phelan, *Rebellions and Revolts*, 161–207.

54. Legalization of the reparto gave corregidores certain advantages over priests in the parish-level competition for control over labor and payments, and many priests responded by raising fees for their services. Ibid., 53–57, 109–17.

55. The regions' priests and corregidores were also hacendados, and they

probably sought to make up for their losses in the grain trade by relying even more heavily on the reparto and other mechanisms of surplus extraction. See Glave and Remy, *Estructura agraria y vida rural*, 519–20.

56. "Well over a hundred times during the years 1720–1790," writes Steve Stern, Andeans "rose up in violent defiance of colonial authorities"; he notes the wide influence of the 1742 rebellion of Juan Santos Atahualpa ("The Age of Andean Insurrection," 34).

57. Brooke Larson, *Colonialism and Agrarian Transformation in Bolivia: Cochabamba, 1550–1900* (Princeton: Princeton University Press, 1988), 234; Escandell-Tur, "Producción y comercio de tejidos coloniales."

58. Guillermo Céspedes del Castillo, *Lima y Buenos Aires: Repercusiones económicas y políticas de la creación del Virreinato del Plata* (Seville: Consejo Superior de Investigaciones Científicas, 1947).

59. O'Phelan, in *Rebellions and Revolts*, 170, notes that Indian and mestizo muleteers and traders were "the principal participants" in the uprisings against customs houses that took place at Arequipa in 1777 and at La Paz in 1777 and 1780. The proposed establishment of a customs house in Cuzco led to plans for an uprising there as well (194–203).

60. See Charles Walker's analytical synthesis of the rebellion in *Smoldering Ashes: Cuzco and the Creation of Republican Peru* (Durham: Duke University Press, forthcoming). According to Manuel de Mendiburu, *Diccionario histórico biográfico del Perú*, 2d ed., 11 vols. (Lima: Imprenta Enrique Palacios, 1931–34), 11:32, Túpac Amaru owned thirty-five mule trains of ten mules each and was involved in trade with Lima and Potosí. O'Phelan, in *Rebellions and Revolts*, 265, cites evidence that at the time of the rebellion Túpac Amaru himself was being pursued by customs house officials for a tax debt of 300 pesos.

61. The most complete account of the rebellion is that of Boleslao Lewin, *La revolución de Túpac Amaru y los orígenes de la emancipación americana* (Buenos Aires: Librería Hachette, 1957); for a condensed, well-referenced account, see Walker, *Smoldering Ashes*.

62. Leon G. Campbell, "Ideology and Factionalism during the Great Rebellion, 1780–82," in Steve J. Stern, ed., *Resistance, Rebellion, and Consciousness in the Andean Peasant World, Eighteenth to Twentieth Centuries* (Madison: University of Wisconsin Press, 1987), 124.

63. AAC, XIX, 1, 20.

64. *La rebelión de Túpac Amaru*, ed. Valcárcel, 2:301–2.

65. In the words of Cúneo Harrison ("Descendientes y herederos," 192), "they did not act as they were supposed to and as they had promised Túpac Amaru." Although Cúneo Harrison gives no evidence that an understanding had been reached between Túpac Amaru and the Ugartes prior to the rebellion, clearly the Spanish authorities were prepared to believe that that was the case (192–93).

66. See Carlos Daniel Valcárcel, *La rebelión de Túpac Amaru* (Mexico City: Fondo de Cultura Económica, 1947), 80–87.

67. *La rebelión de Túpac Amaru*, ed. Valcárcel, 2:386–87.

68. Cahill ("Repartos ilícitos," 462–63) cites a report of the Cuzco audiencia indicating that Túpac Amaru took 14,000 pesos' worth of goods from the obraje of Lucre and 10,000 pesos in cash from the hacienda.

69. *La rebelión de Túpac Amaru*, ed. Valcárcel, 3:221, 223–25.

70. AAC, XIX, 1, 20. Santa Catalina repaid the loan to the juzgado eclesiástico two years later.

71. This and the following information about María Mejía and Mariano Túpac Amaru is drawn from BN, ms. C1081 (1782), "Autos del depósito de María Mejía en el monasterio de Santa Cathalina," transcribed in Kathryn Burns, "Amor y rebelión en 1782: El caso de Mariano Túpac Amaru y María Mejía," *Histórica* 16 (1992), 131–76.

72. Ibid., 163.

73. Legal cases involving the *pragmática* of 1776 against "unequal marriages" generally prohibited marriage between whites and nonwhites of African ancestry. Thus the allegations that Mejía was "half *zamba*" may have been intended—perhaps fabricated—to ensure that she would fit the legal definition of an "unequal" mate for Túpac Amaru. Ibid., 140–43.

74. *La rebelión de Túpac Amaru*, ed. Valcárcel, 3:380–401, 426–27.

75. Mata Linares, a judge of the Lima audiencia, was made intendant of Cuzco in 1784. Luis Durand Florez focuses on Mata Linares and his enmity with Cuzco's criollos in *Criollos en conflicto: Cuzco después de Túpac Amaru* (Lima: Universidad de Lima, 1985).

76. ADC, Intendencia, Gobierno, leg. 130, 1785–86, expediente regarding the election of alcaldes on January 1, 1786, letter of Mata Linares to the viceroy, January 8, 1786. Mata Linares defends his insistence that new elections for alcalde be held after the cabildo had voted for a relative of the Ugartes. He continues: "[L]es sobra habilidad para lo malo, y adverso a el Europeo."

77. Cúneo Harrison, "Descendientes y herederos," 192–93.

78. AGI, Audiencia de Cuzco, 69, letter 567, no. 4, Bishop Moscoso to the Supremo Gobierno, June 1, 1783.

79. AAC, XXXII, 2, 26, "Testimonio de autos seguidos de oficio," 1783, fols. 4–5v.

80. Ibid.

81. In 1792 Rivadeneyra and her rival, Madre Francisca del Tránsito y Valdes, were disqualified by order of the viceroy from running for the office of prioress.

82. AGI, Audiencia de Cuzco, 69, doc. of February 19, 1794, from Aranjuez communicating the king's approval of the Peruvian viceroy's course of action regarding Mata: "[N]o encuentra especie por ridicula que sea a que no de el titulo de sublevacion."

83. Carolyn S. Dean, "(Head)dress for Success: The Use of the *Maskapaycha* in Mid-Colonial Peru," a paper presented at the University of Florida, April 14, 1997, shows how Cuzco's indios nobles jealously guarded the right to use this potent symbol of Inca authority.

84. AGI, Audiencia de Cuzco, 17, doc. 28, contains Mata Linares's report of

March 19, 1786, on the need to abolish the pretensions and customs of Cuzco's noble Incas.

85. ADC, Bernardo José Gamarra, 1791, fols. 147–47v, May 16, 1791, *poder* of the Indian nobles of Cuzco's eight parishes "and the electors." For some idea of what they were up against, see the 1798 proposal by a member of Cuzco's cathedral chapter that Quechua be suppressed and all Indians' dress be changed in order to "españolizarlos": AGI, Audiencia de Cuzco, 70, proposal to the king by the *canónigo* Dr. José Fernández Baeza, June 28, 1798.

86. Mark A. Burkholder and D. S. Chandler provide information on the judges in their *Biographical Dictionary of Audiencia Ministers in the Americas, 1687–1821* (Westport, Conn.: Greenwood Press, 1982). Criollos were not among the oidores of the Audiencia of Cuzco until 1806.

87. Ignacio de Castro, *Relación del Cuzco,* ed. Carlos Daniel Valcárcel (Lima: Universidad Nacional Mayor de San Marcos, 1978), 81, 141.

88. Ibid., 42.

89. AAC, XX, 2, 23 (1785). This case, argued with great verve, sent both sides scrambling for legal books. The prioress of Santa Catalina tried to come up with a volume by Pablo Salazar, cited in the work of Gerónimo de Seballos, but none could not be found in Cuzco or Lima.

90. AAC, LXXXIII, 4, 61 (1793), containing the contract entered into by Don Fernando Ochoa in 1786 with Santa Teresa, placing a censo on the hacienda Guaylla.

91. Ibid. This censo may also be found in ADC, Bernardo José Gamarra, 1786, fols. 407–12, October 3, 1786.

92. ADC, Bernardo José Gamarra, 1789, fols. 512–17, December 31, 1789. The Tronconis heirs owed Santa Clara a total of 25,700 pesos.

93. Manuel Espinavete López, "Descripción de la provincia de Abancay," *Mercurio Peruano* 12 (1795), 144.

94. Ibid., 158.

95. Eleazar Crucinta Ugarte, "Haciendas cañaverales de Abancay y Aymaraes, siglo XVIII" (licentiate thesis, Universidad Nacional San Antonio Abad del Cuzco, 1989), 12, 32. "Concolorcorvo" was the pseudonym adopted by Alonso Carrió de la Vandera.

96. See, for example, ADC, Bernardo José Gamarra, 1784 and 1785. This trend seems to correspond to the rise of chorrillos that Escandell-Tur charts in "Producción y comercio de tejidos coloniales." As big institutions (like the region's obrajes) suffered, smaller, more flexible ones might do relatively well.

97. In his study *Compraventas,* 51, Mörner observed that censos facilitated rapid turnover in the ownership of Cuzco's haciendas. While this observation pertained to a later period (1825–69), the same structural phenomenon can be observed much earlier, and deserves closer study.

98. In 1689, Guallgua belonged to Lic. Cristóbal Calero, *presbítero,* according to *Cuzco 1689,* ed. Villanueva Urteaga, 288.

99. ASCS, *papeles sueltos* relating to Guallgua. The nuns paid 10,150 pesos of the price in cash, since the censos Guallgua carried amounted to 11,850 pesos.

100. Carmona was to deliver 100 fanegas of flour annually. The specified weight per fanega was 7 *arrobas* and 7 *libras* each. At the stipulated price of 5 pesos per fanega of flour, this amounted to 500 pesos' worth of flour each year.

101. AAC, LVI, 2, 24.

102. More research will have to be done before patterns come clear; the Ferros, Garmendias, and others may originally have been part of the intendant system that replaced the corregidores.

103. AAC, LXI, 3, 53. In her 1806 profession at Santa Catalina a nun offered her cell to satisfy payment of her dowry. The prioress expressed her approval, for the cell was large enough to be made into new novices' quarters; the old ones had lapsed into disuse.

104. Doña Josefa Holgado mentions in the terms of her will "that each year the sacristans spend two or three hundred of their own pesos to adorn the altar for the convent's fiestas, and for this reason everyone refuses the office of sacristan" (ADC, Andrés de Zamora, 1790–94, fols. 56–56v, May 4, 1791).

105. Arbiol, *La religiosa instruida*, 597.

106. AAC, LXVII, 4, 65, March 20–21, 1805.

107. For one thing, there was not yet anything ready to take their place: no banks existed in the region, for example, and none would arrive for several more decades. Merchant houses like Braillard may have played an important credit-providing role, and these merit study.

108. AAC, XIV, 1, 9, however, shows that in 1784 Captain Francisco Beitia paid 10,000 pesos in cash to Santa Catalina to redeem half of the censo obligations weighing on his haciendas in Calca.

109. José Hipólito Unanue, *Guia política, eclesiástica y militar del Virreynato del Perú para el año 1793* (Lima: Imprenta Real de los Huérfanos, 1793), 245.

110. Gaspar Melchor de Jovellanos, *Obras escogidas*, 2 vols., ed. Angel del Río (Madrid: Espasa-Calpe, 1935), 1:141–70.

Chapter 7   Surviving Republicanism

1. ADC, Carlos Rodríguez de Ledezma, 1787–89, fols. 645–46, May 22, 1789; Andrés de Zamora, 1790–94, fols. 53–61v, May 4, 1791.

2. One expuesta complained in 1797 that the prioress of Santa Catalina had borrowed her dowry to meet convent expenses and had never paid it back: AAC, XLVI, 2, 21.

3. Castro, *Relación*, 51.

4. ADC, Bernardo José Gamarra, 1790, fols. 267–73v, June 8, 1790. Don Pascual, "cacique y gobernador" of Cabana in Lampa, offered as collateral two ranches.

5. AGI, Audiencia de Cuzco, 68, letter of August 10, 1795, from Abbess Agueda Zamora to the queen.

6. Alberto Flores Galindo, *Buscando un Inca*, 3d ed. (Lima: Instituto de Apoyo Agrario, 1988), 175–242. The idea of placing an Inca in charge of an independent South America seems to have caught on in the criollo imagination.

According to Gerhard Masur, in *Simón Bolívar* (Albuquerque: University of New Mexico Press, 1948), 73, the Venezuelan Francisco de Miranda was presenting such a proposal to William Pitt by 1790.

7. Brief accounts of the movement often called "the revolution of Pumacahua" may be found in Rubén Vargas Ugarte, *Historia del Perú: Emancipación* (1809–1825) (Buenos Aires: Imprenta López, 1958), 45–72, and Lynch, *The Spanish-American Revolutions*, 164–71.

8. Vidaurre was steeped in Enlightenment literature and was reform-minded, but he nevertheless declined an invitation to take part in the movement of 1814, choosing to leave Cuzco. Thereafter he became a prolific essayist. Reform of the church was a leading concern of his; see his *Proyecto de un código penal* (Boston: Hiram Tupper, 1828).

9. *La revolución del Cuzco de 1814*, ed. Manuel Jesús Aparicio Vega, vol. 3, pt. 7 of *Colección documental de la independencia del Perú* (Lima: Comisión Nacional del Sesquicentenario de la Independencia del Perú, 1974), 658.

10. In 1809, a remarkably similar set of events had occurred in Chuquisaca. See Lynch, *The Spanish-American Revolutions*, 49–51.

11. Consolidación was intended to cover bonds that the Spanish treasury had been issuing (*vales reales*). Richard Herr, in *Rural Change and Royal Finances*, 78–118, traces the deterioration of royal credit and the Crown's decision to adopt "extraordinary measures" affecting the church.

12. Asunción Lavrin, in "The Execution of the Law of *Consolidación* in New Spain: Economic Aims and Results," *Hispanic American Historical Review* 53 (1973), 27, notes that "in the American possessions, a provision for the repayment and consolidation of clerical debts was added."

13. Brian R. Hamnett, in "The Appropriation of Mexican Church Wealth by the Spanish Bourbon Government: The 'Consolidación de Vales Reales,' 1805–1809," *Journal of Latin American Studies* 1 (1969), 93–97, describes the indignant reaction in New Spain.

14. Lavrin ("The Execution of the Law of *Consolidación*," 32–33) describes one strategy that Mexican nuns used: they claimed that all property they had purchased with dowry funds should be exempted. The effects of consolidación in Cuzco must have been mitigated by the desperate state of the local economy, for "all sales were to provide at least three-quarters of the assessed value of the property" (33), a level not many cuzqueños could afford.

15. ADC, Asuntos Eclesiásticos, Junta de Consolidación, leg. 86 (1806–7), June 18, 1806. The "latest tax" was a 1795 levy on all property transferred into entail; see Herr, *Rural Change and Royal Finances*, 82.

16. Timothy E. Anna, *The Fall of the Royal Government in Peru* (Lincoln: University of Nebraska Press, 1979), 16.

17. *Documentación oficial española*, ed. Horacio Villanueva Urteaga, vol. 22, pt. 3 of *Colección documental de la independencia del Perú* (Lima: Comisión Nacional del Sesquicentenario de la Independencia del Perú, 1971), 57–60. The invitation extended to La Serna by Cuzco's audiencia is fascinating: citing the *Siete Partidas*, it urges the last Spanish viceroy to make "the ancient court of the Incas" his base of operations in order to save the "Nation."

18. Cuzco also gained its first printing press and a royal mint. Ibid., 1–52, prologue by Horacio Villanueva Urteaga.

19. BN, ms. D869 (1823).

20. By admitting grain and other agricultural products at a high unit price, the convents might allow tenants to pay less than they would if market prices were used. If, for example, the flour of a tenant owing 200 pesos was accepted at 5 pesos per fanega when the market price was 4 pesos, his payment was forty fanegas instead of fifty.

21. It is worth noting that Valer writes not of censuatarios but of "inquilinos," a choice of words that reflects the convents' reliance in these years on rentals and ventas a censo rather than on censos al quitar.

22. AAC, paquete no. 45 (319–20), años 1692–1922, exp. 5 (1827) concerning the case of Sor Rosa Vergara y Cárdenas. Vergara cites both the 1822 and the 1826 measure; the latter was part of a broader republican reform of the regular orders.

23. AAC, XVI, 3, 51, expediente on the January 1823 flight of Rivas from Santa Clara.

24. AAC, paquete no. 45 (319–20), años 1692–1922, exp. 5 (1827) concerning the case of Sor Rosa Vergara y Cárdenas.

25. ADC, Intendencia, Gobierno, leg. 151, 1816–18, "Sobre rebaja de censos" (emphasis mine).

26. This rewriting of the past represents a dramatic shift in belief: to believe that the encumbrances weighing on their properties were "merely" pious obligations, unproductive, not connected to anything modern or fruitful.

27. Horacio Villanueva Urteaga, *Gamarra y la iniciación republicana en el Cuzco* (Lima: Banco de los Andes, 1981), 4–11.

28. Manco Cápac's byline appears in *El Sol de Cuzco*, no. 29, July 16, 1825.

29. Ibid. These assets would soon be bolstered with those of the Augustinian monastery, suppressed in Cuzco in 1826.

30. Ibid.

31. Jorge Basadre, in his *Historia de la República del Perú, 1822–1933*, 6th ed., 16 vols. (Lima: Editorial Universitaria, 1968–69), 2:426, notes that another state-supported school for girls, the Colegio de Educandas del Espíritu Santo, was founded in Lima in 1830.

32. *El Sol del Cuzco*, no. 30, July 23, 1825. The Mercedarians, the Franciscan nuns of Santa Clara, and the Augustinians were assigned contributions of 3,000 pesos, 2,500 pesos, and 2,000 pesos respectively.

33. Félix Denegri Luna, ed., *Diario del viaje del presidente Orbegoso al sur del Perú*, 2 vols. (Lima: Pontificia Universidad Católica, Instituto Riva-Agüero, 1974), 1:264.

34. Ibid., 1:266–67, 2:163.

35. AAC, C-LXI, 2, 28, draft letter of November 11, 1825, from the Gobierno Eclesiástico to the Secretario General del Supremo Consejo de Gobierno. The anonymous draft was clearly written by a nun or by someone close to the nuns, possibly the abbess or administrator.

36. Not everyone could do favors for free, or defer payment indefinitely.

In 1802, for example, a physician who had attended the Dominican nuns for many years brought suit against Santa Catalina to recover 1,000 pesos the nuns owed him for his services. See AAC, C-L, 3, 65.

37. "M.T.M.," *El Sol del Cuzco,* September 24, 1825. The reader explained his bewilderment by using Santa Catalina as a case study. If two hundred women had professed and paid dowry before 1825, then assuming a dowry of 3,333 and one-third pesos, a total of 666,693 pesos, 6 reales should have entered Santa Catalina's coffer. The daily did not respond. Perhaps the editor believed the reader had answered his own question: i.e., that convents were sinkholes into which hundreds of thousands of pesos disappeared.

38. Pilar García Jordán, *Iglesia y poder en el Perú contemporáneo, 1821–1919* (Cuzco: Centro de Estudios Regionales Andinos "Bartolomé de Las Casas," [1991]), 72–73.

39. AAC, LXXIV, 2, 42, "Cuadro que manifiesta el estado actual del monasterio de Santa Clara," October 15, 1826. In 1855, Santa Clara provided more details on properties expropriated by the government, listing their value at 80,364 pesos, 4 reales; see AAC, LXVIII, 2, 27.

40. ADC, Pablo del Mar y Tapia, 1824–26, fols. 194–96, December 9, 1825. The prioress lists the amounts she owes to twenty people for a total of 4,725 pesos.

41. *Anales de la Hacienda Pública del Perú,* 1st ser., 10 vols., comp. P[edro] Emilio Dancuart (Lima: Imprenta de Guillermo Stolte et al., 1902–8), 1:271–72. Precedents existed for a reduction. Following the devastating 1746 earthquake along Peru's central coast, the Crown had granted temporary relief to censuatarios over the church's objections: AGI, Audiencia de Lima, 509. (Relief consisted of a grace period and a temporary reduction of réditos.)

42. In ADC, Pablo del Mar y Tapia, 1820–28, fols. 459–59v, 493–95, 497–98, the three ecónomos of the nunneries come forward in 1828 with their guarantors to deposit surety (*fianzas*) before assuming their duties.

43. AAC, XXI, 2, 37. In 1774 Galeano was brought before ecclesiastical authorities for beating a mestiza servant in Santa Catalina; though ordered not to go near the convent, he returned to thrash Bernarda Palomino, an elderly white woman, with his cane.

44. AAC, LXXIV, 2, 42, October 15, 1826, "Cuadro que manifiesta el estado actual del monasterio de Santa Clara."

45. AAC, C-LXXXVII, 3, 32, letter of June 1, 1829, Madre Paula de los Remedios, prioress, to Bishop Miguel Orozco.

46. García Jordán, *Iglesia y poder,* 74.

47. AAC, C-XXXIV, 1, 1, letter of March 10, 1826.

48. AAC, C-L, 3, 65, doc. of September 12, 1800. It is unclear whether Fernández got her "cholita" back the second time.

49. AAC, XXXIV, 3, 50, docs. regarding the *visita general* of Santa Clara on March 3, 1852.

50. On one occasion, a woman who had been sentenced to a convent as punishment for an offense eventually became a servant there: see the case of Cecilia Aymulo, AAC, XLIII, 4, 68 (1771). Her change in status was considered

the result of the woman's preference for the cloistered life, however, and raised no doubts or suspicions about the nuns' handling of the case. Half a century later, when the categories of depositada and criada had become the focus of intense scrutiny, the case would probably have raised calls for an investigation.

51. AAC, XLV, 3, 48, contains a letter of 1856 from the prioress of Santa Catalina regarding "what happened with Catalina Flores."

52. AAC, C-XVIII, 4, 48, circular dated October 25, 1853.

53. AAC, C-XXII, 1, 15, 1864.

54. AAC, XVII, 2, 33, docs. of 1853 concerning the proposed demolition of part of Santa Catalina.

55. Ibid.

56. Ibid.

57. AAC, paquete no. 45 (319–20), años 1692–1922, exp. 18, fols. 19–21, letter of Abbess Josefa del Corazón de Jesús Ochoa to Bishop Farfán, May 7, 1923.

58. AAC, C-LXXIV, 2, 42, May 24, 1860, razón in response to a request for information from the state. According to Abbess Manuela Espinosa, the convent could expect to collect 6,893 pesos a year; the nuns had given up on an additional 704 pesos of "rentas incobrables."

59. AAC, C-XVIII, 4, 48, May 5, 1869, letter of Abbess Manuela Gastelu to the bishop of Cuzco.

60. AAC, XLV, 3, 48, May 22, 1860, report on Santa Catalina.

61. José Tamayo Herrera, Historia social del Cuzco republicano, 2d ed. (Lima: Editorial Universo, 1981), 27–54.

62. According to José Hipólito Unanue (Guía política, eclesiástica y militar del Virreynato del Perú para el año 1794 [Lima: Imprenta Real de los Huérfanos, 1794], 73) Cuzco had 32,082 inhabitants in 1794. The Diario del viaje del presidente Orbegoso, ed. Denegri Luna, 2:185, cites census data placing Cuzco's population at 20,371 in 1846 and 17,370 in 1876.

63. Alberto Flores Galindo, Arequipa y el sur andino, siglos XVIII–XX (Lima: Editorial Horizonte, 1977). The Arequipans, in turn, were satellites of a number of foreign commercial interests, to which they became linked by both business and kinship during the nineteenth century. Tamayo Herrera (Historia social, 43–45) notes the role of steamships in Cuzco's decline and the rise of Arequipa and its port Islay.

64. Anales de la Hacienda Pública, ed. Dancuart, 7:241–42.

65. BN, ms. D8449, "Representación elevada al arzobispo de Lima Don José Sebastián de Goyeneche y Barreda por el Cabildo Metropolitano de Lima," January 5, 1865. The Peruvian government had already shown itself to be wholly unreliable at making payments of all sorts, and the clergy had felt the impact.

66. Santa Clara lost the most. Even if these principals had yielded Santa Clara only 2 percent annually (just under 1,500 pesos), the nuns still lost about a fifth of their annual income.

67. BN, ms. D2898, "Proyecto de ley presentado al Congreso Constituyente por el diputado Fernando Casos," 1867.

68. AAC, C-XLV, 1, 1, letter of February 23, 1867, Archbishop José Sebastián Goyeneche to Bishop Julián Ochoa.

69. BN, ms. D2898.

70. AAC, XXXVI, 2, 28, doc. of 1880 from Santa Clara concerning the sale of a *custodia* (monstrance). The nuns fretted that a Jewish jeweler might buy their custodia and break it up to make frivolous jewelry.

71. AAC, C-XXXII, 2, 50, letter of November 15, 1859, from the abbess of Santa Clara, Sor Manuela Espinosa, to the *vicario capitular*.

72. Insistence on the common life had been a salient point in the Bourbon reform of the regular orders in New Spain, and some efforts to (re)institute the common life were made in Peru. See Lavrin, "Ecclesiastical Reform of Nunneries," 182–203; and Vargas Ugarte, *Historia de la Iglesia en el Perú*, 4:292–94. In Arequipa, attempts to enforce the common life in Santa Catalina during the 1780s and 1790s caused serious conflict; see Mary A. Y. Gallagher, "Pocket Money and Political Power: The Reform of Santa Catalina of Arequipa (1788–1800)," a paper presented to the American Historical Association, Washington, D.C., December 1992.

73. AAC, XVI, 2, 38, letter of February 3, 1861.

74. AAC, XVII, 2, 24, 1862.

75. Ibid. The priest also ordered the walling up of a second *portería*, a back entrance that can still be seen (now duly walled up) along the Calle Loreto.

76. According to AAC, C-X, 3, 30, report of Friar Francisco Farfán, January 7, 1888, Santa Clara began observing the common life in 1886.

77. See Luis E. Valcárel's recollections of the nunneries in his *Memorias*, ed. José Matos Mar, José Deustua C., José Luis Rénique (Lima: Instituto de Estudios Peruanos, 1981).

78. The history of the credit-providing function of Cuzco's commercial houses has yet to be written. By the turn of the century, even the nuns had started placing their money in such houses, as well as in the city's new banks: the Banco de Perú y Londres, Banco Italiano, and others. See AAC, C-LIII, 3, 57, doc. 6 regarding Santa Teresa's investments in 1921.

79. AAC, C-LXVIII, 2, 27, doc. of March 7, 1889.

80. AAC, C-LVIII, 4, 47, lists in detail Santa Clara's sources of income for 1872. Censos and loans (mutuos) brought in 3,161 pesos; rentals of property brought in 939 pesos; and the government paid just over 4,000 pesos on redeemed censos. The convent's total income came to 8,113 pesos, 5 reales.

81. AAC, C-X, 3, 30, contains a report of January 7, 1888, on the state of Santa Clara by the Franciscan friar Francisco Farfán, "Vicario y Reformador" of the Clares, according to which the Peruvian government owed the convent almost 300,000 pesos ("por los censos redimidos y por los prestamos").

Epilogue

1. Gaining admission to a locutorio meant negotiating at the torno to speak to someone—the abbess or prioress—and to be handed the key; that, in turn,

meant knowing at least a bit about who was inside. I am very grateful to Gabriela Martínez Escobar, César Itier, the late Jesús Lambarry, Antonio Acosta, and J. B. Lassegue for helping me make these contacts.

2. AAC, C-XLIX, 2, 13, doc. of July 26, 1945, from Abbess M. Jesús de la Cruz Urquizo to Archbishop Santiago Hermoza. Forty-five years later, the threatening interlopers at the locutorio had changed (or diversified) their guise. They were no longer "esos señores comunistas" but "esos señores protestantes": the Mormons, Baptists, and others who by the 1990s were busily attempting to win converts to their brand-new churches and away from the Roman Catholic church.

3. AAC, C-LXI, 2, 28, doc. 11, January 18, 1940, cancellation of a censo payable to Santa Clara by "el Diputado Dr. D. Francisco Ponce de León, propietario de la finca nominada Bandoja en Anta." Ponce de León paid one-sixth of the face value of his censo to the juzgado eclesiástico, thus ending a lawsuit with the Clares that had dragged on for some twenty-five years. AAC, C-LXVII, 3, 55, doc. 5, reflects Santa Teresa's loan of 10,000 soles to Cleofé Tisoc at 8 percent; Tisoc offered her house as collateral. She borrowed the money "to cancel her debt to Dr. Augusto de la Barra."

4. Juana Marín Farfán's dowry to become a nun of Santa Clara was waived, according to AAC, C-XXXII, 2, 50, doc. 3, August 4, 1958.

5. See J. B. Lassegue and F. Letona, "Catálogo general del Archivo del Monasterio de Santa Catalina del Cusco, Peru," *Revista Andina* 1 (1983), 127–33.

Glossary

The meaning (and the spelling) of most of the Spanish and Quechua terms below may vary a great deal, depending on context. Here, and throughout the book, I have opted for what seems the most accessible, useful version of non-English words to ease the imagined reader's way, but this glossary may also be taken as an invitation to further explorations of meaning.

aclla: A virgin woman chosen to serve the Inca.

acllahuasi: House of women chosen to serve the Inca.

audiencia: A Spanish viceregal court and governing body, made up of judges (*oidores*) and a president.

ayllu: Andean kinship group, made up of people claiming descent from a common ancestor.

beata: A woman living under informal religious vows.

beaterio: Community or house of women living under informal religious vows (also known as *recogimiento*).

cabildo: A municipal council.

cacique: Caribbean term used by Spaniards throughout the Americas to refer to indigenous chiefs; in the Andes, a synonym for *kuraka*.

censo al quitar: Colonial Peruvian term for a *censo consignativo,* a credit transaction giving the creditor the right to collect a yearly income (*réditos*) on the sum extended as credit (*principal*), until such time as the borrower decided to pay the creditor the full amount of the principal. The transaction is often compared to a mortgage, since the borrower was required to secure the deal by offering a piece of property as collateral. (For the attendant risks, see below, *concurso de acreedores.*)

censualista: The creditor in a censo transaction.

censuatario: The borrower in a censo al quitar, or lessee in a *venta a censo.* This usage, common in colonial Peru, varied elsewhere: *censuario; censatario.*

chorrillo: An urban textile-producing workshop; such operations were generally much smaller than Cuzco's *obrajes.*

concurso de acreedores: Legal action by creditors to recover the principal and annual payments owed on a piece of real property. A *concurso* involved the seizure and sale at auction of the debtor's collateral to satisfy his or her unpaid creditors.

conventos grandes: Colloquial term for the largest, most populous colonial convents (e.g., the Poor Clares and the Dominicans of Cuzco), as distinct from the relatively small, austere ones (e.g., Carmelites).

corregidor: A Spanish magistrate, charged with administering a district (*corregimiento*).

criolla, criollo: An American-born woman or man considered to be of Spanish descent.

depositada: A woman sent into a convent or beaterio for disciplinary reasons.

dominio: The right to control property, a right subdivided in colonial times into further categories; e.g., *dominio útil* (usufruct).

donada: In colonial Peruvian usage, a convent servant who brought her community a small dowry (about one-sixth of the full amount) and professed simple vows.

encomendero: The possessor of an *encomienda*, a grant from the Spanish Crown of the right to receive labor and tribute from a particular group of "Indians."

forastero, forastera: Outsider, foreigner; an Andean immigrant no longer attached to his or her ayllu.

hija natural, hijo natural: A daughter or son born to parents who were not married at the time of the child's birth but might have been (i.e., neither parent had committed adultery).

indios nobles: In Cuzco, those distinguished by their descent from high-ranking Incas, as well as those of other Andean ethnicities who occupied positions of local authority in or near Cuzco (e.g., *kurakas*).

ingenio: A cane-growing, sugar-producing estate.

kuraka: An Andean ethnic lord, chief, or headman, usually styled *cacique* in Spanish documents.

locutorio: The visitors' parlor of a convent.

madres de consejo: Nuns chosen for their probity and experience to advise the abbess or prioress on a convent's important business decisions.

mayordomo: Steward or administrator. Nuns often used the term to refer to the individuals whom they hired to administer particular properties, as well as to the overall manager of their business affairs. Synonyms for the latter, generally a distinguished local layman, included *administrador, síndico.*

mestiza, mestizo: A woman or man considered to be of mixed European and Indian descent.

mestizaje: A postcolonial term for cultural, ethnic, or "racial" mixture.

monja: A woman who has completed her novitiate and professed solemn vows; a nun.

obraje: A textile-producing workshop, dependent on unfree indigenous labor and often located near its source (i.e., in the countryside).

penitenciada: A woman sent into a convent or beaterio for correction; the term is virtually synonymous with *depositada.*

principal: An indigenous leader of lesser rank than a *kuraka*. The term also refers to the amount of credit extended to a borrower in a *censo* transaction.

recogimiento: Community or house of women living under informal religious vows; i.e., a beaterio.

regidor: A person serving on a municipal council; a councilman.

seglar: A secular person; a woman or girl boarding in a convent.

segundón: Second son; younger son.

siglo: A hundred years, or century. Nuns used the term, derived from the Latin *seculum*, to refer to the secular world beyond their cloisters.

Tahuantinsuyo: The Inca state, or "land of the four quarters."

velo blanco: Literally, "white veil," the colonial Peruvian term for a half-dowry nun. Women in this category of profession were second only to the nuns of the black veil in their convent's hierarchy and ranked above *donadas* (who might also be known as *legas*), servants, and slaves.

velo negro: Literally, "black veil," the term for a full-dowry nun (also known as a *monja de coro*, or "choir nun").

venta a censo: Colonial Peruvian term for a long-term lease of property. Such transactions had many informal names (*venta de por vidas; venta por tres vidas*) and were formally *ventas enfiteúticas*.

zamba, zambo: A woman or man considered to be of mixed European and African descent.

Works Cited

Primary Sources: Manuscripts

Cuzco, Archivo Arzobispal del Cuzco (AAC)
    Sección Colonial
    Sección Republicana
    Sección Libros Parroquiales
        Parroquia del Sagrario, Bautismos, 1577–1609, 1608–51
        Parroquia del Sagrario, Matrimonios, 1628–86, 1692–1728

Cuzco, Archivo Departamental del Cusco (ADC; formerly Archivo Histórico
del Cusco)
    Asuntos Eclesiásticos
    Beneficencia
    Cabildo
    Colegio de Ciencias
    Corregimiento
    Intendencia
    Protocolos Notariales:
        Juan de Quiroz
        Luis de Quesada
        Antonio Sánchez
        Cristóbal de Luzero
        Francisco Hurtado
        Alonso Beltrán Luzero
        Lorenzo de Messa Andueza
        Juan de Pineda
        Pedro de Cáceres
        Antonio Pérez de Vargas
        Matías Ximénez Ortega
        Francisco Maldonado
        Gregorio Básquez Serrano
        Alejo Fernández Escudero
        Alejo González Peñalosa

José Tapia Sarmiento
Bernardo José Gamarra
Pedro José Gamarra
Juan Bautista Gamarra
Anselmo Vargas
Andrés de Zamora
Carlos Rodríguez de Ledesma
Pablo del Mar y Tapia
Testimonios Compulsos

Cuzco, Archivo de Santa Catalina de Sena (ASCS) [private]
"Inventario de los instrumentos respectivos a la fundación de este monasterio de Santa Catalina de Sena"
Inventarios de Protocolos (organized by month, January–December)
Inventarios (supplementary)

Cuzco, Archivo de Santa Clara (ASC) [private]
"Volúmen de varias escrituras que pueden servir de títulos"

Lima, Archivo Arzobispal de Lima (AAL)
Apelaciones del Cuzco
Papeles Importantes

Lima, Archivo General de la Nación (AGN)
Campesinado: Derecho Indígena
Juzgado de Aguas
Superior Gobierno

Lima, Archivo de San Francisco (ASF)
Registro 10
Registro 15

Lima, Biblioteca Nacional (BN), Sala de Investigaciones
Manuscripts A155, B457, B702, C1081, D869, D2898, D8449

Lima, Ministerio de Relaciones Exteriores (RR. EE.), Archivo de Límites
Signatura CSG-2 (1559–1613)

Madrid, Archivo Histórico Nacional (AHN)
Sección de Ordenes Militares: Santiago

Seville, Archivo General de Indias (AGI)
Audiencia de Cuzco
Audiencia de Lima
Justicia

Primary Sources: Printed Works

Albornoz, Bartolomé de. *Arte de los contractos.* Valencia: Pedro de Huete, 1573.
Alcaraz y Castro, Isidoro. *Breve instrucción del método, y práctica de los quatro juicios,*

civil ordinario, sumario de partición, executivo, y general de concurso de acreedores. 4th ed. Madrid: Imprenta de la Viuda e Hijo de Marin, 1794.

Angulo, Domingo, ed. "Libro original que contiene la fundación del monesterio de monxas de señora Sta. Clara desta cibdad del Cuzco; por el qual consta ser su patrono el insigne Cabildo, Justicia y Reximiento desta dicha cibdad: Año de 1560." Revista del Archivo Nacional del Perú 11 (1939), 55–95, 157–84.

Aparicio Vega, Manuel Jesús, ed. La revolución del Cuzco de 1814. Vol. 3, pt. 7 of Colección documental de la independencia del Perú. Lima: Comisión Nacional del Sesquicentenario de la Independencia del Perú, 1974.

Arbiol, Antonio. La religiosa instruida. Madrid: Imprenta Real de la Gazeta, 1776.

Arzáns de Orsúa y Vela, Bartolomé. Historia de la villa imperial de Potosí. 3 vols. Edited by Lewis Hanke and Gunnar Mendoza. Providence: Brown University Press, 1965.

Barriga, Víctor M., ed. Documentos para la historia de Arequipa. 3 vols. Arequipa: Editorial "La Colmena," 1939–55.

Calancha, Antonio de la. Crónica moralizada de Antonio de la Calancha. 6 vols. Edited by Ignacio Prado Pastor. Lima: Universidad Nacional Mayor de San Marcos, 1976.

Castro, Ignacio de. Relación del Cuzco. Edited by Carlos Daniel Valcárcel. Lima: Universidad Nacional Mayor de San Marcos, 1978.

Cieza de León, Pedro de. Crónica del Perú, Primera Parte. 2d ed. Edited by Franklin Pease G. Y. Lima: Pontificia Universidad Católica, 1986.

Constituciones generales para todas las monjas, y religiosas sujetas a la obediencia de la orden de N. P. S. Francisco, en toda esta familia cismontana. Mexico City: Imprenta de la Viuda de Francisco Rodríguez Lupercio, 1689.

Contreras y Valverde, Vasco de. Relación de la ciudad del Cuzco. Edited by María del Carmen Martín Rubio. Cuzco: Imprenta Amauta, 1983.

Cook, Noble David, ed. Tasa de la visita general de Francisco de Toledo. Lima: Universidad Nacional Mayor de San Marcos, 1975.

Córdova Salinas, Diego de. Crónica franciscana de las provincias del Perú. Edited by Lino G. Canedo. Washington, D.C.: Academy of American Franciscan History, 1957.

Covarrubias, Sebastián de. Tesoro de la lengua castellana o española. Edited by Martín de Riquer. Barcelona: Editorial Alta Fulla, 1987.

Dancuart, P[edro] Emilio, comp. Anales de la Hacienda Pública del Perú. 1st ser. 10 vols. Lima: Imprenta de Guillermo Stolte et al., 1902–8.

Denegri Luna, Félix, ed. Diario del viaje del presidente Orbegoso al sur del Perú. 2 vols. Lima: Pontificia Universidad Católica, Instituto Riva-Agüero, 1974.

Díaz de Valdepeñas, Hernando. Suma de notas copiosas y muy sustanciales y compendiosas. Toledo: Hernando Díaz and Juan de Medina, 1544.

Espinavete López, Manuel. "Descripción de la provincia de Abancay." Mercurio Peruano 12 (1795), 112–64.

Espino y Cáceres, Diego de. Quaderno de las Leyes de Toro y nuevas decisiones, hechas y ordenadas en la ciudad de Toro, sobre las dudas de derecho que continuamente solian, y suelen occurrir en estos reynos. Salamanca: Diego Cussio, 1599.

Espinosa, Tomás de, ed. *Regla de N. P. S. Agustín, águila de los doctores, luz de la Iglesia. Manual, y espejo espiritual de sus hijas*. Granada: Imprenta Real de Francisco de Ochoa, 1677.

Esquivel y Navia, Diego de. *Noticias cronológicas de la gran ciudad del Cuzco*. 2 vols. Edited by Félix Denegri Luna. Lima: Banco Wiese, 1980.

Garcilaso de la Vega, el Inca. *Royal Commentaries of the Incas and General History of Peru, Part Two*. Translated by Harold V. Livermore. Austin: University of Texas Press, 1966.

Guaman Poma de Ayala, Felipe. *El primer nuevo corónica y buen gobierno*. 3 vols. Edited by John V. Murra and Rolena Adorno. Mexico City: Siglo XXI Editores, 1980.

Hanke, Lewis, ed. *Los virreyes españoles en América durante el gobierno de la Casa de Austria: Perú*. 7 vols. Biblioteca de Autores Españoles 280–86. Madrid: Atlas, 1978–80.

Jovellanos, Gaspar Melchor de. *Obras escogidas*. 2 vols. Edited by Angel del Río. Madrid: Espasa-Calpe, 1935.

Juan, Jorge, and Antonio de Ulloa. *Discourse and Political Reflections on the Kingdoms of Peru*. Edited by John J. TePaske; translated by John J. TePaske and Besse A. Clement. Norman: University of Oklahoma Press, 1978.

Konetzke, Richard, ed. *Colección de documentos para la historia de la formación social de Hispanoamérica, 1493–1810*. 3 vols. Madrid: Consejo Superior de Investigaciones Científicas, 1953–62.

Levillier, Roberto, ed. *Audiencia de Lima: Correspondencia de presidentes y oidores*. Madrid: Imprenta de Juan Pueyo, 1922.

———. *Gobernantes del Perú: Cartas y papeles, siglo XVI*. 14 vols. Madrid: Sucesores de Rivadeneyra et al., 1921–26.

Lohmann Villena, Guillermo. *Los americanos en las órdenes nobiliarias (1529–1900)*. 2 vols. Madrid: Consejo Superior de Investigaciones Científicas, 1947.

Mendoza, Diego de. *Chrónica de la provincia de S. Antonio de los Charcas*. La Paz: Editorial Casa Municipal de la Cultura "Franz Tamayo," 1976.

Mercado, Tomás de. *Summa de tratos y contratos de mercaderes*. Seville: Hernando Díaz, 1571.

———. *Tratos y contratos de mercaderes y tratantes*. Salamanca: Matías Gast, 1569.

Monterroso y Alvarado, Gabriel de. *Prática civil y criminal e instrucción de scrivanos*. Valladolid: Francisco Fernández de Córdova, 1563.

Ordenanza hecha por el muy reverendo señor prior del monesterio de Nuestra Señora Santa María de Guadalupe, en la qual se contienen las condiciones conque se deven hazer los contratos del censso al quitar para que sean sin offensa de Nuestro Señor. Guadalupe: Francisco Díaz, 1548.

Polo de Ondegardo, Juan. *El mundo de los incas*. Edited by Laura González and Alicia Alonso. Crónicas de América 58. Madrid: Historia 16, 1990.

Porras Barrenechea, Raúl. "Dos documentos esenciales sobre Francisco Pizarro y la conquista del Perú." *Revista Histórica* 17 (1948), 5–95.

Recopilación de las leyes destos reynos. 3 vols. Madrid: Catalina de Barrio y Angulo and Diego Díaz de la Carrera, 1640.

Recopilación de leyes de los reynos de las Indias. 3d ed. 4 vols. Madrid: Andrés Ortega, 1774.

Rezabal y Ugarte, José de. *Tratado del real derecho de las medias-anatas seculares y del servicio de lanzas a que están obligados los títulos de Castilla.* Madrid: Don Benito Cano, 1792.

Sancho, Pero. *La relación de Pero Sancho.* Translated by Luis A. Arocena. Buenos Aires: Editorial Plus Ultra, 1986.

Schroeder, H. J., ed. *Canons and Decrees of the Council of Trent.* Rockford, Ill.: TAN Books & Publishers, 1978.

Las Siete Partidas del Rey Alfonso el Sabio, cotejadas con varios códices antiguos por la Real Academia de la Historia. 3 vols. Madrid: Imprenta Real, 1807.

Teresa de Jesús, Saint. *The Collected Works of St. Teresa of Avila.* Vol. 1: *The Book of Her Life, Spiritual Testimonies, Soliloquies.* 2d rev. ed. Translated by Kieran Kavanaugh, O.C.D. and Otilio Rodriguez, O.C.D. Washington, D.C.: Institute of Carmelite Studies, ICS Publications, 1987.

—————. *Libro de las fundaciones.* 3d ed. Edited by Antonio Comas. Madrid: Alianza Editorial, 1984.

Torres de Mendoza, Luis, ed. *Colección de documentos inéditos relativos al descubrimiento, conquista y colonización de las posesiones españolas en América y Oceanía.* 48 vols. Madrid: Imprenta de Manuel G. Hernández, 1864–84.

Unanue, José Hipólito. *Guía política, eclesiástica y militar del Virreynato del Perú para el año 1793.* Lima: Imprenta Real de los Huérfanos, 1793.

—————. *Guía política, eclesiástica y militar del Virreynato del Perú para el año 1794.* Lima: Imprenta Real de los Huérfanos, 1794.

Urteaga, Horacio H., and Carlos A. Romero, eds. *Fundación española del Cuzco y ordenanzas para su gobierno.* Lima: Talleres Gráficos Sanmartí, 1926.

Valcárcel, Carlos Daniel, ed. *La rebelión de Túpac Amaru.* Vol. 2, pts. 1–4 of *Colección documental de la independencia del Perú.* Lima: Comisión Nacional del Sesquicentenario de la Independencia del Perú, 1971–73.

Vargas Ugarte, Rubén, ed. *Concilios limenses (1551–1772).* 3 vols. Lima: Tipografía Peruana, 1951–54.

Vázquez de Espinosa, Antonio. *Compendio y descripción de las Indias occidentales.* Edited by B. Velasco Bayón. Biblioteca de Autores Españoles 231. Madrid: Ediciones Atlas, 1969.

Vidaurre, Manuel de. *Proyecto de un código penal.* Boston: Hiram Tupper, 1828.

Villanueva Urteaga, Horacio. *Cuzco 1689: Economía y sociedad en el sur andino.* Archivos de Historia Andina 2. Cuzco: Centro de Estudios Rurales Andinos "Bartolomé de Las Casas," 1982.

—————, ed. *Documentación oficial española.* Vol. 22, pt. 3 of *Colección documental de la independencia del Perú.* Lima: Comisión Nacional del Sesquicentenario de la Independencia del Perú, 1973.

Xerez, Francisco de. *Verdadera relación de la conquista del Perú.* Edited by Concepción Bravo. Crónicas de América 14. Madrid: Historia 16, 1985.

Secondary Works

Anderson, Benedict. *Imagined Communities: Reflections on the Origins and Spread of Nationalism.* Rev. ed. New York: Verso, 1991.

Andrien, Kenneth. *Crisis and Decline: The Viceroyalty of Peru in the Seventeenth Century.* Albuquerque: University of New Mexico Press, 1985.

Andrien, Kenneth, and Rolena Adorno, eds. *Transatlantic Encounters: Europeans and Andeans in the Sixteenth Century.* Berkeley and Los Angeles: University of California Press, 1991.

Anna, Timothy E. *The Fall of the Royal Government in Peru.* Lincoln: University of Nebraska Press, 1979.

Arenal, Electa, and Stacey Schlau. *Untold Sisters: Hispanic Nuns in Their Own Works.* Translations by Amanda Powell. Albuquerque: University of New Mexico Press, 1989.

Armas Medina, Fernando de. *Cristianización del Perú (1532–1600).* Seville: Escuela de Estudios Hispano-Americanos, 1953.

Assadourian, Carlos Sempat. *El sistema de la economía colonial: Mercado interno, regiones y espacio económico.* Lima: Instituto de Estudios Peruanos, 1982.

———. *Transiciones hacia el sistema colonial andino.* Lima: Instituto de Estudios Peruanos, 1994.

Basadre, Jorge. *Historia de la República del Perú, 1822–1933.* 6th ed. 16 vols. Lima: Editorial Universitaria, 1968–69.

Bauer, Arnold J. "The Church in the Economy of Spanish America: Censos and Depósitos in the Eighteenth and Nineteenth Centuries." *Hispanic American Historical Review* 63 (1983), 707–33.

Bilinkoff, Jodi. *The Avila of Saint Teresa: Religious Reform in a Sixteenth-Century City.* Ithaca: Cornell University Press, 1989.

Bourdieu, Pierre. *Outline of a Theory of Practice.* Translated by Richard Nice. New York: Cambridge University Press, 1977.

Burkholder, Mark A., and D. S. Chandler. *Biographical Dictionary of Audiencia Ministers in the Americas, 1687–1821.* Westport, Conn.: Greenwood Press, 1982.

Burns, Kathryn. "Amor y rebelión en 1782: El caso de Mariano Túpac Amaru y María Mejía." *Histórica* 16 (1992), 131–76.

Cahill, David P. "Repartos ilícitos y familias principales en el sur andino: 1780–1824." *Revista de Indias* 48 (1988), 449–73.

Campbell, Leon G. "Ideology and Factionalism during the Great Rebellion, 1780–82." In Steve J. Stern, ed., *Resistance, Rebellion, and Consciousness in the Andean Peasant World, Eighteenth to Twentieth Centuries.* Madison: University of Wisconsin Press, 1987.

Ceballos López, Vilma. "La Caja de Censos de Indios y su aporte a la economía colonial (1565–1613)." *Revista del Archivo Nacional del Perú* 26 (1962), 269–352.

Certeau, Michel de. *The Practice of Everyday Life.* Translated by Steven Rendall. Berkeley and Los Angeles: University of California Press, 1984.

Céspedes del Castillo, Guillermo. *Lima y Buenos Aires: Repercusiones económicas y políticas de la creación del Virreinato del Plata.* Seville: Consejo Superior de Investigaciones Científicas, 1947.

Cohen, Sherill. *The Evolution of Women's Asylums since 1500: From Refuges for Ex-

Prostitutes to Shelters for Battered Women. New York: Oxford University Press, 1992.

Colin, Michèle. *Le Cuzco à la fin du XVIIe et au début du XVIIIe siècle.* Paris: Institut des Hautes Etudes de l'Amérique Latine, 1966.

Cook, Noble David. *Demographic Collapse: Indian Peru, 1520–1620.* New York: Cambridge University Press, 1981.

Crucinta Ugarte, Eleazar. "Haciendas cañaverales de Abancay y Aymaraes, siglo XVIII." Licenciate thesis, Universidad Nacional San Antonio Abad del Cuzco, 1989.

Cummins, Victoria Hennessey. "The Church and Business Practices in Late Sixteenth-Century Mexico." *The Americas* 44 (1988), 421–40.

Cúneo Harrison, Luis. "Descendientes y herederos del conquistador Don Juan de Pancorvo." *Revista del Instituto Peruano de Investigaciones Genealógicas* 11 (1958) 183–95.

Davies, Keith A. *Landowners in Colonial Peru.* Austin: University of Texas Press, 1984.

de la Cadena, Marisol. "Race, Ethnicity, and the Struggle for Indigenous Self-representation: De-indianization in Cuzco, Peru (1919–1992)." Ph.D. diss., University of Wisconsin, 1996.

de la Puente Brunke, José. *Encomienda y encomenderos en el Perú.* Seville: Diputación Provincial de Sevilla, 1992.

Dean, Carolyn S. "Ethnic Conflict and Corpus Christi in Colonial Cuzco." *Colonial Latin American Review* 2 (1993), 93–120.

———. "(Head)dress for Success: The Use of the *Maskapaycha* in Mid-Colonial Peru." Paper presented at the University of Florida, April 14, 1997.

del Busto Duthurburu, José Antonio. "Maldonado, el Rico, Señor de los Andahuaylas." *Revista Histórica* 26 (1962–63), 113–45.

Durand Florez, Luis. *Criollos en conflicto: Cuzco después de Túpac Amaru.* Lima: Universidad de Lima, 1985.

Escandell-Tur, Neus. "Producción y comercio de tejidos coloniales: Cusco, 1570–1820." Ph.D. diss., University of California–San Diego, 1993.

Feierman, Steven. *Peasant Intellectuals: Anthropology and History in Tanzania.* Madison: University of Wisconsin Press, 1990.

Flores Galindo, Alberto. *Arequipa y el sur andino, siglos XVIII–XX.* Lima: Editorial Horizonte, 1977.

———. *Buscando un Inca.* 3d ed. Lima: Instituto de Apoyo Agrario, 1988.

Foucault, Michel. *The Order of Things: An Archaeology of the Human Sciences.* New York: Vintage Books, 1973.

Franco, Jean. *Plotting Women: Gender and Representation in Mexico.* New York: Columbia University Press, 1989.

Fraser, Valerie. *The Architecture of Conquest: Building in the Viceroyalty of Peru, 1535–1635.* Cambridge: Cambridge University Press, 1990.

Gallagher, Mary A. Y. "Pocket Money and Political Power: The Reform of Santa Catalina of Arequipa (1788–1800)." Paper presented to the American Historical Association, Washington, D.C., December 1992.

García Jordán, Pilar. *Iglesia y poder en el Perú contemporáneo, 1821–1919.* Archivos de

Historia Andina 12. Cuzco: Centro de Estudios Regionales Andinos "Bartolomé de Las Casas," [1991].

Garner, Richard L. "Long-Term Silver Mining Trends in Spanish America: A Comparative Analysis of Peru and Mexico." *American Historical Review* 93 (1988), 898–935.

Gibbs, Donald L. "Cuzco, 1680–1710: An Andean City Seen through Its Economic Activities." Ph.D. diss., University of Texas–Austin, 1979.

———. "The Economic Activities of Nuns, Friars, and their Convents in Mid-Colonial Cuzco." *The Americas* 45 (1989), 343–62.

Glave, Luis Miguel. *Trajinantes: Caminos indígenas en la sociedad colonial, siglos XVI–XVII.* Lima: Instituto de Apoyo Agrario, 1989.

Glave, Luis Miguel, and María Isabel Remy. *Estructura agraria y vida rural en una región andina: Ollantaytambo entre los siglos XVI y XIX.* Archivos de Historia Andina 3. Cuzco: Centro de Estudios Rurales Andinos "Bartolomé de Las Casas," 1983.

Goldwert, Marvin. "La lucha por la perpetuidad de las encomiendas en el Perú virreinal, 1550–1600." *Revista Histórica* 22 (1955–56), 350–60, and 23 (1957–58), 207–20.

Grice-Hutchinson, Marjorie. *The School of Salamanca: Readings in Spanish Monetary Theory, 1544–1605.* Oxford: Clarendon Press, Oxford University, 1952.

Guevara Gil, Jorge A. *Propiedad agraria y derecho colonial.* Lima: Pontificia Universidad Católica del Perú, 1993.

Hamnett, Brian R. "The Appropriation of Mexican Church Wealth by the Spanish Bourbon Government: The 'Consolidación de Vales Reales,' 1805–1809." *Journal of Latin American Studies* 1 (1969), 85–113.

———. "Church Wealth in Peru: Estates and Loans in the Archdiocese of Lima in the Seventeenth Century." *Jahrbuch für Geschichte von Staat, Wirtschaft und Gesellschaft Lateinamerikas* 10 (1973), 113–32.

Hemming, John. *The Conquest of the Incas.* New York: Harcourt Brace Jovanovich, 1970.

Herr, Richard. *The Eighteenth-Century Revolution in Spain.* Princeton: Princeton University Press, 1958.

———. *Rural Change and Royal Finances in Spain at the End of the Old Regime.* Berkeley and Los Angeles: University of California Press, 1989.

Hoffman, Philip T. "Confidence in Your Notary: The Business of Intermediation in Eighteenth-Century Parisian Credit Markets." Paper presented at the Shelby Cullom Davis Center for Historical Studies, Princeton University, January 26, 1996.

Johnson, Penelope D. *Equal in Monastic Profession: Religious Women in Medieval France.* Chicago: University of Chicago Press, 1991.

Jordan, William Chester. *Women and Credit in Pre-Industrial and Developing Societies.* Philadelphia: University of Pennsylvania Press, 1993.

Kealy, Thomas M. *Dowry of Women Religious.* Canon Law Studies 134. Washington, D.C.: Catholic University of America Press, 1941.

Kuznesof, Elizabeth Anne. "Ethnic and Gender Influences on 'Spanish' Creole Society in Colonial Spanish America." *Colonial Latin American Review* 4 (1995), 153–76.

Larson, Brooke. *Colonialism and Agrarian Transformation in Bolivia: Cochabamba, 1550–1900*. Princeton: Princeton University Press, 1988.

Larson, Brooke, and Olivia Harris, eds. *Ethnicity, Markets, and Migration in the Andes*. Durham: Duke University Press, 1995.

Lassegue, J. B., and F. Letona. "Catálogo general del Archivo del Monasterio de Santa Catalina del Cusco, Peru." *Revista Andina* 1 (1983), 127–33.

Lavallé, Bernard. *El mercader y el marqués: Las luchas de poder en el Cusco (1700–1730)*. Lima: Banco Central de Reserva del Perú, 1988.

Lavrin, Asunción. "Ecclesiastical Reform of Nunneries in New Spain in the Eighteenth Century." *The Americas* 22 (1965), 182–203.

———. "The Execution of the Law of *Consolidación* in New Spain: Economic Aims and Results." *Hispanic American Historical Review* 53 (1973), 27–49.

———. "The Role of Nunneries in the Economy of New Spain in the Eighteenth Century." *Hispanic American Historical Review* 46:4 (1966), 371–93.

———, ed. *Latin American Women: Historical Perspectives*. Westport, Conn.: Greenwood Press, 1978.

Lehfeldt, Elizabeth. "Sacred and Secular Spaces: The Role of Religious Women in Golden-Age Valladolid." Ph.D. diss., Indiana University, 1995.

Leiva Viacava, Lourdes. "En torno al primer monasterio limeño en el Virreinato del Perú, 1550–1650." In Manuel Ramos Medina, ed., *El monacato femenino en el imperio español*. Mexico City: Condumex, 1995.

Lewin, Boleslao. *La revolución de Túpac Amaru y los orígenes de la emancipación americana*. Buenos Aires: Librería Hachette, 1957.

Little, Lester K. *Religious Poverty and the Profit Economy in Medieval Europe*. Ithaca: Cornell University Press, 1978.

Llopis Agelán, Enrique. "Las economías monásticas al final del antiguo régimen en Extremadura." Ph.D. diss., Universidad Complutense de Madrid, 1980.

Lockhart, James. *The Men of Cajamarca*. Austin: University of Texas Press, 1972.

———. *Spanish Peru 1532–1560: A Colonial Society*. Madison: University of Wisconsin Press, 1968.

López Martínez, Héctor. "Un motín de mestizos en el Perú (1567)." *Revista de Indias* 24 (1964), 367–81.

Ludlow, Leonor, and Jorge Silva Riquer, eds. *Los negocios y las ganancias de la colonia al México moderno*. Mexico City: Instituto Mora and UNAM, 1993.

Lynch, John. *The Spanish-American Revolutions, 1808–1826*. New York: W. W. Norton & Co., 1973.

Mannarelli, María Emma. "Inquisición y mujeres: Las hechiceras en el Perú durante el siglo XVII." *Revista Andina* 3:1 (1985), 141–55.

———. *Pecados públicos: La ilegitimidad en Lima, siglo XVII*. Lima: Ediciones Flora Tristán, 1993.

Martín, Luis. *Daughters of the Conquistadores: Women of the Viceroyalty of Peru*. Albuquerque: University of New Mexico Press, 1983.

Martín Rubio, María del Carmen. "La Caja de Censos de Indios en el Cuzco." *Revista de Indias* 39 (1979), 187–208.

Martínez López-Cano, María del Pilar. *El crédito a largo plazo en el siglo XVI: Ciudad de México (1550–1620)*. Mexico City: UNAM, 1995.

————. "El crédito particular en España: Formas y controversias." In Leonor Ludlow and Jorge Silva Riquer, eds., *Los negocios y las ganancias de la colonia al México moderno*. Mexico City: Instituto Mora and UNAM, 1993.

————, ed. *Iglesia, estado y economía, siglos XVI al XIX*. Mexico City: Instituto Mora and UNAM, 1995.

Masur, Gerhard. *Simón Bolívar*. Albuquerque: University of New Mexico Press, 1948.

McKnight, Kathryn Joy. *The Mystic of Tunja: The Writings of Madre Castillo, 1671–1742*. Amherst: University of Massachusetts Press, 1997.

Mendiburu, Manuel de. *Diccionario histórico biográfico del Perú*. 2d ed. 11 vols. Lima: Imprenta Enrique Palacios, 1931–34.

Moreno Cebrián, Alfredo. *El corregidor de Indias y la economía peruana del siglo XVIII (los repartos forzosos de mercancías)*. Madrid: Consejo Superior de Investigaciones Científicas, 1977.

Mörner, Magnus. *Compraventas de tierras en el Cuzco, 1825–1869*. Stockholm: Instituto de Estudios Latinoamericanos de Estocolmo, 1984.

————. *Perfil de la sociedad rural del Cuzco a fines de la colonia*. Lima: Universidad del Pacífico, 1978.

Murra, John V. " 'Nos Hazen Mucha Ventaja': The Early European Perception of Andean Achievement." In Kenneth J. Andrien and Rolena Adorno, eds., *Transatlantic Encounters: Europeans and Andeans in the Sixteenth Century*. Berkeley and Los Angeles: University of California Press, 1991.

Myers, Kathleen. *Word from New Spain: The Spiritual Autobiography of Madre María de San José (1656–1719)*. Liverpool: Liverpool University Press, 1993.

Nelson, Benjamin. *The Idea of Usury: From Tribal Brotherhood to Universal Otherhood*. 2d ed. Chicago: University of Chicago Press, 1969.

Noonan, John T., Jr. *The Scholastic Analysis of Usury*. Cambridge: Harvard University Press, 1957.

O'Phelan Godoy, Scarlett. *Rebellions and Revolts in Eighteenth-Century Peru and Upper Peru*. Cologne: Böhlau Verlag, 1985.

Pagden, Anthony. *The Fall of Natural Man*. New York: Cambridge University Press, 1982.

Paz, Octavio. *Sor Juana; or, The Traps of Faith*. Translated by Margaret Sayers Peden. Cambridge: Harvard University Press, 1988.

Pease, Franklin. *Curacas, reciprocidad y riqueza*. Lima: Pontificia Universidad Católica del Perú, 1992.

Perry, Mary Elizabeth. *Gender and Disorder in Early Modern Seville*. Princeton: Princeton University Press, 1990.

Polo y La Borda, Jorge. "La hacienda Pachachaca (segunda mitad del siglo XVIII)." *Histórica* 1 (1977), 223–47.

Portal, Ismael. *Lima religiosa (1535–1924)*. Lima: Librería e Imprenta Gil, 1924.

Quiroz, Alfonso W. *Deudas olvidadas: Instrumentos de crédito en la economía colonial peruana, 1750–1820*. Lima: Pontificia Universidad Católica del Perú, 1993.

———. "Reassessing the Role of Credit in Late Colonial Peru: Censos, Escrituras, and Imposiciones." *Hispanic American Historical Review* 74 (1994), 193–230.

Ramírez, Susan Elizabeth. *The World Upside Down: Cross-cultural Contact and Conflict in Sixteenth-Century Peru*. Stanford: Stanford University Press, 1996.

Ramos Medina, Manuel, ed. *El monacato femenino en el imperio español*. Mexico City: Condumex, 1995.

Reyna, María del Carmen. *El convento de San Jerónimo: Vida conventual y finanzas*. Mexico City: Instituto Nacional de Antropología e Historia, 1990.

Roover, Raymond de. *Business, Banking, and Economic Thought in Late Medieval and Early Modern Europe: Selected Studies of Raymond de Roover*. Edited by Julius Kirschner. Chicago: University of Chicago Press, 1974.

Rostworowski de Diez Canseco, María. *Doña Francisca Pizarro: Una iluste mestiza, 1534–1598*. Lima: Instituto de Estudios Peruanos, 1989.

———. "El repartimiento de Doña Beatriz Clara Coya en el valle de Yucay." *Historia y Cultura* 4 (1970), 153–267.

Rowe, John Howland. "Genealogía y rebelión." *Histórica* 6 (1982), 65–85.

———. "The Incas under Spanish Colonial Institutions." *Hispanic American Historical Review* 37 (1957), 155–99.

———. "El movimiento nacional inca en el siglo XVIII." *Revista Universitaria* [Cuzco] 43 (1954), 17–47.

Scott, Joan Wallach. *Gender and the Politics of History*. New York: Columbia University Press, 1988.

Seed, Patricia. "'Failing to Marvel': Atahualpa's Encounter with the Word." *Latin American Research Review* 26 (1991), 7–32.

Silverblatt, Irene. *Moon, Sun, and Witches: Gender Ideologies and Class in Inca and Colonial Peru*. Princeton: Princeton University Press, 1987.

Soeiro, Susan A. "The Feminine Orders in Colonial Bahia, Brazil: Economic, Social, and Demographic Implications, 1677–1800." In Asunción Lavrin, ed., *Latin American Women: Historical Perspectives*. Westport, Conn.: Greenwood Press, 1978.

Spalding, Karen. *Huarochirí: An Andean Society under Inca and Spanish Rule*. Stanford: Stanford University Press, 1984.

Stern, Steve J. "The Age of Andean Insurrection, 1742–1782: A Reappraisal." In Stern, ed., *Resistance, Rebellion, and Consciousness in the Andean Peasant World, Eighteenth to Twentieth Centuries*. Madison: University of Wisconsin Press, 1987.

———. *Peru's Indian Peoples and the Challenge of Spanish Conquest*. Madison: University of Wisconsin Press, 1982.

———, ed. *Resistance, Rebellion, and Consciousness in the Andean Peasant World, Eighteenth to Twentieth Centuries*. Madison: University of Wisconsin Press, 1987.

Suárez, Margarita. *Comercio y fraude en el Perú colonial: Las estrategias mercantiles de un banquero*. Lima: Banco Central de la Reserva and Instituto de Estudios Peruanos, 1995.

Tamayo Herrera, José. *Historia social del Cuzco republicano*. 2d ed. Lima: Editorial Universo, 1981.

Tandeter, Enrique. *Coercion and Market: Silver Mining in Colonial Potosí, 1692–1826*. Albuquerque: University of New Mexico Press, 1993.

Tapia Franco, Luis Alfredo. "Análisis histórico institucional del censo consignativo en el derecho peruano." B.A. thesis, Pontificia Universidad Católica del Perú, Lima, 1991.

Thurner, Mark. *From Two Republics to One Divided: Contradictions of Postcolonial Nation-making in Andean Peru*. Durham: Duke University Press, 1997.

Tibesar, Antonine. "The *Alternativa*: A Study in Spanish–Creole Relations in Seventeenth-Century Peru." *The Americas* 11 (1955), 229–83.

———. *Franciscan Beginnings in Colonial Peru*. Washington, D.C.: Academy of American Franciscan History, 1953.

Ugarte, César Antonio. *Los antecedentes históricos del régimen agrario peruano*. Lima: Librería e Imprenta Gil, 1918.

Valcárcel, Carlos Daniel. *La rebelión de Túpac Amaru*. Colección Popular 72. Mexico City: Fondo de Cultura Económica, 1947.

Valcárcel, Luis E. *Memorias*. Edited by José Matos Mar, José Deustua C., and José Luis Renique. Lima: Instituto de Estudios Peruanos, 1981.

van Deusen, Nancy. *Dentro del cerco de los muros: El recogimiento en la época colonial*. Lima: CENDOC, 1988.

———. "Los primeros recogimientos para doncellas mestizas en Lima y Cusco, 1550–1580." *Allpanchis* 35/36:1 (1990), 249–91.

Vargas Ugarte, Rubén. *Historia de la Iglesia en el Perú*. 5 vols. Lima and Burgos: Editorial Santa María et al., 1953–62.

———. *Historia del Perú: Emancipación (1809–1825)*. Buenos Aires: Imprenta López, 1958.

Villanueva Urteaga, Horacio. *Gamarra y la iniciación republicana en el Cuzco*. Lima: Banco de los Andes, 1981.

von Wobeser, Gisela. "Mecanismos crediticios en la Nueva España: El uso del censo consignativo." *Mexican Studies/Estudios Mexicanos* 5 (1989), 1–23.

Walker, Charles. *Smoldering Ashes: Cuzco and the Creation of Republican Peru*. Durham: Duke University Press, forthcoming.

Wethey, Harold. *Colonial Architecture and Sculpture in Peru*. Cambridge: Harvard University Press, 1949.

Wightman, Ann M. *Indigenous Migration and Social Change: The Forasteros of Cuzco, 1570–1720*. Durham: Duke University Press, 1990.

Yuste, Carmen. "Los comerciantes de la Ciudad de México en la negociación transpacífica." In Leonor Ludlow and Jorge Silva Riquer, eds., *Los negocios y las ganancias de la colonia al México moderno*. Mexico City: Instituto Mora and UNAM, 1993.

Zavala, Silvio. *La encomienda indiana*. 2d ed. Mexico City: Editorial Porrúa, 1973.

Zegarra López, Dante E. *Monasterio de Santa Catalina de Sena de Arequipa y Doña Ana de Monteagudo, priora*. Arequipa: Corporación Departamental de Desarrollo de Arequipa, 1985.

Index

Cusi Huarcay, Doña María, 25, 27, 29, 222
Cusimantur, Doña Juana Tomasa, 124
Cuzco: audiencia of, 177, 185, 189; cabildo (city council) of, 15–40 passim, 47–50, 59, 61–62, 92, 119, 166, 246–47 n.36; "golden age" of, 78–82, 122–25, 129, 152, 251–52 n.24, 267 n.78; municipal government of, 188, 199–204, 210–13; population of, 18, 204, 237 n.16, 241 n.57, 251 n.23, 252 n.30; Spanish conquest of, 18–20

Dance, 71, 107, 177, 193, 230
Debt: censuatarios' efforts to obtain relief from, 153, 161–65, 178, 184, 192, 196–97, 205, 277 n.41; late colonial burden of, 9, 152–54, 160–67, 178–85, 192 (see also Censo saturation); as a means of creating relationships, 9, 71, 145, 149–54, 192; prosecution for, 145–46, 150, 159, 164–65, 180–81
Dejaciones, 164, 179–80
De la Bandera, Damián, 88
De la Raya, Don Antonio (bishop of Cuzco), 76–77, 82–83, 85, 229–31
Depositadas, 117, 126, 172–73, 186, 207, 210
Desprendimiento. See Poverty, religious
Devil, 16, 80, 106, 128, 183
Díaz Calisaya, Don Pascual, 187
Díaz Uscamaita, Don Antonio, 150
Discipline, 108, 111–12, 117–18, 126, 207, 260 n.90
Disease, impact of, 20, 56, 79, 160–61, 246 n.31
Disentailment of church property, 206
Dominicans: friars, 23, 42, 137, 174; nuns (see Santa Catalina, convent of)
Dominio: defined, 6, 44, 63; dilem-

mas of, 45–48, 52–53, 57, 159, 187, 244 n.5; exercise of, 85, 115, 215
Donadas, 112, 115–16, 119–20, 138–39, 175, 233, 257 n.46
Donations: charitable, 62, 114, 150, 154; in support of Santa Catalina, 83–85, 186, 227–31; in support of Santa Clara, 15, 23, 42–43, 46–47, 81–82, 91–93, 213; in support of Santa Teresa, 128–30
Dowry: discounting and waiving of spiritual, 33, 86–88, 124; investment of spiritual, 47, 67, 87–88, 134, 136–39, 143, 146, 154; loss of spiritual, 159; spiritual, 3, 6, 24–25, 45, 62, 109, 119–22, 247–48 n.53; temporal, 31, 45, 146, 240 n.47
Dueñas Castillejo brothers, 139–40, 153

Earthquakes, 70, 76, 95–96, 137, 161, 229
Economic thought, 159, 167, 178–79, 184–85, 192, 196, 205
Ecónomos, 197–98
Education. See Children; Girls
Elections, convent, 111–12, 120–21, 174–76
Elites, Cuzco. See Criollo aristocracy; Indian nobles; Kurakas; Nobility, titled
Encomenderos: as fathers, 15–18, 21–22, 25–26, 34–36, 38, 217–24; marriage and inheritance strategies of, 19–22, 25, 34–36, 73–76, 238 n.28, 238–39 n.29
Encomiendas: struggles for, 17–20, 34–36, 42, 47, 51, 58, 238 n.20
Enlightenment critique of church wealth, 159, 166–67, 178–79, 184–85, 189, 192
Esquivel, Doña Bernarda de, 162
Esquivel, Doña Leonor de (Doña Melchora Clara Coya), 89–90, 124

"Idolatries," 53–54

Illegitimacy, 21, 24, 33–35, 88, 121–22

Inca, Don Melchor Carlos, 80, 90, 124, 252 n.32

"Inca nationalism," 176–77, 193, 203, 270 n.51, 274–75 n.6, 275 n.17

Incas: criollos' sense of kinship with, 162, 170, 173, 177–78; empire of the (*see* Tahuantinsuyo); Spanish invasion of the, 3, 18–19; symbolic conquest and containment of the, 8, 68, 88–90, 123–24. *See also* Land tenure: Inca

Income, convent. *See* Convents: annual income of

Independence, Peruvian, 188–93

Indian laborers. *See* Labor power: Andean

Indian nobles (indios nobles), 2, 9, 79–80, 123–27, 149–52, 160, 168, 176–77, 260 n.99. *See also* Kurakas

Inflation, 163

Ingenios. *See* Sugar production

Inheritance, 115–16, 124, 147, 227–28, 266 n.62. *See also* Encomenderos: marriage and inheritance strategies of; Family strategies

Insults, 117, 126, 159, 172, 183, 256 n.36

Investment strategies. *See* Convents: financial role of; Credit; Spiritual economy

Irrigation, 55–57, 142, 153

Jesuits, 23, 53–54, 137, 141, 166–67; schooling of indios nobles, 79, 123, 193–94

Jovellanos, Gaspar Melchor de, 159, 184, 192

Juan, Jorge, 168

Juana Inés de la Cruz, Sor, 4–5

Kurakas: daughters of, 8–9, 113, 123–27, 134, 150–52; role of, 8–9, 34, 52–59, 68–69, 79–81, 123–27, 149–57, 160, 168–70, 176–77

Kurakazgos: abolition of, 177

Labor power: Andean, 17, 20, 73–74, 78–81, 86, 161; nuns' claims to, 42, 60, 86; used to construct cloisters, 92, 106

La Encarnación, convent of (Lima), 23–24, 239 n.39

Land grants, 49–50, 52–61, 85–86, 246–47 n.36. *See also* "Lands of the Inca and the Sun"

"Lands of the Inca and the Sun," 8, 52–57, 68, 85, 246 n.34

Land tenure: disputes over, 52–58, 67–69, 144, 246 n.25; Inca, 49–50, 53, 57–58, 67–68, 247 n.41 (*see also* "Lands of the Inca and the Sun"); Spanish, 52–57, 63, 67–68

Land titles: regularization of (composiciones), 79, 140

La Paz (city of), 2, 74, 188, 222–23, 228

Larrazabal, Don Agustín de, 157–58

Las Casas, Bartolomé de, 34, 241 n.63

La Serna, Don José de (viceroy), 190, 193

Las Nazarenas, beaterio of, 126

Lavrin, Asunción, 5

Lay sisters, 112, 119–20, 130, 208. *See also* Convents: stratification within; Donadas; Veil

Leasing, 63, 143, 166, 179, 207

Legal proceedings, nuns' and beatas' involvement in: to collect income and/or recover property, 84–85, 132–34, 145–46, 149–50, 163–64, 178–81, 197; concerning elections, 121, 174–76; concerning indigenous land and labor, 53–60, 86, 144; concerning violation of monastic enclosure, 116–17; in defense of honor, 126, 183; to determine patrons' rights, 92

century redefinition of, 187; as a
gendered activity, 6–7, 41–48, 67,
107, 130, 254 n.72

Prayer: nuns' hours of, 101, 109, 111;
the purchase of, 3, 23, 61

Prioress. *See* Mother superior

Prisoners, convent (depositadas), 117,
126, 172–73, 186, 207, 210

Profession: "free will" and, 109, 148;
as spiritual matrimony, 6, 39, 45,
109 (*see also* Nuns: as brides)

Property: collateral, 3, 65, 69, 145,
149–50, 165; culturally different
definitions of, 8, 48, 52–58, 67;
liberal ideology concerning, 205–
6; seizure of, for indebtedness,
3, 66, 145, 164–65, 180 (*see also*
Concursos de acreedores; Debt:
prosecution for)

Protector of Natives (protector de
los naturales), 126, 136

Pumacahua, Don Mateo García, 170,
189

Puraca, Doña Marta, 125

Quechua language, 123, 150, 171, 273
n.85; nuns' business transactions
in, 103, 125

Queso Yupanqui, Don Melchor, 151

Quicho, Juan, 144

Quicho, Pedro, 144

Quispe Guaman, Don Diego, 124

Quispe Sisa, Doña Catalina, 90

Quispe Titu, 29

Quispicanchis, 178–79

"Race," the gendered construction
of, 15–18, 37–38, 40, 242 n.65,
244 n.87

Ranches (estancias): Caco, 49, 63,
144; Chunoguana, 85–86; Churucalla, 85; Corcora (encomienda
and estancia), 42–43, 60–61, 225–
26; Pallata, 85–86; Patallacta, 86;
Quehue, 170–71; and ranching,
63, 85–86, 143–44, 170–71; Suri-

guaylla (estancia and hacienda),
61, 133–34

Real estate, urban, 64–65, 143, 150,
166, 180

Rebellion against Spanish rule,
Andean, 152, 160, 168–71, 188

Rebolledo, Eustaquio de, 199–200

Recogimientos (beaterios), 23–24,
125–27, 182, 201, 239 n.32

Réditos. *See* Annual payments

Reducciones, 79

Reform of convent life, efforts to
effect, 107, 166–67, 207–9, 212

Refugiadas, 118, 186, 210

Rentals, 63, 143, 150, 166, 180, 207,
215

Republican institutions, 187–88,
193–94, 198

Rivadeneyra, Doña María de la
Concepción y, 172, 174–76

Rivas, Vicentina, 191

Riveros, María, 51, 91–92

Rules and constitutions, monastic,
41–45, 67, 102–3, 107–13, 128–31,
163, 208

Saints, 108, 111, 214, 226

Salinas, Doña Antonia, 124

Sampac, Doña Francisca, 120

Sampac, Don Matías, 120

San Agustín, monastery of, 23–24,
133, 138, 196

San Bernardo, Colegio de, 141, 167,
193

San Blas (parish of), 125, 226

San Buenaventura, Colegio de, 141

San Cristóbal, Doña Josefa de, 124–
25

San Cristóbal (parish of), 149

San Francisco de Borja, Colegio de,
167, 193

Sangarara, battle of, 169, 171, 178

San Gerónimo (parish of), 61, 191

San Ignacio de Loyola, Universidad
de, 167

San Juan Bautista, Magdalena de, 126

Kathryn Burns is Assistant Professor, Department of History, University of Florida.

Library of Congress Cataloging-in-Publication Data
Burns, Kathryn
Colonial habits : convents and the spiritual economy of
Cuzco, Peru / Kathryn Burns.
p.   cm.
Includes bibliographical references and index.
ISBN 0-8223-2259-5 (alk. paper). — ISBN 0-8223-2291-9
(pbk. : alk. paper)
1. Cuzco (Peru)—Social life and customs.   2. Cuzco
(Peru)—History.   3. Convents—Social aspects—Peru—
Cuzco—History.   4. Convents—Economic aspects—Peru—
Cuzco—History.   5. Women—Peru—Cuzco—Social
conditions.   6. Mestizos—Peru—Cuzco—History.
7. Social structure—Peru—Cuzco—History.   I. Title.
F3611.C9B87   1999
985'.37—dc21   98-8099   CIP